# TAKING SIDES

Clashing Views on

## Political Issues

# TAKING SIDES

## Clashing Views on
# Political Issues

**EIGHTEENTH EDITION**

**Selected, Edited, and with Introductions by**

**George McKenna**
*City College, City University of New York*

**and**

**Stanley Feingold**
*City College, City University of New York*

Connect
Learn
Succeed™

TAKING SIDES: CLASHING VIEWS ON POLITICAL ISSUES, EIGHTEENTH EDITION

Published by McGraw-Hill, a business unit of The McGraw-Hill Companies, Inc., 1221 Avenue of the Americas, New York, NY 10020. Copyright © 2013 by The McGraw-Hill Companies, Inc. All rights reserved. Printed in the United States of America. Previous edition © 2012, 2011, and 2010. No part of this publication may be reproduced or distributed in any form or by any means, or stored in a database or retrieval system, without the prior written consent of The McGraw-Hill Companies, Inc., including, but not limited to, in any network or other electronic storage or transmission, or broadcast for distance learning.

Some ancillaries, including electronic and print components, may not be available to customers outside the United States.

This book is printed on acid-free paper.

Taking Sides® is a registered trademark of the McGraw-Hill Companies, Inc.
Taking Sides is published by the **Contemporary Learning Series** group within the McGraw-Hill Higher Education division.

1 2 3 4 5 6 7 8 9 0 DOC/DOC 0 9 8 7 6 5 4 3 2

MHID: 0-07-805032-4
ISBN: 978-0-07-805032-9
ISSN: 1080-580X (print)
ISSN: 2153-2850 (online)

Managing Editor: *Larry Loeppke*
Senior Developmental Editor: *Jill Meloy*
Permissions Supervisor: *Lenny Behnke*
Marketing Specialist: *Alice Link*
Lead Project Manager: *Jane Mohr*
Design Coordinator: *Brenda A. Rolwes*
Cover Graphics: *Rick D. Noel*
Buyer: *Nicole Baumgartner*
Media Project Manager: *Sridevi Palani*

Compositor: MPS Limited
Cover Image: © Comstock/Corbis RF

# Editors/Academic Advisory Board

Members of the Academic Advisory Board are instrumental in the final selection of articles for each edition of TAKING SIDES. Their review of articles for content, level, and appropriateness provides critical direction to the editors and staff. We think that you will find their careful consideration well reflected in this volume.

## TAKING SIDES: Clashing Views on POLITICAL ISSUES

Eighteenth Edition

### EDITORS

**George McKenna**
*City College, City University of New York*

and

**Stanley Feingold**
*City College, City University of New York*

## ACADEMIC ADVISORY BOARD MEMBERS

# Preface

**D**ialogue means two people talking about the same issue. This is not as easy as it sounds. Play back the next debate between the talking heads you see on television. Listen to them trying to persuade each other—actually, the TV audience—of the truth of their own views and of the irrationality of their opponents' views.

What is likely to happen? At the outset, they will probably fail to define the issue with enough clarity and objectivity to make it clear exactly what it is that they are disputing. As the philosopher Alasdair MacIntyre has put it, the most passionate pro and con arguments are often "incommensurable"—they sail past each other because the two sides are talking about different things. As arguments proceed, both sides tend to employ vague, emotion-laden terms without spelling out the uses to which the terms are put. When the heat is on, they may resort to shouting epithets at one another, and the hoped-for meeting of minds will give way to the scoring of political points and the reinforcement of existing prejudices. For example, when the discussion of affirmative action comes down to both sides accusing the other of "racism," or when the controversy over abortion degenerates into taunts and name-calling, then no one really listens and learns from the other side.

It is our conviction that people *can* learn from the other side, no matter how sharply opposed it is to their own cherished viewpoint. Sometimes, after listening to others, we change our view entirely. But in most cases, we either incorporate some elements of the opposing view—thus making our own richer—or else learn how to answer the objections to our viewpoint. Either way, we gain from the experience. For these reasons, we believe that encouraging dialogue between opposed positions is the most certain way of enhancing public understanding.

The purpose of this 18th edition of *Taking Sides* is to continue to work toward the revival of political dialogue in America. As we have done in the past 17 editions, we examine leading issues in American politics from the perspective of sharply opposed points of view. We have tried to select authors who argue their points vigorously but in such a way as to enhance our understanding of the issue.

We hope that the reader who confronts lively and thoughtful statements on vital issues will be stimulated to ask some of the critical questions about American politics. What are the highest priority issues with which government must deal today? What positions should be taken on these issues? What should be the attitude of Americans toward their government? Our conviction is that a healthy, stable democracy requires a citizenry that considers these questions and participates, however indirectly, in answering them. The alternative is apathy, passivity, and, sooner or later, the rule of tyrants.

**Plan of the book**   Each issue has an issue *introduction,* which sets the stage for the debate as it is argued in the YES and NO selections. Each issue concludes with a *postscript* that makes some final observations and points the way to other questions related to the issue. In reading the issue and forming your own opinions you should not feel confined to adopt one or the other of the positions presented. There are positions in between the given views or totally outside them, and the *suggestions for further reading* that appear in each issue postscript should help you find resources to continue your study of the subject. We have also provided relevant Internet site addresses (URLs) on the *Internet References* page that accompanies each part opener. At the back of the book is a listing of all the *contributors to this volume,* which will give you information on the political scientists and commentators whose views are debated here.

**Changes to this edition**   Over the last 35 years, *Taking Sides* has undergone extensive changes and improvements, and we have continued to keep up with the changing times. In this edition, we present five new issues: Is the Welfare State Obsolete? (Issue 12), Should Same-Sex Marriage Be a Constitutional Right? (Issue 15), Do Corporations Have the Same Free Speech Rights as Persons? (Issue 17), Should "Recreational" Drugs Be Legalized? (Issue 18), and Do We Need to Curb Global Warming? (Issue 20). We worked hard on what we hope will be a truly memorable 18th edition, and we think you will like the result. Let us know what you think by writing to us in care of McGraw-Hill Contemporary Learning Series, 501 Bell St., 4th Floor, Dubuque, IA 52001 or e-mailing us at GMcK1320@optonline.net or left@stanleyfeingold.com. Suggestions for further improvements are most welcome!

**A word to the instructor**   An *Instructor's Resource Guide with Test Questions* (multiple-choice and essay) is available through the publisher for the instructor using *Taking Sides* in the classroom. A general guidebook, *Using Taking Sides in the Classroom,* which discusses methods and techniques for integrating the pro-con approach into any classroom setting, is also available. An online version of *Using Taking Sides in the Classroom* and a correspondence for *Taking Sides* adopters can be found at www.mhhe.com/cls. *Taking Sides: Clashing Views on Political Issues* is only one title in the *Taking Sides* series. If you are interested in seeing the table of contents for any of the other titles, please visit the *Taking Sides* Web site at www.mhhe.com/cls.

**Acknowledgments**   We are grateful to Laura McKenna for her help and suggestions in preparing this edition. Thanks also to the Morris Raphael Cohen Library of City College and the public library of Tenafly, New Jersey—especially to Agnes Kolben.

We also appreciate the spontaneous letters from instructors and students who wrote to us with comments and observations. Many thanks to Larry Loeppke, Jill Meloy, and David Welsh for their able editorial assistance. Needless to say, the responsibility for any errors of fact or judgment rests with us.

**George McKenna**
**Stanley Feingold**

# Contents in Brief

# Contents

## UNIT 1   DEMOCRACY AND THE AMERICAN POLITICAL PROCESS   1

### Issue 1.   Should Americans Believe in a Unique American "Mission"?   2

**YES:   Wilfred M. McClay**, from "The Founding of Nations," *First Things* (March 2006)   *4*

**NO:   Howard Zinn**, from "The Power and the Glory: Myths of American Exceptionalism," *Boston Review* (Summer 2005)   *13*

Humanities professor Wilfred M. McClay argues that America's "myth," its founding narrative, helps to sustain and hold together a diverse people. Historian Howard Zinn is convinced that America's myth of "exceptionalism" has served as a justification for lawlessness, brutality, and imperialism.

### Issue 2.   Does the Tea Party Represent a Revival of America's Revolutionary Ideals?   22

**YES:   Dick Armey and Matt Kibbe**, from *Give Us Liberty: A Tea Party Manifesto* (HarperCollins, 2010)   *24*

**NO:   Jill Lepore**, from *The Whites of Their Eyes: The Tea Party's Revolution and the Battle over American History* (Princeton University Press, 2010)   *30*

FreedomWorks founder Dick Armey and FreedomWorks president Matt Kibbe believe that the Tea Party movement is a reawakening of the spirit of the American Revolution. Harvard University professor of American history Jill Lepore believes that the modern Tea Party movement is antihistorical, anti-intellectual, and antipluralist.

### Issue 3.   Is Bigger Government Better Government?   39

**YES:   Jeff Madrick**, from *The Case for Big Government* (Princeton University Press, 2008)   *41*

**NO:   Jim DeMint**, from *Saving Freedom* (Fidelis, 2009)   *46*

Humanities professor Jeff Madrick surveys the numerous government interventions in the economy since the end of World War II and concludes that they have been essential to America's growth and well being. Senator Jim DeMint compares government to a genie that can protect a nation from its enemies and ensure fair and equal treatment of its citizens but which needs to be "caged" lest it overwhelm and destroy the nation.

# UNIT 2   THE INSTITUTIONS OF GOVERNMENT   71

Columnist Ezra Klein contends that institutional deadlock and partisan rancor have paralyzed Congress, causing it to lose power to the president and the bureaucracy. Former representative Lee H. Hamilton contends that many of the Congress's so-called flaws are actually faithful reflections of how the American public thinks and feels.

George Caram Steeh, U.S. judge for the Southern Division of Michigan, maintains that there is a rational basis for the federal government's "individual mandate," for without it individuals could shift the cost of health insurance onto others, driving up the cost for everyone. Henry Hudson, U.S. judge for the Eastern District of Virginia, argues that the "individual mandate" exceeds the regulatory powers granted to the U.S. government under the Commerce Clause because it penalizes the mere failure to purchase a product.

Public policy professor Mark J. Rozell believes that executive privilege is needed for the proper functioning of the executive branch, because presidents need candid advice from their staffs. Political science professor David Gray Adler concludes that neither debate in the Constitutional Convention nor the text of the Constitution provide any support for the view that the Framers supported giving the president the power to conceal information from Congress.

Political scientist Glenn Loury argues that the prudent use of "race-sighted" policies is essential to reducing the deleterious effects of race stigmatization, especially the sense of "racial otherness," which still remain in America. Economist Walter Williams argues that the use of racial preferences sets up a zero-sum game that reverses the gains of the civil rights movement, penalizes innocent people, and ends up harming those they are intended to help.

Legal philosopher Robert P. George asserts that, since each of us was a human being from conception, abortion is a form of homicide and should be banned. Writer Mary Gordon maintains that having an abortion is a moral choice that women are capable of making for themselves, that aborting a fetus is not killing a person, and that antiabortionists fail to understand female sexuality.

Yuval Levin, a Fellow at the Ethics and Public Policy Center in Washington, DC argues that democratic capitalism provides a compelling contrast to the shortcomings of the socialist welfare state. Social scientists Irwin Garfinkel, Lee Rainwater, and Timothy Smeeding believe that the welfare state enriches nations and should be maintained.

Economist Curtis S. Dubay believes that raising the already high taxes on high incomes would stifle job creation, slow the growth of already stagnant wages, and lead to larger deficits. Author Steve Brouwer maintains that higher and more progressive taxes on high incomes would enable the government to finance health care, higher education, and the rebuilding of the nation's infrastructure.

Center on Budget and Policy Priorities Executive Director Robert Greenstein maintains that the long-term trend of inequality of income in the United States continues to grow greater as a consequence of public policy. American Enterprise Institute president Christopher C. DeMuth asserts that Americans have achieved an impressive level of wealth and equality and that a changing economy ensures even more opportunities.

Attorney Theodore B. Olson argues that the right of homosexual people to marry, is the logical extension of the equality proclaimed in the Declaration of Independence and guaranteed by the Fourteenth Amendment. Columnist Sam Shulman sees gay marriage as a burlesque of marriage that will harm the interests of women.

United States Supreme Court Justice John Paul Stevens believes that the Constitution creates "a wall of separation" between church and state that can be rarely broached and only insofar as the state recognition of religion does not express a bias in support of particular religious doctrines. United States Supreme Court Justice Antonin Scalia believes that both the Constitution and American history support the sympathetic acknowledgement of the nearly universal American belief in monotheistic religion as reflected in presidential proclamations, public oaths, public monuments, and other displays.

Supreme Court Justice Anthony Kennedy, for the majority, hold the view that corporations have all the rights and privileges of citizens under the Constitution, so their free speech rights are not to be violated. Supreme

Court Justice John Paul Stevens insists that corporations are not citizens under the Constitution, so Congress may restrict their political speech prior to an election.

Law professor Bryan Stevenson focuses on how the criminalization of drugs has led to mass imprisonment with negative consequences for law enforcement. Theodore Dalrymple, a writer for the Manhattan Institute, describes the consequences of illegal drug use and the potential for further illness and crime if drugs are legalized.

# UNIT 4  AMERICA AND THE WORLD  329

Former Department of Justice attorney Jack Goldsmith argues that, in dealing with terrorism, the elective branches have the authority and justification to establish procedures for noncriminal military detention of an extended nature. Department of State counselor Sarah H. Cleveland believes that unlimited detention of suspected terrorists does not contribute to national security, while it undermines the constitutional defense of habeas corpus.

Editor Gregg Easterbrook argues that global warming, causing deleterious changes in the human condition, is a near certainty for the next few generations. Professor Larry Bell insists that the climate models predicting global warming are speculative at best, and in some cases based upon manipulated data.

Former federal prosecutor Andrew C. McCarthy supports the National Security Agency program of surveillance without a warrant as an effective means of protecting national security that employs the inherent power of the president to protect the country against subversion. Former vice president Al Gore views the warrantless wiretapping of American citizens as a brazen violation of the Constitution and of specific acts of Congress that have spelled out the circumstances under which a president may receive judicial permission to wiretap or otherwise invade the privacy of citizens.

# Correlation Guide

The *Taking Sides* series presents current issues in a debate-style format designed to stimulate student interest and develop critical thinking skills. Each issue is thoughtfully framed with an issue summary, an issue introduction, and critical thinking and reflection questions. The pro and con essays—selected for their liveliness and substance—represent the arguments of leading scholars and commentators in their fields.

**Taking Sides: Clashing Views on Political Issues, 18/e** is an easy-to-use reader that presents issues on important topics such as *democracy and the American political process, the institutions of government, social change and public policy,* and *America and the world.* For more information on *Taking Sides* and other *McGraw-Hill Contemporary Learning Series* titles, visit www.mhhe.com/cls.

This convenient guide matches the units in **Taking Sides: Political Issues, 18/e** with the corresponding chapters in three of our best-selling McGraw-Hill Political Science textbooks by Harrison/Harris, Patterson, and Losco/Baker.

| Taking Sides: Political Issues, 18/e | American Democracy Now, 2/e by Harrison/Harris | The American Democracy, 10/e by Patterson | American Government 2012, 3/e by Losco/Baker |
|---|---|---|---|
| **Issue 1:** Should Americans Believe in a Unique American "Mission"? | **Chapter 1:** People, Politics, and Participation **Chapter 6:** Political Socialization and Public Opinion | **Chapter 1:** Political Thinking: Becoming a Responsible Citizen **Chapter 2:** Constitutional Democracy: Promoting Liberty and Self-Government **Chapter 3:** Federalism: Forging a Nation | **Chapter 1:** Citizenship in Our Changing Democracy **Chapter 4:** Civil Liberties: Expanding Citizens' Rights **Chapter 6:** Public Opinion: Listening to Citizens |
| **Issue 2:** Does the Tea Party Represent a Revival of America's Revolutionary Ideals? | **Chapter 1:** People, Politics, and Participation **Chapter 6:** Political Socialization and Public Opinion **Chapter 7:** Interest Groups **Chapter 8:** Political Parties | **Chapter 1:** Political Thinking: Becoming a Responsible Citizen **Chapter 6:** Public Opinion and Political Socialization: Shaping the People's Voice **Chapter 7:** Political Participation: Activating the Popular Will **Chapter 8:** Political Parties, Candidates, and Campaigns: Defining the Voter's Choice **Chapter 9:** Interest Groups: Organizing for Influence | **Chapter 6:** Public Opinion: Listening to Citizens **Chapter 9:** Parties and Political Campaigns: Citizens and the Electoral Process **Chapter 11:** Congress: Doing the People's Business **Chapter 13:** Bureaucracy: Citizens as Owners and Consumers |

*(Continued)*

| Taking Sides: Political Issues, 18/e | American Democracy Now, 2/e by Harrison/Harris | The American Democracy, 10/e by Patterson | American Government 2012, 3/e by Losco/Baker |
|---|---|---|---|
| **Issue 3:** Is Bigger Government Better Government? | **Chapter 1:** People, Politics, and Participation<br>**Chapter 3:** Federalism<br>**Chapter 13:** The Bureaucracy<br>**Chapter 15:** Economic Policy | **Chapter 3:** Federalism: Forging a Nation<br>**Chapter 13:** The Federal Bureaucracy: Administering the Government | **Chapter 1:** Citizenship in Our Changing Democracy |
| **Issue 4:** Should America Adopt Public Financing of Political Campaigns? | **Chapter 7:** Interest Groups<br>**Chapter 8:** Political Parties<br>**Chapter 9:** Elections, Campaigns, and Voting | **Chapter 8:** Political Parties, Candidates, and Campaigns: Defining the Voter's Choice<br>**Chapter 12:** The Presidency: Leading the Nation | **Chapter 9:** Parties and Political Campaigns: Citizens and the Electoral Process |
| **Issue 5:** Does the President Have Unilateral War Powers? | **Chapter 16:** Domestic Policy<br>**Chapter 17:** Foreign Policy and National Security | **Chapter 12:** The Presidency: Leading the Nation<br>**Chapter 17:** Foreign Policy: Protecting the American Way | **Chapter 11:** Congress: Doing the People's Business<br>**Chapter 12:** The Presidency: Power and Paradox<br>**Chapter 16:** Foreign and Defense Policy: Protecting American Interests in the World |
| **Issue 6:** Should the Courts Seek the "Original Meaning" of the Constitution? | **Chapter 2:** The Constitution<br>**Chapter 4:** Civil Liberties<br>**Chapter 5:** Civil Rights<br>**Chapter 14:** The Judiciary | **Chapter 2:** Constitutional Democracy: Promoting Liberty and Self-Government<br>**Chapter 14:** The Federal Judicial System: Applying the Law | **Chapter 2:** The Constitution: The Foundation of Citizens' Rights<br>**Chapter 14:** The Courts: Judicial Power in a Democratic Setting |
| **Issue 7:** Is Congress a Dysfunctional Institution? | **Chapter 11:** Congress | **Chapter 2:** Constitutional Democracy: Promoting Liberty and Self-Government<br>**Chapter 11:** Congress: Balancing National Goals and Local Interests | **Chapter 11:** Congress: Doing the People's Business |
| **Issue 8:** May Congress Require People to Buy Health Insurance? | **Chapter 11:** Congress<br>**Chapter 12:** The Presidency | **Chapter 2:** Constitutional Democracy: Promoting Liberty and Self-Government<br>**Chapter 11:** Congress: Balancing National Goals and Local Interests<br>**Chapter 12:** The Presidency: Leading the Nation | **Chapter 3:** Federalism: Citizenship and the Dispersal of Power<br>**Chapter 11:** Congress: Doing the People's Business<br>**Chapter 13:** Bureaucracy: Citizens as Owners and Consumers |

| Taking Sides: Political Issues, 18/e | American Democracy Now, 2/e by Harrison/ Harris | The American Democracy, 10/e by Patterson | American Government 2012, 3/e by Losco/ Baker |
|---|---|---|---|
| **Issue 9:** Should the President Be Allowed "Executive Privilege"? | **Chapter 11:** Congress **Chapter 12:** The Presidency | **Chapter 2:** Constitutional Democracy: Promoting Liberty and Self-Government **Chapter 11:** Congress: Balancing National Goals and Local Interests **Chapter 12:** The Presidency: Leading the Nation | **Chapter 11:** Congress: Doing the People's Business **Chapter 12:** The Presidency: Power and Paradox |
| **Issue 10:** Does Affirmative Action Advance Racial Equality? | **Chapter 4:** Civil Liberties **Chapter 5:** Civil Rights **Chapter 6:** Political Socialization and Public Opinion **Chapter 7:** Interest Groups **Chapter 14:** The Judiciary | **Chapter 5:** Equal Rights: Struggling Toward Fairness **Chapter 6:** Public Opinion and Political Socialization: Shaping the People's Voice **Chapter 14:** The Federal Judicial System: Applying the Law | **Chapter 2:** the Constitution: The Foundation of Citizens' Rights **Chapter 4:** Civil Liberties: Expanding Citizens' Rights **Chapter 5:** Civil Rights: Toward a More Equal Citizenry |
| **Issue 11:** Should Abortion Be Restricted? | **Chapter 4:** Civil Liberties **Chapter 5:** Civil Rights **Chapter 6:** Political Socialization and Public Opinion **Chapter 7:** Interest Groups **Chapter 14:** The Judiciary | **Chapter 4:** Civil Liberties: Protecting Individual Rights **Chapter 6:** Public Opinion and Political Socialization: Shaping the People's Voice **Chapter 9:** Interest Groups: Organizing for Influence **Chapter 12:** The Presidency: Leading the Nation **Chapter 14:** The Federal Judicial System: Applying the Law | **Chapter 2:** the Constitution: The Foundation of Citizens' Rights **Chapter 6:** Public Opinion: Listening to Citizens **Chapter 8:** Interest Groups in America |
| **Issue 12:** Is the Welfare State Obsolete? | **Chapter 4:** Civil Liberties **Chapter 5:** Civil Rights **Chapter 6:** Political Socialization and Public Opinion | **Chapter 6:** Public Opinion and Political Socialization: Shaping the People's Voice **Chapter 7:** Political Participation: Activating the Popular Will **Chapter 16:** Welfare and Education Policy: Providing for Personal Security and Need | **Chapter 3:** Federalism: Citizenship and the Dispersal of Power **Chapter 4:** Civil Liberties: Expanding Citizens' Rights **Chapter 6:** Public Opinion: Listening to Citizens **Chapter 13:** Bureaucracy: Citizens as Owners and Consumers **Chapter 15:** Public Policy: Responding to Citizens |

*(Continued)*

| Taking Sides: Political Issues, 18/e | American Democracy Now, 2/e by Harrison/ Harris | The American Democracy, 10/e by Patterson | American Government 2012, 3/e by Losco/ Baker |
|---|---|---|---|
| **Issue 13:** Are Americans Overtaxed? | **Chapter 6:** Political Socialization and Public Opinion<br>**Chapter 15:** Economic Policy<br>**Chapter 16:** Domestic Policy | **Chapter 6:** Public Opinion and Political Socialization: Shaping the People's Voice<br>**Chapter 15:** Economic and Environmental Policy: Contributing to Prosperity<br>**Chapter 16:** Welfare and Education Policy: Providing for Personal Security and Need | **Chapter 6:** Public Opinion: Listening to Citizens<br>**Chapter 13:** Bureaucracy: Citizens as Owners and Consumers<br>**Chapter 15:** Public Policy: Responding to Citizens |
| **Issue 14:** Is America Becoming More Unequal? | **Chapter 4:** Civil Liberties<br>**Chapter 5:** Civil Rights<br>**Chapter 6:** Political Socialization and Public Opinion | **Chapter 5:** Equal Rights: Struggling Toward Fairness<br>**Chapter 7:** Political Participation: Activating the Popular Will<br>**Chapter 16:** Welfare and Education Policy: Providing for Personal Security and Need | **Chapter 5:** Civil Rights: Toward a More Equal Citizenry<br>**Chapter 7:** Political Participation: Equal Opportunities and Unequal Voices |
| **Issue 15:** Should Same-Sex Marriage be a Constitutional Right? | **Chapter 4:** Civil Liberties<br>**Chapter 5:** Civil Rights<br>**Chapter 6:** Political Socialization and Public Opinion<br>**Chapter 7:** Interest Groups<br>**Chapter 14:** The Judiciary | **Chapter 4:** Civil Liberties: Protecting Individual Rights<br>**Chapter 5:** Equal Rights: Struggling Toward Fairness<br>**Chapter 9:** Interest Groups: Organizing for Influence | **Chapter 2:** The Constitution: The Foundation of Citizens' Rights<br>**Chapter 4:** Civil Liberties: Expanding Citizens' Rights<br>**Chapter 5:** Civil Rights: Toward a More Equal Citizenry<br>**Chapter 7:** Political Participation: Equal Opportunities and Unequal Voices |
| **Issue 16:** Should There Be a "Wall of Separation" Between Church and State? | **Chapter 1:** People, Politics, and Participation<br>**Chapter 2:** The Constitution<br>**Chapter 3:** Federalism<br>**Chapter 6:** Political Socialization and Public Opinion<br>**Chapter 14:** The Judiciary | **Chapter 1:** Political Thinking: Becoming a Responsible Citizen<br>**Chapter 4:** Civil Liberties: Protecting Individual Rights<br>**Chapter 14:** The Federal Judicial System: Applying the Law | **Chapter 1:** Citizenship in Our Changing Democracy<br>**Chapter 3:** Federalism: Citizenship and the Dispersal of Power<br>**Chapter 14:** The Courts: Judicial Power in a Democratic Setting |
| **Issue 17:** Do Corporations Have the Same Free Speech Rights as Persons? | **Chapter 2:** The Constitution<br>**Chapter 4:** Civil Liberties<br>**Chapter 5:** Civil Rights | **Chapter 4:** Civil Liberties: Protecting Individual Rights<br>**Chapter 5:** Equal Rights: Struggling Toward Fairness | **Chapter 7:** Political Participation: Equal Opportunities and Unequal Voices<br>**Chapter 13:** Bureaucracy: Citizens as Owners and Consumers |

| Taking Sides: Political Issues, 18/e | American Democracy Now, 2/e by Harrison/ Harris | The American Democracy, 10/e by Patterson | American Government 2012, 3/e by Losco/ Baker |
| --- | --- | --- | --- |
| **Issue 18:** Should "Recreational" Drugs Be Legalized? | **Chapter 4:** Civil Liberties<br>**Chapter 5:** Civil Rights<br>**Chapter 17:** Foreign Policy and National Security | **Chapter 4:** Civil Liberties: Protecting Individual Rights<br>**Chapter 5:** Equal Rights: Struggling Toward Fairness<br>**Chapter 14:** The Federal Judicial System: Applying the Law | **Chapter 3:** Federalism: Citizenship and the Dispersal of Power<br>**Chapter 4:** Civil Liberties: Expanding Citizens' Rights<br>**Chapter 6:** Public Opinion: Listening to Citizens<br>**Chapter 14:** The Courts: Judicial Power in a Democratic Setting |
| **Issue 19:** Is Indefinite Detention of Suspected Terrorists Justified? | **Chapter 4:** Civil Liberties<br>**Chapter 5:** Civil Rights<br>**Chapter 17:** Foreign Policy and National Security | **Chapter 4:** Civil Liberties: Protecting Individual Rights<br>**Chapter 17:** Foreign Policy: Protecting the American Way | **Chapter 2:** The Constitution: The Foundation of Citizens' Rights<br>**Chapter 12:** The Presidency: Power and Paradox<br>**Chapter 16:** Foreign and Defense Policy: Protecting American Interests in the World |
| **Issue 20:** Do We Need to Curb Global Warming? | **Chapter 1:** People, Politics, and Participation<br>**Chapter 7:** Interest Groups<br>**Chapter 10:** The Media | **Chapter 1:** Political Thinking: Becoming a Responsible Citizen<br>**Chapter 9:** Interest Groups: Organizing for Influence<br>**Chapter 10:** The News Media: Communicating Political Images | **Chapter 8:** Interest Groups in America<br>**Chapter 10:** Media: Tuning In or Tuning Out Nation<br>**Chapter 15:** Public Policy: Responding to Citizens |
| **Issue 21:** Is Warrantless Wiretapping Ever Justified to Protect National Security? | **Chapter 4:** Civil Liberties<br>**Chapter 5:** Civil Rights<br>**Chapter 10:** The Media<br>**Chapter 14:** The Judiciary<br>**Chapter 17:** Foreign Policy and National Security | **Chapter 4:** Civil Liberties: Protecting Individual Rights<br>**Chapter 10:** The News Media: Communicating Political Images<br>**Chapter 11:** Congress: Balancing National Goals and Local Interests<br>**Chapter 12:** The Presidency: Leading the Nation<br>**Chapter 14:** The Federal Judicial System: Applying the Law<br>**Chapter 14:** The Federal Judicial System: Applying the Law | **Chapter 2:** The Constitution: The Foundation of Citizens' Rights<br>**Chapter 12:** The Presidency: Power and Paradox<br>**Chapter 16:** Foreign and Defense Policy: Protecting American Interests in the World |

# Topic Guide

This topic guide suggests how the selections in this book relate to the subjects covered in your course. You may want to use the topics listed in these pages to search the Web more easily. On the following pages, a number of Web sites have been gathered specifically for this book. They are arranged to reflect the issues of this *Taking Sides* reader. You can link to these sites by going to www.mhhe.com/cls. All issues and their articles that relate to each topic are listed below the boldfaced term.

## Abortion

11. Should Abortion Be Restricted?

## Affirmative Action

10. Does Affirmative Action Advance Racial Equality?

## American "Mission"

1. Should Americans Believe in a Unique American "Mission"?

## Capitalism

17. Do Corporations Have the Same Free Speech Rights as Persons?

## Congress

7. Is Congress a Dysfunctional Institution?
8. May Congress Require People to Buy Health Insurance?

## Corporations

17. Do Corporations Have the Same Free Speech Rights as Persons?

## Discrimination

10. Does Affirmative Action Advance Racial Equality?

## Drugs

18. Should "Recreational" Drugs Be Legalized?

## Environment

20. Do We Need to Curb Global Warming?

## Equality

10. Does Affirmative Action Advance Racial Equality?
14. Is America Becoming More Unequal?

## Executive Privilege

9. Should the President Be Allowed "Executive Privilege"?

## Free Speech

17. Do Corporations Have the Same Free Speech Rights as Persons?

## Gays

15. Should Same-Sex Marriage Be a Constitutional Right?

## Global Warming

20. Do We Need to Curb Global Warming?

## Government

3. Is Bigger Government Better Government?

## Health Insurance

8. May Congress Require People to Buy Health Insurance?

# Introduction

## Labels and Alignments in American Politics

George McKenna
Stanley Feingold

As the 2012 presidential and congressional elections got underway, Republicans and Democrats struggled for control of the White House and Congress. Republicans accused President Obama of trying to govern a largely "conservative" and "moderate" country from the "far left." The president countered that the Republican Party had been captured by the "the right." As the rhetoric reached fever-pitch, some political pundits and commentators worried that these confrontations might lead to the emergence of constantly dueling "radical" ideologies in America—"progressive liberalism" versus "classical" economics, secularism versus "the religious right"—and they urged the contending parties to remember America's heritage of "pluralism," which leaves room for both radicals and those sometimes called "reactionaries." Meantime, far beyond the White House and the Capitol building— although on occasion they marched in front of both—were the various movements of the right and the left, the right represented by the Tea Party movement and the left by the Occupy Wall Street movement.

Liberal, conservative, moderate, pluralist, radical, right wing, left wing, "classical" economics, "progressive"—what do these terms mean? Or do they have any meaning? Some political analysts regard them as arbitrary labels slapped on by commentators seeking quick ways to sum up candidates (or in some cases to demonize them). The reaction against the ideological labels is understandable, not only because they are often used too loosely but, as we shall see, because the terms themselves can evolve over time. Nevertheless, we think there are some core meanings left, so if they are used carefully, they can help us locate positions on the political stage and the actors who occupy them. In this Introduction we shall try to spell out the meanings of these terms, at least as they are used in American politics, and illustrate these terms by showing how they fit some of the issues presented in this book.

## Liberals Versus Conservatives: An Overview

Let us examine, very briefly, the historical evolution of the terms *liberalism* and *conservatism*. By examining the roots of these terms, we can see how these philosophies have adapted themselves to changing times. In that way, we can avoid using the terms rigidly, without reference to the particular contexts in which liberalism and conservatism have operated over the past two centuries.

## Classical Liberalism

The classical root of the term *liberalism* is the Latin word *libertas,* meaning "liberty" or "freedom." In the early nineteenth century, liberals dedicated themselves to freeing individuals from all unnecessary and oppressive obligations to authority—whether the authority came from the church or the state. They opposed the licensing and censorship of the press, the punishment of heresy, the establishment of religion, and any attempt to dictate orthodoxy in matters of opinion. In economics, liberals opposed state monopolies and other constraints upon competition between private businesses. At this point in its development, liberalism defined freedom primarily in terms of freedom *from.* It appropriated the French term *laissez-faire,* which literally means "leave to be." Leave people alone! That was the spirit of liberalism in its early days. It wanted government to stay out of people's lives and to play a modest role in general. Thomas Jefferson summed up this concept when he said, "I am no friend of energetic government. It is always oppressive."

Despite their suspicion of government, classical liberals invested high hopes in the political process. By and large, they were great believers in democracy. They believed in widening suffrage to include every white male, and some of them were prepared to enfranchise women and blacks as well. Although liberals occasionally worried about "the tyranny of the majority," they were more prepared to trust the masses than to trust a permanent, entrenched elite. Liberal social policy was dedicated to fulfilling human potential and was based on the assumption that this often-hidden potential is enormous. Human beings, liberals argued, were basically good and reasonable. Evil and irrationality were believed to be caused by "outside" influences; they were the result of a bad social environment.

A liberal commonwealth, therefore, was one that would remove the hindrances to the full flowering of the human personality. The basic vision of liberalism has not changed since the nineteenth century. What has changed is the way it is applied to modern society. In that respect, liberalism has changed dramatically. Today, instead of regarding government with suspicion, liberals welcome government as an instrument to serve the people. The change in philosophy began in the latter years of the nineteenth century, when businesses—once small, independent operations—began to grow into giant structures that overwhelmed individuals and sometimes even overshadowed the state in power and wealth. At that time, liberals began reconsidering their commitment to the *laissez-faire* philosophy. If the state can be an oppressor, asked liberals, can't big business also oppress people? By then, many were convinced that commercial and industrial monopolies were crushing the souls and bodies of the working classes. The state, formerly the villain, now was viewed by liberals as a potential savior. The concept of freedom was transformed into something more than a negative freedom *from;* the term began to take on a positive meaning. It meant "realizing one's full potential." Toward this end, liberals believed, the state could prove to be a valuable instrument. It could educate children, protect the health and safety of workers, help people through hard times, promote a healthy economy, and—when necessary—force business to act more humanely and responsibly. Thus was born the movement that culminated in New Deal liberalism.

# New Deal Liberalism

In the United States, the argument in favor of state intervention did not win an enduring majority constituency until after the Great Depression of the 1930s began to be felt deeply. The disastrous effects of a depression that left a quarter of the workforce unemployed opened the way to a new administration—and a promise. "I pledge you, I pledge myself," Franklin D. Roosevelt said when accepting the Democratic nomination in 1932, "to a new deal for the American people." Roosevelt's New Deal was an attempt to effect relief and recovery from the Depression; it employed a variety of means, including welfare programs, public works, and business regulation—most of which involved government intervention in the economy. The New Deal liberalism relied on government to liberate people from poverty, oppression, and economic exploitation. At the same time, the New Dealers claimed to be as zealous as the classical liberals in defending political and civil liberties.

The common element in *laissez-faire* liberalism and welfare-state liberalism is their dedication to the goal of realizing the full potential of each individual. Some still questioned whether this is best done by minimizing state involvement or whether it sometimes requires an activist state. The New Dealers took the latter view, although they prided themselves on being pragmatic and experimental about their activism. During the heyday of the New Deal, a wide variety of programs were tried and—if found wanting—abandoned. All decent means should be tried, they believed, even if it meant dilution of ideological purity. The Roosevelt administration, for example, denounced bankers and businessmen in campaign rhetoric but worked very closely with them while trying to extricate the nation from the Depression. This set a pattern of pragmatism that New Dealers from Harry Truman to Lyndon Johnson emulated.

# Progressive Liberalism

Progressive liberalism emerged in the late 1960s and early 1970s as a more militant and uncompromising movement than the New Deal had ever been. Its roots go back to the New Left student movement of the early 1960s. New Left students went to the South to participate in civil rights demonstrations, and many of them were bloodied in confrontations with southern police; by the mid-1960s they were confronting the authorities in the North over issues like poverty and the Vietnam War. By the end of the decade, the New Left had fragmented into a variety of factions and had lost much of its vitality, but a somewhat more respectable version of it appeared as the New Politics movement. Many New Politics crusaders were former New Leftists who had traded their jeans for coats and ties; they tried to work within the system instead of always confronting it.

Even so, they retained some of the spirit of the New Left. The civil rights slogan "Freedom Now" expressed the mood of the New Politics. The young university graduates who filled its ranks had come from an environment where "nonnegotiable" demands were issued to college deans by leaders of sit-in protests. There was more than youthful arrogance in the New Politics movement, however; there was a pervasive belief that America had lost, had compromised away, much of its idealism. The New Politics liberals sought to recover some of that spirit by linking up with an older tradition of militant reform, which went back to the time of the Revolution. These new liberals saw themselves as the authentic heirs of Thomas Paine and Henry David Thoreau, of the abolitionists, the radical populists, the suffragettes, and the great progressive reformers of the early twentieth century.

While New Deal liberals concentrated almost exclusively on bread-and-butter issues such as unemployment and poverty, the New Politics liberals introduced what came to be known as social issues into the political arena.

These included: the repeal of laws against abortion, the liberalization of laws against homosexuality and pornography, the establishment of affirmative action programs to ensure increased hiring of minorities and women, and the passage of the Equal Rights Amendment.

In foreign policy, too, New Politics liberals departed from the New Deal agenda. Because they had keener memories of the unpopular and (for them) unjustified war in Vietnam than of World War II, they became doves, in contrast to the general hawkishness of the New Dealers. They were skeptical of any claim that the United States must be the leader of the free world or, indeed, that it had any special mission in the world; some were convinced that America was already in decline and must learn to adjust accordingly. The real danger, they argued, came not from the Soviet Union but from the mad pace of America's arms race with the Soviets, which, as they saw it, could bankrupt the country, starve its social programs, and culminate in a nuclear Armageddon. New Politics liberals were heavily represented at the 1972 Democratic national convention, which nominated South Dakota senator George McGovern for president. By the 1980s the New Politics movement was no longer new, and many of its adherents preferred to be called progressives.

By this time their critics had another name for them: radicals. The critics saw their positions as inimical to the interests of the United States, destructive of the family, and fundamentally at odds with the views of most Americans. The adversaries of the progressives were not only conservatives but many New Deal liberals, who openly scorned the McGovernites. This split still exists within the Democratic party, although it is now more skillfully managed by party leaders. In 1988 the Democrats paired Michael Dukakis, whose Massachusetts supporters were generally on the progressive side of the party, with New Dealer Lloyd Bentsen as the presidential and vice presidential candidates, respectively.

In 1992 the Democrats won the presidency with Arkansas governor Bill Clinton, whose record as governor seemed to put him in the moderate-to-conservative camp, and Tennessee senator Albert Gore, whose position on environmental issues could probably be considered quite liberal but whose general image was middle-of-the-road. Both candidates had moved toward liberal positions on the issues of gay rights and abortion. By 1994 Clinton was perceived by many Americans as being "too liberal," which some speculate may have been a factor in the defeat of Democrats in the congressional elections that year. Clinton immediately sought to shake off that perception, positioning himself as a "moderate" between extremes and casting the Republicans as an "extremist" party. (These two terms will be examined presently.)

President Obama comes from the progressive liberal wing of the Democratic Party, although in his campaign for office he attempted to appeal to moderates and even some conservatives by stressing his determination to regard the country not in terms of red (Republican) states and blue (Democratic) states but as a nation united. Once in office, however, his agenda, which included an $830-billion "stimulus" expenditure to jump-start the economy and an ambitious social insurance program, came from the playbook of progressive liberalism; by 2010 it faced unanimous resistance from the Republican minority in Congress. In the 2010 congressional races its unpopularity in so-called "swing" districts and states, that had swung Democrat in the 2008 election, cost many moderate Democrats their seats in Congress.

## Conservatism

Like liberalism, conservatism has undergone historical transformation in America. Just as early liberals (represented by Thomas Jefferson) espoused less government, early conservatives (whose earliest leaders were Alexander Hamilton and John Adams) urged government support of economic enterprise and government intervention on behalf of certain groups. But today, in reaction to the growth of the welfare state, conservatives argue strongly that more government means more unjustified interference in citizens' lives, more bureaucratic regulation of private conduct, more inhibiting control of economic enterprise, more material advantage for the less energetic and less able at the expense of those who are prepared to work harder and better, and, of course, more taxes—taxes that will be taken from those who have earned money and given to those who have not.

Contemporary conservatives are not always opposed to state intervention. They may support larger military expenditures in order to protect society against foreign enemies. They may also allow for some intrusion into private life in order to protect society against internal subversion and would pursue criminal prosecution zealously in order to protect society against domestic violence. The fact is that few conservatives, and perhaps fewer liberals, are absolute with respect to their views about the power of the state. Both are quite prepared to use the state in order to further *their* purposes. It is true that activist presidents such as Franklin Roosevelt and John Kennedy were likely to be classified as liberals. However, Richard Nixon was also an activist, and, although he does not easily fit any classification, he was far closer to conservatism than to liberalism. It is too easy to identify liberalism with statism and conservatism with antistatism: it is important to remember that it was liberal Jefferson who counseled against "energetic government" and conservative Alexander Hamilton who designed bold powers for the new central government and wrote,

"Energy in the executive is a leading character in the definition of good government."

# The Religious Right

The terms "right" and "left," as in "right wing of the Republican Party" and "leftist Democrats," came from an accident of seating in the French National Assembly during the Revolution of the early 1790s. It just happened that the liberals flocked to the left side of the assembly hall while conservatives went to the right. "Left" and "right," then, are almost synonyms for liberals and conservatives, the main difference being that they give a sense of continuum and degree—someone can be "center-left" or "center-right" instead of at the extremes.

Even so, the terms have a certain hard edge. To call someone a "leftist" or a "right-winger" is to give an impression that they are strident or excessively zealous. That impression is conveyed in the term "religious right," a term few of its adherents would use to describe themselves, preferring softer terms like "religious conservatives" or "cultural conservatives."

For better or worse, although, the term "religious right" has entered the media mainstream, so we shall use it here to designate observant Christians or Jews whose concerns are not so much high taxes and government spending as the decline of traditional Judeo-Christian morality, a decline they attribute in part to wrongheaded government policies and judicial decisions. They oppose many of the recent judicial decisions on socio-cultural issues such as abortion, school prayer, pornography, and gay rights, and they were outspoken critics of the Clinton administration, citing everything from President Clinton's views on gays in the military to his sexual behavior while in the White House.

Spokesmen for progressive liberalism and the religious right stand as polar opposites: The former regard abortion as a woman's right; the latter see it as legalized murder. The former tend to regard homosexuality as a lifestyle that needs protection against discrimination; the latter are more likely to see it as a perversion. The list of issues could go on. The religious right and the progressive liberals are like positive and negative photographs of America's moral landscape. Sociologist James Davison Hunter uses the term *culture wars* to characterize the struggles between these contrary visions of America. For all the differences between progressive liberalism and the religious right, however, their styles are very similar. They are heavily laced with moralistic prose; they tend to equate compromise with selling out; and they claim to represent the best, most authentic traditions of America.

This is not to denigrate either movement, for the kinds of issues they address are indeed moral issues, which do not generally admit much compromise. These issues cannot simply be finessed or ignored, despite the efforts of conventional politicians to do so. One of them, abortion (Issue 11), is included in this volume.

# Neoconservatism

The term *neoconservatism* came into use in the early 1970s as a designation for former New Deal Democrats who had became alarmed by what they saw as the drift of their party's foreign policy toward appeasing Communists. When

Senator George McGovern, the party's presidential nominee in 1972, stated that he would "crawl to Hanoi on my knees" to secure peace in Vietnam, he seemed to them to exemplify this new tendency. They were, then, "hawks" in foreign policy, which they insisted was the historic stance of their party; they regarded themselves as the true heirs of liberal presidents such as Truman and Kennedy and liberal senators such as Henry ("Scoop") Jackson of Washington State. On domestic policy, they were still largely liberal, except for their reactions to three new liberal planks added by the "progressives": gay rights, which neoconservatives tended to regard as a distortion of civil rights; abortion, which to some degree or another went against the grain of their moral sensibilities; and affirmative action, which some compared to the "quota system" once used to keep down the number of Jews admitted to elite universities. In fact, a number of prominent neoconservatives were Jews, including Norman Podhoretz, Midge Decter, Gertrude Himmelfarb, and Irving Kristol (although others, such as Michael Novak and Daniel Patrick Moynihan, were Roman Catholics, and one, Richard John Neuhaus, was a Lutheran pastor who later converted to Catholicism and became a priest).

The term *neoconservative* seemed headed for oblivion in the 1980s, when some leading neoconservatives dropped the "neo" part and classified themselves as conservatives, period. By the time the Soviet Union collapsed in 1991, it appeared that the term was no longer needed—the Cold War with "world Communism" was over. But the rise of Islamic terrorism in the 1990s, aimed at the West in general and the United States in particular, brought back alarms analogous to those of the Cold War period, with global terrorism now taking the place of world Communism. So, too, was the concern that liberal foreign policy might not be tough enough for the fight against these new, ruthless enemies of Western democracy. The concern was ratcheted up considerably after the events of 9/11, and now a new generation of neoconservatives was in the spotlight—some of its members literally the children of an earlier "neo" generation. They included Bill Kristol, John Podhoretz, Douglas Feith, Paul Wolfowitz, Richard Perle, David Brooks, and (although he was old enough to overlap with the previous generation) Bill Bennett.

## Radicals, Reactionaries, and Moderates

The label *reactionary* is almost an insult, and the label *radical* is worn with pride by only a few zealots on the banks of the political mainstream. A reactionary is not a conserver but a backward-mover, dedicated to turning the clock back to better times. Most people suspect that reactionaries would restore us to a time that never was, except in political myth. For most Americans, the repeal of industrialism or universal education (or the entire twentieth century itself) is not a practical, let alone desirable, political program.

Radicalism (literally meaning "from the roots" or "going to the foundation") implies a fundamental reconstruction of the social order. Taken in that sense, it is possible to speak of right-wing radicalism as well as left-wing radicalism—radicalism that would restore or inaugurate a new hierarchical society as well as radicalism that calls for nothing less than an egalitarian society. The term is sometimes used in both of these senses, but most often the word *radicalism* is reserved to characterize more liberal change. While the liberal would effect change through conventional democratic processes, the radical is likely to be skeptical about the ability of the established machinery to bring about the needed change and might be prepared to sacrifice "a little" liberty to bring about a great deal more equality.

*Moderate* is a highly coveted label in America. Its meaning is not precise, but it carries the connotations of sensible, balanced, and practical. A moderate person is not without principles, but he or she does not allow principles to harden into dogma. The opposite of moderate is *extremist,* a label most American political leaders eschew. Yet there have been notable exceptions. When Arizona senator Barry Goldwater, a conservative Republican, was nominated for president in 1964, he declared, "Extremism in defense of liberty is no vice! . . . Moderation in the pursuit of justice is no virtue!" This open embrace of extremism did not help his electoral chances; Goldwater was overwhelmingly defeated. At about the same time, however, another American political leader also embraced a kind of extremism, and with better results. In a famous letter written from a jail cell in Birmingham, Alabama, the Reverend Martin Luther King, Jr., replied to the charge that he was an extremist not by denying it but by distinguishing between different kinds of extremists. The question, he wrote, "is not whether we will be extremist but what kind of extremist will we be. Will we be extremists for hate, or will we be extremists for love?" King aligned himself with the love extremists, in which category he also placed Jesus, St. Paul, and Thomas Jefferson, among others. It was an adroit use of a label that is usually anathema in America.

# Pluralism

The principle of pluralism espouses diversity in a society containing many interest groups and in a government containing competing units of power. This implies the widest expression of competing ideas, and in this way, pluralism is in sympathy with an important element of liberalism. However, as James Madison and Alexander Hamilton pointed out when they analyzed the sources of pluralism in their *Federalist* commentaries on the Constitution, this philosophy springs from a profoundly pessimistic view of human nature, and in this respect it more closely resembles conservatism. Madison, possibly the single most influential member of the convention that wrote the Constitution, hoped that in a large and varied nation, no single interest group could control the government. Even if there were a majority interest, it would be unlikely to capture all of the national agencies of government—the House of Representatives, the Senate, the presidency, and the federal judiciary—each of which was chosen in a different way by a different constituency for a different term of office. Moreover, to make certain that no one branch exercised excessive power, each was equipped with "checks and balances" that enabled any agency of national government to curb the powers of the others. The clearest statement of Madison's, and the Constitution's, theory can be found in the 51st paper of the *Federalist:* It may be a reflection on human nature that such devices should be necessary to control the abuses of government. But what is government itself, but the greatest of all reflections on human nature? If men were angels, no government would be necessary.

This pluralist position may be analyzed from different perspectives. It is conservative insofar as it rejects simple majority rule; yet it is liberal insofar as it rejects rule by a single elite. It is conservative in its pessimistic appraisal of human nature; yet pluralism's pessimism is also a kind of egalitarianism, holding as it does that no one can be trusted with power and that majority interests no less than minority interests will use power for selfish ends. It is possible to suggest that in America pluralism represents an alternative to both liberalism and conservatism. Pluralism is anti-majoritarian and anti-elitist and combines some elements of both.

# Some Applications

Despite our effort to define the principal alignments in American politics, some policy decisions do not fit neatly into these categories. Readers will reach their own conclusions, but we suggest some alignments here in order to demonstrate the variety of viewpoints.

In Issue 1, concerning the notion of a unique American "mission," Howard Zinn expresses a view common among New Politics liberals: skepticism of any claim that the United States must be the leader of the free world or, indeed, that it has ever had any special mission in the world. Wilfred McClay's view that the "myth" of America is a noble one is still shared today by many New Deal liberals, but it is embraced more conspicuously by conservatives. In Issue 4, Mark Green favors taxpayer funding of political campaigns, based upon the progressive liberal argument that our democratic system needs not just an honest ballot count but a playing field leveled through the elimination of money as a factor in elections; John Samples adopts the conservative view that taxpayers should not be forced to fund the electoral campaigns of politicians.

In Issue 6, on courts seeking the "original meaning" of the Constitution, Supreme Court Justice Stephen Breyer believes that constitutional interpretation must reflect what he believes to be the democratic trajectory of the Constitution, a long-held liberal position, while his colleague on the bench, Justice Antonin Scalia, takes a position long argued by conservatives when he insists that the Constitution, unlike statutes, was not meant to be changed, except by amendment. Warrantless wiretapping by the president, covered in Issue 21, also taps into liberal-conservative dichotomies. Andrew McCarthy insists, as do many conservatives, that it is necessary, long practiced by presidents during wartime, and authorized by the president's wartime powers, while former Vice President Al Gore takes the liberal position that it violates essential liberties.

Issue 12, on whether the welfare state is obsolete, pits the New Deal liberalism of Irwin Garfinkel and Timothy Smeeding against Yuval Levin's brand of conservatism (or perhaps neoconservatism), which does not trust entirely to markets but relies also on family, church, and civil society as "counterweights." Issue 14, on whether or not the gap between the rich and the poor is increasing, points up another disagreement between liberals and conservatives. Most liberals would agree with Robert Greenstein that socioeconomic inequality is increasing and that this undermines the basic tenets of American democracy. Christopher DeMuth, representing the conservative viewpoint, maintains that Americans are becoming more equal and that virtually all people benefit from increased prosperity because it takes place in a free market. Then there is national health insurance, which liberals and conservatives have been fighting about since President Harry Truman introduced the proposal in 1945. Here is a classic liberal–conservative split, and in Issue 8 U.S. District Court Judge Henry Hudson sides with conservatives by arguing that the federal government has no right to tell people they must buy health insurance. But in another District Court, Judge Caram Steeh takes the liberal position that the federal government possesses broad powers to tax, spend, and regulate.

Affirmative action (Issue 10) has become a litmus test of the newer brand of progressive liberalism. The progressives say that it is not enough for the laws of society to be color-blind or gender-blind; they must now reach out to remedy the ills caused by racism and sexism. New Deal liberals, along with conservatives and libertarians, generally oppose affirmative action.

Another example of progressive liberalism is the movement to promote the right of homosexuals to marry. New Deal liberals might or might not support gay marriage, but they would not consider the issue within the framework of liberalism versus conservatism. Their fight was largely over bread-and-butter issues, not issues involving cultural norms. Because it is so remote from the traditional liberal/conservative dichotomy, Ted Olson is able to label his case for gay marriage as a "conservative" case, even though it sounds more like that of progressive liberalism. Opposing him is Sam Shulman, who makes a nuanced but boldly conservative case against same-sex marriage. There are also liberal-conservative splits in foreign policy, and they often figure into debates on national security. Both sides claim to support both civil liberties and national security, but liberals seem to emphasize the former and conservatives the latter. We can see this in the debates on indefinite detention (Issue 19) and warrantless wiretapping (Issue 21). Both of these issues were the subjects of fierce arguments between liberals and conservatives during the Bush administration, and they still are, although on the issue of indefinite detention the Democrats are not as likely to join the liberal side of the debate today. That is because the Obama administration was forced by members of its own party to give up plans for civilian trials of terrorist suspects being held at the Guantanamo base in Cuba. The plan now is to put them on trial before military tribunals, but even here some trials are being postponed indefinitely because evidence used in the trials could seriously compromise national security. There are prisoners in Guantanamo who may sit there for the rest of their lives without a trial.

Global warming (Issue 20) is also an international issue, for if the emission of carbon dioxide and other "greenhouse" gases is indeed causing the earth's temperature to rise, it affects every nation on earth. That is why it has been the subject of international conferences and agreements. And it is, or at least has become, embedded in the larger argument between liberals and conservatives. In the debates between the ten candidates seeking the Republican nomination for president in 2012, only one, John Huntsman of Utah, said he believed in man-made global warming. The rest seemed to agree with Texas Governor Rick Perry that science has not proven the thesis. Liberals, almost without exception, subscribe to the global-warming thesis. (Their complaint is that too many Democratic office-holders, jittery about the costs of eliminating global warming, have grown silent on the subject.) To Gregg Easterbrook, the evidence for global warming is so overwhelming that the debate is over. But obviously it isn't, because Larry Bell, among many others, is still presenting contrary evidence. Our readers can examine both sides before concluding that the case is closed.

This book contains some arguments that are not easy to categorize. Issue 11, on whether or not abortion should be restricted, is one such issue. The pro-choice position, as argued by Mary Gordon, is not a traditional liberal position. Less than a generation ago legalized abortion was opposed by liberals such as Senator Edward Kennedy (D-Massachusetts) and the Reverend Jesse Jackson, and more recently some liberals, such as the late Pennsylvania governor Robert Casey and columnist Nat Hentoff, have opposed it. Nevertheless, most liberals now adopt some version of Gordon's pro-choice views. (President Obama said that the question of when life begins was "above my pay grade" but is firmly on the pro-choice side.) Opposing Gordon is Robert George, whose argument here might be endorsed by many traditional liberals like Hentoff.

The arguments in Issue 7, on Congress, are also difficult to classify, if only because *nobody* seems to like Congress much anymore. Presidential approval ratings below 30 percent are considered abysmal, but Congress's ratings go down to the low teens. Distaste for Congress cuts across partisan and ideological lines: typically, liberals hate Congress because it takes so long to get anything done there; conservatives hate it because it passes too many laws micromanaging the economy. In Issue 7, Ezra Klein gives vent to some of the popular complaints about Congress, while former Congressman Lee Hamilton puts up a spirited defense of the branch in which he served for more than three decades.

The issue of "recreational" drug legalization (Issue 18) also doesn't squarely fit into a liberal-conservative framework. The cause of drug legalization is usually embraced by liberals, but the dean of conservatism, William F. Buckley, famously took up the cause, even admitting he once tried "pot" on his yacht in international waters. In our selections, Bryan Stevenson actually uses a law-and-order argument (usually associated with conservatives) to call for drug legalization, while Theodore Dalrymple uses some of the same law-and-order premises to oppose legalization.

Obviously one's position on the issues in this book will be directed by circumstances. However, we would like to think that the essays in this book are durable enough to last through several seasons of events and controversies.

We can be certain that the issues will survive. The search for coherence and consistency in the use of political labels underlines the options open to us and reveals their consequences. The result must be more mature judgments about what is best for America. That, of course, is the ultimate aim of public debate and decision making, and it transcends all labels and categories.

# *Internet References . . .*

In addition to the Internet sites found below, type in key words, such as "American mission," "American exceptionalism," "democracy fight terror," and "public financing campaigns" to find other listings.

## The Federal Web Locator

Use this handy site as a launching pad for the Web sites of U.S. federal agencies, departments, and organizations. It is well organized and easy to use for informational and research purposes.

**www.lib.auburn.edu/madd/docs/fedloc.html**

## The Library of Congress

Examine this Web site to learn about the extensive resource tools, library services/resources, exhibitions, and databases available through the Library of Congress in many different subfields of government studies.

**www.loc.gov**

## U.S. Founding Documents

Through this Emory University site you can view scanned originals of the Declaration of Independence, the Constitution, and the Bill of Rights. The transcribed texts are also available, as are the *Federalist Papers*.

**www.law.emory.edu/FEDERAL/**

## Hoover Institution Public Policy Inquiry: Campaign Finance

Use this Stanford University site to explore the history of campaign finance as well as the current reforms and proposals for future change.

**www.campaignfinancesite.org**

## Poynter.org

This research site of the Poynter Institute, a school for journalists, provides extensive links to information and resources about the media, including media ethics and reportage techniques. Many bibliographies and Web sites are included.

**www.poynter.org/research/index.htm**

## Freedom House

Founded over sixty years ago by Eleanor Roosevelt, Wendell Wilke, and others concerned about the suppression of democracy in the world, Freedom House charts the progress and retrogression of freedom in the nations of the world. You can view its annual "map of freedom" to see which countries it lists each year as "free" (in green), "partly free" (in yellow) and "not free" (in blue).

**www.freedomhouse.org**

# UNIT 1

# Democracy and the American Political Process

*D*emocracy is derived from two Greek words, demos *and* kratia, *which mean, respectively, "people" and "rule." But who are "the people," and how much "rule" should there be? Does the Tea Party accurately represent the opinions of the people? Do the people need more, or fewer, "rules"? Does "special interest" money in elections undermine the general interest? Some analysts of democracy believe that a viable democratic system requires widespread belief in their country's unique mission? But is that necessary?*

- Should Americans Believe in a Unique American "Mission"?
- Does the Tea Party Represent a Revival of America's Revolutionary Ideals?
- Is Bigger Government Better Government?
- Should America Adopt Public Financing of Political Campaigns?

# ISSUE 1

# Should Americans Believe in a Unique American "Mission"?

**YES: Wilfred M. McClay,** from "The Founding of Nations," *First Things* (March 2006)

**NO: Howard Zinn,** from "The Power and the Glory: Myths of American Exceptionalism," *Boston Review* (Summer 2005)

### ISSUE SUMMARY

**YES:** Humanities professor Wilfred M. McClay argues that America's "myth," its founding narrative, helps to sustain and hold together a diverse people.

**NO:** Historian Howard Zinn is convinced that America's myth of "exceptionalism" has served as a justification for lawlessness, brutality, and imperialism.

Take a dollar from your wallet and look at the back of it. On the left side, above an unfinished pyramid with a detached eye on top, are the words "Annuit Coeptis," Latin for, "He has favored our endeavors." The "He" is God.

Since the time of the Puritans, Americans have often thought of themselves collectively as a people whose endeavors are favored by God. "We shall be as a city upon a hill, the eyes of all people are upon us," said Puritan leader John Winthrop aboard the *Arbella*, the Puritans' flagship, as it left for the New World in 1630. Later in that century another Puritan, the Rev. Samuel Danforth, famously spoke of New England's divinely assigned "errand into the wilderness." By the eighteenth century, the role of New England had become the role of America: God had led his people to establish a new social order, a light to the nations. "Your forefathers," John Jay told New Yorkers in 1776, "came to America under the auspices of Divine Providence." For Patrick Henry, the American Revolution "was the grand operation, which seemed to be assigned by the Deity to the men of this age in our country." In his First Inaugural Address, George Washington saw an "invisible hand" directing the people of the United States. "Every step they have taken seems to have been distinguished by some token of providential agency." Even the most secular-minded founders thought of their nation in providential terms. Thomas Jefferson paid homage to the "Being . . . who led our fathers, as Israel of old, from their native land and planted them in a country flowing with all the necessaries and comforts of life; who has covered our infancy with His providence and our riper years with his wisdom and power." At the Constitutional Convention in Philadelphia, Benjamin Franklin declared that "God governs in the affairs of men," adding: "And if a sparrow cannot fall to the ground without his notice, is it probable that an empire cannot rise without his aid?"

Throughout the nineteenth and twentieth centuries, this notion of America as "a people set apart" was a perennial feature of American public discourse. Its most eloquent expression came in the speeches of Abraham Lincoln. Perhaps in deference to biblical literalists, Lincoln did not call Americans a "chosen people" (a name limited to the Jews in the Bible), but he came close: he said Americans were God's "almost chosen people." In other speeches, particularly in his Second Inaugural Address, he stressed the role of Divine Providence in directing the course of American history. Frederick Douglass, the black abolitionist leader, called the Second Inaugural "more like a sermon than a state paper."

So it has gone, down through the nation's history. Herbert Croly, the influential Progressive writer in the early twentieth century, called on Americans to realize "the promise of American life." In 1936 Franklin Roosevelt told a newer generation of Americans that they had a "rendezvous with destiny." John F. Kennedy proclaimed that "God's work must truly be our own." Martin Luther King, in his prophetic "I Have a Dream" speech identified his dream with the God-given promises of America. Ronald Reagan, paraphrasing John Winthrop's speech of 1630, saw America as a "shining city on a hill."

All of this sounds inspiring, and no doubt it did help inspire many worthy reforms, from the abolition of slavery in the 1860s to the landmark civil rights laws a century later. But is there a darker side to it? To its critics, American "exceptionalism" is a dangerous notion. They remind us that other nations, too, such as the ancient Romans, the Dutch, the Spanish, the British, and the Germans, have at various times boasted of themselves as an exceptional people, and that this has led them down the path to chauvinism, imperialism, and even genocide. To them, the invocation, "God bless America" sounds like hubris, as if God is being asked to bless whatever it is that America decides to do. Such a spirit lay behind "Manifest Destiny," a slogan from the mid-nineteenth century that was used to justify American expansion into territory claimed by Mexico, and in the 1890s American imperialists justified American expansion into Cuba and the Philippines in nearly similar language. From Indian removal at home to imperial adventures abroad, there have been few dark episodes in American history that have not found defenders ready to put them in terms of American exceptionalism.

In the selections that follow, humanities professor Wilfred M. McClay looks at the brighter side of American providentialism, while historian Howard Zinn argues that what he calls "American exceptionalism" is a dangerous idea because it has served as a justification for lawlessness, brutality, and imperialism.

# YES ↩                    Wilfred M. McClay

# The Founding of Nations

**D**id the United States really have a beginning that can be called its "Founding"? Can any society, for that matter, be said to have a founding moment in its past that ought to be regarded as a source of guidance and support?

Much of the intellectual culture of our time stands resolutely opposed to the idea of a founding as a unique moment in secular time that has a certain magisterial authority over what comes after it. The cult of ancestors, in its many forms, is always one of the chief objects of modernity's deconstructive energies. Kant's famous command, *Sapere Aude*—"Dare to Reason," the battle cry of the Enlightenment—always ends up being deployed against arguments claiming traditional authority.

Foundings, in this view, are fairy tales that cannot be taken seriously—indeed, that it is dangerous to take seriously, since modern nation-states have used them as tools of cultural hegemony. One has a moral obligation to peek behind the curtain, and one ought to have a strong presupposition about what one will find there. There is a settled assumption in the West, particularly among the educated, that every founding was in reality a blood-soaked moment, involving the enslavement or exploitation of some for the benefit of others. Foundational myths are merely attempts to prettify this horror. Our ancestors were not the noble heroes of epic. They were the primal horde or the Oedipal usurpers, and their authority derived ultimately from their successful monopolization of violence—and then their subsequent monopolization of the way the story would be told.

The perfect expression of this view is Theodor Adorno's dictum, "There is no monument of civilization that is not at the same time a monument of barbarism." Every achievement of culture involves an elaborate concealment of the less-than-licit means that went into its making. Property is theft, in Proudhon's famous phrase, which means that legitimacy is nothing more than the preeminent force, and our systems of law are the ways that the stolen money is laundered and turned into Carnegie libraries and Vanderbilt universities and other carved Corinthian pillars of society. From this point of view, the credulous souls who speak of the American founding are merely trying to retail a heroic myth about the Founding Fathers, a group of youthful and idealistic patriarchs who somehow reached up into the heavens and pulled down a Constitution for all time.

Admittedly, American filiopietism about the Founding can get out of hand. On the ceiling of the rotunda of the United States Capitol building—the inside of the dome which, in its external aspect, is arguably the single most recognizable symbol of American democracy—there is painted a fresco called "The Apotheosis of George Washington." It is as if the Sistine Chapel were transposed into an American key. The first president sits in glory, flanked by the Goddess of Liberty and the winged figure Fame sounding a victorious trumpet and holding aloft a palm frond. The thirteen female figures in a semi-circle around Washington represent the thirteen original states. On the outer ring stand six allegorical groups representing classical images of agriculture, arts and sciences, commerce, war, mechanics, and seafaring. This figure of a deified Washington, painted significantly enough in the year 1865, reflects a vision that appealed powerfully to the American public. But it is actually a rather disturbing image, and it cries out for debunking.

Still, debunking is a blunt instrument of limited value, despite the modern prejudice in its favor. To the question "What is a man?" André Malraux once gave the quintessential modern debunking answer: "A miserable little pile of secrets." That answer is too true to dismiss—but not quite true enough to embrace. And it is, in its way, the exact opposite number to the saccharin image of a deified and perfected George Washington dwelling in the clouds atop the Capitol dome. Such a conflict between grand moral oversimplications impoverishes our thinking and sets us a false standard of greatness—one that is too easily debunked and leaves us too easily defrauded. . . .

When we speak of American national identity, one of the chief points at issue arises out of the tension between *creed* and *culture*. This is a tension between, on the one hand, the idea of the United States as a nation built on the foundation of self-evident, rational, and universally applicable propositions about human nature and human society; and, on the other hand, the idea of the United States as a very unusual, historically specific and contingent entity, underwritten by a long, intricately evolved, and very particular legacy of English law, language, and customs, Greco-Roman cultural antecedents, and Judeo-Christian sacred texts and theological and moral teachings, without whose presences the nation's flourishing would not be possible.

All this makes a profound tension, with much to be said for both sides. And the side one comes down on will say a lot about one's stance on an immense number of issues, such as immigration, education, citizenship, cultural assimilation, multiculturalism, pluralism, the role of religion in public life, the prospects for democratizing the Middle East, and on and on.

Yet any understanding of American identity that entirely excluded either creed or culture would be seriously deficient. Any view of American life that failed to acknowledge its powerful strains of universalism, idealism, and crusading zeal would be describing a different country from the America that happens to exist. And any view of America as simply a bundle of abstract normative ideas about freedom and democracy and self-government that can flourish just as easily in any cultural and historical soil, including a multilingual, post-religious, or post-national one, takes too much for granted and will be in for a rude awakening.

The antagonism of creed and culture is better understood not as a statement of alternatives but as an antinomy, one of those perpetual oppositions that can never be resolved. In fact, the two halves of the opposition often reinforce each other. The creed needs the support of the culture—and the culture, in turn, is imbued with respect for the creed. For the creed to be successful, it must be able to presume the presence of all kinds of cultural inducements—toward civility, restraint, deferred gratification, nonviolence, loyalty, procedural fairness, impersonal neutrality, compassion, respect for elders, and the like. These traits are not magically called into being by the mere invocation of the Declaration of Independence. Nor are they sustainable for long without the support of strong and deeply rooted social and cultural institutions that are devoted to the formation of character, most notably the traditional family and traditional religious institutions. But by the same token, the American culture is unimaginable apart from the influence of the American creed: from the sense of pride and moral responsibility Americans derive from being, as Walter Berns has argued, a carrier of universal values—a vanguard people.

Forcing a choice between creed and culture is not the way to resolve the problem of cultural restoration. Clearly both can plausibly claim a place in the American Founding. What seems more urgent is the repair of some background assumptions about our relation to the past. It is a natural enough impulse to look back in times of turbulence and uncertainty. And it is especially natural, even obligatory, for a republican form of government to do so, since republics come into being at particular moments in secular time, through self-conscious acts of public deliberation. Indeed, philosophers from Aristotle on have insisted that republics *must* periodically recur to their first principles, in order to adjust and renew themselves through a fresh encounter with their initiating vision.

A constitutional republic like the United States is uniquely grounded in its foundational moment, its time of creation. And a founding is not merely the instant that the ball started rolling. Instead, it is a moment that presumes a certain authority over all the moments that will follow—and to speak of a founding is to presume that such moments in time are possible. It most closely resembles the moment that one takes an oath or makes a promise. One could even say that a constitutional founding is a kind of covenant, a meta-promise entered into with the understanding that it has a uniquely powerful claim on the future. It requires of us a willingness to be constantly looking back to our initiating promises and goals, in much the same way that we would chart progress or regress in our individual lives by reference to a master list of resolutions.

Republicanism means self-government, and so republican liberty does not mean living without restraint. It means, rather, living in accordance with a law that you have dictated to yourself. Hence the especially strong need of republics to recur to their founding principles and their founding narratives, is a never-ending process of self-adjustment. There should be a constant interplay between founding ideals and current realities, a tennis ball bouncing back and forth between the two.

And for that to happen, there need to be two things in place. First, founding principles must be sufficiently fixed to give us genuine guidance, to *teach* us something. Of course, we celebrate the fact that our Constitution was created with a built-in openness to amendment. But the fact that such ideals are open to amendment is perhaps the least valuable thing about them. A founding, like a promise or a vow, means nothing if its chief glory is its adaptability. The analogy of a successful marriage, which is also, in a sense, a *res publica* that must periodically recur to first principles, and whose flourishing depends upon the ability to distinguish first principles from passing circumstances, is actually a fairly good guide to these things.

❧

Second, there needs to be a sense of connection to the past, a reflex for looking backward, and cultivating that ought to be one of the chief uses of the formal study of history. Unfortunately, the fostering of a vital sense of connection to the past is not one of the goals of historical study as it is now taught and practiced in this country. The meticulous contextualization of past events and ideas, arising out of a sophisticated understanding of the past's particularities and discontinuities with the present, is one of the great achievements of modern historiography. But we need to recognize that this achievement comes at a high cost when it emphasizes the *pastness* of the past—when it makes the past completely unavailable to us, separated from us by an impassable chasm of contextual difference.

In the case of the American Founding, a century-long assault has taken place among historians, and the sense of connection is even more tenuous. The standard scholarly accounts insist this heated series of eighteenth-century debates—among flawed, unheroic, and self-interested white men—offers nothing to which we should grant any abiding authority. That was then, and this is now.

The insistence on the pastness of the past imprisons us in the present. It makes our present antiseptically cut off from anything that might really nourish, surprise, or challenge it. It erodes our sense of being part of a common enterprise with humankind. An emphasis on scholarly precision has dovetailed effortlessly with what might be called the debunking imperative, which generally aims to discredit any use of the past to justify or support something in the present, and is therefore one of the few gestures likely to win universal approbation among historians. It is professionally safest to be a critic and extremely dangerous to be too affirmative.

Scholarly responsibility thus seems to demand the deconstruction of the American Founding into its constituent elements, thereby divesting it of any claim to unity or any heroic or mythic dimensions, deserving of our admiration or reverence. There was no coherence to what they did, and looking backward to divine what they meant by what they were doing makes no sense.

The Founders and Framers, after all, fought among themselves. They produced a document that was a compromise, that waffled on important issues, that remains hopelessly bound to the eighteenth century and inadequate to our contemporary problems, etc. And so—in much the same manner as the source criticism of the Bible, which challenges the authority of Scripture by understanding the text as a compilation of haphazardly generated redactions—the Constitution is seen as a concatenation of disparate elements, a mere political deal meant to be superseded by other political deals, and withal an instrument of the powerful. The last thing in the world you would want to do is treat it as a document with any intrinsic moral authority. Every text is merely a pretext. This is the kind of explanation one has learned to expect from the historical guild.

⋅⟡⋅

In this connection, it is amusing to see the extent to which historians, who are pleased to regard the Constitution as a hopelessly outdated relic of a bygone era, are themselves still crude nineteenth-century positivists at heart. They still pride themselves on their ability to puncture myths, relying on a shallow positivistic understanding of a myth as a more or less organized form of falsehood, rather than seeing myth as a structure of meaning, a manner of giving a manageable shape to the cosmos, and to one's own experience of the world, a shape that expresses cultural ideals and shared sentiments, and that guides us through the darkness of life's many perils and unanswerable questions by providing us with what Plato called a "likely story."

To be sure, there are good things to be said of a critical approach to history, and there are myths aplenty that richly deserve to be punctured. I am glad, for example, that we know beyond a shadow of a doubt that Washington, D.C., in the Kennedy years had very little in common with the legendary Camelot, aside from the ubiquity of adulterous liaisons in both places. That kind of ground-clearing is important, and we are better off without that kind of propagandistic myth. We might even be better off without the Apotheosis of George Washington sitting atop the Capitol dome.

But ground-clearing by itself is not enough. And to think otherwise is to mistake an ancillary activity for the main thing itself—as if agriculture were nothing more than the application of insecticides and weedkillers. History as debunking is ultimately an empty and fruitless undertaking, which fails to address the reasons we humans try to narrate and understand our pasts. It fails to take into account the ways in which a nation's morale, cohesion, and strength derive from a sense of connection to its past. And it fails to acknowledge how much a healthy sense of the future—including the economic and cultural preconditions for a critical historiography to ply its trade—depends on a mythic sense of the nation. The human need to encompass life within the framework of myth is not merely a longing for pleasing illusion. Myths reflect a fundamental human need for a larger shape to our collective aspirations. And it is an illusion to think that we can so ignore that need, and so cauterize our souls, that we will never again be troubled by it.

Indeed, the debunking imperative operates on the basis of its own myth. It presumes the existence of a solid and orderly substratum, a rock-solid reality lying just beneath the illusory surfaces, waiting to be revealed in all its direct and unfeigned honesty when the facades and artifices and false divisions are all stripped away. There is a remarkable complacency and naiveté about such a view. The near-universal presumption that the demise of the nation-state and the rise of international governance would be very good things has everything, except a shred of evidence, to support it. And as for the debunking of bourgeois morality that still passes for sophistication in some quarters and has been the stock-in-trade of Western intellectuals for almost two centuries now—well, this has always been a form of moral free-riding, like the radical posturing of adolescents who always know they can call Mom when they get into trouble.

❧

One residue of the debunking heritage is the curious assumption that narratives of foundings are mere fairy tales—prettified, antiseptic flights of fancy, or wish-fulfillment fantasies, telling of superlative heroes and maidens acting nobly and virtuously to bring forth the status quo or its antecedents. I think it's fair to say that foundational narratives, including creation myths, tend to be conservative in character, in the sense that they tend to provide historical and moral support for existing regimes and social arrangements. It's hard to imagine them being any other way. But the part about their being prettifying fairy tales is demonstrably wrong. In fact, one could say that the most amazing feature of the great foundational myths is their moral complexity.

One need not even consider the appalling creation myths of Greek antiquity, such as the story of Kronos, who castrated his father Ouranos with a sickle given him by his mother, and then, in order to protect himself against the same dismal fate, swallowed his own children until his youngest child, Zeus, also aided by his mother, was able to overthrow him and assume primacy among the gods.

Consider instead the great Biblical stories of the Pentateuch, foundational texts not only for the Jewish people but for the entire family of monotheistic Abrahamic religious faiths—which is to say, those faiths that have been most constitutive of Western civilization. These Biblical texts are anything but tracts of unrelieved patriotism. In fact, one would be justified in seeing them as an exercise in collective self-humiliation. They are replete with the disreputable deeds of their imperfect and dissembling patriarchs, who pawn off their wives as sisters, deceive their fathers, cheat their brothers, murder, and commit incest—together with tales of an incorrigibly feckless people, the people of Israel, sheep-like fools who manage to forget every theophany and divine favor shown them, and prove unable and unwilling to follow the law that has been given to them.

The narrative does not blink at those things. It is itself the harshest critic of the things it describes, and every one of its human heroes is presented as deeply flawed. But what holds all this together is not the greatness of the heroes but the enduring quality of God's successive covenants with them and with His people. The God of the Hebrew Bible makes promises and keeps them, operating through covenants and laws that superintend and take precedence over the force of passing events. In that sense, the complexity of the Biblical account registers, in a remarkably accurate way, the same set of moral directives regarding the authority of the past—and the elements of pain and suffering and shame in that past—that goes into the making of any durable founding. The Passover seder, which is also the template for the Christian gospel story, is not a story of heroic triumph but of deliverance from slavery by a promise-keeping Deity. . . .

Perhaps the most interesting question about these foundational stories is why they are so complex. And the answer is surely to be found in the complexity of the mythic dimension itself, the ways in which it can register and mirror and instruct a civilization, precisely by virtue of its being a rich and truthful narrative that is widely shared. This quality can be neglected in an overly politicized or rationalized age, which wants to see the play of tangible and measurable material interests or causes always at the bottom of things. And it certainly eludes a culture that has ceased to understand the human necessity of looking backward.

❧❦❧

Human knowledge about human affairs always has a reflexive quality about it. It is never a matter of the tree falling unheard and unwitnessed in the forest. There is always someone listening and watching, always a feedback effect—and most prophecies tend to be either self-fulfilled or self-averted. The best social scientists understand this perfectly well (after all, they were the ones who gave us the term "self-fulfilling prophecy"), but they give us such knowledge in a vocabulary and form that are often all but self-subverting. Who, after all, wants to embrace a myth while *calling* it a myth?

But to do so may be preferable to the alternative of nineteenth-century positivism, so long as we are able to proceed with a capacious understanding of "myth," as something more than a mere tall tale, something that can be both life-giving and true. In this connection, there may be particular value in revisiting Ernest Renan's celebrated 1882 essay "What is a Nation?", a rich evocation of the nation's mythic dimension. For Renan, a nation was fundamentally "a soul, a spiritual principle," constituted not only by "present-day consent" but also by the residuum of the past, "the possession in common of a rich legacy of memories" which form in the citizen "the will to perpetuate the value of the heritage that one has received in an undivided form." He declared:

> The nation, like the individual, is the culmination of a long past of endeavors, sacrifice, and devotion. Of all cults, that of the ancestors is the most legitimate, for the ancestors have made us what we are. A heroic past, great men, glory (by which I understand genuine glory),

this is the social capital upon which one bases a national idea. To have common glories in the past and to have a common will in the present, to have performed great deeds together, to wish to perform still more—these are the essential conditions for being a people. . . . A nation is therefore a large-scale solidarity, constituted by the feeling of the sacrifices that one has made in the past and of those that one is prepared to make in the future.

Renan strongly opposed the then-fashionable view that nations should be understood as entities united by racial or linguistic or geographical or religious or material factors. None of those factors were sufficient to account for the emergence of this "spiritual principle." Active consent had to be a part of it. But it was insufficient without the presence of the past—the past in which that consent was embedded and through which it found meaning.

The ballast of the past, and our intimate connection to it, is similarly indispensable to the sense of American national identity. It forms a strain in our identity that is in some respects far less articulate (and less frequently articulated) than the universalistic principles that some writers have emphasized, precisely because it seems to conflict with American assertions of universalism, and its intellectual basis is less well-defined. But it is every bit as powerful, if not more so, and just as indispensable. And it is a very *particular* force. Our nation's particular triumphs, sacrifices, and sufferings—and our memories of those things—draw and hold us together, precisely because they are the sacrifices and sufferings, not of all humanity, but of us in particular.

No one has spoken of American national identity with greater mastery than Abraham Lincoln. In his 1838 speech on "The Perpetuation of Our Political Institutions," delivered to the Young Men's Lyceum of Springfield, Illinois, Lincoln responded to the then-raging violence directed at blacks and abolitionists in Southern and border states with an admonition that could have come from Toynbee: "If destruction be our lot, we must ourselves be its author and finisher. As a nation of freemen, we must live through all time, or die by suicide." The danger he most feared was that rampant lawlessness would dissolve the "attachment of the People" to their government. And the answer he provides to this danger is remarkable for the way it touches on the same themes that Renan recounts:

> Let every American, every lover of liberty, every well wisher to his posterity, swear by the blood of the Revolution, never to violate in the least particular, the laws of the country; and never to tolerate their violation by others. As the patriots of seventy-six did to the support of the Declaration of Independence, so to the support of the Constitution and Laws, let every American pledge his life, his property, and his sacred honor;—let every man remember that to violate the law, is to trample on the blood of his father, and to tear the character of his own, and his children's liberty. Let reverence for the laws, be breathed by every American mother, to the lisping babe, that prattles on her lap—let it be taught in schools, in seminaries, and in colleges;—let it be written in Primmers, spelling books, and in Almanacs;—let it be preached from

the pulpit, proclaimed in legislative halls, and enforced in courts of justice. And, in short, let it become the political religion of the nation; and let the old and the young, the rich and the poor, the grave and the gay, of all sexes and tongues, and colors and conditions, sacrifice unceasingly upon its altars.

The excerpt shows Lincoln's remarkable ability to intertwine the past and the present, and evoke a sense of connection between them. The speech performs the classic republican move, back to the founding origins, connecting the public order explicitly with something so primal as a son's love of, and respect for, his father. Obedience to the law and reverence for the Constitution—these are directly connected with memory, the reverence owed to the sufferings of the patriot generation, and the blood of one's own father. Such words gesture toward his even more famous invocation of "the mystic chords of memory" in his First Inaugural Address, chords "stretching from every battlefield and patriot grave to every living heart and hearthstone all over this broad land," chords that provide the music of the Union. He performs a similar move of memorial linkage in the Gettysburg Address, beginning with the Founding Fathers and ending with a rededication and recommitment, drawn from knowledge of the "honored dead" who hallowed the ground with their sacrifice.

It is pointless to ask whether such a vision of the Union reflects an "objective" reality. The mythic reality on which such rhetoric depends, and which it helps to create and sustain, is powerful in its own right, too compelling to be dismissed or deconstructed into the language of "state formation" or "cultural hegemony." You could say that the antiseptic scholarly language offers insights that Lincoln cannot give us, and you would be right. But you could also say that Lincoln's reverent and hortatory language offers insights that the antiseptic scholars cannot provide, and you would be equally right. The real question is which language tells us more, and for what purposes.

A belief in the particularly instructive and sustaining qualities of the American Founding does not depend on a belief in the moral perfection of the Founders themselves, or the presumption that they were completely pure and disinterested regarding the measures they sought, or that they were invariably wise or prudent or far-sighted, or that they agreed in all important things, or that the Constitution they created is perfect in every way. The stories that we tell ourselves about ourselves, in order to remember who we are, should not neglect to tell us the ways we have fallen short and the ways we have suffered, both needfully and needlessly, by necessity or by chance.

We should not try to edit out those stories' strange moral complexity, because it is there for a reason. Indeed, it is precisely our encounter with the surprise of their strangeness that reminds us of how much we have yet to learn from them.

**Howard Zinn**
 ➡ **NO**

# The Power and the Glory: Myths of American Exceptionalism

The notion of American exceptionalism—that the United States alone has the right, whether by divine sanction or moral obligation, to bring civilization, or democracy, or liberty to the rest of the world, by violence if necessary—is not new. It started as early as 1630 in the Massachusetts Bay Colony when Governor John Winthrop uttered the words that centuries later would be quoted by Ronald Reagan. Winthrop called the Massachusetts Bay Colony a "city upon a hill." Reagan embellished a little, calling it a "shining city on a hill."

The idea of a city on a hill is heartwarming. It suggests what George Bush has spoken of: that the United States is a beacon of liberty and democracy. People can look to us and learn from and emulate us.

In reality, we have never been just a city on a hill. A few years after Governor Winthrop uttered his famous words, the people in the city on a hill moved out to massacre the Pequot Indians. Here's a description by William Bradford, an early settler, of Captain John Mason's attack on a Pequot village.

> Those that escaped the fire were slain with the sword, some hewed to pieces, others run through with their rapiers, so as they were quickly dispatched and very few escaped. It was conceived that they thus destroyed about 400 at this time. It was a fearful sight to see them thus frying in the fire and the streams of blood quenching the same, and horrible was the stink and scent thereof; but the victory seemed a sweet sacrifice, and they gave the praise thereof to God, who had wrought so wonderfully for them, thus to enclose their enemies in their hands and give them so speedy a victory over so proud and insulting an enemy.

The kind of massacre described by Bradford occurs again and again as Americans march west to the Pacific and south to the Gulf of Mexico. (In fact our celebrated war of liberation, the American Revolution, was disastrous for the Indians. Colonists had been restrained from encroaching on the Indian territory by the British and the boundary set up in their Proclamation of 1763. American independence wiped out that boundary.)

Expanding into another territory, occupying that territory, and dealing harshly with people who resist occupation has been a persistent fact of

As seen in *Boston Review,* Summer 2005. Copyright © 2005 by Howard Zinn. This piece originally appeared as the foreword in *Iraq: The Logic of Withdrawal.* Reprinted by permission of The New Press. www.thenewpress.com

American history from the first settlements to the present day. And this was often accompanied from very early on with a particular form of American exceptionalism: the idea that American expansion is divinely ordained. On the eve of the war with Mexico in the middle of the 19th century, just after the United States annexed Texas, the editor and writer John O'Sullivan coined the famous phrase "manifest destiny." He said it was "the fulfillment of our manifest destiny to overspread the continent allotted by Providence for the free development of our yearly multiplying millions." At the beginning of the 20th century, when the United States invaded the Philippines, President McKinley said that the decision to take the Philippines came to him one night when he got down on his knees and prayed, and God told him to take the Philippines.

Invoking God has been a habit for American presidents throughout the nation's history, but George W. Bush has made a specialty of it. For an article in the Israeli newspaper *Ha'aretz*, the reporter talked with Palestinian leaders who had met with Bush. One of them reported that Bush told him, "God told me to strike at al Qaeda. And I struck them. And then he instructed me to strike at Saddam, which I did. And now I am determined to solve the problem in the Middle East." It's hard to know if the quote is authentic, especially because it is so literate. But it certainly is consistent with Bush's oft-expressed claims. A more credible story comes from a Bush supporter, Richard Lamb, the president of the Ethics and Religious Liberty Commission of the Southern Baptist Convention, who says that during the election campaign Bush told him, "I believe God wants me to be president. But if that doesn't happen, that's okay."

Divine ordination is a very dangerous idea, especially when combined with military power (the United States has 10,000 nuclear weapons, with military bases in a hundred different countries and warships on every sea). With God's approval, you need no human standard of morality. Anyone today who claims the support of God might be embarrassed to recall that the Nazi storm troopers had inscribed on their belts, "Gott mit uns" ("God with us").

Not every American leader claimed divine sanction, but the idea persisted that the United States was uniquely justified in using its power to expand throughout the world. In 1945, at the end of World War II, Henry Luce, the owner of a vast chain of media enterprises—*Time, Life, Fortune*—declared that this would be "the American Century," that victory in the war gave the United States the right "to exert upon the world the full impact of our influence, for such purposes as we see fit and by such means as we see fit."

This confident prophecy was acted out all through the rest of the 20th century. Almost immediately after World War II the United States penetrated the oil regions of the Middle East by special arrangement with Saudi Arabia. It established military bases in Japan, Korea, the Philippines, and a number of Pacific islands. In the next decades it orchestrated right-wing coups in Iran, Guatemala, and Chile, and gave military aid to various dictatorships in the Caribbean. In an attempt to establish a foothold in Southeast Asia it invaded Vietnam and bombed Laos and Cambodia.

The existence of the Soviet Union, even with its acquisition of nuclear weapons, did not block this expansion. In fact, the exaggerated threat of "world communism" gave the United States a powerful justification for expanding all over the globe, and soon it had military bases in a hundred countries. Presumably, only the United States stood in the way of the Soviet conquest of the world.

Can we believe that it was the existence of the Soviet Union that brought about the aggressive militarism of the United States? If so, how do we explain all the violent expansion before 1917? A hundred years before the Bolshevik Revolution, American armies were annihilating Indian tribes, clearing the great expanse of the West in an early example of what we now call "ethnic cleansing." And with the continent conquered, the nation began to look overseas.

On the eve of the 20th century, as American armies moved into Cuba and the Philippines, American exceptionalism did not always mean that the United States wanted to go it alone. The nation was willing—indeed, eager—to join the small group of Western imperial powers that it would one day supersede. Senator Henry Cabot Lodge wrote at the time, "The great nations are rapidly absorbing for their future expansion, and their present defense all the waste places of the earth. . . . As one of the great nations of the world the United States must not fall out of the line of march." Surely, the nationalistic spirit in other countries has often led them to see their expansion as uniquely moral, but this country has carried the claim farthest.

American exceptionalism was never more clearly expressed than by Secretary of War Elihu Root, who in 1899 declared, "The American soldier is different from all other soldiers of all other countries since the world began. He is the advance guard of liberty and justice, of law and order, and of peace and happiness." At the time he was saying this, American soldiers in the Philippines were starting a bloodbath which would take the lives of 600,000 Filipinos.

The idea that America is different because its military actions are for the benefit of others becomes particularly persuasive when it is put forth by leaders presumed to be liberals, or progressives. For instance, Woodrow Wilson, always high on the list of "liberal" presidents, labeled both by scholars and the popular culture as an "idealist," was ruthless in his use of military power against weaker nations. He sent the navy to bombard and occupy the Mexican port of Vera Cruz in 1914 because the Mexicans had arrested some American sailors. He sent the marines into Haiti in 1915, and when the Haitians resisted, thousands were killed.

The following year American marines occupied the Dominican Republic. The occupations of Haiti and the Dominican Republic lasted many years. And Wilson, who had been elected in 1916 saying, "There is such a thing as a nation being too proud to fight," soon sent young Americans into the slaughterhouse of the European war.

Theodore Roosevelt was considered a "progressive" and indeed ran for president on the Progressive Party ticket in 1912. But he was a lover of war and a supporter of the conquest of the Philippines—he had congratulated the general who wiped out a Filipino village of 600 people in 1906. He had promulgated the 1904 "Roosevelt Corollary" to the Monroe Doctrine, which justified the occupation of small countries in the Caribbean as bringing them "stability."

During the Cold War, many American "liberals" became caught up in a kind of hysteria about the Soviet expansion, which was certainly real in Eastern Europe but was greatly exaggerated as a threat to western Europe and the United States. During the period of McCarthyism the Senate's quintessential liberal, Hubert Humphrey, proposed detention camps for suspected subversives who in times of "national emergency" could be held without trial.

After the disintegration of the Soviet Union and the end of the Cold War, terrorism replaced communism as the justification for expansion. Terrorism was real, but its threat was magnified to the point of hysteria, permitting excessive military action abroad and the curtailment of civil liberties at home.

The idea of American exceptionalism persisted as the first President Bush declared, extending Henry Luce's prediction, that the nation was about to embark on a "new American Century." Though the Soviet Union was gone, the policy of military intervention abroad did not end. The elder Bush invaded Panama and then went to war against Iraq.

The terrible attacks of September 11 gave a new impetus to the idea that the United States was uniquely responsible for the security of the world, defending us all against terrorism as it once did against communism. President George W. Bush carried the idea of American exceptionalism to its limits by putting forth in his national-security strategy the principles of unilateral war.

This was a repudiation of the United Nations charter, which is based on the idea that security is a collective matter, and that war could only be justified in self-defense. We might note that the Bush doctrine also violates the principles laid out at Nuremberg, when Nazi leaders were convicted and hanged for aggressive war, preventive war, far from self-defense.

Bush's national-security strategy and its bold statement that the United States is uniquely responsible for peace and democracy in the world has been shocking to many Americans.

But it is not really a dramatic departure from the historical practice of the United States, which for a long time has acted as an aggressor, bombing and invading other countries (Vietnam, Cambodia, Laos, Grenada, Panama, Iraq) and insisting on maintaining nuclear and non-nuclear supremacy. Unilateral military action, under the guise of prevention, is a familiar part of American foreign policy.

Sometimes bombings and invasions have been cloaked as international action by bringing in the United Nations, as in Korea, or NATO, as in Serbia, but basically our wars have been American enterprises. It was Bill Clinton's secretary of state, Madeleine Albright, who said at one point, "If possible we will act in the world multilaterally, but if necessary, we will act unilaterally." Henry Kissinger, hearing this, responded with his customary solemnity that this principle "should not be universalized." Exceptionalism was never clearer.

Some liberals in this country, opposed to Bush, nevertheless are closer to his principles on foreign affairs than they want to acknowledge. It is clear that 9/11 had a powerful psychological effect on everybody in America, and for certain liberal intellectuals a kind of hysterical reaction has distorted their ability to think clearly about our nation's role in the world.

In a recent issue of the liberal magazine *The American Prospect,* the editors write, "Today Islamist terrorists with global reach pose the greatest immediate threat to our lives and liberties. . . . When facing a substantial, immediate, and provable threat, the United States has both the right and the obligation to strike preemptively and, if need be, unilaterally against terrorists or states that support them."

Preemptively and, if need be, unilaterally; and against "states that support" terrorists, not just terrorists themselves. Those are large steps in the direction of the Bush doctrine, though the editors do qualify their support for preemption by adding that the threat must be "substantial, immediate, and provable." But when intellectuals endorse abstract principles, even with qualifications, they need to keep in mind that the principles will be applied by the people who run the U.S. government. This is all the more important to keep in mind when the abstract principle is about the use of violence by the state—in fact, about preemptively initiating the use of violence.

There may be an acceptable case for initiating military action in the face of an immediate threat, but only if the action is limited and focused directly on the threatening party—just as we might accept the squelching of someone falsely shouting "fire" in a crowded theater if that really were the situation and not some guy distributing anti-war leaflets on the street. But accepting action not just against "terrorists" (can we identify them as we do the person shouting "fire"?) but against "states that support them" invites unfocused and indiscriminate violence, as in Afghanistan, where our government killed at least 3,000 civilians in a claimed pursuit of terrorists.

It seems that the idea of American exceptionalism is pervasive across the political spectrum.

The idea is not challenged because the history of American expansion in the world is not a history that is taught very much in our educational system. A couple of years ago Bush addressed the Philippine National Assembly and said, "America is proud of its part in the great story of the Filipino people. Together our soldiers liberated the Philippines from colonial rule." The president apparently never learned the story of the bloody conquest of the Philippines.

And when the Mexican ambassador to the UN said something undiplomatic about how the United States has been treating Mexico as its "backyard" he was immediately reprimanded by then–Secretary of State Colin Powell. Powell, denying the accusation, said, "We have too much of a history that we have gone through together." (Had he not learned about the Mexican War or the military forays into Mexico?) The ambassador was soon removed from his post.

The major newspapers, television news shows, and radio talk shows appear not to know history, or prefer to forget it. There was an outpouring of praise for Bush's second inaugural speech in the press, including the so-called liberal press (*The Washington Post, The New York Times*). The editorial writers eagerly embraced Bush's words about spreading liberty in the world, as if they were ignorant of the history of such claims, as if the past two years' worth of news from Iraq were meaningless.

Only a couple of days before Bush uttered those words about spreading liberty in the world, *The New York Times* published a photo of a crouching, bleeding Iraqi girl. She was screaming. Her parents, taking her somewhere in their car, had just been shot to death by nervous American soldiers.

One of the consequences of American exceptionalism is that the U.S. government considers itself exempt from legal and moral standards accepted by other nations in the world. There is a long list of such self-exemptions: the refusal to sign the Kyoto Treaty regulating the pollution of the environment, the refusal to strengthen the convention on biological weapons. The United States has failed to join the hundred-plus nations that have agreed to ban land mines, in spite of the appalling statistics about amputations performed on children mutilated by those mines. It refuses to ban the use of napalm and cluster bombs. It insists that it must not be subject, as are other countries, to the jurisdiction of the International Criminal Court.

What is the answer to the insistence on American exceptionalism? Those of us in the United States and in the world who do not accept it must declare forcibly that the ethical norms concerning peace and human rights should be observed. It should be understood that the children of Iraq, of China, and of Africa, children everywhere in the world, have the same right to life as American children.

These are fundamental moral principles. If our government doesn't uphold them, the citizenry must. At certain times in recent history, imperial powers—the British in India and East Africa, the Belgians in the Congo, the French in Algeria, the Dutch and French in Southeast Asia, the Portuguese in Angola—have reluctantly surrendered their possessions and swallowed their pride when they were forced to by massive resistance.

Fortunately, there are people all over the world who believe that human beings everywhere deserve the same rights to life and liberty. On February 15, 2003, on the eve of the invasion of Iraq, more than ten million people in more than 60 countries around the world demonstrated against that war.

There is a growing refusal to accept U.S. domination and the idea of American exceptionalism. Recently, when the State Department issued its annual report listing countries guilty of torture and other human-rights abuses, there were indignant responses from around the world commenting on the absence of the United States from that list. A Turkish newspaper said, "There's not even mention of the incidents in Abu Ghraib prison, no mention of Guantánamo." A newspaper in Sydney pointed out that the United States sends suspects—people who have not been tried or found guilty of anything—to prisons in Morocco, Egypt, Libya, and Uzbekistan, countries that the State Department itself says use torture.

Here in the United States, despite the media's failure to report it, there is a growing resistance to the war in Iraq. Public-opinion polls show that at least half the citizenry no longer believe in the war. Perhaps most significant is that among the armed forces, and families of those in the armed forces, there is more and more opposition to it.

After the horrors of the first World War, Albert Einstein said, "Wars will stop when men refuse to fight." We are now seeing the refusal of soldiers to fight, the refusal of families to let their loved ones go to war, the insistence of the parents of high-school kids that recruiters stay away from their schools.

These incidents, occurring more and more frequently, may finally, as happened in the case of Vietnam, make it impossible for the government to continue the war, and it will come to an end.

The true heroes of our history are those Americans who refused to accept that we have a special claim to morality and the right to exert our force on the rest of the world. I think of William Lloyd Garrison, the abolitionist. On the masthead of his antislavery newspaper, *The Liberator*, were the words, "My country is the world. My countrymen are mankind."

# EXPLORING THE ISSUE

## Should Americans Believe in a Unique American "Mission"?

## Critical Thinking and Reflection

1. What does Wilfred McClay mean by America's "myth"? Does he mean it disparagingly, as in "falsehood," or does he use it approvingly?
2. What does Howard Zinn mean by American "exceptionalism"? What does he think is wrong with that concept?
3. Is it good for a nation to remind itself of its past sins? Can this collective contrition be pushed too far?
4. What does the term "city upon a hill" mean?

## Is There Common Ground?

In the 1960s, the former Socialist candidate for president, Norman Thomas, admonished an angry crowd of antiwar demonstrators not to burn the flag but to wash it. Thomas was one of many critics of American policies who would insist that they love America more, not less, because they can acknowledge how far their country falls short of achieving its professed goals of "liberty and justice for all." That suggests that perhaps there is common ground between both sides, if each is able to say, "America is a country founded on great principles which on memorable occasions it has put into effect, though on other occasions it has shamefully contradicted its ideals. May this nation always and forevermore live by its grand principles!" There is at least a chance that both Zinn and McClay might say "amen" to that.

## Additional Resources

Howard Zinn's *People's History of the United States: 1492 to Present* (Harper Perennial Modern Classics, 2005) presents a more sweeping presentation of his argument here, while Stephen H. Webb makes the case for a doctrine of providence in *American Providence: A Nation With a Mission* (Continuum, 2004). James H. Hutson's edited *The Founders on Religion: A Book of Quotations* (Princeton, 2005) served as the source for the quotations from the founders presented in the Introduction to this issue. Alexis de Tocqueville is credited with inventing the term "American exceptionalism," and in his classic *Democracy in America* (Knopf, 1951) he seemed to endorse the idea by stating his belief that "the people of the United States [are] that portion of the English people who are commissioned to explore the forests of the new world." Seymour Martin Lipset's *American Exceptionalism: A Double-Edged Sword* (Norton, 1997) thinks

America is different not so much because of its founding narrative but because, unlike Europe, it was "born modern," with a distinct creed. Neil Baldwin, *The American Revelation: Ten Ideals That Shaped Our Country from the Puritans to the Cold War* (St. Martin's Griffin, 2006), explores the basic ideals of "fundamental Americanism," correlating them with famous Americans, from John Winthrop to George Marshall, prominently associated with them.

Samuel P. Huntington's *Who Are We?* (Simon & Schuster, 2004) highlights America's uniqueness among industrial nations today, especially in terms of its highly charged mixture of piety and patriotism. In *Hellfire Nation*, James A. Morone (Yale, 2004) finds both good and bad effects following from America's belief in its "mission"—on the one hand, utopian and reformist impulses, which he likes, and on the other hand, Victorian censoriousness, which he doesn't like.

# ISSUE 2

## Does the Tea Party Represent a Revival of America's Revolutionary Ideals?

**YES: Dick Armey and Matt Kibbe,** from *Give Us Liberty: A Tea Party Manifesto* (HarperCollins, 2010)

**NO: Jill Lepore,** from *The Whites of Their Eyes: The Tea Party's Revolution and the Battle over American History* (Princeton University Press, 2010)

### ISSUE SUMMARY

**YES:** FreedomWorks founder Dick Armey and FreedomWorks president Matt Kibbe believe that the Tea Party movement is a reawakening of the spirit of the American Revolution.

**NO:** Harvard University professor of American history Jill Lepore believes that the modern Tea Party movement is antihistorical, anti-intellectual, and antipluralist.

O n the evening of December 16, 1773, American colonists boarded English ships in Boston harbor and tossed crates of British tea into the sea to protest the British government's new tax on tea. Their bold action was a seminal moment in inciting the revolution that ended with the independence of the American colonies and the creation of the United States of America.

The contemporary Tea Party movement began early in 2008, gathered momentum during that year's election, and began to challenge the traditional leadership of the Republican Party in the congressional primaries and elections in 2010. For the Tea Partiers, there are clear parallels with the tyrannical exercise of power by the British government against the American colonies.

As the Boston Tea Party did then, the modern Tea Party movement sees an improper and illegal exercise of power by the national government. It believes that its success will lead to the restoration of individual liberty and constitutional government, which have been undermined by the present national government.

The immediate incitement for the Tea Party movement was the economic decline of middle-class and working-class people in the sharply diminished economy that followed the banking and housing crises. Many conservatives (as well as many liberals) resented the government's decision to bailout banks and financial institutions because they were "too big to fail," unlike the ordinary Americans who were too small to save.

The modern Tea Party movement is a loosely affiliated combination of a number of political groups, like Tea Party Nation, Tea Party Patriots, and Tea Party Express. Some add conservative social issues to their agenda, such as opposition of abortion rights, same-sex marriage, and illegal immigration, while other Tea Party supporters would confine their goals to economic ends.

An intriguing element in the modern movement is that some Tea Partiers express support for libertarianism, a hostility to governmental interference in personal or social affairs except when absolutely necessary for a secure and stable society. Where traditional Republicans saw President George W. Bush as a true conservative, Tea Party speakers are often critical of Bush policies that increased the national debt. Where traditional Democrats see President Barack Obama as a moderate liberal, the Tea Party condemns him as a socialist. Still seeking a dominant role within the Republican Party, the Tea Party movement has started to convert its antitax, antigovernment stance into concrete political programs, seeking to cut taxes and federal programs.

The modern Tea Party is not (any more than the Boston Tea Party) a political party. Almost always, its impact upon the political process has been directed to influencing the Republican Party by securing the nomination of candidates who share its views, even if this means defeating Republican incumbents that do not adequately subscribe to Tea Party principles.

Critics of the Tea Party movement believe that there is no real parallel between the contemporary Tea Party movement and the protest movements preceding and accompanying the American Revolution. The Boston Tea Party was fundamentally inspired by colonial resentment of being unrepresented in the British government. By contrast, today's Tea Party movement freely seeks and has already won political representation.

Recent polls indicate that a majority of Democratic voters believe the Tea Party's opposition to President Obama surpasses simple political differences. Many see evidence of racial bias in widespread suspicion of the president's native citizenship despite the existence of his birth certificate, as well as a persisting conviction among his critics that Obama is a Muslim despite the evidence of his Christian adherence. Liberal opponents see something sinister in what they perceive as an intolerant coalition opposed not only to President Obama, but also to liberals, intellectuals, minorities, and the mainstream media.

Dick Armey and Matt Kibbe believe that this movement can "take country back" from powerful government and privileged interests by a grassroots citizen rebellion, which they see is already well under way. Jill Lepore argues that today's Tea Partiers have a superficial and largely incorrect understanding of what the American Revolution was about and what the Constitution established, permitted, and denied. Whatever its future may be, the Tea Party movement clearly is an important element in determining how the national government moves in this decade.

# YES ↵

**Dick Armey and
Matt Kibbe**

# Give Us Liberty:
# A Tea Party Manifesto

**A**n on-air commentator for cable news network CNBC, Rick Santelli was a fixture at the Chicago Mercantile Exchange, where he offered news and commentary on corn futures, yield rates, and other market data. On the morning of February 19, 2009, news coverage was dominated by Obama's proposal for yet another housing bailout. CNBC studio analysts calmly reported the news, discussing vast sums of taxpayer money in a tone ordinarily reserved for reporting on weather patterns over the Midwest. Standing by for a floor report, Santelli heard the commentary on his earpiece and began to fume.

After reporting on the latest housing bailouts, an anchor tossed to Santelli for his usual update. Santelli unexpectedly unleashed an impassioned rant.

"The government is promoting bad behavior!" Santelli shouted. "This is America! How many people want to pay for your neighbor's mortgages that have an extra bathroom and can't pay their bills? Raise your hand! President Obama, are you listening? You know Cuba used to have mansions and a relatively decent economy. They moved from the individual to the collective. Now they're driving '54 Chevys. It's time for another Tea Party. What we are doing in this country will make Thomas Jefferson and Benjamin Franklin roll over in their graves. We're thinking of having a Chicago Tea Party in July, all you capitalists. I'm organizing."

As he spoke, a group of traders formed around him on the trading floor. Capitalists to a man, they cheered the outburst and drowned out the planned transition, extending the segment and creating an indelible TV moment. Within hours, Santelli's rant had gone viral, earning more than a million views on YouTube and countless watercooler and dinner-table discussions across the country. The frustration that had been building, and which had begun to turn into street action, now had a name. The Tea Party was ready for the national stage.

## Conceived in Liberty

Across the nation, private citizens who had never protested, never agitated, never taken a public political stand were gathering and organizing to make a difference. United by common principles and outraged by the complacence and indifference of their elected leaders, these individuals were ready to do something. Early meetings were filled with entrepreneurs, retirees, school-teachers, civil rights leaders, lawyers, those who had prospered in recent years, and some who had fallen on hard times. All believed that the time to act had come, that their children and grandchildren deserved better and it was up to them to change the course of a nation.

But for all the excitement, the first wave of Tea Party activists faced significant challenges. They were poorly funded. They lacked national organization. They were greeted with skepticism by the political establishment. They included none of the political intelligentsia in their ranks, none of the gatekeepers and message experts and focus group gurus. How could they hope to influence a Congress of incumbent leaders with strong ties to interest groups and well-funded corporate backers? How could they challenge an administration that had swept into the White House with a landslide victory in the presidential campaign?

To many, the answer could be found in another group of unlikely activists who were overmatched and outgunned but fought anyway. Also comprised of ordinary citizens, this group had toppled an entrenched regime that seemed invincible. In fact, it had happened in 1773, right here in America.

. . . History teaches us that nothing could be more American than a protest. What made the opening salvos of the Tea Party movement so jarring to political, academic, and news media observers was its unlikely source—an irate group of citizens from across the political spectrum who were agitating and demanding change. For generations, guerrilla tactics had been a trademark of the Left, best demonstrated in ecoterrorism and virulent antiwar campaigns. Accustomed to Code Pink public disturbance stunts and blood-tossing animal rights' activists, students of political activism had come to understand public protest as left-leaning by definition and reserved for those who were willing to damage public property and disrupt legal activities. Now that middle-class Americans of all backgrounds were taking to the Internet, airwaves, and streets, conventional wisdom was turned on its head and the original Tea Party was seen in a new light. . . .

The spark that ignited the modern Tea Party movement was not just a question of bad economics—it cut to the core of basic American values of individual choice and individual accountability. Millions of Americans were still angry over the new culture of bailouts that had taken Washington by storm since the popping of the housing bubble in 2008 and they were just itching for a fight. They thought that candidate Obama would prove different, having run on a mantra of fiscal responsibility. Regardless of their limited choices at the ballot box, the American people were hungry for accountability, for the American way of doing things.

The entire founding enterprise, including America's Declaration of Independence from the British Crown in 1776 happened only because of the Tea Party ethos, the tradition of rising up against tyranny and taking to the streets in protest. Indeed, the period of American history leading up to the signing of the Declaration is the definitive case study in effective grassroots organization and the power of a committed, organized minority to defeat powerful, entrenched interests.

For any activist who fought in the trenches against Obama's hostile take-over of the health care system, the process that produced the Declaration will sound all too familiar: debate inside the Continental Congress was often dominated by lies, vote buying, and the influence of deep-pocketed business interests enjoying the favored treatment of the executive branch (King George III, that is). Does any of this ring a bell?

How did the advocates of liberty prevail over the entrenched interests and apathetic citizens that might have stifled the efforts of Thomas Jefferson and Benjamin Franklin? The answer, of course, is grassroots activism of citizens outside of the formal political process. The Declaration was radical in principle and revolutionary in practice—sweeping political change driven by a grassroots cadre of committed individuals armed only with their passion and their principles. Politics as usual did not stop them, and neither did lack of popular support. The political momentum for liberty was in large part created by the efforts of citizen patriots from Massachusetts, later joined by men in the other colonies. These so-called Sons of Liberty, led by a struggling entrepreneur named Samuel Adams—yes, the guy on the beer label—used targeted grassroots activism to undercut American support for British rule and create the political conditions that made ratification of the Declaration of Independence and the American Revolution possible.

Speaking truth to power was important, Adams knew, but nothing beat the power of grassroots activism. In the early 1750s Adams began recruiting activists to the cause of liberty, targeting men in taverns and workers in the shipyards and on the streets of Boston. His tactics often involved antitax protests under the Liberty Tree, a large elm across from Boylston Market. Tax collectors were hung in effigy and Crown-appointed governors mocked, belittled, and verbally abused. The Sons of Liberty organized boycotts of British goods and monopolistic practices that were de facto taxes on the colonists. Adams packed town hall meetings at Faneuil Hall, filling the room with patriots so that Tory voices were overwhelmed. Every oppressive new policy handed down by King George and the House of Commons was used to build the ranks of the Sons of Liberty. Taxes imposed by the Stamp Act of 1765, trade duties created by the Townshend Acts—each was an excuse to rally new recruits to the cause of American independence.

The most famous act of Whig defiance against the Crown—the Boston Tea Party—is now viewed as a tipping point in the battle for American independence. It had a profound impact on public opinion among the uncommitted population. It was not a spontaneous looting by angry tea drinkers but an operation carefully choreographed by Samuel Adams and the Sons of Liberty. When a Parliament-granted monopoly to the East India Trading Company dramatically drove up the price of tea in the colonies, Adams saw an opportunity to channel outrage into action. The "Mohawks" who emptied British tea into Boston Harbor on December 16, 1773, were his activists disguised by Indian war paint to protect their identities from Tory spies. Because property was not destroyed (other than the tea) and the ships' crews not harmed, the Boston Tea Party gave the Sons of Liberty broader public acceptance in the colonies. . . .

. . . The Tea Party is the product of a perfect storm of (1) broken Republican commitments, (2) the aggressive left-wing agenda of a Democratic regime motivated by redistributionist values that are antithetical to the values of most Americans, and (3) technological innovations that allow people to find one another, organize, and get essential information in real time from competitive sources.

We call this complex and diverse movement "beautiful chaos." Or better yet, to borrow Nobel Prize–winning economist F. A. Hayek's weighty notion: "spontaneous order." By this we [refer to] what is now the dominant understanding in organizational management theory: decentralization of personal knowledge is the best way to maximize the contributions of people, their talents, and the total productivity of any enterprise, no matter how big. Let the "leaders" be the regional activists who have the best knowledge of the local personalities and issues. In the real world, this is common sense. In Washington, D.C., this is known as radical. Even dangerous. . . .

. . . When you think about it, a decentralized model for social change is most consistent with the values of independence self-reliance, and personal liberty that embody America. Those activists who gathered at Boston's Old South Meeting House in 1773 knew it. Thomas Jefferson understood this when he wrote, "I would rather be exposed to the inconveniences attending too much liberty than to those attending too small a degree of it."

The big government crowd, on the other hand, is naturally drawn to the compulsion demanded by a centralized authority. They can't imagine an undirected social order. *Someone needs to be in charge.* "We can't give people a choice or they might take it," said Senator Ted Kennedy during a closed-door House–Senate conference committee dealing with health savings accounts.

Big government is audacious. It is conceited. It knows better. Government is, by definition, the means by which you are compelled by force to do that, which you would not do voluntarily. Like pay high taxes. Or "purchase," by federal mandate, a government-defined health insurance plan that you cannot afford, do not need, or simply do not want. For the Left, and for today's monolithically liberal Democratic Party, every solution to every perceived problem involves more government: top-down dictates from new laws enforced by new bureaucrats who are presumed to care more and, most important, know better what you need. "I'm from the government, and I'm going to help you whether you want it or not." . . .

Those liberals now in control of our government seem bent on apologizing for the United States, striving to, in the words of Barack Obama, "remake America." They want to remake us to look more like European social democracies. Liberals don't talk about democratic socialism anymore; they prattle on about "social justice." They misuse the phrase. Justice means treating every individual with respect and decency and exactly the same as anyone else is treated under the laws of the land. As best we can tell, "social justice" translates to really wise elected officials (you know, smarter than you) redistributing your hard-earned income to their favored social agendas, all dutifully administered by a well-intentioned bureaucrat. In Europe, this translates into bloated social welfare programs that punish work; massive tax burdens, particularly on the working class through hidden value-added taxes that crush economic expansion; and structural barriers to opportunity for younger generations of have-nots trying to enter the workforce.

The politics of greed is always wrapped in the language of love. When you hear someone go on about social justice, read between the lines. More government control of health care is not really about improving access to health care; it's about controlling your health care.

If you want to comprehend the energy and passion behind the citizen activists who are fighting this corrosive ideology of redistribution, understand this: we believe that America's founders got it right and that Europe got it wrong. America is different because we are all about the individual over the collective. . . .

It is time to take America back. We need to reclaim America from the advocates of big government in both political parties, from the rent-seeking corporations eager to use the power of government to enrich themselves at the expense of consumers and taxpayers, and from the web of left-wing special interests who feed at the public trough and consider it their right to do so.

The political potential of the broad grassroots movement against big government that we are witnessing today should not be underestimated. There is a small-"l" libertarian, commonsense fiscal conservatism out there that transcends partisan definitions. These are independent voters who are united around the idea that government is spending too much money it does not have, and that government is getting involved in things, like controlling health care and running car companies, that it cannot do effectively, and should not try to do at all.

These highly motivated concerns about fiscal issues now represent the very center of electoral opinion among Republicans, most independents, and a growing number of Democrats who have developed buyer's remorse. Today the liberals who control Congress make even Bill Clinton look conservative by comparison and they are scaring Americans with their fiscal lasciviousness. This overreach is the stage upon which to build a revolt. We can take America back from moneyed special interests, leftist advocacy groups, and arrogant politicians. We can stop the monumental legislative threats to our economic liberties. Most important, perhaps, we can do these things by building a national community of activists—organized on the ground and connected online—that will be able to hold the next generation of political leaders, whether they are Democrats or Republicans, accountable for their actions.

The Tea Party is different. Consider the comparable events that led to the political backlash in 1994. That was a voter uprising that too quickly waned when the imminent threat of one-party rule under the Democratic establishment seemed contained. The new activists who had risen up to throw the bums out of power eventually left the playing field again, leaving our political system in the hands of politicians. Left unattended, these politicians, as they all eventually will, returned to tending to their own self-indulgent needs. At best, they became inconvenience-minimizers, eager to compromise for the lesser of two evils. At worst, they grew their own power at the expense of the American people and the fiscal health of our economy. All of the corruptions that followed—the ballooning federal debt, the frenzied spending, the political favors, the bailouts, and the government takeovers—now confront our economy, our futures, and the American way of life built upon freedom, opportunity, and prosperity.

This political boom-and-bust cycle, not unlike the government-generated business cycle that caused the housing bubble and the massive mistakes that went with it, generates periods of accountability followed by years of neglect and an inevitable slip back to business as usual. The problem with this cycle, beyond the policy damage done, is the difficulty in reversing the trend toward more government spending and more government control over our lives. With each new government program, the baseline of total spending is raised, phony budget estimates become very real red ink, and the federal take grows as a percentage of the total private economy. When a constitutional barrier is breached, as happened with the extraordinary ceding of power to an unelected secretary of the treasury under TARP, there is permanent damage done to that constitutional wall that stands between free citizens and a tyrannical government. When informal constraints against hasty legislative actions are torn, as happened with the Democrats' decision to create a massive new health care entitlement through parliamentary chicanery, there is no going back to the way it was before. A future Congress will certainly try to use its new power to enact sweeping legislation with similar tactics, permanently end-running the "cooling off" function the authors of the Constitution envisioned in their design of a deliberative Congress.

The Tea Party movement is rising up because we know we cannot leave public policy to the politicians, or to the "experts," or to someone else with a parochial agenda, a concentrated benefit that comes first, before the public good, and at your expense. The broad community of patriotic citizens that have stood up to take their country back from an unholy alliance of government power and privileged interests are making a difference in ways that defy easy comparisons to the boom and bust of other recent shifts in the political winds. The Tea Party has evolved from political revolt to social movement. We the people are that force more powerful, a force that can save our great nation for future generations.

The establishment doesn't like it one bit. They will kick and scream and throw every possible roadblock in our path.

But we suspect George Washington would love it. He, after all, demanded as much of us. "The preservation of the sacred fire of liberty, and the destiny of the Republican model of government are justly considered as deeply, perhaps as finally staked, on the experiment entrusted to the hands of the American people."

Or, as we like to say, freedom works.

Jill Lepore

→ **NO**

# The Whites of Their Eyes:
# The Tea Party's Revolution and the
# Battle over American History

. . . **O**n March 5, 2010, the 240th anniversary of the Boston Massacre, Glenn Beck issued a special Fox News report on "Indoctrination in America": "Tonight, America, I want you to sit down and talk to your kids and hold your kids close to you," he began. "Get the kids out of this indoctrination or our republic will be lost." He was talking about environmentalism and about a lot of other things, too: "Our kids are being brainwashed with the concept of— I've shown it to you before, earth worship. Earth worship. I pledge allegiance to the earth. Social justice. What is social justice? God is being eliminated from the equation entirely." He found occasion to reach back to the Revolution: "Let me give you the words of George Washington, 'It is impossible to rightly govern a nation without God and the Bible.'" Like Hannity, Beck had begun giving history lessons. He outfitted his studio with chalk and a blackboard and even old-fashioned oak school chairs and desks, as if from a one-room schoolhouse. What our children are learning, Beck warned, darkly, is nothing short of learn-to-hate-America lunacy.

. . . From the start, the Tea Party's chief political asset was its name: the echo of the Revolution conferred upon a scattered, diffuse, and confused movement a degree of legitimacy and the appearance, almost, of coherence. Aside from the name and the costume, the Tea Party offered an analogy: rejecting the bailout is like dumping the tea; health care reform is like the Tea Act; our struggle is like theirs. Americans have drawn Revolutionary analogies before. They have drawn them for a very long time. When in doubt, in American politics, left, right, or center, deploy the Founding Fathers. Relying on this sort of analogy, advocates of health care reform could have insisted that, since John Hancock once urged the Massachusetts legislature to raise funds for the erection of lighthouses, he would have supported state health care reform, because, like a lighthouse, health care coverage concerns public safety. That might sound strained, at best, but something quite like it has been tried. In 1798, John Adams signed an "Act for the relief of sick and disabled Seamen": state and later federal government officials collected taxes from shipmasters, which were used to build hospitals and provide medical care for merchant and naval seamen. In the 1940s, health care reformers used this precedent to bolster their case. Government-sponsored health care wasn't un-American, these reformers argued; Adams had thought of it.

That political tradition is long-standing. But the more I looked at the Tea Party, at Beck and Hannity as history teachers, and at the Texas School Board reforms, the more it struck me that the statement at the core of the far right's version of American history went just a bit further. It was more literal than an analogy. It wasn't "our struggle is like theirs." It was "we are there" or "they are here." The unanswered question of the Bicentennial was, "What ails the American spirit?" Antihistory has no patience for ambiguity, self-doubt, and introspection. The Tea Party had an answer: "We have forsaken the Founding Fathers." Political affiliates are, by nature, motley. But what the Tea Party, Beck and Hannity, and the Texas School Board shared was a set of assumptions about the relationship between the past and the present that was both broadly anti-intellectual and, quite specifically, antihistorical, not least because it defies chronology, the logic of time. To say that we are there, or the Founding Fathers are here, or that we have forsaken them and they're rolling over in their graves because of the latest, breaking political development—the election of the United States' first African American president, for instance—is to subscribe to a set of assumptions about the relationship between the past and the present stricter, even, than the strictest form of constitutional originalism, a set of assumptions that, conflating originalism, evangelicalism, and heritage tourism, amounts to a variety of fundamentalism.

Historical fundamentalism is marked by the belief that a particular and quite narrowly defined past—"the founding"—is ageless and sacred and to be worshipped; that certain historical texts—"the founding documents"—are to be read in the same spirit with which religious fundamentalists read, for instance, the Ten Commandments; that the Founding Fathers were divinely inspired; that the academic study of history (whose standards of evidence and methods of analysis are based on skepticism) is a conspiracy and, furthermore, blasphemy; and that political arguments grounded in appeals to the founding documents, as sacred texts, and to the Founding Fathers, as prophets, are therefore incontrovertible.

The past haunts us all. Just how is a subject of this book. But time moves forward, not backward. Chronology is like gravity. Nothing falls up. We cannot go back to the eighteenth century, and the Founding Fathers are not, in fact, here with us today. They weren't even called the Founding Fathers until Warren G. Harding coined that phrase in his keynote address at the Republican National Convention in 1916. Harding also invoked the Founding Fathers during his inauguration in 1921—"Standing in this presence, mindful of the solemnity of this occasion, feeling the emotions which no one may know until he senses the great weight of responsibility for himself, I must utter my belief in the divine inspiration of the founding fathers"—in what is quite possibly the worst inaugural address ever written. . . .

The Founding Fathers haven't been rolling over in their graves for very long, either. Not one was roused from his eternal slumber with any regularity until about the time that Harding called the founders our fathers (and, more particularly, his) and said they were divinely inspired (which had the curious effect of granting to his presidency something akin to the divine right of kings). . . .

On March 20, 2010, the day before the U.S. House of Representatives was scheduled to vote on the health care bill, the Boston Tea Party held an Anti-Obamacare rally in front of Faneuil Hall. A few dozen people turned up. Most carried signs: "The Constitution SPEAKS." Some waved flags of thirteen stars. Acolytes of Ayn Rand urged, "READ ATLAS SHRUGGED." Christen Varley told a woman who showed up with a Hitler sign to leave. The place was bustling with tourists on their way to shop at Quincy Market. Austin Hess, wearing his tricorn and a mock–Obama campaign T-shirt that read NOPE instead of HOPE, summed up his objectives for the Tea Party movement: "I want to replace the current political establishment, get all incumbents out and replace them with fiscal conservatives who will abide by the Constitution."

Hess had moved to Massachusetts from Virginia three years before. "We're trying to get back to what the founders had," he told me. "We're trying to bring people back to Boston's roots. Liberty above all." A nurse from Worcester who grew up in the Midwest and was registered as an Independent explained what getting back to those eighteenth-century roots meant to her: "I don't want the government giving money to people who don't want to work. Government is for the post office, and to defend our country, and maybe for the roads. That's all."

"The history of our revolution will be one continued lye from one end to the other," Johns Adams once predicted. He was right to worry. In every nation, as in every family, some stories are remembered, others are forgotten, and there are always some stories too painful to tell. Adams expected that the Revolution, a messy, sprawling, decades-long affair, would, over time, be shortened and simplified. In the national imagination, the Revolution is a fable. Much of what most people picture when they think about the Revolution comes from the world of juvenilia—*Johnny Tremain,* paper dolls, elementary school art projects, and family vacations—which isn't surprising, and wouldn't be a problem, except that every history of a nation's founding makes an argument about the nature of its government. . . .

On Sunday, March 21, 2010, the U.S. House of Representatives passed the health care bill, in a vote that fell along partisan lines. All but 34 Democrats voted for it, and all 178 Republicans voted against it. On Monday, eleven state attorneys general announced a plan to challenge the law as a violation of state sovereignty. Across the country, there followed scattered threats of violence against legislators who had voted in favor of the bill and against the president who signed it into law on Tuesday, by which time there had already been talk of nullification.

The next night, I met Austin Hess and Kat Malone at the Warren Tavern in Charlestown. The tavern, built in 1784, was named after Dr. Joseph Warren, who died in the Battle of Bunker Hill, and was just a cobbled street away from Monument Square, where a granite obelisk commemorated the patriots who died alongside him. We sat near the bar, beneath a dark ceiling of massive oak timbers. Tin lanterns hung from the wall. Hess took off his tricornered hat and set it down on the table between us. Malone was quiet. Hess was frustrated.

"I have recently started a committee to elect the corpse of Calvin Coolidge," he said, "because anyone's better than Obama." He was dismayed by the vote, but he was also, as always, courteous and equable. "It's the law of the land now, so, it's up to us to blunt its impact and overturn it if we can." The vote, and House Speaker Nancy Pelosi's maneuvering around a potential filibuster made possible by Brown's election to the Senate, had deepened Hess's conviction about the aptness of his analogy. "One of the things people like to say about us is that they like to think that we don't know what we're talking about, that we don't know what the tea party was about. But to the people who say we have taxation with representation, I would just say that they should look to the bill that just passed. We sent Scott Brown to Washington to kill this bill, but the people in Washington did everything they could to thwart the will of the people, and especially the people of Massachusetts. How is my voice being represented?" . . .

"I really feel like this is a modern-day Intolerable Act," Austin Hess said, about the new health care law, when we met at the Warren Tavern. Every time Hess talked about the Intolerable Acts, I got to thinking about the limits of tolerance, tolerance of racial equality, of religious diversity, of same-sex marriage, of a global economy, of democracy, of pluralism, of change. Hess labored in a world of uneasy alliances. I asked him if he was troubled by Christen Varley's work with the Coalition for Marriage and the Family. "We do not discuss social issues and foreign policy issues," he said. He was frustrated that journalists kept getting the Tea Party wrong. Hess's girlfriend was black. He was tired of people calling the movement racist. "I will simply say this," he e-mailed me. "I know what is in my heart."

In 2010, nationwide polls reported that people who identified themselves as sympathetic with the Tea Party were overwhelmingly white, although estimates varied, and the Tea Party didn't appear to be much whiter than, say, the Republican Party. Whatever else had drawn people into the movement— the bailout, health care, taxes, Fox News, and, above all, the economy—some of it, for some people, was probably discomfort with the United States' first black president, because he was black. But it wasn't the whiteness of the Tea Party that I found most striking. It was the whiteness of their Revolution. The Founding Fathers were the whites of their eyes, a fantasy of an America before race, *without* race. There were very few black people in the Tea Party, but there were no black people at all in the Tea Party's eighteenth century. Nor, for that matter, were there any women, aside from Abigail Adams, and no slavery, poverty, ignorance, insanity, sickness, or misery. Nor was there any art, literature, sex, pleasure, or humor. There were only the Founding Fathers with their white wigs, wearing their three-cornered hats, in their Christian nation, revolting against taxes, and defending their right to bear arms. . . .

The scholarship academic historians have written since the 1960s, uncovering the lives of ordinary people and examining conflict among groups and especially races, sexes, classes, and nations, was not without substantial shortcomings. Critics, both within and outside the academy, had charged scholars of American history not only with an inability to write for general readers and an unwillingness to examine the relationship between the past and the present, but also with a failure to provide a narrative synthesis, to tell a big story instead of many little ones. Those criticisms were warranted. They were also criticisms academic historians had made of themselves. Scholars criticize and argue—and must, and can—because scholars share a common set of ideas about how to argue, and what counts as evidence. But the far right's American history—its antihistory—existed outside of argument and had no interest in evidence. It was much a fiction as the Lost Cause of the Confederacy, reductive, unitary, and, finally, dangerously antipluralist. It erased slavery from American history and compressed a quarter century of political contest into "the founding," as if ideas worked out, over decades of debate and fierce disagreement, were held by everyone, from the start. "Who's your favorite Founder?" Glenn Beck asked Sarah Palin. "Um, you know, well," she said. "All of them."

There was, though, something heartbreaking in all this. Behind the Tea Party's Revolution lay nostalgia for an imagined time—the 1950s, maybe, or the 1940s—less riven by strife, less troubled by conflict, less riddled with ambiguity, less divided by race. In that nostalgia was the remembrance of childhood, a yearning for a common past, bulwark against a divided present, comfort against an uncertain future. "History is not a dry academic subject for us," as Hess put it. "It is our heritage." . . .

The National Center for Constitutional Studies was started in Utah in 1967, to promote originalism, the idea that the original intent of the framers is knowable and fixed and the final word. When the framers were still alive, people who wanted to know what they meant, by, say, a particular phrase, couldn't really ask them. Delegates to the Constitutional Convention pledged themselves to secrecy. And the more time passed, the remoter the Revolution, the more inscrutable the documents (even the meaning of the *words* changed), the greater the distance between now and then, the more demanding the act of interpretation. In 1816, when Jefferson was seventy-three, many of his Revolutionary generation having already died, he offered this answer, when asked what the framers would suggest about how to deal with this problem. "This they would say themselves, were they to rise from the dead": "laws and institutions must go hand in hand with the progress of the human mind." (To paraphrase the historian Carl Becker, the question the Enlightenment asked was not, "What would our forefathers do?" but "How can we make society better?") Jefferson put it this way: "Some men look at constitutions with sanctimonious reverence, and deem them like the ark of the covenant, too sacred to be touched. They ascribe to the men of the preceding age a wisdom more than human." In Federalist 14, Madison asked, "Is it not the glory of the people of America, that, whilst they have paid a decent regard to the opinions of former times and other nations, they have not suffered a blind veneration for antiquity, for custom, or for names, to overrule the suggestions of their own good sense, the knowledge of their own situation, and the lessons of their own experience?" The founders were not prophets. Nor did they hope to be worshipped. They believed that to defer without examination to what your forefathers believed is to become a slave to the tyranny of the past. . . .

Precisely what the founders believed about God, Jesus, sin, the Bible, churches, and hell is probably impossible to discover. They changed their minds and gave different accounts to different people: Franklin said one thing to his sister, Jane, and another thing to David Hume; Washington prayed with his troops, but, while he lay slowly dying, he declined to call for a preacher. This can make them look like hypocrites, but that's unfair, as are a great many attacks on these men. They approached religion more or less the same way they approached everything else that interested them: Franklin invented his own, Washington proved diplomatic, Adams grumbled about it (he hated Christianity, he once said, but he couldn't think of anything better, and he also regarded it as necessary), Jefferson could not stop tinkering with it, and Madison defended, as a natural right, the free exercise of it. That they wanted to preserve religious liberty by separating church and state does not mean they were irreligious. They wanted to protect religion from the state, as much as the other way around.

Nevertheless, if the founders had followed their forefathers, they would have written a Constitution establishing Christianity as the national religion. Nearly every British North American colony was settled with an established religion; Connecticut's 1639 charter explained that the whole purpose of government was "to mayntayne and presearve the liberty and purity of the gospel of our Lord Jesus." In the century and a half between the Connecticut charter and the 1787 meeting of the Constitutional Convention lies an entire revolution, not just a political revolution but also a religious revolution. Following the faith of their fathers is exactly what the framers did not do. At a time when all but two states required religious tests for office, the Constitution prohibited them. At a time when all but three states still had an official religion, the Bill of Rights forbade the federal government from establishing one.

Originalism in the courts is controversial, to say the least. Jurisprudence stands on precedent, on the stability of the laws, but originalism is hardly the only way to abide by the Constitution. Setting aside the question of whether it makes good law, it is, generally, lousy history. And it has long since reached well beyond the courts. Set loose in the culture, and tangled together with fanaticism, originalism looks like history, but it's not; it's historical fundamentalism, which is to history what astrology is to astronomy, what alchemy is to chemistry, what creationism is to evolution.

In eighteenth-century America, I wouldn't have been able to vote. I wouldn't have been able to own property, either. I'd very likely have been unable to write, and, if I survived childhood, chances are that I'd have died in childbirth. And, no matter how long or short my life, I'd almost certainly have died without having once ventured a political opinion preserved in any historical record, except that none of these factors has any meaning or bearing whatsoever on whether an imaginary eighteenth-century me would have supported the Obama administration's stimulus package or laws allowing the carrying of concealed weapons or the war in Iraq, because I did not live in eighteenth-century America, and no amount of thinking that I could, not even wearing petticoats, a linsey-woolsey calico smock, and a homespun mobcap, can make it so. Citizens and their elected officials have all sorts of reasons to support or oppose all sorts of legislation and government action, including constitutionality, precedence, and the weight of history. But it's possible to cherish the stability of the law and the durability of the Constitution, as amended over two and a half centuries of change and one civil war, and tested in the courts, without dragging the Founding Fathers from their graves. To point this out neither dishonors the past nor relieves anyone of the obligation to study it. To the contrary.

"What would the founders do?" is, from the point of view of historical analysis, an ill-considered and unanswerable question, and pointless, too. Jurists and legislators need to investigate what the framers meant, and some Christians make moral decisions by wondering what Jesus would do, but no NASA scientist decides what to do about the Hubble by asking what Isaac Newton would make of it. People who ask what the founders would do quite commonly declare that they know, they know, they just know what the founders would do and, mostly, it comes to this: if only they could see us now, they would be rolling over in their graves. They might even rise from the dead and walk among us. We have failed to obey their sacred texts, holy writ. They suffered for us, and we have forsaken them. Come the Day of Judgment, they will damn us.

That's not history. It's not civil religion, the faith in democracy that binds Americans together. It's not originalism or even constitutionalism. That's fundamentalism.

# EXPLORING THE ISSUE

## Does the Tea Party Represent a Revival of America's Revolutionary Ideals?

## Critical Thinking and Reflection

1. What does the Tea Party movement stand for in American national politics?
2. Is it more unified on economic, civil liberty, or foreign policy issues?
3. Are parallels with the Boston Tea Party justified or unjustified?
4. How did the election of President Obama influence the rise of the movement?
5. How successful was the mid-term congressional elections in 2010?
6. What role does it play in the presidential nominating system?
7. How might the primary nominating process influence the Tea Party's role?
8. Which of the prospective presidential candidates in 2012 receive Tea Party support?
9. Is it more or less likely to win over independent voters than the traditional Republican leadership?
10. Are there circumstances under which the Tea Party movement might nominate an independent candidate?

## Is There Common Ground?

There is no basis for common ground between those who are persuaded that there is one true meaning of the American constitutional system and those who maintain that the convictions of the Founding Fathers are open to differing interpretations. This has the potential to make the ideological opposition of the major parties more divisive, leaving little or no room for compromise. At the same time, there is a similar resentment of what is characterized as the "bailout of Wall Street" on the part of both much of the Tea Party movement and the radical sentiment that led to the Occupy Wall Street sit-ins. Whether this convergence of views can go further is doubtful in view of the basic distinction between the radical support for liberal government intervention in other areas and the adamant Tea Party opposition to taxation and any substantial government role in dealing with economic issues.

## Additional Resources

Supporting the modern Tea Party movement is Scott Rasmussen and Doug Schoen, *Mad as Hell: How the Tea Party Movement Is Fundamentally Remaking Our Two-Party System* (Harper, 2010). Like other sympathetic books, it expresses the conviction that expensive government policies are incompatible with America's founding principles and unsustainable in future generations. It goes further in arguing that the recent financial crisis produced strong reactions on both the left and the right of American politics, but the conservative movement will be more successful. John M. O'Hara played a role in the creation of the Tea Party movement, and he has written an account of its evolution, philosophy, and strategy in *A New American Tea Party: The Counterrevolution Against Bailouts, Handouts, Reckless Spending, and More Taxes* (John Wiley, 2010).

Kate Zernike, *Boiling Mad: Inside Tea Party America* (Times Books, 2010), critical of the modern Tea Party movement, places it in the context of hostility to a concentration of government power that is as old as the United States. Zernike notes that many of the recent government policies that the Tea Party condemns are those that improved race relations.

Max Blumenthal in *Republican Gomokrrah: Inside the Movement That Shattered the Party* (Nation Books, 2009) condemns the Tea Party movement as a powerful element of a toxic conservative rage that opposes an African American president. Blumenthal believes that the economic focus hides the influence of the Christian Right within the movement in advancing a broader social and moral agenda.

# ISSUE 3

## Is Bigger Government Better Government?

**YES: Jeff Madrick**, from *The Case for Big Government* (Princeton University Press, 2008)

**NO: Jim DeMint**, from *Saving Freedom* (Fidelis, 2009)

### ISSUE SUMMARY

**YES:** Humanities professor Jeff Madrick surveys the numerous government interventions in the economy since the end of World War II and concludes that they have been essential to America's growth and well being.

**NO:** Senator Jim DeMint compares government to a genie that can protect a nation from its enemies and ensure fair and equal treatment of its citizens but which needs to be "caged" lest it overwhelm and destroy the nation.

**A** continuing debate about government runs through the course of American history. The debate is between those who see government as an instrument for doing good versus those who see it as a potentially oppressive institution. Those who take the latter view usually concede that, yes, we do need government for strictly limited purposes—but, in the words of Tom Paine, government "even in its best state, is but a necessary evil."

Paine wrote those words in 1776, when America was still governed by a foreign nation. Does the situation change when a nation becomes self-governed? Alexander Hamilton thought so. Hamilton fought fiercely against the imperial government of Great Britain, but once American independence was achieved he became a champion of what he called "energetic" government, a term that included the pursuit of public programs aimed at increasing the nation's prosperity. He helped create the first federally owned Bank of the United States, encouraged the government to subsidize domestic industries, and he even experimented with government-owned mills in New Jersey. Opposing him was Secretary of State Thomas Jefferson. Jefferson wanted government to stay out of the domestic economy.

Despite the protestations of Jefferson and those who followed him, government became increasingly energetic during the nineteenth century. Though Andrew Jackson killed the rechartering of the Bank of the United States with his presidential veto, the federal government passed tariffs and financed the building of roads, canals, and railroads; during and after the Civil War federal power expanded into areas such as civil rights and higher education, areas once reserved to the states. By the close of the nineteenth century, government began tentatively moving into the areas of social welfare and business regulation—though not without resistance.

In the twentieth century, government growth expanded during World War I, contracted in the 1920s, and exploded during the years of President Franklin Roosevelt, 1933–1945. A host of "alphabet" bureaucracies (e.g., WPA, PWA, NLRB, NRA, and so on) were created, government spending increased to unprecedented levels, and new entitlement programs such as Social Security and Aid to the Families of Dependent Children (AFDC) were created. During this period the terms "liberal" and "conservative" crystallized into descriptions of the two sides in the debate: liberals were those who championed government activism and conservatives were those resisting it. Today, almost seventy years later, "liberal" and "conservative" still work reasonably well, at least in the economic sphere, as thumbnail labels for those who favor government and those who don't.

Liberals and conservatives have won some and lost some since the end of the 1940s. President Dwight Eisenhower was a moderate conservative, yet it was under his administration that the Federal-Aid Highway Act was passed, which put the federal government into the business of financing the construction of 41,000 miles of instate highways throughout the nation; Eisenhower also established a new cabinet department, Health, Education and Welfare (later renamed the Department of Health and Human Services).

During President Lyndon Johnson's, term 1964–68, the largest expansion of the federal government since the Roosevelt administration took place. Johnson boldly declared an "unconditional war on poverty." He created a variety of new federal agencies to teach job skills, stimulate community action, and dispense welfare. He pushed Medicaid and Medicare through Congress, and led Congress in passing new civil rights laws.

During Ronald Reagan's administration there was a serious challenge in the White House to liberal economic programs. The number of pages added to the Federal Register, which records the rules and regulations issued by federal agencies, declined each year of Reagan's presidency, breaking a sharp increase since 1960. The centerpiece of his economic program was his tax cuts, enacted in 1981, which lowered the top personal tax bracket from 70 to 28 percent in seven years. Reagan failed, however, to lower government expenditures, and the deficit soared.

Today's conservatives have made Reagan's approach their model, while liberals seek to build on Franklin Roosevelt's legacy. The Obama administration's plan to establish some form of universal health insurance, first proposed by President Harry Truman in 1945, rests on assumptions about government broadly shared by liberals since Roosevelt's time but whose philosophical roots can be traced to Alexander Hamilton.

Professor Jeff Madrick takes the liberal view that activist government has done much to enhance the quality of life and increase American prosperity. However, Senator Jim DeMint warns that when governments venture beyond keeping the peace and enforcing the rules of fair play, they begin to crush vital liberties and wreck the economy.

# YES ←

Jeff Madrick

# The Case for Big Government

After World War II, almost all economists feared a reprise of the Depression. It was hard to imagine what could replace all the lost military demand. But the opposite occurred. After a pause in 1947, the economy grew as rapidly on average as it ever did before, and the incomes of most working Americans grew faster than ever before. The progressive turn of policy, despite a resurgence of antigovernment sensibility, did not deter growth. Nor did higher income tax rates, which were raised by Roosevelt during the Depression and were raised again to record levels during World War II, where they remained for more than a decade. The highest tax bracket reached approximately 90 percent, where it remained until 1964. To the contrary, bigger government seemed to go along with ever faster growth. Roosevelt had proposed a G.I. Bill of Rights in 1943, among other things, to provide aid for veterans to go to college and to buy a house. Congress raised objections, but in 1944 the G.I. Bill was passed. By the late 1950s, half of the returning sixteen million soldiers financed college or other training programs as a result. Millions of mortgages were guaranteed. The nation was thus directed in a particular way. The Marshall Plan under President Truman, and named after the secretary of state who strongly advocated it, provided billion of dollars of aid to rebuild Europe.

Dwight Eisenhower, as a former president, incurred the ire of the Republican right wing by proposing to expand Social Security coverage to another ten million workers—to include farm workers and professionals such as teachers, accountants, and dentists. He also increased benefits. Eisenhower said that it was simply clear that not all could save enough for retirement. Eisenhower also advocated the development and federal financing of a national highway system. He had strong support from the major auto companies, of course, and the bill passed in 1956. By the late 1950s, 90 percent of all homes in America were reachable by road, and often by highway. It was an explicit case of national government coordination and investment that deeply influenced the development of the nation into a new geography of suburbs, based on cheap gas, cheap property, and mostly free roads.

In these decades, the federal government financed and administered the antipolio vaccines. In the wake of the Soviet launch of the first space satellite, Sputnik, Congress passed the National Defense Education Act, providing billions of dollars of annual grants and loans to support higher education, technical training, and other educational programs. Young people were further spurred to go to college. The National Institutes of Health, as an extension of late nineteenth-century government investment in health research, were expanded dramatically after World War II, and accounted for a high proportion of medical breakthroughs. Research and development (R&D) was undertaken in many federal agencies, not least the Defense Department, where the Internet had its origins. The federal government accounted for most of America's R&D, in fact, through the 1960s, topping out at 67 percent of all such research in 1963. Many economists contend that such intense research efforts account for greater American economic superiority in these years than any other single factor. The Supreme Court under Eisenhower, led by Johnson's appointee as chief justice, Earl Warren, ordered that public schools be integrated.

In the 1960s, President Johnson passed Medicare and implemented his War on Poverty, including health care for the poor under Medicaid. Regulatory changes were significant, and included landmark civil rights legislation, which protected voting rights for blacks, ended Jim Crow laws once and for all, and forbade gender and racial discrimination in labor markets. Other regulatory reforms involved cigarettes, packaging, motor vehicle safety, consumer credit, and the expansion of the authority of the Food and Drug Administration.

Between 1948 and 1970, the share of spending in GDP by the federal, state, and local governments rose from 16.5 percent to 27.5 percent, nearly eleven percentage points. Most of this increase was in social expenditures. Yet productivity, wages, and overall GDP grew very rapidly, as noted. What is the complaint then in light of all this success? It is hard to escape the conclusion as noted earlier in this section that government did not hurt but significantly helped economies to grow.

## The Economic Benefits of Government

. . . Few economists disagree with the theory that some measure of public investment in infrastructure, education, and health care is necessary. Because public goods such as roads and schools benefit society overall more than any individual or business, such investment would not have been adequately undertaken by private firms. . . . Government support is required for primary education, roads, and the poor.

Far less frequently discussed is the fact that government can be the focus of needed and useful coordination. When railroads used different size track (gauge), government was needed to standardize them. By organizing communities to use a single public water system, government creates economies of scale for such a public good. The highway system was an immense act of coordination that probably couldn't have been attained through a private network; there is no example of one in the world, in any case. The system of international trade and currency valuation is a government-led example of coordination.

Similarly, regulations can and often do make economies work better. They can make information about products and services more open. They can reduce corruption, monopolistic pricing, and anticompetitive policies regarding research, innovation, and new products. They can temper financial speculation, which distorts the flow of capital toward inefficient uses and can often lead to costly corrections and serious recessions, as occurred yet again in 2008.

Some regulations can be poorly administered and reduce economic efficiency. Others will outlive their usefullness; they should be pruned and streamlined over time. But other regulations will be a short-term cost to business that the nation chooses to bear for quality of life and even a better economy. Maintaining the safety of products that consumers cannot judge for themselves is an example; but the safety and effectiveness of products also makes consumers more confident buyers of products. Environmental regulations adopted in the early 1970s have probably been costly to all of us, but they are a cost we bear for cleaner air and water and the diminution of global warming. It is no cause for alarm that regulations have multiplied as the economy supplies so many more goods and services to the people. As economies change and grow more complex, it is only natural that more oversight is needed.

At the still more liberal end of the political spectrum, some economists will argue—though not the American mainstream—that programs that help raise and make wages more equal, such as laws that facilitate union organizing, minimum wages, and equal rights, may well aid economic growth, not undermine productivity, by creating demand for goods and services, and also reinforcing faith in workers that they will be fairly rewarded for their effort. . . .

One of the key benefits of the larger post–World War II government, if in some quarters still a controversial one, is also that it makes the economy more stable. Well before Keynes's work during the Depression there were calls for government spending to create jobs and support incomes. Massive public works projects that reignited economic growth, such as Baron Hausmann's rebuilding of Paris, are common in history. But in the post–World War II era, such activities gained new theoretical justification from Keynes's theories. Both Keynesian liberals and some Friedmanite conservatives accepted, to one degree or another, that fiscal and monetary policy—deficit spending by the treasury or the adjustment of interest rates by the central bank—could help avoid or ameliorate recessions and thereby raise the rate of growth over time. A large government is itself, despite conservative arguments cited earlier, a bulwark against rapidly declining spending. Unemployment insurance, Social Security, and government employment itself are stabilizing factors.

If the size of government truly and directly caused the inflation of the 1970s and contributed demonstrably to slower economic growth, it would be reason for concern. But we have seen that it did not in the United States, and nations with far larger governments have produced neither more rapid inflation nor substandard levels of income for their citizens. The public goods and social programs of many countries—from Sweden and Norway to France and Germany—are significantly more generous than America's. . . .

In fact, enlightened regulation has been imperative for economic growth at least since Jefferson's policies for governing the distribution of land. When done well, regulation keeps competition honest and free, enables customers to know and understand the products they receive, and fosters new ideas. When neglected, abuse becomes easy, information in markets is suppressed, capital investment is channeled to wasteful and inefficient uses, and dangerous excesses occur. The open flow of products and services information is critical to a free-market economy. The conditions for healthy competition have simply not been maintained under a free-market ideology of minimal government that professes great faith in competition. Competition requires government oversight; the wool has been pulled over our eyes.

We now know the following. If federal, state, and local governments absorb roughly 35 percent of GDP in America, rather than the current roughly 30 percent, it will not inhibit growth and undermine entrepreneurial spirits, productivity, or prosperity if the spending is well-channeled. Government absorbs much more of national income in other nations whose prosperity is the equivalent of or perhaps superior to America's. In European nations, government spending absorbs approximately 40 percent of all spending, and standards of living are high. If government programs are managed well, they will on balance enhance productivity. A rise to 35 percent will raise approximately $700 billion a year to the federal, state, and local governments to provide protections to workers, finance social programs, maintain an adequate regulatory presence, and raise significantly the level of investment in transportation, energy, education, and health care. Part and perhaps all of this $700 billion can be paid for with higher taxes. . . .

. . . The most productive way to address rising global competition is not trade restrictions per se but for the government to invest in the nation. Consumer spending leaks to foreign imports and business investment leaks across borders. But potential returns to the economy from spending on transportation projects are at this point significant, partly due to years of neglect, and the jobs created to implement them largely stay at home. The proportion of the federal budget spent on investment in the nation—including transportation, science, technology, and energy—are well down from the levels of the 1970s. Federal spending on education as a proportion of GDP fell under Clinton but was raised under his successor, George Bush, and it remains slightly higher as a proportion of GDP than it was in the 1970s. Overall, public investment equaled nearly 3 percent of GDP in the 1970s, which would come to more than $400 billion today. Under Clinton it fell to half of that proportion, and under Bush it rose but remains at less than 2 percent of GDP. Merely raising it to 1970s levels would produce $140 billion more a year to spend. To reemphasize, such spending usually creates domestic jobs and builds future productivity at the same time.

To take one estimate, a House Transportation Committee report cites a Federal Highway Administration model that claims that a $75 billion investment will create more than 3.5 million jobs and $464 billion in additional nationwide sales. Every $1 billion, in other words, yields 47,500 jobs and another $6 billion in sales. Spending has been so inadequate that such estimates can be accepted confidently. The Society of Civil Engineers suggest that much of America's infrastructure should get a grade of D. While these studies are hardly definitive, they are suggestive of the possibilities.

The most exciting potential returns are for high-quality pre-K education. A wide range of studies has been undertaken on several high-quality programs that have long been underway in the United States. The benefits of such programs include not only improving the ability of children to learn, but also long-term reduction in crime rates, reduced need for special education and repeating grades, and lower welfare enrollment rates. A conventional conservative economist such as James Heckman, a Nobel laureate who opposes college subsidies, nevertheless favors significant funding of preschool programs. Some estimate these programs create benefits that exceed costs by five to ten times. A highly sophisticated recent analysis by two economists estimates that if a high-quality program was instituted nationwide, the federal moneys spent would be fully paid for in increased tax revenues due to improved incomes and would reduce welfare, crime, and special education expenses. In other words, it would pay for itself. . . .

As a consequence of neglect and change, an adequate agenda for America is a lengthy one, but it is not an antigrowth agenda. It favors growth. Growing personal income is more necessary to a full life than is recognized, in part because the cost of some key needs rise very fast, in part because a wealthy society can finance innovation, and in part because a wealthy populace will find it easier and more congenial to pay for communal needs through taxes. But for too long, mainstream economists have accepted the notion that more savings and technology will alone lead to faster growth. The agenda for government is therefore inappropriately limited; government spending, for example, will allegedly erode savings. America has been able to test this economic philosophy for a full generation and it has failed. Years of below-par productivity growth, low and stagnating wages, inattention to basic needs, persistent poverty, and the undermining of assets necessary to future growth, including education, health care, energy alternatives, and transportation infrastructure are the consequences.

The gap between a growing economy and falling wages is the major contemporary mystery. Global competition and off-shoring may explain part of the gap, but the trend began decades ago. Research shows that a gap in worker compensation and productivity began to open up slowly in the late 1980s: typical workers got less than their historical share, while capital (profits) and high-income workers got more. This gap widened explosively in the 2000s.

Furthermore, there was little explanation as to why male incomes in particular fared especially poorly over this long period we have described. A major reason is the withdrawal of government from its traditional purposes.

Jim DeMint

⟶ **NO**

# Saving Freedom

## Big Government's Impossible Dream: Making Everything Right for Everyone

The proliferation of special interests in Washington has created a threat to freedom quite different from the "tyranny of the majority." Majority interests in America are now secondary to the politics of special interests. The election of 2008 demonstrated how a political party could bundle the interests of numerous groups and create a new ruling majority—a new tyranny of special interests.

This new political dynamic is the antithesis of the intent of our Constitution and a serious blow to the cause of freedom. The rights of individuals, protected by equal justice and the rule of law, are now subjugated to the special rights of groups that are guaranteed by a strong, centralized government. The "common good" is now viewed as a conglomeration of disparate interests of multiple groups demanding special treatment.

There are a lot of good reasons for Americans to fight back against this centralization of special interest power in Washington, but the most important reason is it creates a dysfunctional government. It may be a cliché, but it's true; Washington is broken. Almost everything our federal government attempts to do becomes a disaster. We mandate that cars burn corn ethanol and cause a world food crisis. We combine social engineering with monetary policy and create a worldwide financial crisis. . . . We have left one catastrophe after another in our wake as we have attempted to save the world, dry every tear, and solve every problem. . . .

Freedom is protected by a wide range of public and private institutions guarding against the concentration of power. The concentration of power at the federal level destroys this balance, weakens other institutions of freedom, and destroys freedom itself. Americans must not continue to allow one institution of freedom, the federal government, to dominate and diminish the role of other institutions or to demean the individual values that made our country great and free.

America needs champions of freedom at the state and local levels who will challenge the growing concentration of power in Washington. Governors and state legislatures could take much more control of education, health care, transportation, energy, and other services that would give their citizens more independence from the federal government. This could help begin the process of downsizing the federal government. Business leaders could unite around common goals to reduce corporate taxes, duplicative regulations, and frivolous lawsuits at the state and federal levels. Every dollar and decision we keep from Washington today means more freedom for all Americans tomorrow.

## Freedom versus Big Government: *Unlimited Government Leads to Unlimited Debt and Socialism*

*Long ago in a distant land, a very old man called his son to his dying bed. There he revealed an amazing secret: the old man's father had bequeathed him a genie he kept locked in a small cage and hidden in a closet. The genie provided two services to the kingdom where the man's family lived for generations. First, he protected the people from any person or country that attempted to harm them. Second, he guaranteed all the citizens of the kingdom were treated equally and fairly. Because of these two protections, their kingdom was the happiest and most prosperous in the land.*

*The man told his son to bring the genie's cage to his bedside. "The genie is now your responsibility," he said, "but you must never ask him to do any more than the two services he has provided for years. If you do, he will grow in size and strength with every new request. Then he will break out of his cage and become a threat to the kingdom instead of a blessing."*

*The son promised to heed his father's warning, and for several years he kept his promise. Then a neighbor's home burned along with all of the possessions in the house. Instead of waiting for the community to help the man rebuild his home as was the kingdom's custom, the son decided to ask the genie to help. The whole community was amazed at the beautiful new home with all the man's possessions restored. They held a great celebration for the son and gave him a beautiful award. But soon another man's home was destroyed by a flood, and instead of rushing to help, the community came to the son's house and demanded that the genie restore the man's home.*

*The son relented and asked the genie to help. This time the genie grew large enough to break out of the cage. He escaped, and everywhere he went someone asked him to do something new. He grew and grew and began to demand more and more food and possessions from the kingdom. The genie built a huge castle on a hill and demanded that all citizens bring him half of everything they produced. But citizens continued to ask for more and more, and the genie continued to grow and demand more and more from the citizens. The people became weaker and poorer, and their kingdom eventually disappeared from the land.*

America's founders knew they were putting a powerful genie in a cage when they formed the federal government. They knew that historically all democratic governments grew until they consumed the freedom of the people and ultimately collapsed under their own weight. They knew the American people would have to remain constantly vigilant to restrain the growth of government. And they knew, like the genie in the story above, the federal government would grow every time we asked it to do something new. But our founders left us a "cage" to protect ourselves against the genie of government growth: the Constitution.

After my first election to Congress in 1998, I spent November, December, and the first few weeks in January 1999 setting up my office, hiring staff, and fighting to get on the committees that aligned with my priorities: tax reform, Social Security reform, health-care reform, and education choice. Most of these issues were handled by the powerful Ways and Means Committee that was reserved for senior members or "vulnerable" Republicans who needed to raise a lot of money. Apparently, outside groups gave a lot of money to committee members who could tinker with the tax code. They were less interested in people like me who really wanted to reform the tax code. I never got on the Ways and Means Committee during my six years in the House.

Swearing-in ceremonies for the new Congress were in late January. My wife and four children traveled to D.C. to watch from the House gallery as I took the oath of office. Every member of the House has to stand in the House chamber, raise his right hand, and recite the oath of office at the beginning of each new Congress. I had never given a lot of thought to the oath until I took it, and frankly was a little surprised by what it actually said. I guess I expected to swear allegiance to my country and agree to do whatever I thought was best for my state and the American people. But the oath was a simple pledge to defend the Constitution:

> I, Jim DeMint, do solemnly swear that I will support and defend the Constitution of the United States against all enemies, foreign or domestic; that I will bear true faith and allegiance to the same; that I take this obligation freely, without any mental reservation or purpose of evasion; and that I will faithfully discharge the duties of the office on which I am about to enter. So help me God.

There is nothing in this oath about representing my district and state or helping the poor and downtrodden. There was nothing about responding to the woes of the American people. There was no list of duties because everything we were supposed to do in Congress was written in the Constitution. All federal officers, the president and his cabinet, justices on the Supreme Court, and members of the armed services all take an oath to protect and defend the Constitution. It must have been really important at one time. . . .

I rarely heard the Constitution spoken of again—not when considering legislation, not when considering any new government program. It was never used as justification for legislation because there was little we did that fit within the limited powers of the federal government specified by the Constitution. . . .

The Constitution gives Congress the power to make laws for specific federal purposes, raise revenues (taxes), and spend money; it charges the president with the responsibility to execute the laws and command the military, and it gives the Supreme Court and other federal courts the responsibility of ensuring equal justice under the law. The areas in which Congress is allowed to make laws and spend money are confined primarily to protecting Americans against "enemies foreign and domestic" by establishing and funding the military and by punishing counterfeiters and pirates on the high seas (Article I, Sec. 8). Congress is also given the power to regulate commerce *between* (not within) the states and foreign nations and to establish post offices and post roads.

Section 9 of Article I then tells Congress several things it can't do, including showing preference to states and spending money unless it is properly appropriated by law. This is where most of Congress's mischief originates. Politicians and even some judges have said this section gives Congress "the power of the purse" to spend money on anything it pleases. This is categorically absurd! It is clear in context that Congress only has authority to fund actions consistent with those powers given to Congress in Section 8.

The modern-day interpretation of Section 9 of Article I completely undermines all the restraints in size and scope of the federal government that were the primary purpose of the Constitution. Today Congress makes laws, spends money, and raises taxes for small local projects (traffic lights and water projects), for preferential requests from specific states (museums), and to satisfy demands from special interest groups (farmers, unions, minorities, senior citizens, veterans, etc). It won't be easy to turn this around because most American voters are now dependent in some way on federal beneficence.

The federal government now provides funding and heavily regulates public education, health care, retirement income (Social Security), farming, transportation, research, water and sewer services, banking and financial services, electric utilities, environmental standards, business and labor relations, and a myriad of other activities not found in the Constitution. It is perhaps naive and unrealstic to believe that Americans who are heavily dependent on these federal services would ever support a return to a pure Constitutional framework. I do believe, however, that if Americans could grasp the disastrous long-term impact of allowing our federal "genie" continued growth, they would force elected officials and judges to focus more on the protective "cage" provided by the Constitution. Then we could begin to restrain the growth of the federal government.

## Why Restrain the Growth of the Federal Government?

Most members of Congress act like the Constitution is no longer relevant and seem to believe we should continue to expand federal programs whenever and wherever we see fit. But no reasonably informed, thinking American could believe unrestrained government spending would be good for our country. I will discuss in later chapters the corruption, incompetence, mismanagement, and devastating societal impact of congressional meddling in all areas of American cultural and economic life. The focus of this chapter, however, is the financial condition of our country. The most compelling arguments to stop the growth of the federal government are our government's unsustainable levels of spending and debt, which could result in the financial collapse of our government and our private sector economic structure.

. . . Government spending represented only a small fraction of the private economy until the twentieth century. Since World War II government spending has hovered around 20 percent of GDP.

Economic cycles over the past several decades have confirmed that good economic growth can occur when government spending stays below 20 percent.

The U.S. economy has usually slowed and declined as government spending exceeded 20 percent. . . . Government spending now exceeds 20 percent and will surpass 40 percent in about thirty years. . . .

Equally troubling is the growing national debt owed by the American people. Over recent decades America's debt has grown but has stayed below 50 percent of GDP because our economy has continued to grow. Based on current projections, however, our debt will soon explode and dramatically eclipse our total economy. Unless major reforms are enacted quickly, Americans will face devastating economic consequences. . . .

Americans have been told so many times about an impending "crisis" they no longer take these alarms seriously: the energy crisis, the Social Security crisis, the housing crisis, the mortgage crisis, the Wall Street crisis, the auto industry crisis, the recession crisis, and of course, the global warming crisis are all examples of recent problems used for political manipulation. Global warming, which is now being used as an excuse to expand dramatically the power and control of government, may not even be a man-made phenomenon. The science on this issue is far from conclusive. Yet Congress is in a virtual panic to implement massive taxes on our economy to punish the users of coal and gas.

Unlike politically manufactured crises, the catastrophic financial course of the federal government is an absolute fact. Without major reforms there is no plausible survivable scenario for our economy. This is not a problem that might occur in the distant future. The nation's debt, out-of-control spending, and loose monetary policy are creating worldwide economic insecurity. It seems inexplicable that Congress is completely ignoring this problem.

## Ignoring the Warnings

During the hurried debate and political panic of the Wall Street debacle in late 2008, I remember many of my Senate and House colleagues expressing disbelief that there had been no warning of the crisis. The fact is there were ample warnings for more than ten years. Congressional leaders chose not to act because the government-sponsored entities (Fannie Mae and Freddie Mac) and Wall Street were doing their bidding, in addition to making consistently large financial contributions to their campaign accounts.

Easy and cheap credit were allowing more people to buy homes and cars, accomplishing the dual goals of artificially raising the standard of living for lower-income Americans and keeping our economy running on steroids. The problem with steroids is they eventually destroy the people who use them. Loose monetary policy created a financial house of cards destined to crash. But unqualified borrowers and unscrupulous lenders were not the only ones who suffered. Much of the savings of responsible, hardworking Americans evaporated almost overnight.

Once the panic ensued, many politicians were quick to blame others and claim "they had sent a letter" warning of the coming crisis. Baloney. Congress, well-known for its doublespeak and dishonesty, outdid itself during the "economic rescue" debate. The people who blocked reforms and received the most campaign contributions from the guilty parties were the ones in charge of negotiating the irresponsible bailouts. The result was several trillion dollars borrowed against America's future and an unprecedented intrusion by the federal government into the private economy.

I'm afraid neither Congress nor the majority of the American people learned their lesson. We are now ignoring a much more serious warning. America's massive and growing debt is today's greatest threat to America's prosperity. Early in 2008 the comptroller general of the United States, David M. Walker, began to travel the country trying to warn Americans about our unsustainable level of spending and debt. Almost no one paid attention. His warnings did not appear on the nightly news of the major television networks.

Mr. Walker's presentation, titled "Saving Our Future Requires Tough Choices Today," revealed that mandatory spending (required by law) for Social Security, Medicare, and Medicaid (entitlements) had grown from 16 percent of federal spending in 1966 to 40 percent of the entire federal budget in 2006. The large wave of baby boomers now reaching retirement age promises to make this problem much worse.

Most of this spending has been taken from funds that should have been used for the primary constitutional responsibility of the federal government—defense. Military spending dropped from 43 percent in 1966 to 20 percent in 2006. While "smart bombs" and other new high-tech weapons systems have lulled Americans into a false sense of security, our military is fighting with one hand tied behind its back. In the age of terrorism, our intelligence capabilities are woefully lacking. Our Air Force is flying many antiquated planes (often more than forty years old), and the scheduled replacement rates guarantee a worsening situation. So much of our military spending is directed by political earmarks from congressmen and senators with parochial interests that we make it harder for our military leaders to develop coherent plans to defend our nation.

My point is this: there is a terrible cost to unrestrained government spending and debt. Part of that cost is the neglect of real national priorities such as defense. The other costs are the devaluation of our currency, the destruction of our private-sector economy, and the loss of wealth and quality of life for all Americans. . . .

## Principles and Institutions

Government is an essential *institution* for the development and protection of freedom. We must have a framework of law, order, and justice for freedom to grow and thrive. Government makes the rules and enforces them much like the officials at a football game. Players and coaches have the freedom to do whatever they want as long as they follow the rules. When they don't, the officials throw a flag and impose a penalty. But the officials don't call the plays or decide who gets to play. Officials don't manage the game, and the federal government shouldn't try to manage America.

America's government has grown well beyond the constitutional framework provided by our founders. Our federal government is no longer the referee for our economy and culture; it is now the biggest player on the field. Our federal government is trying to manage many aspects of America's economy and social services. It is not an exaggeration to say the results have been catastrophic. Not only has the government inhibited the growth of our economy and undermined our culture, it has put our country on an unsustainable financial course that must be reversed immediately. . . .

# EXPLORING THE ISSUE

## Is Bigger Government Better Government?

## Critical Thinking and Reflection

1. Madrick argues that the federal government's expansion since World War II has been good for the country. Why does he reach that conclusion? What sort of evidence does he cite?
2. Madrick often refers to the success of big government in Western Europe and cites it as a model for this country. Do you think the European model fits the United States? Why, or why not?
3. What does DeMint mean by big government's "impossible dream"? Why does he think it is impossible?
4. What is the point DeMint is trying to make in his fable about the dying man's "genie"? Would this be a plausible prediction of America's future?

## Is There Common Ground?

There *might* be common ground between Madrick and DeMint if the latter could convince the former to limit government to (a) protecting people from other people or countries that want to harm them and (b) guaranteeing that all citizens be treated equally and fairly. But it does not seem likely that Madrick would consent to these limited functions of government, unless of course terms like "fairness" and "equality" were given very expansive definitions—which is what DeMint complains that liberals always do!

## Additional Resources

In 1962, economist Milton Friedman published *Capitalism and Freedom* (University of Chicago Press), which is now considered a classic of economic conservatism (although Friedman, using an older definition, preferred to be called a liberal). In it, he argued that even toll roads and national parks should be run by private enterprise. It was just this kind of privatization that liberal economist John K. Galbraith scorned in *The Affluent Society* (Houghton Mifflin, 1960); he argued that it was leading to urban sleaziness and vulgarity in America. More recent works arguing the case for and against big government include Max Neiman, *Defending Government: Why Big Government Works* (Prentice Hall, 2009), which contends that big government is essential to improve the lives of people and that its critics really harbor a resentment against democracy; and Timothy P. Carney, *The Big Ripoff: How Big Business and Big Government Steal*

*Your Money* (Wiley, 2006), which argues that there really isn't much difference between Big Business Republicans and Tax-and-Spend Democrats, for together they have built an empire of exploitation.

A large part of Madrick's argument for government activism rests on the success of President Roosevelt's policies during the Great Depression and World War II.

For an absorbing history of America during the Depression, see Amity Shlaes, *The Forgotten Man* (Harper Perennial, 2007). Shlaes is generally critical of Franklin Roosevelt's policies. For another point of view, see David M. Kennedy, *Freedom from Fear: The American People in Depression and War, 1929–1945* (Oxford University Press, 2001). Kennedy lauds Roosevelt as a true visionary who also possessed the political skills to bring together people of very diverse views.

# ISSUE 4

# Should America Adopt Public Financing of Political Campaigns?

**YES: Mark Green**, from "Change, for Good," *Selling Out: How Big Corporate Money Buys Elections, Rams Through Legislation, and Betrays Our Democracy* (HarperCollins, 2002)

**NO: John Samples**, from "Taxpayer Financing of Campaigns," in John Samples, ed., *Welfare for Politicians? Taxpayer Financing of Campaigns* (Cato Institute, 2005)

### ISSUE SUMMARY

**YES:** Political activist and author Mark Green sums up his thesis in the subtitle of his book, a work that urges adoption of public financing of election campaigns in order to make politics more honest and to reduce the dependency of elected officials on selfish interests.

**NO:** Cato Institute director and political scientist John Samples opposes public financing of candidates for public office because it does not achieve any of the goals of its advocates and it forces voters to underwrite the financing of candidates they do not support.

**A**pproximately $4 billion was spent on the 2004 presidential and congressional elections, nearly $1 billion more than in the election four years earlier. It was the most expensive election in American history, but it will almost certainly be exceeded in 2008. Internet advertising has been added on to print, radio, television, and live campaigning, resulting not in altering how the money is spent but in adding to it.

This has occurred despite the efforts of Congress to regulate and restrict campaign expenditures. In 2000, Congress established disclosure requirements for nonparty political groups known as Section 527 organizations, which were not required to register with the Federal Elections Commission because their principle purpose was alleged to be something other than influencing federal elections. In 2002, the first important revision of federal campaign finance law in more than two decades, the Bipartisan Campaign Reform Act, was adopted. The following year, the U.S. Supreme Court upheld its major provisions: the elimination of party soft money and the regulation of candidate-specific issue advertising. Nevertheless, the presidential candidacies of President George W. Bush and Senator John Kerry inspired vaster contributions and expenditures in accordance with—and sometimes in circumvention of—the law.

What is wrong with this increased spending? A great deal, say those who believe that rampant spending on political campaigns discourages less prosperous citizens from seeking elective office, diverts office-holders from doing their jobs to seeking contributions and bending their convictions to conform to those of their contributors, exaggerates the political influence of special interests, and discourages would-be voters who conclude that money matters more than their votes.

Soft money is money that is contributed not to individual campaigns but to political parties, ostensibly for the purpose of "party-building" activities, such as get-out-the-vote drives. The Federal Election Commission (FEC), an agency created in 1974, began allowing this practice in 1978, and within a decade fund-raisers in both parties began to realize its usefulness as a way around existing contribution limits. Under then-existing law, "hard money" contributions (funds contributed directly to the campaigns of particular candidates) were limited to $1,000 per person for each candidate; the assumption was that no candidate can be "bought" for a mere $1,000. But unlimited soft money allowed wealthy donors and interest groups to contribute huge sums to the parties at dinners, coffees, and other such gatherings—thus subtly (or not-so-subtly) reminding them of who was buttering their bread. Another concern of those who supported the new law was what they saw as the misuse of "issue advocacy" during campaigns. Interest groups had been able to get around the legal limits on contributions by pouring millions of unregulated dollars into "attack" ads that did not explicitly ask people to vote for or against a candidate. Instead, they said something like "Call Senator Smith and tell him to stop supporting polluters."

The new law sought to plug these loopholes and to bring the existing system of federal campaign finance regulation up-to-date. Among its major provisions are the following:

- A ban on soft money contributions to the national political parties.
- An increase in hard money contribution limits. For example, limits to individual candidates were increased from $1,000 to $2,000 per candidate per election. The increase was meant to take inflation into account.
- Restrictions on the ability of corporations, labor unions, and other interest groups to run "issue ads" featuring the names or likenesses of candidates within 60 days of a general election and 30 days of a primary election.

Some critics of existing campaign finance methods believe that the recent changes do not go far enough. Mark Green, in the selection that follows, concludes that nothing less than public financing of campaigns and elections will serve the public interest and further democracy. Critics of public financing maintain that these changes in the law are contrary to democracy because they use public tax money to support views that many citizens oppose. One of these critics, John Samples, argues that the changes would have a negative effect on voter participation and would limit competition.

# YES ↵       Mark Green

## Change, for Good

The evidence . . . makes it clear: our campaign finance system is broken, citizens of all persuasions want change, and successful alternatives exist.

The alibis of apologists—change helps incumbents; money is speech; money doesn't buy votes—are shallow and unpersuasive. So now the defenders of the status quo have shifted to political and free-market arguments. Voters don't really care, they say; or, as Mitch McConnell argued in 2000, they assert that no candidate has ever been elected or defeated on the issue of campaign reform, and thus it can be safely ignored. Yet McConnell's Senate nemesis, John McCain, made campaign finance reform the heart and soul of his electrifying 2000 presidential campaign. Only by vastly outspending McCain did George W. Bush squeak by him in a tight primary battle that was supposed to be a coronation—and not before soft money became a dinner-table conversation staple. That same year, Maria Cantwell believes, making campaign finance reform a centerpiece of her Washington State U.S. Senate race was a major reason for her squeaker of a victory.

Senators McCain and Cantwell ran against what big money buys for special interests—tax breaks and loopholes for big corporations, weakened environmental regulations for manufacturers, and price protections for drug companies. But they also ran against what those purchases cost Americans: higher taxes, more pollution, and expensive health care, respectively.

To be successful, a pro-democracy movement like campaign finance reform cannot be merely an abstract, good-government ideal. It must be tied to the issues that Americans care most about: affordable child care, education, health care, and housing; a clean environment and safe streets; and tax rates that are fair. Do we want children with lower rates of asthma? Then we need campaign finance reform. Do we want enough funds for smaller class sizes and qualified, well-paid teachers? Then we need campaign finance reform. Do we want seniors to have access to lifesaving medicine? Then we need campaign finance reform. Do we want to keep guns out of the hands of kids and criminals? Then we need campaign finance reform. . . .

Both Republicans and Democrats came to agree that the problem with welfare was not necessarily the result of bad people but of a very bad system that—by paying more if a recipient had no work and no husband—discouraged employment and marriage. Ditto campaign finance. The sin is the *system*. How else can we explain how such provably honorable people as John Glenn, Alan Cranston, and John McCain felt it necessary to go to bat for the likes of a big, sleazy contributor like Charles Keating?

A comprehensive campaign finance reform program is ideally suited to achieve the conservative goals on which our economy and society are built— competition, efficiency, accountability, open markets, and market integrity. Specifically, four reforms would restore our electoral democracy by elevating voters over donors: spending limits, public financing, a restructured enforce-ment agency, and free broadcast time and mailings.

Limits on campaign spending are an integral part of restoring our democracy; Congress understood this fact when it included expenditure limits in the 1971 and 1974 campaign finance laws. Furthermore, the experi-ence of the last quarter century has taught us that without caps on campaign spending to complement contribution limits, money will always find ways back into the system. But as long as *Buckley v. Valeo* remains the law, the courts are likely to strike down any attempts to place limits on campaign spending.

The Court in *Buckley* concluded that expenditures did not raise the prob-lem of corruption in the same way contributions did. The Court's conclusion is based on two critical errors: (1) subjecting expenditure limits to a higher standard than contribution limits, and (2) considering only the anticorruption rationale while dismissing the other interests.

Why should campaign expenditures be entitled to much greater consti-tutional protection than campaign contributions? Neither expenditures nor contributions actually are speech; both merely facilitate expressive activities. And the argument that contributions pose a greater danger of quid pro quo corruption than expenditures seems ridiculous on its face: Are we really to believe that a $2000 contribution to a candidate will create a greater sense of obligation than millions of dollars in independent expenditures for that candidate?

And what makes preventing quid pro quo corruption so much more important than any other governmental interest? Of course, it is unaccept-able for public officials to sell votes, access, or influence to the highest bidder. Why? Not because of the quid pro quo–ness of it all; we exchange money for goods and services all the time in our daily lives. Rather, it is because the sale of our government undermines the most fundamental principles of our democracy: competitive elections, effective government, and—most impor-tant of all—the guarantee that our public officials answer to their true con-stituents, not a handful of wealthy benefactors. Quid pro quo arrangements are surely egregious violations of these democratic norms, but they are not the only ones. . . .

Until *Buckley* falls and a spending cap is found constitutional, funding limits can only be encouraged by offering public funds to candidates who voluntarily accept them. Only spending limits can end the arms race for cam-paign cash and reduce the power of war chests that incumbents build to scare off competition. And only the combination of spending limits and public funds can level the political playing field.

Spending limits that are set too high tend to favor incumbents, because few others can raise the resources to compete with them. Limits that are set too low, however, also favor incumbents, since challengers need to spend enough to overcome the natural advantages that accrue to incumbents through years of constituent service, free media, and use of the franking privilege. So the porridge must not be too hot or too cold. When weighing these two considerations, a third must also be taken into account: incumbents and the well-connected will not voluntarily join a public financing program if they feel its spending limits are significantly below what they could otherwise raise. If limits are too low, so too will be participation rates, and the program's purposes will be seriously compromised.

Of these three considerations, two point toward higher spending limits, which suggests that it is better to err on the side of caution. The average House winner spent $842,245 in 2000; the average candidate who challenged an incumbent spent just $143,685. In 1988, only 22 House campaigns hit the million-dollar mark; in 2000, the number reached 176. To control costs without discouraging participation or diminishing a challenger's ability to compete, House candidates should be held to inflation-adjusted spending limits of $900,000–$450,000 each for the primary and general election. A strong argument may be made that a $900,000 limit, which memorializes a level of spending that is about the current average, does not do enough to suppress campaign spending. But to undercut opponents who will use inadequate spending limits as an excuse to oppose reform, and to ensure that challengers can spend at significant levels, it is in the reform coalition's best interests to support limits around the current average cost of a winning campaign. By definition, this amount can't be too low or too high if it's the average amount it takes to win.

Senate candidates should be able to spend $1 million, plus fifty cents for each voting-age person in the state—which would come to about $8 million (for the primary and general election combined) in New York State, $7 million in Florida, $5 million in Ohio and Pennsylvania, and $2 million in Arkansas— or about one-fourth to one-half of what's recently been spent in these states. But in comparison to House contests, Senate races have higher profiles and receive significantly more media attention, making it harder for incumbents to dominate. Consequently, spending limits lower than current averages will protect challengers from the war chests that Senate incumbents can build over six years, and still ensure—because of free media coverage—that challengers will have ample opportunity to get their message out.

For instance, in Michigan's 2000 Senate race Debbie Stabenow spent $8 million in her victory over incumbent Senator Spencer Abraham, who spent $14.5 million. Under the spending-limit formula just outlined, both candidates would have been held to about $5 million. Similarly, in Pennsylvania, a $5 million limit would have helped challenger Ron Klink, who was outspent by nearly $10 million in his losing 2000 campaign against incumbent Senator Rick Santorum.

Separate limits for the primary and general election ensure that the winner of a hard-fought primary will not be placed at a disadvantage by facing a general-election opponent who suffered no primary challenge. To ensure equity, of course, candidates without primary election opponents should be allowed to spend up to the limit in the primary election period, although no public funds should be given to candidates without serious opponents, whether in primary or general elections.

**A bonus provision**   Again, so long as *Buckley* is the constitutional standard, legislation cannot prevent the super-rich from spending tens of millions of dollars on their campaigns. We can, however, help their opponents by eliminating the spending limit. It is unfair to keep a lid on a non-rich candidate when his or her opponent effectively says the sky's the limit. . . .

The airwaves belong to us, the public. We provide broadcasters with federal licenses—for free—on the condition that they agree to serve "the public interest, convenience, and necessity." They have not lived up to their end of the bargain.

How have they gotten away with it? (You'll never guess.) The powerful broadcast industry vehemently opposes reforms affecting their bottom lines. The industry gave $6.8 million to candidates and parties in the presidential election year of 2000, with half coming in soft money. Their annual largesse has allowed them to skirt their public duty, and then some: despite a thirty-year-old law designed to hold down campaign ad rates, broadcasters routinely gouge candidates. When the Senate included a provision in McCain-Feingold to close the loophole that allows for such price gouging, the industry went on the attack, showering both parties with hard and soft money. Their efforts paid off: the House stripped the provision from Shays-Meehan and the loophole remains.

Why is the broadcast industry unwilling to live up to its public service obligations? In the 2000 elections, broadcasters pulled down revenue from political commercials that approached $1 billion. Reducing that revenue would mean cutting into profit margins that average between 30 and 50 percent. So it makes perfect business sense for the industry to invest a relatively minute amount in contributions to candidates and parties, because the payoff is astronomical. Dan O'Connor, the general sales manager of WSYT-TV in Syracuse, New York, put it this way: Ad buyers for candidates "call you up and say, 'Can you clear $40,000 [in TV ad time] next week?' It's like, 'What? Am I dreaming? Of course I can clear that!' And they send you a check in the mail overnight. It's like Santa Claus came to town. It's a beautiful thing."

Paul Taylor, executive director of the Alliance for Better Campaigns, a nonpartisan group that advocates for free airtime, sums up the scam this way: "Let's follow the bouncing ball. Our government gives broadcasters free licenses to operate on the public airwaves on the condition that they serve the public interest. During the campaign season, broadcasters turn around and sell access to these airwaves to candidates at inflated prices. Meanwhile, many candidates sell access to the government in order to raise special-interest money to purchase access to the airwaves. It's a wonderful arrangement for the broadcasters, who reap windfall profits from political campaigns. It's a good system for incumbents, who prosper in the big-dollar, high-ante political culture of paid speech. But it's a lousy deal for the rest of us."

Walter Cronkite, the iconic American newsman, is chairman of the Alliance for Better Campaigns. According to Cronkite, "In the land of free speech, we've permitted a system of 'paid speech' to take hold during the political campaigns on the one medium we all own—our broadcast airwaves. It's long past time to turn that around. Free airtime would help free our democracy from the grip of the special interests." That's the way it is, and even Senator Mitch McConnell, the self-described Darth Vader of campaign finance reform, agrees that the broadcasters are not giving the public a fair shake. And for the rest of the world, this is a no-brainer. "America is almost alone among the Atlantic democracies in declining to provide political parties free prime time on television during elections," writes historian Arthur Schlesinger Jr. "[If it did so], it could do much both to bring inordinate campaign costs under control and revitalize the political parties."

It's time for electronic consumers to negotiate a better deal with those we give free licenses to. Cronkite's alliance is pushing an innovative and market-based proposal—first discussed in a 1982 monograph from the Democracy Project, Independent Expenditures in Congressional Campaigns: The Electronic Solution—that would provide free broadcast vouchers to candidates and parties. Here's how it would work: Qualifying candidates who win their parties' nominations would receive vouchers for use in their general election campaigns. Candidates, particularly those from urban areas who don't find it cost-effective to advertise on television or radio, could trade their vouchers to their party in exchange for funds to pay for direct mail or other forms of communication. Parties, in turn, could use the vouchers themselves or give them to other candidates. The system creates a market for broadcast vouchers that, because of pricing incentives, ensures their efficient distribution.

A comprehensive campaign finance reform program should provide candidates with a right of access to the public airwaves. Until then, the alliance's voucher proposal should be restricted to those candidates who accept spending limits. Whether vouchers were used for airtime or exchanged for party monies for direct mail, candidates would report them as expenditures. Under such a system, spending limits would retain their integrity. The value of the vouchers should be set at $250,000 for House candidates and vary by population for Senate candidates, with candidates in midsize states receiving up to $2.5 million in vouchers. As in public financing, candidates should be required to reach contribution thresholds to qualify for vouchers.

One might argue that vouchers would simply encourage the proliferation of slickly produced thirty-second advertisements. Yet the reality, for better or worse, is that political commercials are part of elections in America, and there's little chance that will change. The voucher proposal bows to that reality, but it also offers hope: candidates who accept the vouchers should be required to feature their own voices in at least 50 percent of all their ads—whether paid for by vouchers, private contributions, or public funds. There is a growing public distaste for anonymous negative advertising, and candidates, given free access to the airwaves, should be held accountable for their ads.

And there are other ways to promote civic discourse. Cronkite's alliance has put forth a complement to its voucher proposal, called "Voters' Time," that would require broadcasters to air a minimum of two hours a week of candidate discussion in the month preceding every election. At least half of the programs would have to be aired in prime time or drive time, and the formats—debates, interviews, town hall meetings—would be of the broadcasters' choosing. A voters' time requirement is necessary, because broadcasters are airing less and less campaign news and candidate discourse.

In the 2000 election campaign, despite the closest presidential election in a generation, ABC, CBS, and NBC devoted 28 percent less time to campaign coverage than in 1988. In a nationwide survey conducted two days prior to the 2000 elections, more than half the population could not answer basic questions about Bush's and Gore's positions on the issues. There are many factors contributing to that result, but two of them—the domination of election by big money interests, and the unwillingness of the broadcast industry to be a part of the solution—can be cured.

Mandating free airtime for candidates and candidate discussion would appropriately hold broadcasters to a minimal standard of what it means, under the Federal Communications Commission Act, to serve "the public interest, convenience, and necessity." But this will require a committed Congress standing up to an unusually powerful industry, one that gives big contributions and confers access to voters via the airwaves.

At a minimum, two other useful methods of encouraging civic discourse and facilitating candidate communication should be part of any reform bill. First, candidates who accept public funds should be required to debate. Kentucky, New Jersey, Los Angeles, and New York City all require debates of publicly funded candidates. Especially when the public has invested its money in public campaigns, it deserves to see the candidates in public face-to-face meetings. In March 2000, Al Gore proposed that he and George W. Bush eliminate campaign television advertisements and instead hold issue debates twice a week until the elections. Bush declined, but a CBS News poll showed that voters responded positively, with 65 percent calling it a "good idea."

Second, cities like New York and Seattle mail a voters' guide to registered voters before elections. The guides include candidate statements and biographical information, as well as information on voting. New York City's guide costs fifty cents a copy to publish and mail, a bargain by any standard. The federal government should do the same. Or it could create and promote a Web-based guide to serve as a clearing-house for candidate and election information. Before voting, citizens could log on to the site, read statements for federal candidates, and find out information about their polling stations. In the age of information technology, demology, democracy should not be left behind.

John Samples

→ **NO**

# Taxpayer Financing of Campaigns

Candidates and parties need money to fight election campaigns. In the United States, this money comes largely from individuals and groups, not the government, that is, the taxpayers. Some critics decry such private financing of politics. They argue that private donations advance special interests and corrupt politics and government. Some of them argue that government should ban private campaign contributions in favor of public financing. Since public funding comes from everyone, they reason, it actually comes from no one, thereby precluding the influence of private interests on public affairs. That argument has found few converts at the national level. States and cities have been more willing to experiment with taxpayer support for campaigns. . . .

Proponents claim government financing of campaigns serves the public interest in three ways: it advances the integrity of elections and lawmaking, promotes political equality, and fosters electoral competitiveness.

## Corruption

The Supreme Court held in *Buckley v. Valeo* that the government has a compelling interest in preventing corruption or the appearance of corruption in campaigns and policymaking, an interest that may outweigh the First Amendment rights implicated in contributing to a political campaign. Allegations of corruption thus increase the probability that a law regulating campaign finance will pass constitutional muster.

Advocates of government financing claim the current system of largely private financing of campaigns fosters corruption (or its appearance) in several ways. They say campaign contributions buy favors from elected officials, the quid-pro-quo corruption noted in *Buckley*. Others say contributors receive favorable action on policies that attract little public attention and debate. Advocates also say private money fosters more subtle forms of favoritism; for example, members of Congress may allocate their time and effort in committees to help contributors. If private money corrupts, the advocates conclude, the private financing system should be abolished in favor of government financing.

In their contribution to this volume, Jeffrey Milyo and David Primo summarize the academic studies of Congress and campaign contributions, almost all of which provide little evidence to support allegations of corruption. Having surveyed the field, even Andrew Geddis, a supporter of government financing, concludes, "One obstacle is that various studies have failed to produce the sort of evidence of a strong correlation between campaign donations and a representative's public actions needed to back up suspicions of general quid pro quo understandings." Should we not have strong evidence to uproot our current system of campaign finance, especially when money is tied to the exercise of free speech?

If corruption involves using public power for private ends, government financing itself provides an example of corruption; after all, the program takes money from everyone and gives it to particular interests. One might counter with Richard Briffault's argument that government financing cannot be corrupt because tax revenue "comes from everyone, and thus, from no one in particular." But that leaves out an important part of the story. Tax money used to finance campaigns may come from everyone, but it goes predominantly, and is designed to go predominantly, to particular interests and groups within the American polity. Government subsidies for ethanol are no less corrupt because everyone pays for them and neither are government subsidies to particular candidates.

## Equality

Some Americans contribute to political campaigns, but most do not. For advocates of government financing, these differences create intolerable inequalities that are "in sharp tension with the one person-one vote principle enshrined in our civic culture and our constitutional law. Public funding is necessary to bring our campaign finance system more in line with our central value of political equality." Similarly, Public Campaign, a leading organization advocating taxpayer financing, argues that private financing "violates the rights of all citizens to equal and meaningful participation in the democratic process." The principle of one person–one vote means "one man's vote in a congressional election is to be worth as much as another's" because assigning different weights to different votes in various House districts would violate Article 1, § 2 of the Constitution. The principle applies to state elections because of the equal protection clause of the 14th Amendment. Is one person–one vote thus "our central value of political equality"? A look at American institutions suggests otherwise.

The representation of states in the U.S. Senate assigns different weights to different votes in different states. Because the Electoral College also recognizes state representation, the election of the president also accords greater weight to votes in small states compared with those in large states. Moreover, the Supreme Court has not subjected judicial elections to the principle of one person–one vote.

One person–one vote applies only to voting. No American has a right to "equal and meaningful participation in the democratic process" if that means the whole of political life. In particular, the rights of association and speech set out in the First Amendment have been explicitly protected from government efforts to compel "equal . . . participation." In *Buckley*, the Supreme Court noted that federal election law sought to equalize the influence of individuals and groups over the outcome of elections. The justices demurred:

> But the concept that government may restrict the speech of some elements of our society in order to enhance the relative voice of others is wholly foreign to the First Amendment, which was designed "to secure 'the widest possible dissemination of information from diverse and antagonistic sources,'" and "to assure unfettered interchange of ideas for the bringing about of political and social changes desired by the people."

Far from being "our central value of political equality," equal participation remains "wholly foreign to the First Amendment."

Moreover, even if the government financed all campaigns, we would not have equal participation in elections. Proponents of government financing focus on one source of political inequality: money. They ignore all other sources of inequality such as a talent for speaking, the ability to write, good looks, media ownership and access, organizational ability, and so on. The proponents do not propose to restrain the many nonmonetary sources of influence perhaps because such talents are often found among the proponents of government financing of campaigns. The leveling impulse, they imply, should not restrict such political talents; only people with money should be excluded from political influence. Sometimes in public policy what is not regulated tells you more about a piece of legislation than what is covered. So it is with government financing of campaigns. . . .

Proponents of government financing argue that public subsidies will enable new candidates to run who would otherwise be excluded from the race. They argue the candidates who now obtain funding reflect the investment and consumption preferences of wealthy and conservative individuals. They believe contributions reproduce the inequalities of wealth in the economy and lead to a government that is unrepresentative of America. This argument depends crucially on the stereotypical image of "fat cat" contributors devoted to conservative causes. Large donors may be unrepresentative of the United States as a whole—they do have more money than the average American—but that does not mean they hold vastly different political views than most Americans. In fact, a recent study indicates large contributors often identify themselves as Democrats and as liberal on the issues. That should not be so surprising. In 1998, National Election Studies found that almost one-third of the richest Americans identified themselves as liberals.

Finally, we should be clear how extensive, intrusive, and dangerous a government financing system would be. Keep in mind that the goal of equalizing financial resources in an election requires extensive control and oversight of all electoral spending. The election authority must immediately know about all spending by privately financed candidates and every dollar laid out by any group participating in an election. Public Campaign's model legislation states that government-financed candidates must use a government-issued debit card that draws solely on funds in an account created by the government. Those who believe government usually acts benevolently will not worry about such extensive oversight and control of political activity. Those who expect abuses when government takes total control over anything—and especially over campaigns—will worry.

## Competition

Over the past 40 years, the percentage of the vote an incumbent member of Congress receives simply for being an incumbent has risen from 2 percent to 6 or 7 percent. Similar increases in the advantages of incumbency have been observed in executive and legislature elections in the states. Advocates of government subsidies say the need to raise large sums to challenge an incumbent explains why incumbents are hard to challenge. Government financing, they say, would overcome this barrier to entry by giving challengers tax money leading to a more competitive system.

Much depends on who designs the system of government financing. Spending levels strongly influence the competitiveness of challengers to incumbents. If a challenger can spend enough to make his name and causes known, a government financing scheme might foster more competition. If legislatures enact the system, of course, incumbents will design and pass the law. They will be tempted to set spending limits low to favor their own reelections. For example, in 1997, Congress debated a government financing proposal that included spending caps: every challenger spending less than the proposed limits in Senate campaigns in 1994 and 1996 had lost; every incumbent spending less than the limits had won. Similarly, in the House, 3 percent of the challengers spending less than the proposed limits won in 1996, while 40 percent of the incumbents under the limits won.

Such legislative design issues may explain why government financing of campaigns has not *in fact* increased the competitiveness of elections. The leading study of government financing in the states concluded, "There is no evidence to support the claim that programs combining public funding with spending limits have leveled the playing field, countered the effects of incumbency, and made elections more competitive." Believing that government financing will increase competitiveness seems to be a triumph of hope over experience. . . .

Experience indicates that government financing tends to favor certain types of candidates. The political scientists Michael Malbin and Thomas Gais found sharp partisan differences in candidate participation. They studied gubernatorial elections in 11 states from 1993 to 1996 and found that 82 percent of Democratic candidates took taxpayer funding, while only 55 percent of Republican candidates participated. Their data on legislative elections in Minnesota and Wisconsin show a similar partisan divide. Malbin and Gais attribute these partisan variations to the libertarianism of Republicans: candidates who philosophically oppose government subsidies often do not accept them. In other words, government financing in practice provides an advantage to nonlibertarian candidates.

Full government financing of campaigns in Arizona and Maine tells a similar story. In the 2000 election in Arizona, 41 percent of Democratic candidates and 50 percent of Green Party candidates received public subsidies for their campaigns; 8 percent of Republicans accepted government money in the general election, while no candidates of the Libertarian Party took the subsidy.

In Maine's 2000 election, 43.4 percent of Democratic Party candidates chose government financing compared with 24 percent of Republicans.

Government financing of campaigns looks a lot like other political activity by individuals and groups that do not do well in private markets. Declining parts of the economy—say, small farmers and large steel mill owners—want government help to overcome their own mistakes or unfavorable economic changes. Similarly, candidates who have little appeal to voters and campaign contributors seek public subsidies (like farmers) and regulatory protections from competition (like steel mill owners).

Government subsidies for candidates, however, are crucially different from funding for ethanol. Government financing of campaigns takes money from taxpayers and gives it to a subset of all political candidates. For that reason, government financing seems either unnecessary or immoral. It is unnecessary if a taxpayer agrees with the candidate supported by the subsidy; the taxpayer may simply give the money directly to the candidate.

If, however, the taxpayer disagrees with the candidate, taxing him to support that candidate is immoral. An example will make clear the immorality of the policy. Imagine I had the power to force Nick Nyhart, the Executive Director of Public Campaign, to contribute to the Cato Institute, thereby supporting the writing and marketing of the very arguments against government financing you are reading right now. Such compulsion would strike most Americans as wrong. We think individuals should not be forced to support ideas that contravene their deepest commitments, whether those commitments are religious, social, or political. Government financing schemes, however, transfer money from taxpayers to political candidates and their campaigns. Inevitably they force liberals to support conservatives, Democrats to support Republicans, and vice versa.

Advocates of government financing of campaigns employ emotionally charged rhetoric at every turn. They implore us to "reform" the system to root out "corruption" and attain "clean elections." The reality of government financing belies this expansive rhetoric. Such proposals, especially the "clean elections" variant, simply transfer wealth from taxpayers to a preferred set of candidates and causes. That preferred set inevitably excludes candidates who believe forced transfers of wealth are immoral (such as Libertarians and Republican candidates with a libertarian outlook). Not surprisingly, government financing in the states has favored candidates of the left (such as Democrats and third parties like the Greens). For that reason, government financing of campaigns serves private goals through public means. Far from being a reform, government financing offers more "politics as usual," understood as the struggle to obtain special favors from government.

Those who wish to support the candidates and causes favored by government financing may do so now; they need only send their check to the candidate or cause they favor. Government financing forces all taxpayers to financially support candidates they would not otherwise support, candidates whose views they may find repugnant. On the question of government financing of campaigns, Thomas Jefferson should have the last word: "To compel a man to furnish contributions of money for the propagation of opinions which he disbelieves, is sinful and tyrannical."

# EXPLORING THE ISSUE

## Should America Adopt Public Financing of Political Campaigns?

## Critical Thinking and Reflection

1. How has Congress sought to limit campaign spending?
2. Do state primaries influence the spending and strategy of candidates?
3. What are the democratic arguments in support of spending limits?
4. What are the constitutional arguments in opposition to spending limits?
5. Are American political campaigns too long or not long enough?
6. What impact has campaign spending had on the outcome of elections?
7. Does it make sense to distinguish between issue advocacy and clear support for candidates?
8. Do primary candidate debates have any impact on candidate spending?
9. How would public financing alter political campaigns?

## Is There Common Ground?

Between those who would keep government out of political campaigns and those who would have elections wholly publicly financed, there is a wide gap. In recent presidential elections, the federal government has offered candidates a choice between limited public financing and virtually unlimited private financing. Some states have offered a similar choice. Access to free televised debates has supplemented private financing of televised commercials. Congress has sought to impose limits, but these have been challenged, often successfully, in the federal courts. The example of substantial public subsidization of election campaigns in European democracies has not received much support in American political parties.

Because so large a proportion of campaign expenses is borne by private groups not attached to the political parties, the possibility of a common ground seems remote. In fact, despite efforts at placing limits, the amount of money spent in conducting campaigns has risen sharply in every recent national election.

## Additional Resources

Most studies of political campaigns do not attempt to achieve objectivity, and tend to support extreme positions, as the titles of two books suggest. Darrell M. West strongly supports public finance in *Checkbook Democracy: How Money*

*Corrupts Political Campaigns* (Northeastern University Press, 2000). In total opposition to this policy, Bradley Smith offers a vigorous critique in *Unfree Speech: The Folly of Campaign Finance Reform* (Princeton University Press, 2001), contending that all restrictions on campaign contributions should be eliminated. In *Sold to the Highest Bidder: The President from Dwight D. Eisenhower to George W. Bush* (Prometheus Books, 2002), Daniel M. Friedenberg contends that "money controls the actions of both the executive and legislative branches of our government on the federal and state levels."

The most comprehensive overall examination of the role of money in elections is in *The New Campaign Finance Sourcebook*, by Anthony Corrado, Thomas E. Mann, Daniel R. Ortiz, and Trevor Potter (Brookings Institution, 2005). The authors conclude that campaign finance will always be a work in progress, dealing with but never resolving the inherent problems associated with money in politics.

# Internet References . . .

In addition to the Internet sites listed below, type in key words, such as "American federalism," "commerce power," "presidential appointments," and "government regulation," to find other listings.

## U.S. House of Representatives

This page of the U.S. House of Representatives will lead you to information about current and past House members and agendas, the legislative process, and so on. You can learn about events on the House floor as they happen.

**www.house.gov**

## The United States Senate

This page of the U.S. Senate will lead you to information about current and past Senate members and agendas, legislative activities, committees, and so on.

**www.senate.gov**

## The White House

Visit the White House page for direct access to information about commonly requested federal services, the White House Briefing Room, and the presidents and vice presidents. The Virtual Library allows you to search White House documents, listen to speeches, and view photos.

**www.whitehouse.gov/index.html**

## Supreme Court Collection

Open this Legal Information Institute (LII) site for current and historical information about the Supreme Court. The LII archive contains many opinions issued since May 1990 as well as a collection of nearly 600 of the most historic decisions of the Court.

**http://supct.law.cornell.edu/supct/index.html**

## National Security Agency

Find out more about the agency that has been at the center of controversy over the President's power to intercept telecommunications in and out of the country. Its home page explains its many functions, relates its storied past in breaking the Japanese code during World War II, and boasts its continued role "in keeping the United States a step ahead of its enemies." It contains links to fourteen other federal agencies, including the C.I.A., the Defense Intelligence Agency, and the National Reconnaissance Office.

**www.nsa.gov/about/index.cfm**

# The Institutions of Government

*T*he Constitution divides authority between the national government and the states, delegating certain powers to the national government and providing that those not thus delegated "are reserved to the states respectively, or to the people." The national government's powers are further divided between three branches, Congress, the president, and the federal judiciary, each of which can exercise checks on the others. How vigorously and faithfully are these branches performing their respective functions? Do they remain true to the authentic meaning of the Constitution? What legitimate defenses does each branch possess against encroachment by the others? These issues have been debated since the earliest years of the Republic, and the debate continues today.

- Does the President Have Unilateral War Powers?
- Should the Courts Seek the "Original Meaning" of the Constitution?
- Is Congress a Dysfunctional Institution?
- May Congress Require People to Buy Health Insurance?
- Should the President Be Allowed "Executive Privilege"?

# ISSUE 5

## Does the President Have Unilateral War Powers?

**YES: John C. Yoo,** from *Memorandum Opinion for the Deputy Counsel to the President* (September 25, 2001)

**NO: Michael Cairo,** from "The 'Imperial Presidency' Triumphant," in Christopher S. Kelley, ed., *Executing the Constitution* (SUNY, 2006)

### ISSUE SUMMARY

**YES:** John C. Yoo, a law professor at the University of California, Berkeley, argues that the language of the Constitution, long-accepted precedents, and the practical need for speedy action in emergencies all support broad executive power during war.

**NO:** Michael Cairo, lecturer in International Relations at Southern Illinois University, deplores the unilateral military actions undertaken by Presidents Clinton and Bush; he argues that the Founders never intended to grant exclusive war powers to the president.

**D**ramatic and bitter as they are, the current struggles between the White House and Congress over the president's unilateral authority to conduct military operations and foreign affairs are not without precedent. Episodically, they have been occurring since the administration of George Washington.

The language of the Constitution relating to war powers almost seems to invite struggles between the two branches. Congress is given the power to declare war and "to raise and support armies." The president is authorized to serve as commander-in-chief of the armed forces "when called into actual service of the United States." While the power to "declare" or authorize war rests squarely with the U.S. Congress, the Founders gave some leeway to the president when it came to war *making*. At the Constitutional Convention, some delegates wanted to give Congress the exclusive power to make war, not simply to declare it. That would have ruled out any presidential war making. But James Madison successfully argued the need for "leaving to the Executive the power to repel sudden attacks."

Down through the years, several presidents have interpreted very broadly—these emergency war-making powers. In 1801, President Jefferson ordered his navy to seize the ships of Barbary pirates in the Mediterranean, and 45 years later President Polk sent American troops into territory claimed by Mexico, thus provoking the Mexican-American War. A young congressman named Abraham Lincoln vigorously protested Polk's unilateral assertion of power, but when he came to office and faced the secession of the South, he went much further than Polk in the assertion of power, jailing people without trial, enlarging the size of the army and navy, withdrawing money from the Treasury, and blockading Southern ports without authorization from Congress. In more recent times, President Truman committed America to fight in Korea without a congressional declaration, and President Kennedy ordered a naval blockade of Cuba in 1962 without even consulting Congress.

The mid-1960s marked the high-water period of unchallenged presidential war making. Between 1961 and 1963, Kennedy sent 16,000 armed "advisers" to Vietnam, and between 1964 and 1968, President Johnson escalated American involvement to 500,000 troops—all without a formal declaration of war. But that period of congressional indulgence was soon to end. By the early 1970s, Congress was starting on a course that would culminate in the cutoff of funds for Vietnam and legislative efforts to head off any more undeclared wars. In 1973, over President Nixon's veto, Congress passed the War Powers Resolution, which required the president to notify Congress within 48 hours after putting troops in harm's way, withdraw them within 60 to 90 days absent a congressional authorization, and submit periodic progress reports to Congress during that period. In practice, the War Powers Resolution has been largely ignored—by Ronald Reagan when he sent troops into Grenada, by George H. W. Bush when he sent them to Panama, and by Bill Clinton when he sent them into Somalia, Haiti, and Bosnia.

Perhaps ironically, the War Powers Resolution may even have been useful to President George W. Bush in obtaining congressional authorization for the invasion of Iraq. In October 2002, Congress passed a joint resolution giving the president the authority to use the armed forces "as he determines to be necessary and appropriate" to defend national security and enforce all U.N. resolutions against Iraq. The resolution added that this constituted "specific statutory authorization" for war within the meaning of the War Powers Resolution. Such broadly worded language has come back to haunt many members of Congress who voted for it but now wish they hadn't. The new Democratic Congress elected in 2006 is considering various options for challenging President Bush's war-making ability as it relates to Iraq, including the repeal or modification of the 2002 authorization for going to war.

In the selections that follow, John C. Yoo, a law professor at the University of California, Berkeley, argues that the language of the Constitution, long-accepted precedents, and the practical need for speedy action in emergencies all support broad executive power during war. Opposing that view is Michael Cairo, a lecturer in International Relations at Southern Illinois University, who criticizes the unilateral military actions undertaken by Presidents Clinton and Bush, arguing that the Founders never intended to grant exclusive war powers to the president.

# YES ⤶

## The President's Constitutional Authority to Conduct Military Operations Against Terrorists and Nations Supporting Them: Memorandum Opinion for the Deputy Counsel to the President

Our review establishes that all three branches of the Federal Government—Congress, the Executive, and the Judiciary—agree that the President has broad authority to use military force abroad, including the ability to deter future attacks.

## I.

The President's constitutional power to defend the United States and the lives of its people must be understood in light of the Founders' express intention to create a federal government "cloathed with all the powers requisite to [the] complete execution of its trust." *The Federalist* No. 23 (Alexander Hamilton). Foremost among the objectives committed to that trust by the Constitution is the security of the Nation. As Hamilton explained in arguing for the Constitution's adoption, because "the circumstances which may affect the public safety are [not] reducible within certain determinate limits, . . . it must be admitted, as a necessary consequence that there can be no limitation of that authority which is to provide for the defense and protection of the community in any matter essential to its efficiency."

"It is 'obvious and unarguable' that no governmental interest is more compelling than the security of the Nation." (1981). Within the limits that the Constitution itself imposes, the scope and distribution of the powers to protect national security must be construed to authorize the most efficacious defense of the Nation and its interests in accordance "with the realistic purposes of the entire instrument." (1948) Nor is the authority to protect national security limited to actions necessary for "victories in the field." (1946) The authority over national security "carries with it the inherent power to guard against the immediate renewal of the conflict."

From DOJ Office of Legal Counsel (2001.09.25), available at: www.usdoj.gov/olc/warpowers925 .htm

We now turn to the more precise question of the President's inherent constitutional powers to use military force.

## Constitutional Text

The text, structure and history of the Constitution establish that the Founders entrusted the President with the primary responsibility, and therefore the power, to use military force in situations of emergency. Article II, Section 2 states that the "President shall be Commander in Chief of the Army and Navy of the United States, and of the Militia of the several States, when called into the actual Service of the United States." He is further vested with all of "the executive Power" and the duty to execute the laws. These powers give the President broad constitutional authority to use military force in response to threats to the national security and foreign policy of the United States. During the period leading up to the Constitution's ratification, the power to initiate hostilities and to control the escalation of conflict had been long understood to rest in the hands of the executive branch.

By their terms, these provisions vest full control of the military forces of the United States in the President. The power of the President is at its zenith under the Constitution when the President is directing military operations of the armed forces, because the power of Commander in Chief is assigned solely to the President. It has long been the view of this Office that the Commander-in-Chief Clause is a substantive grant of authority to the President and that the scope of the President's authority to commit the armed forces to combat is very broad. The President's complete discretion in exercising the Commander-in-Chief power has also been recognized by the courts. In the *Prize Cases*, (1862), for example, the Court explained that, whether the President "in fulfilling his duties as Commander in Chief" had met with a situation justifying treating the southern States as belligerents and instituting a blockade, was a question "to be *decided by him*" and which the Court could not question, but must leave to "the political department of the Government to which this power was entrusted."

Some commentators have read the constitutional text differently. They argue that the vesting of the power to declare war gives Congress the sole authority to decide whether to make war. This view misreads the constitutional text and misunderstands the nature of a declaration of war. Declaring war is not tantamount to making war—indeed, the Constitutional Convention specifically amended the working draft of the Constitution that had given Congress the power to make war. An earlier draft of the Constitution had given to Congress the power to "make" war. When it took up this clause on August 17, 1787, the Convention voted to change the clause from "make" to "declare." A supporter of the change argued that it would "leav[e] to the Executive the power to repel sudden attacks." Further, other elements of the Constitution describe "engaging" in war, which demonstrates that the Framers understood making and engaging in war to be broader than simply "declaring" war. . . . If the Framers had wanted to require congressional consent before the initiation of military hostilities, they knew how to write such provisions.

Finally, the Framing generation well understood that declarations of war were obsolete. Not all forms of hostilities rose to the level of a declared war: during the seventeenth and eighteenth centuries, Great Britain and colonial America waged numerous conflicts against other states without an official declaration of war. . . . Instead of serving as an authorization to begin hostilities, a declaration of war was only necessary to "perfect" a conflict under international law. A declaration served to fully transform the international legal relationship between two states from one of peace to one of war. Given this context, it is clear that Congress's power to declare war does not constrain the President's independent and plenary constitutional authority over the use of military force.

## Constitutional Structure

Our reading of the text is reinforced by analysis of the constitutional structure. First, it is clear that the Constitution secures all federal executive power in the President to ensure a unity in purpose and energy in action. "Decision, activity, secrecy, and dispatch will generally characterize the proceedings of one man in a much more eminent degree than the proceedings of any greater number." *The Federalist* No. 70 (Alexander Hamilton). The centralization of authority in the President alone is particularly crucial in matters of national defense, war, and foreign policy, where a unitary executive can evaluate threats, consider policy choices, and mobilize national resources with a speed and energy that is far superior to any other branch. As Hamilton noted, "Energy in the executive is a leading character in the definition of good government. It is essential to the protection of the community against foreign attacks." This is no less true in war. "Of all the cares or concerns of government, the direction of war most peculiarly demands those qualities which distinguish the exercise of power by a single hand." *The Federalist* No. 74.

Second, the Constitution makes clear that the process used for conducting military hostilities is different from other government decisionmaking. In the area of domestic legislation, the Constitution creates a detailed, finely wrought procedure in which Congress plays the central role. In foreign affairs, however, the Constitution does not establish a mandatory, detailed, Congress-driven procedure for taking action. Rather, the Constitution vests the two branches with different powers—the President as Commander in Chief, Congress with control over funding and declaring war—without requiring that they follow a specific process in making war. By establishing this framework, the Framers expected that the process for warmaking would be far more flexible, and capable of quicker, more decisive action, than the legislative process. Thus, the President may use his Commander-in-Chief and executive powers to use military force to protect the Nation, subject to congressional appropriations and control over domestic legislation.

Third, the constitutional structure requires that any ambiguities in the allocation of a power that is executive in nature—such as the power to conduct military hostilities—must be resolved in favor of the executive branch. Article II, section 1 provides that "[t]he executive Power shall be vested in a President of the United States." By contrast, Article I's Vesting Clause gives Congress only the powers "herein granted." This difference in language indicates that Congress's legislative powers are limited to the list enumerated in Article I, section 8, while the President's powers include inherent executive powers that are unenumerated in the Constitution. To be sure, Article II lists specifically enumerated powers in addition to the Vesting Clause, and some have argued that this limits the "executive Power" granted in the Vesting Clause to the powers on that list. But the purpose of the enumeration of executive powers in Article II was not to define and cabin the grant in the Vesting Clause. Rather, the Framers unbundled some plenary powers that had traditionally been regarded as "executive," assigning elements of those powers to Congress in Article I, while expressly reserving other elements as enumerated executive powers in Article II. So, for example, the King's traditional power to declare war was given to Congress under Article I, while the Commander-in-Chief authority was expressly reserved to the President in Article II. Further, the Framers altered other plenary powers of the King, such as treaties and appointments, assigning the Senate a share in them in Article II itself. Thus, the enumeration in Article II marks the points at which several traditional executive powers were diluted or reallocated. Any *other*, unenumerated executive powers, however, were conveyed to the President by the Vesting Clause.

There can be little doubt that the decision to deploy military force is "executive" in nature, and was traditionally so regarded. It calls for action and energy in execution, rather than the deliberate formulation of rules to govern the conduct of private individuals. Moreover, the Framers understood it to be an attribute of the executive. "The direction of war implies the direction of the common strength," wrote Alexander Hamilton, "and the power of directing and employing the common strength forms a usual and essential part in the definition of the executive authority." *The Federalist* No. 74 (Alexander Hamilton). As a result, to the extent that the constitutional text does not explicitly allocate the power to initiate military hostilities to a particular branch, the Vesting Clause provides that it remain among the President's unenumerated powers.

Fourth, depriving the President of the power to decide when to use military force would disrupt the basic constitutional framework of foreign relations. From the very beginnings of the Republic, the vesting of the executive, Commander-in-Chief, and treaty powers in the executive branch has been understood to grant the President plenary control over the conduct of foreign relations. As Secretary of State Thomas Jefferson observed during the first Washington Administration: "the constitution has divided the powers of government into three branches [and] has declared that the executive powers shall be vested in the president, submitting only special articles of it to a negative by the senate." Due to this structure, Jefferson continued, "the transaction of business with foreign nations is executive altogether; it belongs, then, to the head of that department, except as to such portions of it as are specially submitted to the senate. Exceptions are to be construed strictly." In defending President Washington's authority to issue the Neutrality Proclamation, Alexander Hamilton came to the same interpretation of the President's foreign affairs powers. According to Hamilton, Article II "ought . . . to be considered as intended . . . to specify and regulate the principal articles implied in the definition of Executive Power; leaving the rest to flow from the general grant of that power." As future Chief Justice John Marshall famously declared a few years later, "The President is the sole organ of the nation in its external relations, and its sole representative with foreign nations. . . . The [executive] department . . . is entrusted with the whole foreign intercourse of the nation. . . ." Given the agreement of Jefferson, Hamilton, and Marshall, it has not been difficult for the executive branch consistently to assert the President's plenary authority in foreign affairs ever since. . . .

# II.

## Executive Branch Construction and Practice

The position we take here has long represented the view of the executive branch and of the Department of Justice. Attorney General (later Justice) Robert Jackson formulated the classic statement of the executive branch's understanding of the President's military powers in 1941:

> "Article II, section 2, of the Constitution provides that the President "shall be Commander in Chief of the Army and Navy of the United States." By virtue of this constitutional office he has supreme command over the land and naval forces of the country and may order them to perform such military duties as, in his opinion, are necessary or appropriate for the defense of the United States. These powers exist in time of peace as well as in time of war. . . .

> "Thus the President's responsibility as Commander in Chief embraces the authority to command and direct the armed forces in their immediate movements and operations designed to protect the security and effectuate the defense of the United States. . . . [T]his authority undoubtedly includes the power to dispose of troops and equipment in such manner and on such duties as best to promote the safety of the country." . . .

Attorney General (later Justice) Frank Murphy, though declining to define precisely the scope of the President's independent authority to act in emergencies or states of war, stated that: "the Executive has powers not enumerated in the statutes—powers derived not from statutory grants but from the Constitution. It is universally recognized that the constitutional duties of the Executive carry with them the constitutional powers necessary for their proper performance. These constitutional powers have never been specifically defined, and in fact cannot be, since their extent and limitations are largely dependent upon conditions and circumstances. . . . The right to take specific action might not exist under one state of facts, while under another it might be the absolute duty of the Executive to take such action." . . .

## Judicial Construction

Judicial decisions since the beginning of the Republic confirm the President's constitutional power and duty to repel military action against the United States through the use of force, and to take measures to deter the recurrence of an attack. As Justice Joseph Story said long ago, "[i]t may be fit and proper for the government, in the exercise of the high discretion confided to the executive, for great public purposes, to act on a sudden emergency, or to prevent an irreparable mischief, by summary measures, which are not found in the text of the laws." (1824). The Constitution entrusts the "power [to] the executive branch of the government to preserve order and insure the public safety in times of emergency, when other branches of the government are unable to function, or their functioning would itself threaten the public safety." (1946, Stone, C.J., concurring).

If the President is confronted with an unforeseen attack on the territory and people of the United States, or other immediate, dangerous threat to American interests and security, the courts have affirmed that it is his constitutional responsibility to respond to that threat with whatever means are necessary, including the use of military force abroad. . . .

## III.

The historical practice of all three branches confirms the lessons of the constitutional text and structure. The normative role of historical practice in constitutional law, and especially with regard to separation of powers, is well settled. . . . Indeed, as the Court has observed, the role of practice in fixing the meaning of the separation of powers is implicit in the Constitution itself: "'the Constitution . . . contemplates that practice will integrate the dispersed powers into a workable government.'" (1989). In addition, governmental practice enjoys significant weight in constitutional analysis for practical reasons, on "the basis of a wise and quieting rule that, in determining . . . the existence of a power, weight shall be given to the usage itself—even when the validity of the practice is the subject of investigation." (1915). . . .

The historical record demonstrates that the power to initiate military hostilities, particularly in response to the threat of an armed attack, rests exclusively with the President. As the Supreme Court has observed, "[t]he United States frequently employs Armed Forces outside this country—over 200 times in our history—for the protection of American citizens or national security." (1990). On at least 125 such occasions, the President acted without prior express authorization from Congress. Such deployments, based on the President's constitutional authority alone, have occurred since the Administration of George Washington. . . . Perhaps the most significant deployment without specific statutory authorization took place at the time of the Korean War, when President Truman, without prior authorization from Congress, deployed United States troops in a war that lasted for over three years and caused over 142,000 American casualties.

Recent deployments ordered solely on the basis of the President's constitutional authority have also been extremely large, representing a substantial commitment of the Nation's military personnel, diplomatic prestige, and financial resources. On at least one occasion, such a unilateral deployment has constituted full-scale war. On March 24, 1999, without any prior statutory authorization and in the absence of an attack on the United States, President

Clinton ordered hostilities to be initiated against the Republic of Yugoslavia. The President informed Congress that, in the initial wave of air strikes, "United States and NATO forces have targeted the [Yugoslavian] government's integrated air defense system, military and security police command and control elements, and military and security police facilities and infrastructure. . . . I have taken these actions pursuant to my constitutional authority to conduct U.S. foreign relations and as Commander in Chief and Chief Executive." Bombing attacks against targets in both Kosovo and Serbia ended on June 10, 1999, seventy-nine days after the war began. More than 30,000 United States military personnel participated in the operations; some 800 U.S. aircraft flew more than 20,000 sorties; more than 23,000 bombs and missiles were used. As part of the peace settlement, NATO deployed some 50,000 troops into Kosovo, 7,000 of them American. . . .

## Conclusion

In light of the text, plan, and history of the Constitution, its interpretation by both past Administrations and the courts, the longstanding practice of the executive branch, and the express affirmation of the President's constitutional authorities by Congress, we think it beyond question that the President has the plenary constitutional power to take such military actions as he deems necessary and appropriate to respond to the terrorist attacks upon the United States on September 11, 2001. Force can be used both to retaliate for those attacks, and to prevent and deter future assaults on the Nation. Military actions need not be limited to those individuals, groups, or states that participated in the attacks on the World Trade Center and the Pentagon: the Constitution vests the President with the power to strike terrorist groups or organizations that cannot be demonstrably linked to the September 11 incidents, but that, nonetheless, pose a similar threat to the security of the United States and the lives of its people, whether at home or overseas. In both the War Powers Resolution and the Joint Resolution, Congress has recognized the President's authority to use force in circumstances such as those created by the September 11 incidents. Neither statute, however, can place any limits on the President's determinations as to any terrorist threat, the amount of military force to be used in response, or the method, timing, and nature of the response. These decisions, under our Constitution, are for the President alone to make.

Michael Cairo

**➔ NO**

# The "Imperial Presidency" Triumphant: War Powers in the Clinton and Bush Administrations

## War Powers and the Constitution

To the casual observer, the president, as commander in chief, appears entitled to unilateral military powers when deploying and using U.S. troops and forces abroad. One of the many arguments in favor of presidential war powers is the Minority Report of the Congressional Committees Investigating the Iran-Contra Affair. According to the report, no fewer than 118 occasions of force occurred without prior legislative authorization. "The relevance of these repeated examples of the extensive use of armed force," it argues, "is that they indicate how far the President's inherent powers were assumed to have reached when Congress was silent, and even in some cases, where Congress had prohibited an action." Former Senator John Tower also argued that Congress should not encumber presidents in the foreign policy process. Robert Bork concurs, arguing that morality should be a president's guide and Congress should abstain from decisions on the use of force. Supreme Court Justice George Sutherland presented the strongest argument on behalf of presidential war powers, however, in 1936. In his written opinion in *U.S. v. Curtiss-Wright Export Corp. et al.*, Sutherland wrote that the president is the "sole organ of the federal government in the field of international relations" and has "plenary and exclusive" power as president. Congress, he suggested, was meant to play a secondary role in U.S. foreign policy.

Presidential practice has also relegated Congress to a backseat in decisions on the use of force. Since World War II, Congress has never specifically declared war. In the Korean War, the Truman administration argued, "the President's power to send Armed Forces outside the country is not dependent on Congressional authority." Secretary of Defense Richard Cheney echoed this sentiment prior to the Persian Gulf War. Cheney explained that he did "not believe the president requires any additional authority from Congress" to engage U.S. forces abroad. During his 1992 presidential election campaign, President George H. W. Bush stated that he did not need "some old goat" in Congress to evict Saddam Hussein from Kuwait.

Contrary to these arguments and presidential practice in general, the Founders did not intend to grant presidents exclusive authority in war powers. The belief that Congress should not get in the president's way when national security matters arise is clearly popular, but the Constitution contradicts this. According to the Constitution, Congress and the president are given specific foreign policy powers and each plays a role to ensure that U.S. foreign policy is effective. In fact, the Constitution grants broad power to Congress, not the president. Although the president is given the powers to nominate ambassadors, negotiate treaties, and direct the armed forces as commander in chief, the Congress is granted the powers to regulate commerce, raise and support armies, provide and maintain a navy, and declare war. Thus, the Constitution originally empowered Congress in military matters.

In drafting the Constitution, the Founders were concerned about correcting the deficiencies of the Articles of Confederation. The Articles bestowed all legislative and executive authority in the Congress. Article 6 gave Congress control over conduct of foreign affairs, and Article 9 gave Congress "the sole and exclusive right and power of determining on peace and war." Unlike the Articles, the Constitution was founded on the principle of separation of powers—a division of authority between government branches. In foreign policy, that division was ambiguous. Experience under the Articles led the Founders to favor great centralization of executive authority in the Constitution. Alexander Hamilton, writing in *Federalist 70*, explains, "energy in the Executive is a leading character in the definition of good government." When constructing the Constitution, however, the Founders favored less centralization based on their experiences with the monarchy. . . .

The Constitution thus established a shared system. This constitutional division of foreign affairs powers only served to cause confusion. Almost immediately after the founding of the new republic, the question of war powers emerged as a prominent issue of debate. In 1793 President George Washington unilaterally proclaimed U.S. neutrality in the war between France and Great Britain despite the existence of an alliance with France. Alexander Hamilton defended the action, arguing that foreign policy was an executive function and the powers of declaring war and ratifying treaties bestowed on Congress were "exceptions out of the general 'executive power' vested in the President." These powers were to be "construed strictly, and ought to be extended no further than is essential to their execution." Although Congress had the right to declare war, the president had the duty to preserve peace until the Congress did so. "The legislature," he argued, "is still free to perform its duties, according to its own sense of them; though the executive, in the exercise of constitutional powers, may establish an antecedent state of things, which ought to weigh in the legislative decision." In short, each branch had a duty to exercise its power, possessing concurrent authority.

James Madison responded to Hamilton's defense of Washington's proclamation of neutrality, denying that the powers of making wars and treaties were inherently executive. The fact that they were royal prerogative, Madison argued, did not make them presidential prerogatives. The power to declare war must include everything necessary to make that power effective, including the congressional right to judge whether the United States was obliged to declare war. According to Madison, this judgment could not be foreordained by presidential decisions. Thus, whereas Hamilton saw congressional power to declare war as limited, Madison viewed it as very powerful. . . .

## The Clinton Administration and Saddam Hussein

On August 2, 1990, Saddam Hussein, the leader of Iraq, invaded and annexed Kuwait, seizing Kuwait's vast oil reserves and liquidating billions of dollars of loans provided by Kuwait during the Iran-Iraq War. Within months, the George H. W. Bush administration assembled a coalition of forces, supported by the United Nations, to remove the Iraqi army from Kuwait. On January 17, 1991, Operation Desert Storm, which was authorized by UN Resolution 678 and by a congressional vote endorsing the action, ensued.

The international coalition proved victorious and instituted UN Resolution 687, giving the UN Special Commission (UNSCOM) complete access to Iraqi facilities to search for weapons of mass destruction. In addition, the UN Security Council also passed UN Resolution 688, condemning Iraqi actions against the Kurdish population and authorizing relief organizations to provide humanitarian aid. Pursuant to these resolutions, but without specific UN Security Council authorization, a no-fly zone was established, prohibiting Iraqi flights in northern and southern Iraq.

President-elect Clinton inherited this policy toward Iraq and a hostile Hussein. Almost immediately, Clinton faced mounting tensions between the United States and Iraq. In April 1993 former President Bush visited Kuwait. Prior to his visit, the Central Intelligence Agency (CIA) and Federal Bureau of Investigation (FBI) uncovered an assassination plot against Bush and linked the Iraqi government to that plot. As a response to this plot, Clinton responded with an attack, using precision-guided missiles. Clinton justified the bombings in a statement to Congress, noting "our inherent right to self-defense as recognized in Article 51 of the United Nations Charter and pursuant to [his] constitutional authority with respect to the conduct of foreign relations and as Commander in Chief." In an address to the American public about the strikes, Clinton added, "There should be no mistake about the message we intend these actions to convey to Saddam Hussein. . . . We will combat terrorism. We will deter aggression. . . . While the cold war has ended, the world is not free of danger. And I am determined to take the steps necessary to keep our Nation secure."

In 1996 Clinton used force against Hussein in support of Iraq's Kurdish population. One Kurdish faction, the Patriotic Union of Kurdistan (PUK), accepted arms from Iran and Hussein responded by attacking the PUK's headquarters in northern Iraq, attempting to crush the opposition. In response, Clinton ordered a missile attack on targets in southern Iraq. In justifying this attack, Clinton relied on humanitarian arguments stressing UN Resolution 688 explaining, "Earlier today I ordered American forces to strike Iraq. Our missiles sent the following message to Saddam Hussein: When you abuse your own people . . . you must pay a price." During his weekly radio address, Clinton added, "America's policy has been to contain Saddam, to reduce the threat he poses to the region, and to do it in a way that makes him pay a price when he acts recklessly."

The next major crisis with Iraq occurred in 1998 when Saddam Hussein refused UNSCOM weapons inspectors access to certain sites, as the provisions of UN Resolution 687 outlined. Hussein argued that U.S. involvement in the inspections was the problem. The Clinton administration suggested that diplomacy was their main instrument in solving the crisis, but reserved the right to use force. Implicit in the administration's argument for the use of force was that the administration had the authority to do so. In an address at Tennessee State University, Secretary of State Madeleine Albright stated, "We will work for that peaceful solution as long as we can. But if we cannot get such a solution—and we do believe that the time for diplomacy is running out—then we will use force." Days before, in a statement before the House International Relations Committee, Albright remarked, "Let no one miscalculate. We have authority to do this, the responsibility to do this, the means and the will."

By the end of February, however, UN Secretary-General Kofi Annan had negotiated a diplomatic solution to the crisis. The Clinton administration responded by sponsoring a successful resolution in the UN Security Council. Resolution 1154 explained that Iraq would face the "severest consequences" if it failed to comply with UNSCOM. President Clinton made clear that the UN Security Council's decision authorized the use of force against Iraq, despite opposition from other members of the UN Security Council. In remarks the day after the UN Security Council vote on Resolution 1154, Clinton stated, "The Government of Iraq should be under no illusion. The meaning of 'severest consequences' is clear. It provides authority to act if Iraq does not turn the commitment it has now made into compliance."

In December 1998 Clinton attacked Iraq after a series of diplomatic conflicts over UNSCOM. In an address to the American public, Clinton explained that Iraq had been given numerous opportunities to comply and must face the "consequences of defying the U.N." In a letter to Congress, Clinton justified the attacks citing UN Security Council Resolutions 678 and 687, authorizing "all necessary means" to ensure Iraqi compliance. He also referred to the power granted to the president under Public Law 102–1, which authorized President Bush to use force against Iraq in 1991.

Clinton's actions toward Iraq established a pattern that continued into the George W. Bush administration. First, the Clinton administration took action with little congressional consultation. In fact, Congress remained relatively silent on each occasion. Some of this silence can be attributed to public approval of Clinton's actions. For example, in the 1993 case, 61 percent of the public approved of the action taken. Second, the Clinton administration claimed unilateral powers under the commander in chief clause of the Constitution and UN Security Council authorizations. Justifying the attacks based on UN Security Council authorization broadly defined presidential and U.S. power.

## The Clinton Administration and Osama bin Laden

The Clinton administration's abuse of war powers with regard to Iraq paled in comparison to its abuse of war powers in its decision to strike the alleged terrorist bases of Osama bin Laden. The threat of terrorism became a more prominent foreign policy concern in the 1990s. In 1998, President Clinton unilaterally authorized air strikes against alleged terrorist sites. These strikes were not only conducted unilaterally, but also were executed without prior authorization from the United Nations.

Although terrorism was not considered a central threat to U.S. interests when Clinton took office, it quickly became one. By the end of the Clinton administration's first term the federal building in Oklahoma City had been bombed, the World Trade Center had been victimized by terrorists, and U.S. troops were killed in Saudi Arabia when terrorists exploded a car near a military complex. These events, among others, pushed terrorism to the center of U.S. interest. Like its predecessors, the Clinton administration attempted to deal with terrorism through multilateral, diplomatic channels. Despite these efforts, however, terrorists struck the U.S. embassies in Kenya and Tanzania on August 7, 1998. These attacks were soon attributed to Osama bin Laden and his terrorist network, al Qaeda. . . .

When the U.S. embassies in Kenya and Tanzania were bombed, 300 people were killed, including 12 Americans, and nearly 5,000 people were injured. Six days later, the Clinton administration responded with tomahawk missile attacks on alleged bin Laden bases in Afghanistan and Sudan.

In his letter to congressional leaders notifying them of the attack, he added:

> The United States acted in exercise of our inherent right of self-defense consistent with Article 51 of the United Nations Charter. These strikes were a necessary and proportionate response to the imminent threat of future terrorist attacks against U.S. personnel and facilities. . . . I directed these actions pursuant to my constitutional authority to conduct U.S. foreign relations and as Commander in Chief and Chief Executive.

Not only did Clinton rely on the UN Charter and his powers as commander in chief for his actions, but he also suggests that these actions were an inherent right of his power as chief executive. This sounds familiarly like Hamilton's argument that foreign policy was an executive function and the powers of declaring war and ratifying treaties bestowed on Congress were "exceptions out of the general 'executive power' vested in the President. Clinton was relying on the Hamiltonian interpretation of the Constitution. . . .

## The Bush Administration: Increasing Risks, Increasing Power

In the George W. Bush administration, the war on terrorism and policy toward Iraq are intertwined. This became clear after the September 11, 2001, terrorist attacks on the United States. On that day, terrorists struck the World Trade

Center Twin Towers and the Pentagon, killing thousands. Following these attacks, Bush made clear his intentions vowing, "Terrorism against our nation will not stand." He further argued, "War has been waged against us by stealth and deceit and murder," granting the president full authority to defend against the threat. The policy would eventually become the Bush Doctrine, including not only terrorist groups, but rogue states.

On September 12, the UN Security Council adopted a resolution condemning the attacks, declaring that they constituted a "threat to international peace and security." In addition, the resolution recognized the "inherent right of individual or collective self-defense in accordance with the Charter. On September 28, the UN Security Council unanimously adopted a historic resolution directed toward combating terrorism and states that support, harbor, provide safe haven to, supply, finance, help recruit, or aid terrorists. The resolution required cooperation of all member states in a wide range of areas. Resolution 1373 established a comprehensive legal framework for addressing the threat of international terrorism. It also provided a basis for the Bush Doctrine.

On October 7, the U.S. ambassador to the United Nations, John Negroponte, delivered a letter to the president of the UN Security Council stating that the United States, together with other states, had "initiated actions in the exercise of its inherent right of individual and collective self defense." These actions were taken against al Qaeda terrorist camps and military installations in Afghanistan, which had a "central role in the attacks." The letter went on to state that the United States "may find that our self-defense requires further actions with respect to other organizations and other States." This letter was the birth of the Bush Doctrine, which asserted the right of the United States to use military force in "self-defense" against any state that aids, harbors, or supports international terrorism, and it had profound implications. Most significantly, Ambassador Negroponte's letter left open the possibility that a state may intervene in anticipatory self-defense, without UN Security Council authorization, in another state that is alleged to be aiding, harboring, or supporting terrorism. Secretary of Defense Donald Rumsfeld later added:

> The only way to deal with the terrorists . . . is to take the battle to them, and find them, and root them out. And that is self-defense. And there is no question but that any nation on Earth has the right of self-defense. And we do. And what we are doing is going after those people, and those organizations, and those capabilities wherever we're going to find them in the world, and stop them from killing Americans. . . . That is in effect self-defense of a preemptive nature.

In his January 2002 State of the Union address, Bush, referring to North Korea, Iran, and Iraq, argued, "States like these, and their terrorist allies, constitute an axis of evil, arming to threaten the peace of the world. . . . America will do what is necessary to ensure our nation's security. . . . I will not wait on events while dangers gather. I will not stand by as peril draws closer and closer." With this statement, the president made clear his intentions to wage war when he felt preventing threats to the United States was necessary. The

United States had been attacked, and Bush believed his actions did not require congressional authority or consultation.

Although Bush had a strong argument for unilaterally exercising the decision to use force with regard to the terrorist attacks on September 11, he used that argument to extend his authority and shift U.S. foreign policy. Throughout the spring and summer 2002, the Bush administration devised its strategy for approaching the world. The national security strategy that emerged in September 2002 represents the most sweeping transformation in U.S. foreign policy since the beginning of the cold war. The strategy sets forth three tasks: "We will defend the peace by fighting terrorists and tyrants. We will preserve the peace by building good relations among great powers. We will extend the peace by encouraging free and open societies on every continent." . . .

The new strategy is proactive, rejecting the reactive strategies of containment and deterrence; its proactive stance is the basis for expanded presidential power. The strategy suggests that due to the nature of the threat a president may act alone to start a war against a perceived aggressor. The strategy presents an incontestable moral claim that in certain situations preemption is preferable to doing nothing and relies on Article 51 of the UN Charter for its legitimacy. In fact, the entire strategy is based on the presumption that a president can and must act to prevent future attacks on the United States or U.S. interests. Although such a policy may have its merits, it denies the necessity for congressional action of any kind in the use of force.

The irony of this policy is that although it does not require international support, the Bush administration has sought international support for it, using the United Nations and international law to justify the implementation of the national security strategy. On September 13, 2002, Bush addressed the UN General Assembly in New York City. He linked U.S. strategy to the purpose of the United Nations and justified using force against rogue states such as Iraq:

> The United Nations was born in the hope that survived a world war, the hope of a world moving toward justice, escaping old patterns of conflict and fear. The founding members resolved that the peace of the world must never again be destroyed by the will and wickedness of any man. . . . After generations of deceitful dictators and broken treaties and squandered lives, we dedicated ourselves to standards of human dignity . . . and to a system of security defended by all. Today, these standards and this security are challenged. . . . Above all, our principles and our security are challenged today by outlaw groups and regimes that accept no law of morality and have no limit to their violent ambitions.

Bush proceeded to make clear that the new doctrine of preemption, and the United Nations' relevancy, would be tested in Iraq. "In one place—in one regime—we find all these dangers in their most lethal and aggressive forms, exactly the kind of aggressive threat the United Nations was born to confront." Bush proceeded to lay out the case for using force against Iraq, which, he argued, had made a series of commitments to the United Nations, dating back to 1991. Furthermore, Iraq repeatedly failed to meet its commitments. . . .

The administration consequently negotiated a new UN Security Council resolution. The intent of that resolution was to prepare the way toward military action in Iraq. Resolution 1441 passed the UN Security Council unanimously on November 8, 2002, with a 15–0 vote in support of the resolution, and laid out what Iraq had to do to avoid war. The resolution cited Iraq in "material breach of its obligations under relevant resolutions." Furthermore, it offered Iraq "a final opportunity to comply with its disarmament obligations." In its final phrases, the resolution warned Iraq that it would face "serious consequences" because of continued violations of the UN Security Council resolutions.

Iraq responded to Resolution 1441 by inviting UN weapons inspectors back into the country. Throughout late 2002 and early 2003, the weapons inspectors, headed by Hans Blix and Mohammed el Baredei, pursued their task while the world watched and the United States continued to make its case that Iraqi failure to comply would be met with swift action. . . .

Bush, like Clinton before him, stressed the importance of the United Nations and used UN resolutions as a basis for using force against Iraq. . . .

On March 19, citing continued Iraqi noncompliance with international law, Bush announced that a coalition of thirty-five countries, led by the United States, began their attack on Iraq. "Our nation enters this conflict reluctantly," he told the American people, "yet our purpose is sure. The people of the United States and our friends and allies will not live at the mercy of an outlaw regime that threatens the peace with weapons of mass murder.

Following just over one month of warfare, the Iraqi regime crumbled and U.S. troops occupied Baghdad, Iraq's capital. With rebuilding efforts under way in Iraq, Bush immediately began efforts to focus on another member of the axis of evil—Iran, thus extending the Bush Doctrine of preemption. It is clear that the doctrine is firmly in place and presidential power will remain strong as long as U.S. foreign policy continues to emphasize and expand the war on terrorism. Presidential abuse of war powers is not a new phenomenon. Since World War II, however, presidential war power has vastly expanded and increased. . . . Congress is designed to be the primary check on presidential war powers. Since World War II, however, Congress has been rather ineffective in checking presidential war powers. In some cases, Congress not only fails to combat presidential war power, but also even voluntarily surrenders its legislative functions. In both the Clinton and George W. Bush administrations, Congress never declared war, but actively supported the actions each president took. . . .

[C]ontemporary presidents do not believe they need congressional approval and have substituted congressional approval with international legal sanction. Presidents Clinton and George W. Bush both relied on international legal authority in the form of UN Security Council resolutions to pursue military force. This suggests that presidents must no longer garner congressional approval when pursuing war, but must now acquire international support and must meet obligations under international law. This, as the George W. Bush case suggests, opens up the door to an even greater expansion of presidential authority and power in the use of force. . . .

# EXPLORING THE ISSUE

## Does the President Have Unilateral War Powers?

## Critical Thinking and Reflection

1. What legal precedents does John Yoo cite to bolster his case that the president has unilateral war powers?
2. Michael Cairo deplores President Clinton's use of air strikes against suspected terrorist bases in Africa. By that logic, would he also condemn President Obama's drone strikes against suspected terrorists in Pakistan and elsewhere, or are the two cases different?
3. The Congress has the sole power to "declare" war, but does that leave the president the sole power to "make" war? Or is there a real difference between the two? Try making a case using either Yoo or Cairo as a guide.

## Is There Common Ground?

The only thing in common between the two sides is their tendency to occupy each other's position with a change of administration. When a Republican president faced a Democratic Congress in 2007–2009, there was much complaining from the latter about the president's unilateral war-making. But a few years later, with a Democratic president, many of the same practices—targeting terrorists, holding them indefinitely, wiretapping, rendition—continued, this time with tacit approval from many Democrats in Congress. Now it was time for the Republicans to make a show of indignation.

## Additional Resources

Richard Neustadt's *Presidential Power: The Politics of Leadership*, originally published in 1960, has been revised under the title *Presidential Power and the Modern Presidents: The Politics of Leadership from Roosevelt to Reagan* (Free Press, 1991); it remains a useful and readable study of "personal power and its politics: what it is, how to get it, how to keep it, how to use it." For more recent studies, especially those pertinent to the immediate debate, one might begin with Yoo's book-length case for unilateral war powers, *The Powers of War and Peace: The Constitution and Foreign Affairs After 9/11* (University of Chicago, 2006). Sharply contesting that point of view is Louis Fisher's *Presidential War Power* (University Press of Kansas, 2004), which deplores what Fisher sees as the erosion of congressional war powers to a succession of modern presidents. Richard A. Posner's *Not a Suicide Pact: The Constitution in a Time of National*

*Emergency* (Oxford University Press, 2006) generally supports presidential emergency powers, including coercive interrogations, interception of communications within the United States, and tough laws against revealing classified information. Gerald Astor, *Presidents at War: From Truman to Bush, The Gathering of Military Powers to Our Commanders in Chief* (Wiley, 2006), traces the history and evolution of presidential war-making power in the modern era, concluding that it has gotten out of hand, especially under George W. Bush. Congressman John Murtha wrote its Foreword. Mark Brandon et al., *The Constitution in Wartime: Beyond Alarmism and Complacency* (Duke, 2005) is a collection of essays seeking a balanced view of presidential war powers.

# ISSUE 6

## Should the Courts Seek the "Original Meaning" of the Constitution?

**YES: Antonin Scalia,** from "Constitutional Interpretation," Remarks at Woodrow Wilson International Center for Scholars (March 14, 2005)

**NO: Stephen Breyer,** from *Active Liberty: Interpreting Our Democratic Constitution* (Knopf/Vintage, 2005)

### ISSUE SUMMARY

**YES:** Supreme Court Justice Antonin Scalia rejects the notion of a "living Constitution," arguing that the judges must try to understand what the framers meant at the time.

**NO:** Supreme Court Justice Stephen Breyer contends that in finding the meaning of the Constitution, judges cannot neglect to consider the probable consequences of different interpretations.

O n many matters the United States Constitution speaks with crystal clarity. In Article II, it says that "the Senate of the United States shall be composed of two Senators from each State." Even if it were desirable to have more than two Senators, or less, per state, there is no room for interpretation; "two" can only mean "two," and the only way of making it "one" or "three" is by constitutional amendment. (That process is itself clearly spelled out in Article V of the Constitution.) Other clauses, too, are defined in such a way as to put them beyond interpretative argument. Presidents Reagan and Clinton wanted very much to run again after their two terms, but there was no way either of them could get around the unambiguous words of the Twenty-Second amendment: "No person shall be elected to the office of President more than twice." The same clarity is found in many other provisions in the Constitution, such as the age requirements for Senators, Representatives, and Presidents (Articles I and II); direct election of Senators (Amendment XVII); and both Prohibition and its repeal (Amendments XVIII and XXI).

But other clauses in the Constitution are not so clear-cut. The First Amendment states that "Congress shall make no law respecting an establishment of religion. . . ." What is an "establishment of religion"? The Constitution itself does not say. Some constitutional scholars take it to mean that the state may not single out any particular religion for state sponsorship or support; others interpret it to mean that the state may not aid any religions. Which interpretation is correct? And what method do we use to determine which is correct? The same questions have to be asked about other fuzzy-sounding phrases, such as "due process of law" (Article V and Amendment XIV), "cruel and unusual punishment" (Amendment VIII), and "commerce among the several states" (Article I). Down through the years, jurists and legal commentators have tried to devise guiding principles for interpreting these and other phrases that have been subjects of dispute in the courts.

One set of principles made headlines in the 1980s when federal Appeals Court judge Robert Bork was nominated to the Supreme Court by President Ronald Reagan. Bork was a champion of "originalism," interpreting the Constitution according to what he called the "original intent" of its framers. What the courts should do, Bork argued, is to go back to what the framers meant at the time they wrote the particular clauses in dispute. Since the effect of Bork's approach was to call into question some of the more recent decisions by the Court, such as those upholding affirmative action and abortion, his nomination provoked a tumultuous national debate, and in the end he failed to win Senate confirmation.

On its face, originalism seems to comport with common sense. In making a will, to take an analogy, people rightly expect that their will should be interpreted according to *their* intent, not what their heirs might want it to mean. The analogy, however, comes under serious strain when we consider that the Constitution is not, like a will, the product of one person, or even one generation. Its various clauses have been crafted over 220 years; they are the work of many people in various Congresses, and many, many more who ratified them in state conventions or legislatures. Each one of those people may have had a different idea of what those clauses meant. When we come to clauses like "establishment of religion" or "equal protection of the laws," how can we possibly determine what the "original intent" of these clauses was—or even if there was any single intent?

The reply of the originalists is that the goal of determining the framers' intent must be striven for even when it is not perfectly attained. Moreover, what are we going to put in its place? Surely we can't have judges simply making things up, slipping in their own personal policy preferences in place of the Constitution and statutes of the United States.

This is one of the arguments—what he calls the "killer argument"—advanced by Justice Antonin Scalia in the selections that follow. As if replying to him, Justice Stephen Breyer rises to Scalia's challenge by suggesting that in interpreting the Constitution judges should weigh the probable consequences of varying interpretations of disputed clauses in the Constitution.

# YES

**Antonin Scalia**

# Constitutional Interpretation

I am one of a small number of judges, small number of anybody: judges, professors, lawyers; who are known as originalists. Our manner of interpreting the Constitution is to begin with the text, and to give that text the meaning that it bore when it was adopted by the people. I'm not a strict construction-ist, despite the introduction. I don't like the term "strict construction." I do not think the Constitution, or any text should be interpreted either strictly or sloppily; it should be interpreted reasonably. Many of my interpretations do not deserve the description "strict." I do believe, however, that you give the text the meaning it had when it was adopted.

This is such a minority position in modern academia and in modern legal circles that on occasion I'm asked when I've given a talk like this a question from the back of the room—"Justice Scalia, when did you first become an originalist?"—as though it is some kind of weird affliction that seizes some people—"When did you first start eating human flesh?"

Although it is a minority view now, the reality is that, not very long ago, originalism was orthodoxy. Everybody, at least purported to be an originalist. If you go back and read the commentaries on the Constitution by Joseph Story, he didn't think the Constitution evolved or changed. He said it means and will always mean what it meant when it was adopted.

Or consider the opinions of John Marshall in the Federal Bank case,* where he says, we must not, we must always remember it is a constitution we are expounding. And since it's a constitution, he says, you have to give its provisions expansive meaning so that they will accommodate events that you do not know of which will happen in the future.

Well, if it is a constitution that changes, you wouldn't have to give it an expansive meaning. You can give it whatever meaning you want and when future necessity arises, you simply change the meaning. But anyway, that is no longer the orthodoxy.

Oh, one other example about how not just the judges and scholars believed in originalism, but even the American people. Consider the Nineteenth Amendment, which is the amendment that gave women the vote. It was adopted by the American people in 1920. Why did we adopt a constitutional amendment for that purpose? The Equal Protection Clause existed in 1920; it was adopted right after the Civil War. And you know that if that issue of the franchise for women came up today, we would not have to have a

---

*McCulloch v. Maryland,* 4 Wheat, 316 (1819). [*Eds.*]

From a speech delivered at the Woodrow Wilson International Center for Scholars, March 14, 2005.

constitutional amendment. Someone would come to the Supreme Court and say, "Your Honors, in a democracy, what could be a greater denial of equal protection than denial of the franchise?" And the Court would say, "Yes! Even though it never meant it before, the Equal Protection Clause means that women have to have the vote." But that's not how the American people thought in 1920. In 1920, they looked at the Equal Protection Clause and said, "What does it mean?" Well, it clearly doesn't mean that you can't discriminate in the franchise—not only on the basis of sex, but on the basis of property ownership, on the basis of literacy. None of that is unconstitutional. And therefore, since it wasn't unconstitutional, and we wanted it to be, we did things the good old fashioned way and adopted an amendment.

Now, in asserting that originalism used to be orthodoxy, I do not mean to imply that judges did not distort the Constitution now and then, of course they did. We had willful judges then, and we will have willful judges until the end of time. But the difference is that prior to the last fifty years or so, prior to the advent of the "Living Constitution," judges did their distortions the good old fashioned way, the honest way—they lied about it. They said the Constitution means such and such, when it never meant such and such.

It's a big difference that you now no longer have to lie about it, because we are in the era of the evolving Constitution. And the judge can simply say, "Oh yes, the Constitution didn't used to mean that, but it does now." We are in the age in which not only judges, not only lawyers, but even school children have come to learn the Constitution changes. I have grammar school students come into the court now and then, and they recite very proudly what they have been taught: "The Constitution is a living document." You know, it morphs.

Well, let me first tell you how we got to the "Living Constitution." You don't have to be a lawyer to understand it. The road is not that complicated. Initially, the Court began giving terms in the text of the Constitution a meaning they didn't have when they were adopted. For example, the First Amendment, which forbids Congress to abridge the freedom of speech. What does the freedom of speech mean? Well, it clearly did not mean that Congress, or government could not impose any restrictions upon speech. Libel laws for example, were clearly Constitutional. Nobody thought the First Amendment was *carte blanche* to libel someone. But in the famous case of *New York Times v. Sullivan*, the Supreme Court said, "But the First Amendment does prevent you from suing for libel if you are a public figure and if the libel was not malicious." That is, the person, a member of the press or otherwise, thought that what the person said was true. Well, that had never been the law. I mean, it might be a good law. And some states could amend their libel law.

It's one thing for a state to amend its libel law and say, "We think that public figures shouldn't be able to sue." That's fine. But the courts have said that the First Amendment, which never meant this before, now means that if you are a public figure, that you can't sue for libel unless it's intentional, malicious. So that's one way to do it.

Another example is: the Constitution guarantees the right to be represented by counsel; that never meant the State had to pay for your counsel. But you can reinterpret it to mean that.

That was step one. Step two, I mean, that will only get you so far. There is no text in the Constitution that you could reinterpret to create a right to abortion, for example. So you need something else. The something else is called the doctrine of "Substantive Due Process." Only lawyers can walk around talking about substantive process, inasmuch as it's a contradiction in terms. If you referred to substantive process or procedural substance at a cocktail party, people would look at you funny. But lawyers talk this way all the time.

What substantive due process is, is quite simple, the Constitution has a Due Process Clause, which says that no person shall be deprived of life, liberty or property without due process of law. Now, what does this guarantee? Does it guarantee life, liberty or property? No, indeed! All three can be taken away. You can be fined, you can be incarcerated, you can even be executed, but not without due process of law. It's a procedural guarantee. But the Court said, and this goes way back, in the 1920s at least, in fact the first case to do it was Dred Scott. But it became more popular in the 1920s. The Court said there are some liberties that are so important, that no process will suffice to take them away. Hence, substantive due process.

Now, what liberties are they? The Court will tell you. Be patient. When the doctrine of substantive due process was initially announced, it was limited in this way, the Court said it embraces only those liberties that are fundamental to a democratic society and rooted in the traditions of the American people.

Then we come to step three. Step three: that limitation is eliminated. Within the last twenty years, we have found to be covered by Due Process the right to abortion, which was so little rooted in the traditions of the American people that it was criminal for two hundred years; the right to homosexual sodomy, which was so little rooted in the traditions of the American people that it was criminal for two hundred years.

So it is literally true, and I don't think this is an exaggeration, that the Court has essentially liberated itself from the text of the Constitution, from the text, and even from the traditions of the American people. It is up to the Court to say what is covered by substantive due process. What are the arguments usually made in favor of the Living Constitution? As the name of it suggests, it is a very attractive philosophy, and it's hard to talk people out of it: the notion that the Constitution grows. The major argument is the Constitution is a living organism, it has to grow with the society that it governs or it will become brittle and snap.

This is the equivalent of, an anthropomorphism equivalent to what you hear from your stock broker, when he tells you that the stock market is resting for an assault on the eleven-thousand level. The stock market panting at some base camp. The stock market is not a mountain climber and the Constitution is not a living organism for Pete's sake; it's a legal document, and like all legal documents, it says some things, and it doesn't say other things.

And if you think that the aficionados of the Living Constitution want to bring you flexibility, think again. My Constitution is a very flexible Constitution. You think the death penalty is a good idea: persuade your fellow citizens and adopt it. You think it's a bad idea: persuade them the other way and eliminate it. You want a right to abortion: create it the way most rights are created in a democratic society. Persuade your fellow citizens it's a good idea, and enact it. You want the opposite, persuade them the other way. That's flexibility. But to read either result into the Constitution is not to produce flexibility, it is to produce what a constitution is designed to produce: rigidity.

Abortion, for example, is offstage, it is off the democratic stage, it is no use debating it, it is unconstitutional. I mean prohibiting it is unconstitutional. I mean it's no use debating it anymore. Now and forever, coast to coast, I guess until we amend the constitution, which is a difficult thing. So, for whatever reason you might like the Living Constitution, don't like it because it provides flexibility. That's not the name of the game.

Some people also seem to like it because they think it's a good liberal thing. That somehow this is a conservative/liberal battle. And conservatives like the old-fashioned originalist Constitution and liberals ought to like the Living Constitution. That's not true either. The dividing line between those who believe in the Living Constitution and those who don't is not the dividing line between conservatives and liberals.

Conservatives are willing to grow the Constitution to cover their favorite causes just as liberals are. And the best example of that is two cases we a..nounced some years ago on the same day, the same morning. One case was *Romer v. Evans*, in which the people of Colorado had enacted an amendment to the State Constitution by plebiscite, which said that neither the State, nor any subdivision of the State would add to the protected statuses against which private individuals cannot discriminate. The usual ones are: race, religion, age, sex, disability and so forth. Would not add sexual preference. Somebody thought that was a terrible idea, and since it was a terrible idea, it must be unconstitutional. Brought a lawsuit, it came to the Supreme Court. And the Supreme Court said, "Yes, it is unconstitutional." On the basis of . . . I don't know. The Sexual Preference Clause of the Bill of Rights, presumably. And the liberals loved it; and the conservatives gnashed their teeth.

The very next case we announced is a case called *BMW v. [Gore]*. Not the [Gore] you think; this is another [Gore]. Mr. Gore had bought a BMW, which is a car supposedly advertised at least as having a superb finish, baked seven times in ovens deep in the Alps, by dwarfs. And his BMW apparently had gotten scratched on the way over. They did not send it back to the Alps, they took a can of spray-paint and fixed it. And he found out about this and was furious, and he brought a lawsuit. He got his compensatory damages, a couple of hundred dollars, the difference between a car with a better paint job and a worse paint job. Plus, $2 million against BMW for punitive damages for being a bad actor, which is absurd of course, so it must be unconstitutional. BMW appealed to my court, and my court said, "Yes, it's unconstitutional." In violation of, I assume, the Excessive Damages Clause of the Bill of Rights. And if excessive punitive damages are unconstitutional, why aren't excessive compensatory damages unconstitutional? So you have a federal question whenever you get a judgment in a civil case. Well, that one the conservatives liked, because conservatives don't like punitive damages, and the liberals gnashed their teeth.

I dissented in both cases because I say, "A pox on both their houses." It has nothing to do with what your policy preferences are; it has to do with what you think the Constitution is.

Some people are in favor of the Living Constitution because they think it always leads to greater freedom. There's just nothing to lose. The evolving Constitution will always provide greater and greater freedom, more and more rights. Why would you think that? It's a two-way street. And indeed, under the aegis of the Living Constitution, some freedoms have been taken away. . . .

Well, I've talked about some of the false virtues of the Living Constitution, let me tell you what I consider its, principal, vices are. Surely the greatest, you should always begin with principal, its greatest vice is its illegitimacy. The only reason federal courts sit in judgment of the constitutionality of federal legislation is not because they are explicitly authorized to do so in the Constitution. Some modern constitutions give the constitutional court explicit authority to review German legislation or French legislation for its constitutionality. Our Constitution doesn't say anything like that. But John Marshall says in *Marbury v. Madison*: look, this is lawyers' work. What you have here is an apparent conflict between the Constitution and the statute. And, all the time, lawyers and judges have to reconcile these conflicts; they try to read the two to comport with each other. If they can't, it's judges' work to decide which ones prevail. When there are two statutes, the more recent one prevails. It implicitly repeals the older one. But when the Constitution is at issue, the Constitution prevails because it is a "superstatute." I mean, that's what Marshall says: it's judges' work.

If you believe, however, that the Constitution is not a legal text, like the texts involved when judges reconcile or decide which of two statutes prevail; if you think the Constitution is some exhortation to give effect to the most fundamental values of the society as those values change from year to year; if you think that it is meant to reflect, as some of the Supreme Court cases say, particularly those involving the Eighth Amendment, if you think it is simply meant to reflect the evolving standards of decency that mark the progress of a maturing society, if that is what you think it is, then why in the world would you have it interpreted by nine lawyers? What do I know about the evolving standards of decency of American society? I'm afraid to ask.

If that is what you think the Constitution is, then *Marbury v. Madison* is wrong. It shouldn't be up to the judges, it should be up to the legislature. We should have a system like the English. Whatever the legislature thinks is constitutional is constitutional. They know the evolving standards of American society, I don't. So in principle, it's incompatible with the legal regime that America has established.

Secondly, and this is the killer argument, I mean, it's the best debater's argument. They say in politics, you can't beat somebody with nobody, it's the same thing with principles of legal interpretation. If you don't believe in originalism, then you need some other principle of interpretation. Being a non-originalist is not enough. You see, I have my rules that confine me. I know what I'm looking for. When I find it, the original meaning of the Constitution, I am handcuffed. If I believe that the First Amendment meant when it was adopted that you are entitled to burn the American flag, I have to come out that way, even though I don't like to come out that way. When I find that the original meaning of the jury trial guarantee is that any additional time you spend in prison which depends upon a fact, must depend upon a fact found by a jury, once I find that's what the jury trial guarantee means, I am handcuffed. Though I'm a law-and-order type, I cannot do all the mean conservative things I would like to do to this society. You got me.

Now, if you're not going to control your judges that way, what other criterion are you going to place before them? What is the criterion that governs the living constitutional judge? What can you possibly use, besides original meaning? Think about that. Natural law? We all agree on that, don't we? The philosophy of John Rawls? That's easy. There really is nothing else. You either tell your judges, "Look, this is a law, like all laws, give it the meaning it had when it was adopted." Or, you tell your judges, "Govern us. You tell us whether people under eighteen, who committed their crimes when they were under eighteen, should be executed. You tell us whether there ought to be an unlimited right to abortion or a partial right to abortion. You make these decisions for us."

I have put this question, you know I speak at law schools with some frequency just to make trouble, and I put this question to the faculty all the time, or incite the students to ask their living constitutional professors. "OK professor, you are not an originalist, what is your criterion?" There is none other.

And finally, this is what I will conclude with, although it is not on a happy note, the worst thing about the Living Constitution is that it will destroy the Constitution. I was confirmed, close to nineteen years ago now, by a vote of ninety-eight to nothing. The two missing were Barry Goldwater and Jake Garn, so make it a hundred. I was known at that time to be, in my political and social views, fairly conservative. But still, I was known to be a good lawyer, an honest man, somebody who could read a text and give it its fair meaning, had judicial impartiality and so forth. And so I was unanimously confirmed.

Today, barely twenty years later, it is difficult to get someone confirmed to the Court of Appeals. What has happened? The American people have figured out what is going on. If we are selecting lawyers, if we are selecting people to read a text and give it the fair meaning it had when it was adopted, yes, the most important thing to do is to get a good lawyer. If on the other hand, we're picking people to draw out of their own conscience and experience, a new constitution, with all sorts of new values to govern our society, then we should not look principally for good lawyers. We should look principally for people who agree with us, the majority, as to whether there ought to be this right, that right, and the other right. We want to pick people that would write the new constitution that we would want.

And that is why you hear in the discourse on this subject, people talking about moderate, we want moderate judges. What is a moderate interpretation of the text? Halfway between what it really means and what you'd like it to mean? There is no such thing as a moderate interpretation of the text. Would you ask a lawyer, "Draw me a moderate contract?" The only way the word has any meaning is if you are looking for someone to write a law, to write a constitution, rather than to interpret one. The moderate judge is the one who will devise the new constitution that most people would approve of. So for example, we had a suicide case some terms ago, and the Court refused to hold that there is a constitutional right to assisted suicide. We said, "We're not yet ready to say that. Stay tuned, in a few years, the time may come, but we're not yet ready." And that was a moderate decision, because I think most people would not want—if we had gone, looked into that and created a national right to assisted suicide that would have been an immoderate and extremist decision.

I think the very terminology suggests where we have arrived: at the point of selecting people to write a constitution, rather than people to give us the fair meaning of one that has been democratically adopted. And when that happens, when the Senate interrogates nominees to the Supreme Court, or to the lower courts you know, "Judge so and so, do you think there is a right to this in the Constitution? You don't? Well, my constituents think there ought to be, and I'm not going to appoint to the court someone who is not going to find that." When we are in that mode, you realize, we have rendered the Constitution useless, because the Constitution will mean what the majority wants it to mean. The senators are representing the majority. And they will be selecting justices who will devise a constitution that the majority wants.

And that of course, deprives the Constitution of its principle utility. The Bill of Rights is devised to protect you and me against, who do you think? The majority. My most important function on the Supreme Court is to tell the majority to take a walk. And the notion that the justices ought to be selected because of the positions that they will take that are favored by the majority is a recipe for destruction of what we have had for two hundred years.

Stephen Breyer      **NO**

# Active Liberty: Interpreting Our Democratic Constitution

**M**y discussion sees individual constitutional provisions as embodying certain basic purposes, often expressed in highly general terms. It sees the Constitution itself as a single document designed to further certain basic general purposes as a whole. It argues that an understanding of, and a focus upon, those general purposes will help a judge better to understand and to apply specific provisions. And it identifies consequences as an important yardstick to measure a given interpretation's faithfulness to these democratic purposes. In short, focus on purpose seeks to promote active liberty by insisting on interpretations, statutory as well as constitutional, that are consistent with the people's will. Focus on consequences, in turn, allows us to gauge whether and to what extent we have succeeded in facilitating workable outcomes which reflect that will.

Some lawyers, judges, and scholars, however, would caution strongly against the reliance upon purposes (particularly abstractly stated purposes) and assessment of consequences. They ask judges to focus primarily upon text, upon the Framers' original expectations, narrowly conceived, and upon historical tradition. They do not deny the occasional relevance of consequences or purposes (including such general purposes as democracy), but they believe that judges should use them sparingly in the interpretive endeavor. They ask judges who tend to find interpretive answers in those decision-making elements to rethink the problem to see whether language, history, tradition, and precedent by themselves will not yield an answer. They fear that, once judges become accustomed to justifying legal conclusions through appeal to real-world consequences, they will too often act subjectively and undemocratically, substituting an elite's views of good policy for sound law. They hope that language, history, tradition, and precedent will provide important safeguards against a judge's confusing his or her personal, undemocratic notion of what is good for that which the Constitution or statute demands. They tend also to emphasize the need for judicial opinions that set forth their legal conclusions in terms of rules that will guide other institutions, including lower courts.

This view, which I shall call "textualist" (in respect to statutes) or "originalist" (in respect to the Constitution) or "literalist" (shorthand for both), while logically consistent with emphasizing the Constitution's democratic objectives, is not hospitable to the kinds of arguments I have advanced. Nor is it easily reconciled with my illustrations. Why, then, does it not undercut my entire argument?

The answer, in my view, lies in the unsatisfactory nature of that interpretive approach. First, the more "originalist" judges cannot appeal to the Framers themselves in support of their interpretive views. The Framers did not say specifically what factors judges should take into account when they interpret statutes or the Constitution. This is obvious in the case of statutes. Why would the Framers have preferred (1) a system of interpretation that relies heavily on linguistic canons to (2) a system that seeks more directly to find the intent of the legislators who enacted the statute? It is close to obvious in respect to the Constitution. Why would the Farmers, who disagreed even about the necessity of *including* a Bill of Rights in the Constitution, who disagreed about the *content* of that Bill of Rights, nonetheless have agreed about *what school of interpretive thought* should prove dominant in interpreting that Bill of Rights in the centuries to come?

In respect to content, the Constitution itself says that the "enumeration" in the Constitution of some rights "shall not be construed to deny or disparage others retained by the people." Professor Bernard Bailyn concludes that the Framers added this language to make clear that "rights, like law itself, should never be fixed, frozen, that new dangers and needs will emerge, and that to respond to these dangers and needs, rights must be newly specified to protect the individual's integrity and inherent dignity." Given the open-ended nature of *content*, why should one expect to find fixed views about the nature of interpretive practice?

If, however, justification for the literalist's interpretive practices cannot be found in the Framers intentions, where can it be found—other than in an appeal to *consequences*, that is, in an appeal to the presumed beneficial consequences for the law or for the nation that will flow from adopting those practices? And that is just what we find argued. That is to say, literalist arguments often try to show that that approach will have favorable *results*, for example, that it will deter judges from substituting their own views about what is good for the public for those of Congress or for those embodied in the Constitution. They argue, in other words, that a more literal approach to interpretation will better control judicial subjectivity. Thus, while literalists eschew consideration of consequences case by case, their interpretive rationale is consequentialist in this important sense.

Second, I would ask whether it is true that judges who reject literalism necessarily open the door to subjectivity. They do not endorse subjectivity. And under their approach important safeguards of objectivity remain. For one thing, a judge who emphasizes consequences, no less than any other, is aware of the legal precedents, rules, standards, practices, and institutional understanding that a decision will affect. He or she also takes account of the way in which this system of legally related rules, institutions, and practices affects the world.

To be sure, a court focused on consequences may decide a case in a way that radically changes the law. But this is not always a bad thing. For example, after the late-nineteenth-century Court decided *Plessy v. Ferguson*, the case which permitted racial segregation that was, in principle, "separate but equal," it became apparent that segregation did not mean equality but meant disrespect for members of a minority race and led to a segregated society that was totally unequal, a consequence directly contrary to the purpose and demands of the Fourteenth Amendment. The Court, in *Brown v. Board of Education* and later decisions, overruled *Plessy*, and the law changed in a way that profoundly affected the lives of many.

In any event, to focus upon consequences does not automatically invite frequent dramatic legal change. Judges, including those who look to consequences, understand the human need to plan in reliance upon law, the need for predictability, the need for stability. And they understand that too radical, too frequent legal change has, as a consequence, a tendency to undercut those important law-related human needs. Similarly, each judge's individual need to be consistent over time constrains subjectivity. As Justice O'Connor has explained, a constitutional judge's initial decisions leave "footprints" that the judge, in later decisions, will almost inevitably follow.

Moreover, to consider consequences is not to consider simply whether the consequences of a proposed decision are good or bad, in a particular judge's opinion. Rather, to emphasize consequences is to emphasize consequences related to the particular textual provision at issue. The judge must examine the consequences through the lens of the relevant constitutional value or purpose. The relevant values limit interpretive possibilities. If they are democratic values, they may well counsel modesty or restraint as well. And I believe that when a judge candidly acknowledges that, in addition to text, history, and precedent, consequences also guide his decision-making, he is more likely to be disciplined in emphasizing, for example, constitutionally relevant consequences rather than allowing his own subjectively held values to be outcome determinative. In all these ways, a focus on consequences will itself constrain subjectivity.

Here are examples of how these principles apply. The First Amendment says that "Congress shall make no law respecting an establishment of religion." I recently wrote (in dissent) that this clause prohibits government from providing vouchers to parents to help pay for the education of their children in parochial schools. The basic reason, in my view, is that the clause seeks to avoid among other things the "social conflict, potentially created when government becomes involved in religious education." Nineteenth- and twentieth-century immigration has produced a nation with fifty or more different religions. And that fact made the risk of "social conflict" far more serious after the Civil War and in twentieth-century America than the Framers, with their eighteenth-century experience, might have anticipated. The twentieth-century Supreme Court had held in applicable precedent that, given the changing nature of our society, in order to implement the basic value that the Framers wrote the clause to protect, it was necessary to interpret the clause more broadly than the Framers might have thought likely.

My opinion then turned to consequences. It said that voucher programs, if widely adopted, could provide billions of dollars to religious schools. At first blush, that may seem a fine idea. But will different religious groups become concerned about which groups are getting the money and how? What are the criteria? How are programs being implemented? Is a particular program biased against particular sects, say, because it forbids certain kinds of teaching? Are rival sects failing to live up to the relevant criteria, say, by teaching "civil disobedience" to "unjust laws"? How will claims for money, say, of one religious group against another, be adjudicated? In a society as religiously diverse as ours, I saw in the administration of huge grant programs for religious education the potential for religious strife. And that, it seemed to me, was the kind of problem the First Amendment's religion clauses seek to avoid.

The same constitutional concern—the need to avoid a "divisiveness based upon religion that promotes social conflict"—helped me determine whether the Establishment Clause forbade two public displays of the tables of the Ten Commandments, one inside a Kentucky state courthouse, the other on the grounds of the Texas State Capitol. It is well recognized that the Establishment Clause does not allow the government to compel religious practices, to show favoritism among sects or between religion and non-religion, or to promote religion. Yet, at the same time, given the religious beliefs of most Americans, an absolutist approach that would purge all religious references from the public sphere could well promote the very kind of social conflict that the Establishment Clause seeks to avoid. Thus, I thought, the Establishment Clause cannot *automatically* forbid every public display of the Ten Commandments, despite the religious nature of its text. Rather, one must examine the context of the *particular* display to see whether, in that context, the tablets convey the kind of government-endorsed religious message that the Establishment Clause forbids.

The history of the Kentucky courthouse display convinced me and the other members of the Court's majority that the display sought to serve its sponsors' primarily religious objectives and that many of its viewers would understand it as reflecting that motivation. But the context of the Texas display differed significantly. A private civic (and primarily secular) organization had placed the tablets on the Capitol grounds as part of the organization's efforts to combat juvenile delinquency. Those grounds contained seventeen other monuments and twenty-one historical markers, none of which conveyed any religious message and all of which sought to illustrate the historical "ideals" of Texans. And the monument had stood for forty years without legal challenge. These circumstances strongly suggested that the public visiting the Capitol grounds had long considered the tablets' religious message as a secondary part of a broader moral and historical message reflecting a cultural heritage—a view of the display consistent with its promoters' basic objective.

It was particularly important that the Texas display stood uncontested for forty years. That fact indicated, as a practical matter of degree, that (unlike the Kentucky display) the Texas display was unlikely to prove socially divisive. Indeed, to require the display's removal itself would encourage disputes over the the removal of longstanding depictions of the Ten Commandments from public buildings across the nation, thereby creating the very kind of religiously based divisiveness that the Establishment Clause was designed to prevent. By way of contrast, the short and stormy history of the more contemporary

Kentucky display revealed both religious motivation and consequent social controversy. Thus, in the two cases, which I called borderline cases, consideration of likely consequences—evaluated in light of the purposes or values embodied within the Establishment Clause—helped produce a legal result: The Clause allowed the Texas display, while it forbade the display in Kentucky.

I am not arguing here that I was right in any of these cases. I am arguing that my opinions sought to identify a critical value underlying the Religion Clauses. They considered how that value applied in modern-day America; they looked for consequences relevant to that value. And they sought to evaluate likely consequences in terms of that value. That is what I mean by an *interpretive approach* that emphasizes consequences. Under that approach language, precedent, constitutional values, and factual circumstances all constrain judicial subjectivity.

Third, "subjectivity" is a two-edged criticism, which the literalist himself cannot escape. The literalist's tools—language and structure, history and tradition—often fail to provide objective guidance in those truly difficult cases about which I have spoken. Will canons of interpretation provide objective answers? One canon tells the court to choose an interpretation that gives every statutory word a meaning. Another permits the court to ignore a word, treating it as surplus, if otherwise the construction is repugnant to the statute's purpose. Shall the court read the statute narrowly as in keeping with the common law or broadly as remedial in purpose? Canons to the left to them, canons to the right of them, which canons shall the judges choose to follow?

. . . Fourth, I do not believe that textualist or originalist methods of interpretation are more likely to produce clear, workable legal rules. But even were they to do so, the advantages of legal rules can be overstated. Rules must be interpreted and applied. Every law student whose class grade is borderline knows that the benefits that rules produce for cases that fall within the heartland are often lost in cases that arise at the boundaries.

. . . Fifth, textualist and originalist doctrines may themselves produce seriously harmful consequences—outweighing whatever risks of subjectivity or uncertainty are inherent in other approaches.

. . . Literalism has a tendency to undermine the Constitution's efforts to create a framework for democratic government—a government that, while protecting basic individual liberties, permits citizens to govern themselves, and to govern themselves effectively. Insofar as a more literal interpretive approach undermines this basic objective, it is inconsistent with the most fundamental original intention of the Framers themselves.

For any or all of these reasons, I hope that those strongly committed to textualist or literalist views—those whom I am almost bound not to convince—are fairly small in number. I hope to have convinced some of the rest that active liberty has an important role to play in constitutional (and statutory) interpretation.

That role, I repeat, does not involve radical change in current professional interpretive methods nor does it involve ignoring the protection the Constitution grants fundamental (negative) liberties. It takes Thomas Jefferson's statement as a statement of goals that the Constitution now seeks to fulfill: "[A]ll men are created equal." They are endowed by their Creator with certain "unalienable Rights." "[T]o secure these Rights, Governments are instituted among Men, *deriving their just powers from the consent of the governed.*" It underscores, emphasizes, or reemphasizes the final democratic part of the famous phrase. That reemphasis, I believe, has practical value when judges seek to assure fidelity, in our modern society, to these ancient and unchanging ideals.

# EXPLORING THE ISSUE

## Should the Courts Seek the "Original Meaning" of the Constitution?

## Critical Thinking and Reflection

1. What does Justice Scalia mean by the "original meaning" of the Constitution?
2. Why does Justice Breyer reject the concept of an original meaning?
3. If there is no "original meaning," are Justices free to read their views into the Constitution?
4. How would Justice Scalia reconcile *Brown v. Board of Education* (against enforced racial segregation) with his originalist interpretation of the Constitution?
5. How should the Supreme Court determine the constitutional status of actions that the authors of the Constitution could not imagine?
6. Should narrow 5-4 decisions overthrow Acts of Congress or should a larger majority be required?
7. Which side of this issue would the Framers of the Constitution be more likely to take?
8. Should the Constitution be amended to resolve sharply disputed constitutional questions?
9. What impact do divided Supreme Court decisions have on the resolution of controversial issues?

## Is There Common Ground?

The close division on the present United States Supreme Court reflects a division that runs through the nation's history. The size of the two blocs varies, depending on which president fills a vacancy, but the conflict remains. Each side represents itself a truer embodiment of the spirit of the Constitution's authors. Both sides will be respecters of *stare decisis* (to stand by an earlier decision) when it conforms to their views, and both sides will overthrow a precedent when it does not. The only common ground they share is the U. S. Constitution, but it is the point at which they part.

## Additional Resources

Constitutional scholar Ronald Dworkin rejects Justice Scalia's originalism in favor of interpretations that increase liberty and equality; those are his moral values and Dworking frankly declares that they should be read into the

Constitution. See his book, *Freedom's Law: The Moral Reading of the American Constitution* (Harvard University Press, 1996). Mary Ann Glendon warns of the perils of what she regards as "*romantic* judging" in *A Nation Under Lawyers* (Farrar, Straus & Giroux, 1994).

Jeffrey Toobin, *The Nine: Inside the Secret World of the Supreme Court* (Doubleday, 2007), concludes that the High Court's decisions do not derive from the Constitution or the laws or even ideology, but from the personalities of the men and women who sit on it. Jeffrey A. Segal et al., *The Supreme Court in the Legal System* (Cambridge University Press, 2005) is a comprehensive introduction to the Supreme Court and the lower federal courts.

# ISSUE 7

# Is Congress a
# Dysfunctional Institution?

**YES: Ezra Klein**, from "What Happens When Congress Fails to Do Its Job," *Newsweek* (March 27, 2010)

**NO: Lee H. Hamilton**, from "Public Criticisms of Congress," *How Congress Works* (Indiana University Press, 2004)

### ISSUE SUMMARY

**YES:** Columnist Ezra Klein contends that institutional deadlock and partisan rancor have paralyzed Congress, causing it to lose power to the president and the bureaucracy.

**NO:** Former representative Lee H. Hamilton contends that many of the Congress's so-called flaws are actually faithful reflections of how the American public thinks and feels.

Those who teach introductory American government usually look forward to the unit on the American presidency. It sets off lively class participation, especially when students talk about the actions of whoever happens to be in the White House. The same happens when the topic is the Supreme Court; students can argue about controversial decisions like school prayer, flag-burning, and abortion, and the instructor sometimes has to work hard to keep the discussion from getting too hot.

But when Congress, the third branch of the federal government, comes up for discussion, it is hard to get anything going beyond a few cynical shrugs and wisecracks. Seriously intended comments, when they finally emerge, may range from skeptical questions ("What do they *do* for their money?") to harsh pronouncements ("Bunch of crooks!").

Students today can hardly be blamed for these reactions. They are inheritors of a rich American tradition of Congress-bashing. At the end of the nineteenth century, the novelist Mark Twain quipped that "there is no distinctly native American criminal class except Congress." In the 1930s, the humorist Will Rogers suggested that "we have the best Congress money can buy." In the 1940s, President Harry Truman coined the term *do-nothing Congress*, and Fred Allen's radio comedy show had a loudmouth "Senator Claghorn" who did nothing but bluster. In the 1950s, the *Washington Post's* "Herblock" and other cartoonists liked to draw senators as potbellied old guys chewing cigars.

Needless to say, the drafters of the U.S. Constitution did not anticipate that kind of portrayal; they wanted Congress to stand tall in power and stature. Significantly, they listed it first among the three branches, and they gave it an extensive list of powers, eighteen in all, rounding them off with the power to "make all laws which shall be necessary and proper" for executing its express powers.

Throughout the first half of the nineteenth century, Congress played a very visible role in the business of the nation, and some of its most illustrious members, like Daniel Webster, Henry Clay, and John C. Calhoun, were national superstars. Men and women crowded in to the visitors' gallery when Webster was about to deliver one of his powerful orations; during these performances they sometimes wept openly.

What, then, happened to Congress over the years to bring about this fall from grace? A number of factors have come into play, two of which can be cited immediately.

First, Congress has become a very complicated institution. In both houses, especially in the House of Representatives, legislation is not hammered out on the floor but in scores of committees and subcommittees, known to some journalists and political scientists but to relatively few others. Major bills can run hundreds of pages, and are written in a kind of lawyerspeak inaccessible to ordinary people. Congressional rules are so arcane that even a bill with clear majority support can fall through the cracks and disappear. The public simply doesn't understand all this, and incomprehension can easily sour into distrust and suspicion.

A second reason why Congress doesn't get much respect these days is connected with the increased visibility of its sometime rival, the presidency. Ever since Abraham Lincoln raised the possibility of what presidents can do during prolonged emergencies, charismatic presidents like Woodrow Wilson, Franklin Roosevelt, and Ronald Reagan, serving during such times, have aggrandized the office of the president, pushing Congress into the background. They have thus stolen much of the prestige and glamour that once attached to the legislative branch. The president has become a very visible "one" and Congress has faded into a shadowy "many." Everyone knows who the president is, but how many people can name the leaders of Congress? Can you?

In the following selections, *Washington Post* columnist Ezra Klein blames them on the ideological polarization of our two parties in Congress, which, he believes, has virtually paralyzed the institution. Lee H. Hamilton, a former member of Congress, takes a different position, arguing that the noisy clash of viewpoints and interests serves the public by airing controversies and preventing ill-considered measures from passing.

# YES ↵

**Ezra Klein**

# What Happens When Congress Fails to Do Its Job?

**I.** In 2008 Barack Obama almost asked Evan Bayh to be his running mate. It was "a coin toss," recalls David Plouffe, Obama's campaign manager. Bayh lost that toss, but the fact that he was a finalist—much as he'd been for John Kerry four years earlier—was proof that he was doing something right in his day job as junior senator from Indiana. His future seemed bright.

Last month he announced his retirement.

There was no scandal. Bayh wasn't plagued by poor fundraising or low poll numbers. Nor is fatigue a likely explanation: at 54, Bayh is fairly young, at least when you're grading on the curve that is the United States Senate.

What drove Bayh from office, rather, was that he'd grown to hate his job. Congress, he wrote in a *New York Times* op-ed, is "stuck in an endless cycle of recrimination and revenge. The minority seeks to frustrate the majority, and when the majority is displaced it returns the favor. Power is constantly sought through the use of means which render its effective use, once acquired, impossible."

The situation had grown so grim, Bayh said, that continued service was no longer of obvious use. Americans were left with a bizarre spectacle: a member of the most elite legislative body in the most powerful country in the world was resigning because the dysfunctions of his institution made him feel ineffectual. "I simply believe I can best contribute to society in another way," Bayh explained, "creating jobs by helping grow a business, helping guide an institution of higher learning, or helping run a worthy charitable endeavor."

This is what it's come to, then: our senators envy the influence and sway held by university presidents.

**II.** In the months leading up to the health-care-reform vote, there was much talk that Congress is broken and serious reform is necessary. Some would say the bill's passage is a decisive refutation of that position. They are wrong.

What we have learned instead is that even in those rare moments when bold action should be easy, little can be done. Consider the position of the Democrats over the last year: a popular new president, the largest majority either party has held in the Senate since the post-Watergate wave, a 40-seat majority in the House, and a financial crisis. Congress has managed to pass a lot of legislation, and some of it has been historic. But our financial system is not fixed and our health-care problems are not solved. Indeed, when it comes to the toughest decisions Congress must make, our representatives have passed them off to some other body or some future generation.

The architects of the health-care-reform bill, for instance, couldn't bring themselves to propose the difficult reforms necessary to assure Medicare—and the government's—solvency. So they created an independent panel of experts who will have to propose truly difficult reforms to enable the Medicare system to survive. These recommendations would take the fast track through Congress, protected from not just the filibuster but even from revision. In fact, if Congress didn't vote on them, they'd still become law. "I believe this commission is the largest yielding of sovereignty from the Congress since the creation of the Federal Reserve," says Office of Management and Budget Director Peter Orszag, and he meant it as a compliment.

Cap-and-trade, meanwhile, is floundering in the Senate. In the event that it dies, the Environmental Protection Agency has been preparing to regulate carbon on its own. Some senators would like to block the EPA from doing so, and may yet succeed. But those in Congress who want to avert catastrophic climate change, but who don't believe they can pass legislation to help do so, are counting on the EPA to act in their stead.

The financial meltdown was, in many ways, a model of quick congressional action. TARP had its problems, and the stimulus was too small, but both passed, and quickly. After they'd passed, though, it became clear they weren't sufficient, and that Congress wasn't going to be able to muster further action. So the Federal Reserve, in consultation with congressional leaders, unleashed more than a trillion dollars into the marketplace. It was still the American people's money being invested, but it didn't need 60 votes in the Senate.

Congress was reticent to do more about the financial crisis because of concern over the deficit. But even apparent bipartisan agreement wasn't sufficient to compel action. Sens. Kent Conrad (D-N.D.) and Judd Gregg (R-N.H.) [led] the Budget Committee, and they called for their committee—and all the other committees—to be bypassed altogether in favor of a deficit commission operating outside the normal legislative structure. "Some have argued that House and Senate committees with jurisdiction over health, retirement and revenue issues should individually take up legislation to address the imbalance," they wrote in a joint op-ed. "But that path will never work. The inability of the regular legislative process to meaningfully act on this couldn't be clearer." They were right: their proposal was defeated by a filibuster and the president formed a deficit commission by executive order instead.

As for foreign policy and national security, Congress has so abdicated its role over war and diplomacy that Garry Wills, in his new book, *Bomb Power*, says that we've been left with an "American monarch," which is only slightly scarier-sounding than the "unitary executive" theory that the Bush administration advocated and implemented.

This is not a picture of a functioning legislature.

Some might throw up their hands and welcome the arrival of outside cavalries, of rule by commissions and central banks and executive agencies. But there is a cost when Congress devolves power to others. The American public knew much more about the stimulus than about the Federal Reserve's "quantitative easing" program because Congress is much more accessible and paid more attention by the media. The EPA can impose blunt regulations on polluters, but it can't put a price on carbon in order to create a real market for cleaner energy. The debt commission's recommendations will still require a congressional vote. When Congress doesn't work, the federal government doesn't work, no matter how hard it tries.

III. So why doesn't Congress work? The simplest answer is that the country has changed, and Congress has not changed alongside it. Congress used to function despite its extraordinary minority protections because the two parties were ideologically diverse. Democrats used to provide a home to the Southern conservatives known as the Dixiecrats. The GOP used to include a bloc of liberals from the Northeast. With the parties internally divided and different blocs arising in shifting coalitions, it wasn't possible for one party to pursue a strategy of perpetual obstruction. But the parties have become ideologically coherent, leaving little room for cooperation and creating new incentives for minority obstruction.

Take the apparent paradox of the filibuster. It is easier than at any other point in our history to break a filibuster. Until 1917, there was no way to shut down debate, and until 1975, it took 67 votes rather than today's 60. And yet, the United States Senate had to break more filibusters in 2009 than in the 1950s and 1960s combined.

"It's not uncommon today to have things filibustered that, once they get past the filibuster, are passed unanimously," complains Bayh. "So it's clearly for the purpose of preventing action, not because of any underlying, substantive disagreement." Even Bill Frist, the former Republican Senate majority leader, has been surprised by the Senate's embrace of the tactic. "Compared to 10 years ago, 15 years ago, 20 years ago," he said during an appearance on MSNBC, "it's being used way too much."

The problem has become sufficiently severe that senators, who normally cling to their institutional traditions like Vatican cardinals, are talking about addressing it. "Next Congress," Harry Reid said to a group of reporters in March, "we are going to take a look at the filibuster. And we're going to make some changes in it."

But the rise of the filibuster is not just a case of rules-gone-wild: it's evidence of a broader polarization in the United States Congress. As the party heretics lost or switched sides, Republicans and Democrats found themselves more often in agreement with themselves and less often in agreement with each other. According to the political scientists Nolan McCarty, Keith T. Poole, and Howard Rosenthal, Democrats and Republicans now vote against each other more regularly than at any time since Reconstruction.

As the Reconstruction watermark suggests, polarized parties are often the result of a polarized country. In this case, it's the opposite. We are no more divided than we were in the 1950s and '60s, when civil rights and the Vietnam War and the feminist revolution split the country. But where the legislative process once worked to harmonize those differences, today it accentuates them. "When the public sees all Democrats on one side of the issue and all Republicans on the other, it's a cue," explains Ron Brownstein, author of The Second Civil War. "And so people's opinions harden, which in turn hardens the politicians on both sides. Then you have the increasingly politicized media, and the activist groups launching primaries. It's all a machine where the whole system is working to amplify our differences."

Senate Republican leader Mitch McConnell said as much . . . in an interview with National Journal. "Whether it became the stimulus, the budget, Guantánamo, health care," he said, "what I tried to do and what John [Boehner] did very skillfully, as well, was to unify our members in opposition to it. Had we not done that, I don't think the public would have been as appalled as they became."

Minority obstruction works because voters and the media often blame the majority. If nothing is getting done and the two sides bicker ceaselessly, it seems sensible to blame the people who are running the place.

But the lesson that the minority could prosper if Washington failed was a bad one for the system to learn. The rules of the United States Congress made it possible for the minority to make the majority fail by simply obstructing their agenda. And so they did. Republicans won in 1994, after killing health-care reform. Democrats adopted the tactic a decade later, taking Congress back in 2006 after killing Social Security privatization. This year, Republicans' strategy was to kill health-care reform again. That's what Sen. Jim DeMint meant when he promised conservative activists that "if we're able to stop Obama on this, it will be his Waterloo. It will break him."

What's important about all those examples is that at no point did the minority party come to the table and propose a serious alternative. Republicans left the health-care system to deteriorate, and Bob Dole went so far as to vote against two bills that had his name on them in the mid-'90s. Democrats enforced a simple proposition in the Social Security fight: there would be no Democratic Social Security reform bill. This year Sen. Lamar Alexander gave the introductory remarks for the Republicans at the president's recent health-care summit. Alexander said the Republicans—the party that pushed No Child Left Behind, the Iraq War, the Medicare prescription-drug benefit, and a total restructuring of the tax code—had come to the conclusion that the United States Congress shouldn't attempt "comprehensive" reforms.

The strategy behind all this is to deny the other side an accomplishment, not put the minority's stamp of approval on a bill that would strengthen the majority's campaign for reelection. Obstruction, not input, has become the minority's credo. And that means gridlock, not action, has become Washington's usual signature.

IV. We like to think of American politics in terms of individuals. Candidates promise to bring a businessman's eye to Congress, or to be an independent voice from Massachusetts. They tell us about their families and their life trials. By the end of most campaigns, we could pick the winner's golden retriever out of a lineup if we had to.

This is a terrible error, because it leads us to change individuals when we need to change the system. And here is the system's problem: the minority wins when the majority fails, and the minority has the power to make the majority fail. Since the rules work no matter which party is in the minority, it means no one can ever govern.

We've become so accustomed to the current state of affairs that some think it core to the functioning of our democracy. "It's called the filibuster," Senator Gregg lectured Democrats from the floor of the Senate. "That's the way the Senate was structured. . . . The Founding Fathers realized when they structured this[;] they wanted checks and balances."

In fact, the filibuster was not an invention of the Founding Fathers. It was an accident: in the early 19th century, the Senate cleaned out its rule book and deleted the provision that let them call a vote to move from one issue to another. It took decades until anybody realized the filibuster had been created.

But Gregg is right to emphasize the importance of checks and balances to the system. The problem is that gridlock—which is partly the result of the filibuster—is eroding them. If the minority is always obstructing, then Congress can never govern. And when Congress can't act, the body cedes power to others. That worries longtime observers of the institution. "The Founders would be appalled at the notion of Congress delegating its fundamental lawmaking responsibilities to others," says Norm Ornstein, a congressional expert at the American Enterprise Institute.

Meanwhile, those who can act gain power at the expense of the Congress. The office of the president has grown in stature and authority. Early presidents delivered the State of the Union as a written letter because giving a big, dramatic speech to Congress would have been seen as overstepping the boundaries of the executive office. Modern presidents use the State of the Union to set the legislative agenda for Congress's next session, a development that would have shocked the Founders.

But it makes sense to us. The president is the main character in the media's retelling of our politics. His approval ratings are more important than the approval ratings of Congress even when we are voting only for congressmen. And it's getting worse: the political scientist Frances Lee has found that on average, each successive Congress spends a larger percentage of its time on the president's agenda than did its predecessor. The result is that there's the president's party in Congress, which mostly tries to help him out, and the opposition party, which tries to hinder him.

Like a parliamentary system, our politics is now defined by tightly knit teams and organized around the leader of the party or government. When Republicans controlled Congress in the early 2000s, they were so subjugated to the White House that Frist was handpicked by President Bush as the Republican Senate leader when Trent Lott, at Bush's urging, resigned over controversial comments he made.

But unlike a parliamentary system, our institutions are built to require minority cooperation. "We are operating in what amounts to a parliamentary system without majority rule," writes Brownstein in a recent National Journal column. "A formula for futility."

V. Sen. Michael Bennett, a Democrat from Colorado, is an expert at assessing and repairing failing institutions. He began in the world of corporate debt restructuring and recently ran Denver's public schools. The difficulty with saving troubled organizations, he says, is that the creditors and interests fight over the remains rather than banding together to nurse the body back to health. "Every one of those negotiations was about getting people to see their self-interest in moving the institution forward," he recalls.

Last year he was appointed to the United States Senate. After a year in the body, what he sees looks uncomfortably familiar: a culture of mistrust in an institution that requires radical transformation. Stakeholders ferociously trying to eke out every last advantage, and in doing so, destroying the very thing they all have a stake in.

Polls back him up: a recent Gallup survey found that only 18 percent of Americans approve of the job Congress is doing. Compare that with the president's approval ratings, which hover around 50 percent—despite the fact that Congress is largely just considering the president's agenda. One of the implications of these numbers: Americans are so disgusted by Congress that they don't trust it to do anything big. But our problems aren't politely waiting around until Congress gets its act together.

So how to change Congress? Well, carefully. Reform may be impossible in the day-to-day context, as the minority cannot unilaterally disarm itself. But the day-to-day context isn't the only possible context. "You have to do the John Rawls thing," says John Sides, a political scientist at George Washington University. "Go behind the veil of ignorance. Figure out the system we'd want without knowing who will be in charge or what they will be doing."

This work should start with a bipartisan group of legislators charged with reforming the rules that Congress works by, but their recommendations should only go into force in six or eight years, when no one knows who will hold the gavel. That lets everyone think of themselves as a potential majority as well as an embattled minority, and more important, it lets members of Congress focus on the health of the institution rather than their fortunes in the next election. It lets Congress be Congress again, if only in theory.

As for what the rules should say, the technical details should be hashed out by smart people from both parties. But the place to start is by ridding the Senate of the filibuster and its lesser-known friends (holds, unanimous consent to work for longer than two hours at a time, and so on), admitting that they are no longer appropriate given the polarizing realities of our politics.

That may seem like a radical change, but recall that the filibuster is an accident, and there is nothing radical or strange about majority voting: we use it for elections (Scott Brown won with 51 percent of the vote, not 60 percent), Supreme Court decisions, and the House of Representatives. As for a majority using its power unwisely, elections can remedy that. And voters can better judge Washington based on what it has done than on what it has been obstructed from doing.

The irony is that getting rid of the rules meant to ensure bipartisanship may actually discourage partisanship. Obstructionism is a good minority strategy as long as it actually works to stymie the majority's agenda and return you to power. But if it just means you sit out the work of governance while the majority legislates around you, your constituents and interest groups will eventually begin demanding that you include them in the process. And that's as it should be: we hire legislators to legislate. We need a system that encourages them to do so.

**NO**

# Public Criticisms of Congress

**M**any Americans might go along with my general explanation of how Congress works but still feel that it doesn't work particularly well. Public approval of how Congress is handling its job has typically been very low in recent decades, usually hovering around a 40 percent approval rating—sometimes going higher, sometimes falling below 30 percent.

I heard numerous criticisms of Congress while serving, often in fairly blunt terms. Many of the criticisms seemed to be quite perceptive; others were fairly far off the mark—such as when people thought that as a member of Congress I received a limousine and chauffeur, or enjoyed free medical care, or didn't pay Social Security or income taxes. Even though the attacks were sometimes unpleasant, I always felt it was important for constituents to relay their complaints about Congress, and I never took them lightly. When people are upset about Congress, it undermines public confidence in government and fosters cynicism and disengagement. In a representative democracy like ours, in which Congress must reflect the views and interests of the American people as it frames the basic laws of the land, it really does matter what people think about Congress.

This chapter will sort through several of the main public criticisms of Congress and how it works.

## "Legislators Are a Bunch of Crooks"

Several years ago, I was watching the evening news on television when the anchorman announced the death of Wilbur Mills, the legendary former chairman of the House Ways and Means Committee. There was a lot he could have said. He might have recounted the central role Mills had played in creating Medicare. Or he might have talked about how Mills helped to shape the Social Security system and draft the tax code. But he didn't. Instead, he recalled how Mills's career had foundered after he had been found early one morning with an Argentinean stripper named Fanne Foxe. And then he moved on to the next story.

One of the perks of being chairman of an influential committee in Congress, as I was at the time, is that you can pick up the telephone and get through to television news anchors. Which I did: I chided him for summing up the man's career with a scandal. Much to my surprise, he apologized.

The fact is, though, he wasn't doing anything unusual. Americans of all stripes like to dwell on misbehavior by members of Congress. We look at the latest scandal and assume that we're seeing the *real* Congress. But we're not. People might hear repeatedly in the media about missteps, but they hear very little about the House leader who went home on weekends to pastor his local church, or the congressman who devoted decades to championing the needs of the elderly, or the senator who spent one day each month working in a local job to better understand the needs of constituents, or the many members who worked behind the scenes in a bipartisan way to reach the delicate compromises needed to make the system work.

Nor do I see members of Congress as basically out to enrich themselves at the public trough. During my time in office—when I heard numerous complaints about congressional "pay-grabs"—the salaries of members didn't even keep up with inflation. The pay I received in my last year in Congress was $20,000 *less* than if my 1965 pay had been adjusted for inflation. For most members, it is not the money that attracts them to public service; most could be making more in the private sector.

I don't want to claim that all members are saints and that their behavior is impeccable. Improper conduct does occur. Yet I agree with the assessment of historian David McCullough: "Congress, for all its faults, has not been the unbroken parade of clowns and thieves and posturing windbags so often portrayed. What should be spoken of more often, and more widely understood, are the great victories that have been won here, the decisions of courage and vision achieved."

Probity in Congress is the rule rather than the exception, and most experts on Congress agree that it has gotten better over the years. A personal example: Back in the early 1970s, I made an argument in a committee hearing one day favoring military aid for one of our allies. When I got back to my office, I discovered a delegation from that country waiting for me; they wanted to thank me with a fat honorarium, a trip to their country, and an honorary degree from one of their universities. I declined.

The point here isn't my purity. It's that at the time this happened, there was nothing improper about their offer. Today, there would be. When I arrived in Congress, members could accept lavish gifts from special interests, pocket campaign contributions in their Capitol offices, and convert their campaign contributions to personal use. And they were rarely punished for personal corruption. None of that would be tolerated now.

Things still aren't perfect. . . . But the ethical climate at the Capitol is well ahead of where it was a couple of decades ago. And, I might add, it is well ahead of the public perception. From my experience in Congress, getting to know hundreds of members of Congress well over the years, my clear impression is that the vast majority would whole-heartedly agree with Representative Barbara Jordan: "It is a privilege to serve people, a privilege that must be earned, and once earned, there is an obligation to do something good with it."

# "There's Too Much Wasteful, Pork-Barrel Spending by Congress"

Some years back, I was at a public meeting in Tell City, Indiana, when one of its citizens stood up to take me and my colleagues to task for our devotion to pork-barrel spending. How in good conscience, he wanted to know, could we spend so much of the public's money on frivolous projects designed only to get us reelected?

My first instinct was to ask him to step outside—but not in the way you might think. To understand why, you have to know a little about Tell City. It is a small town in southern Indiana, founded by Swiss settlers, not far from where Abraham Lincoln ran a ferry across the mouth of the Anderson River as a young man. What you notice in Tell City, though, is a much bigger river, the Ohio, which runs along the edge of its downtown. Indeed, between the building I was standing in and thousands of cubic feet of water lay only a few yards of ground and a levee. And the levee, as you've probably guessed, was built with federal money. If it weren't for this "pork-barrel" project, a good bit of Tell City would long since have been swept away. Pork, I told my audience, is in the eye of the beholder.

The vast majority of federal spending, I would argue, goes to important, widely supported uses. After all, more than half of total federal spending each year goes just for two things—national defense and seniors programs, both very popular. Yet I would agree that you can find some mighty debatable appropriations in each year's federal budget—$1.5 million aimed at refurbishing a statue in one powerful senator's state, $650,000 for ornamental fish research, $90,000 for the National Cowgirl Museum and Hall of Fame, and millions for various memorials and special projects that, in the scheme of things, will benefit relatively few Americans. Congress never fails to provide plenty of material for groups that make it their business to uncover questionable spending.

But think for a moment about what we characterize as "pork-barrel spending." Much of it is for infrastructure: highways, canals, reservoirs, dams, and the like. There's money for erosion-control projects, federal buildings, and military installations. There's support for museums and arts centers. There's backing for academic institutions, health-care facilities, and job-training institutes. All of these have some value and indeed may prove important to lots of people. When it comes to infrastructure spending, "pork-barrel projects" are rarely worthless. Members of Congress know in considerable detail the needs of their district or state, often better than the unelected federal bureaucrat who would otherwise decide where the money goes. We shouldn't fall into the trap of thinking that simply because a senator or representative directs the money to a specific project, it's waste, whereas if a bureaucrat or even the president does, it's not.

At the same time, my scolder in Tell City was on to something. While "pork" may provide valuable support to worthy projects, it can also shore up projects that most of the country would rightly question. The problem is, Congress often doesn't do a good job of distinguishing between the two.

To begin with, pork-barrel projects are frequently inserted by powerful members in spending bills surreptitiously, literally in the dark of night. It may happen within a day of the final vote on a spending measure, and most legislators don't even notice. Nothing is more frustrating for members than to vote for major national legislation only to discover later that it also contained obscure pork-barrel items like a Lawrence Welk memorial. And when legislators do notice a particular project and have concerns about it, they are often reluctant to object, because they may have legislation or projects of their own they don't want to put at risk.

The current process frequently doesn't allow Congress to weigh the relative merit of spending projects, to look at the interests of the country as a whole, or to weigh the needs of one region against another before deciding how to spend the public's money. The problem is not so much that the spending is wasted (it usually does some good) but whether it could better be spent for other projects. Congress often ignores this question and simply provides the money at the request of a member who is powerful or whose vote is badly needed.

We do need to recognize . . . that much of what Congress passes has an important impact on our lives. But we also need to focus more on wasteful spending, going after the bad apples that get all the attention. A few years ago when I was still in Congress, a reform committee I headed up recommended requiring that no bill could be voted on until all of the funding it earmarked for individual projects was listed clearly in publicly available reports. That would force proponents to justify publicly their provisions for special projects and would help ensure that fewer wasteful projects will pass. Sunshine is still the best disinfectant for wasteful proposals. And on that, I think my critic from Tell City and I could both agree.

## "Legislators Just Bicker and Never Get Anything Done"

One of the most common criticisms of Congress is that members spend too much time arguing. I must have heard it a thousand times: Why can't you folks get together?

Congress is generally perceived as the "broken branch" of government, unable to work together to carry out the nation's wishes. Sometimes the language during debates gets a little rough, such as when a member in 1875 described another as "one who is outlawed in his own home from respectable society; whose name is synonymous with falsehood; who is the champion, and has been on all occasions, of fraud; who is the apologist of thieves; who is such a prodigy of vice and meanness that to describe him would sicken imagination and exhaust invective." These comments make the recent partisan squabbling almost sound mild.

The perception of Congress as paralyzed by its own internal bickering comes up in most discussions of the institution, and it is one that matters. Surveys show it is a major factor in the American public's lack of confidence in Congress.

People get upset because they think that everyone agrees on what's right and necessary, and they can't understand why Congress doesn't simply implement the consensus. Yet the truth is that there is far less consensus in the country than is often thought. It is very difficult to get agreement among a broad cross-section of Americans on current major political issues. Most years there is little agreement on what the main issues are, let alone on what specific steps should be taken to address them. The devil—and the dispute—is often in the details.

Most bills passed by Congress actually receive fairly broad, bipartisan support. Yet dispute and delay often occur because it's a tough and tedious job making federal policy. The issues before Congress are much more numerous than in past years, often very complicated and technical, and intensely debated, with a large number of sophisticated groups knowing that key policies and millions of dollars can hinge on every word or comma. The great variety of our nation's races, religions, regional interests, and political philosophies all bring their often-conflicting views to Congress. It's the job of the House and Senate to hear all sides and to search for a broadly acceptable consensus.

There is bound to be bickering when you bring together 535 duly elected representatives and senators—all of whom feel strongly about issues, all of whom want to represent the best interests of their constituents. People shouldn't fall off their chairs because they see heated debate; that's how we thrash things out in a democratic society.

Much of what the public dislikes is part of the process. We could have chosen to have all decisions made by a single ruler at the top, but that's not the kind of government we wanted. Congress was set up as the forum in which strongly held differences would be aired; conflict is built into the system. Allowing all sides a chance to be heard on the most difficult issues facing our nation almost ensures that the debate will at times be contentious, but it also helps to keep our country from ripping apart.

Dispute is different from dysfunction, and results are what count. Intense debate doesn't mean that issues cannot be resolved. It's just that resolving them can be frustrating and time-consuming. I remember many conversations with disgruntled constituents over the years when I urged patience and suggested that they judge Congress by the final results, not by the bickering they might see during the process.

I'm not defending strongly partisan or harsh personal attacks. Certainly things can sometimes go too far and get out of hand. And Congress does have various means for handling such cases—the member in 1875 was in fact formally censured by the House for his remarks. But overall, people should expect some bickering and arguing within Congress. A democracy without conflict is not a democracy. . . .

## "Congress Almost Seems Designed to Promote Total Gridlock"

People will often complain about a "do-nothing" Congress and think much of the fault lies in the basic design of Congress. When a single senator can hold up action on a popular measure, when thirty committees or subcommittees are all reviewing the same bill, when a proposal needs to move not just through both the House and Senate but also through their multilayered budget, authorization, and appropriations processes, when floor procedures are so complex that even members serving several years can still be confused by them—how can you expect to get anything done?

This feeling is magnified by the major changes American society has undergone in recent decades. The incredible increase in the speed of every facet of our lives from communication to transportation, has made many people feel that the slow, untidy, deliberate pace of Congress is not up to the demands of modern society.

It is not now, nor has it ever been, easy to pass legislation through Congress. But there is actually a method to the madness, and basic roadblocks were put into the process for a reason. We live in a great big complicated country, with enormous regional, ethnic, and economic diversity; it is, quite simply, a difficult country to govern. Moving slowly is required for responsiveness and deliberation.

The quest for consensus within Congress can be painfully slow. Issues involving spending and taxes, health care, and access to guns and abortion stir strong emotions and don't submit easily to compromise. Inside-the-Beltway scuffling annoys many Americans, but think about it: Do we really want a speedy system in which laws would be pushed through before a consensus develops? Do we really want a system in which the viewpoint of the minority gets trampled by a rush to action by the majority? Certainly reforms can be made to improve the system, but the basic process of careful deliberation, negotiation, and compromise lies at the very heart of representative democracy. Ours is not a parliamentary system; the dawdling pace comes with the territory.

We misunderstand Congress's role if we demand that it be a model of efficiency and quick action. Our country's founders never intended it to be. They clearly understood that one of the key roles of Congress is to slow down the process—to allow tempers to cool and to encourage careful deliberation, so that unwise or damaging laws do not pass in the heat of the moment and so that the views of those in the minority get a fair hearing. That basic vision still seems wise today. Proceeding carefully to develop consensus is arduous and exasperating, but it's the only way to produce policies that reflect the varied perspectives of a remarkably diverse citizenry. People may complain about the process, yet they also benefit from its legislative speed bumps when they want their views heard, their interests protected, their rights safeguarded. As Sam Rayburn used to say: "One of the wisest things ever said was, 'Wait a minute.'"

. . . I certainly recognize that sometimes there are too many roadblocks in the system and Congress needlessly gets bogged down. Some streamlining and institutional reform is often needed, and I've been involved in many of those reform efforts. Yet I still believe that the fundamental notion that the structure of Congress should contain roadblocks and barriers to hasty action and unfair action makes sense for our country and needs to be protected and preserved. . . .

## "There's Too Much Money in Politics Today"

People hear the stories about all the fund-raising that members must do today, and so they believe that Congress is a "bought" institution. Often they would tell me that in our system dollars speak louder than words and that access is bought and sold. By a four-to-one margin, Americans believe that elected officials are influenced more by pressures from campaign contributors than by what is in the best interests of the country.

The problem of money in politics has been with us for many years. But it has really emerged as a serious problem in recent decades with the advent of television advertising. The biggest portion of my $1 million campaign budget—for a largely rural seat in southern Indiana—went for television.

Having experienced it firsthand, it is clear to me that the "money chase" has gotten out of hand. A lot of money from special interests is floating around Capitol Hill—in fact, far too much money. I believe it's a problem we ignore at our own peril.

To be fair, many of the claims of special interests buying influence in Congress are overstated. I would be the last to say that contributions have no impact on a member's voting record. But it should also be kept in mind that most of the money comes from groups who already share your views on the issues and want to see you reelected, rather than from groups who are hoping to change your mind. In addition, many influences shape members' voting decisions—including their assessment of the arguments, the opinions of experts and colleagues, their party's position, and, most importantly, what their constituents want. In the end, members know that if their votes aren't in line with what their constituents want, they simply won't be reelected. And that, rather than a campaign contribution, is what is foremost in their minds.

Yet it is still an unusual member of Congress who can take thousands of dollars from a particular group and not be affected by it at all. . . . Overall, this is an area in which I agree that significant reform is needed. It is also, unfortunately, an area in which there are no easy answers. . . .

## "Congress Is Run by Lobbyists and Special Interests"

Americans have different views of lobbyists and special interests. Some see them as playing an essential part in the democratic process. Others look at them with some skepticism, but understand that they have a role to play in developing policy. Yet most see them as sinister forces with too much control of Congress. The recent Enron and Arthur Andersen scandals, and revelations about those companies' extensive lobbying of Congress, have fed this cynicism about the hold that powerful private interests maintain over public policy. Americans continue to remain suspicious that Congress is manipulated by powerful wheeler-dealers who put enormous pressure on legislators or buy votes through extensive campaign contributions and other favors. It is not an unfounded concern, and it is not going to go away, no matter how fervently some might try to dismiss it.

Now, the popular view of lobbyists as nefarious fat cats smoking big cigars and handing out $100 bills behind closed doors is wrong. These days, lobbyists are usually principled people who recognize that their word is their bond. They are aggressive in seeking out members of Congress, offering to take them to dinner for a chance at a longer conversation, and operating from a carefully worked-out game plan that takes into account who might be persuaded to vote their way, when they ought to be approached, and whether they have interested constituents who can be used effectively to put pressure on them. Lobbying is an enormous industry today with billions of dollars riding on its outcomes. Special interest groups will often spend millions of dollars on campaigns to influence a particular decision—through political contributions, grassroots lobbying efforts, television advocacy ads, and the like—because they know they can get a lot more back than they spent. Lobbyists who can get the kind of language they want into a bill can reap very large rewards. They are very good at what they do, and members of Congress can sometimes be easily swayed by them.

The influence of lobbyists on the process is not as simple as it might appear. In the first place, "special interests" are not just the bad guys. If you're retired, or a homeowner, or use public transit, or fly on airplanes, or are concerned about religious freedom, there are people in Washington lobbying on your behalf. With an estimated 25,000 interest groups lobbying in Washington, you can be sure your views are represented in many ways. Advocacy groups help Congress understand how legislation affects their members, and they help focus the public's attention on important issues. They play a vital role in amplifying the flow of information that Thomas Jefferson called the "dialogue of democracy."

In addition, Congress often takes up controversial, attention-grabbing issues on which you'll find an entire spectrum of opinions. Public notice is high, a host of special interests are weighing in, and lobbyists as well as legislators themselves are all over the map. In these circumstances, the prospect is very small that any single interest group or lobbyist can disproportionately influence the results. Quite simply, there are too many of them involved for that to happen, and the process is too public.

Where you have to look out is when things get quiet, when measures come up that are out of the public eye. A small change in wording here, an innocuous line in a tax bill there—that's where specific groups can reap enormous benefits that might not have been granted had they been held up to close public scrutiny.

The answer, it seems to me, is not to decry lobbying or lobbyists. In our system of government, we make a lot of trade-offs, as James Madison warned more than two centuries ago when he argued that "factions" were part of the cost of maintaining a democracy. At heart, lobbying is simply people banding together to advance their interests, whether they are farmers or environmentalists or bankers. Belonging to an interest group—the Sierra Club, the AARP, the Chamber of Commerce—is one of the main ways Americans participate in public life these days.

When I was in Congress, I found that organized groups not only brought a useful perspective to the table. They also pointed out how a given measure might affect my constituents in ways I hadn't considered. Lobbyists are typically professionals with a variety of skills: They are experts in their subject, with a sophisticated knowledge of the political process and the ability to raise large sums of money and make campaign contributions. They maintain extensive contacts, can generate grassroots support, and often have experience in putting together winning coalitions. I came to think of lobbyists as an important part of the *public discussion* of policy.

I emphasize "public discussion" for a reason. Sunshine is a powerful disinfectant, and rather than trying to clamp down on lobbying, I believe we would be better off ensuring that it happens in the open and is part of the broader policy debate.

So our challenge is not to shut it down but to make sure it's a balanced dialogue and that those in power don't consistently listen to the voices of the wealthy and the powerful more intently than to others. Several legislative proposals have been made over the years that would help, including campaign finance reform, strict limits on gifts to members of Congress, travel restrictions for members and their staffs funded by groups with a direct interest in legislation, and effective disclosure of the role lobbyists play in drafting legislation. But in the end, something may be even more important: ongoing conversation between elected officials and the people they represent.

Under our system of government, there is absolutely nothing wrong with lobbyists advocating their point of view. Lobbying is a key element of the legislative process and part of the free speech guaranteed under our Constitution. Members of Congress, I would argue, have a responsibility to listen to lobbyists. But members also have a responsibility to understand where these lobbyists are coming from, to sort through what they are saying, and then to make a judgment about what is in the best interests of their constituents and the nation as a whole.

# EXPLORING THE ISSUE

## Is Congress a Dysfunctional Institution?

## Critical Thinking and Reflection

Lee Hamilton asks:

1. Do we really want a speedy system in which laws would be pushed through before a consensus develops?
2. Do we really want a system in which the viewpoint of the minority gets trampled by a rush to action by the majority?
3. What is your answer to the above questions?
4. Which side was right, and what does the debate tell us about the possibilities of "consensus" in today's Congress?

## Is There Common Ground?

In theory, at least, there is common ground between the assertion that bills should not be hastily run through Congress and the assertion that the passage of laws should not be hamstrung indefinitely by a minority. The problem comes in trying to craft a synthesis of those two assertions in today's polarized Congress. Some hope that a temporary solution—there is never a permanent one—will come when a new election gives one of the parties decisive control of both houses of Congress. Yet that happened in 2008, and, while it did result in the passage of at least three important pieces of legislation, it also set off a powerful backlash against the majority party in the political arena. Lee Hamilton's ideal of "consensus" remains elusive.

## Additional Resources

Richard Fenno's *Home Style: House Members in Their Districts* (Longman, 2002), originally published in 1978, shows how various members connect to their home districts, and reaches the unsurprising conclusion that those with the safest seats can spend most of their energies in Washington rather than back home. But in *Dilemmas of Representation: Local Politics, National Factors, and the Home Styles of Modern U.S. Congress Members* (State University of New York, 2007), Sally Friedman goes further, suggesting that the pull of national politics is even stronger now, affecting all Congress members in one way or another. Lawrence C. Dodd and Bruce Oppenheimer, in *Congress Reconsidered* (CQ Press, 2004), now in its eighth edition, assess the congressional reforms enacted during the 1970s, show how fragile the Democratic majority became at the end of the 1980s, and trace the goings-on in Congress since the Republicans took control in 1995. Although it does not bring us quite up to date on the new Democratic majority, it lets us see how the missteps of Republicans prepared the way for the shift. Diana Evans, *Greasing the Wheels: Using Pork Barrel Projects to Build Majority Coalitions in Congress* (Cambridge University Press, 2004), defends congressional "pork-barreling," arguing—as Lee Hamilton does—that it gets a lot of good things done. Charles Bancroft Cushman's, *An Introduction to the U.S. Congress* (Shape, 2006), is a compact volume that covers the subject competently for introductory students.

# ISSUE 8

## May Congress Require People to Buy Health Insurance?

**YES: George Caram Steeh**, from "Order Denying Plaintiff's Motion," *Thomas More Law Center v. Obama* (October 7, 2010)

**NO: Henry Hudson**, from "Memorandum Opinion," *Virginia v. Sebelius* (December 13, 2010)

### ISSUE SUMMARY

**YES:** George Caram Steeh, U.S. judge for the Southern Division of Michigan, maintains that there is a rational basis for the federal government's "individual mandate," for without it individuals could shift the cost of health insurance onto others, driving up the cost for everyone.

**NO:** Henry Hudson, U.S. judge for the Eastern District of Virginia, argues that the "individual mandate" exceeds the regulatory powers granted to the U.S. government under the Commerce Clause because it penalizes the mere failure to purchase a product.

Its critics call it "ObamaCare," but its short official name is the "Affordable Care Act" (ACA) of 2010. Its stated purposes are to ensure health care coverage for virtually all Americans while reducing costs. To accomplish these aims, the ACA requires individual Americans to purchase health insurance and requires insurance companies to abide by a variety of new regulations, including coverage for those with preexisting conditions.

During the 8-month battle over passage of the ACA, critics launched a variety of complaints about both the substance of the legislation and the methods used to pass it. One challenge to the bill, however, formally began only after its passage, and that was the claim that the new law, or a part of it anyway, violates the U.S. Constitution. Specifically, the charge was that it exceeds the powers granted to the Congress under Article I of the Constitution.

Article I grants many powers to Congress, including the power to "regulate Commerce with foreign Nations, and among the several States, and with the Indian Tribes." Particularly since the time of President Franklin Roosevelt's "New Deal" in the 1930s, the federal government has relied on this clause to justify the expansion of its powers. In 1940, an Ohio farmer named Roscoe Filburn was fined by a federal court for growing 11.9 more acres of wheat than he was allowed under the Agricultural Adjustment Act (AAA) of 1938. The AAA, a Depression-era law, limited the acreage on which farmers could grow crops on the theory that fewer bushels of farm products would mean higher prices for farmers, thus helping to stimulate the economy. Filburn appealed the ruling to the Supreme Court, charging that the federal government had exceeded its authority under the Commerce Clause. Much of those 11.9 acres, Filburn insisted, grew wheat never brought to market but consumed entirely on his farm. But in *Wickard v. Filburn* (1942), the Court rejected that argument, noting that even if the wheat is never marketed, "it supplies a need of a man who grew it which would otherwise be reflected by purchases in the open market." Multiply farmer Filburn by all the other farmers doing the same and in the aggregate it "would have a substantial effect in defeating and obstructing" the government's authority to stimulate commerce.

*Wickard v. Filburn* has never been overturned, but in recent years it has been qualified by the Court. In the 1995 case of *United States v. Lopez*, the Court struck down a federal law prohibiting the possession of guns in a public school zone. Congress, it held, exceeded its authority under the Commerce Clause. "The possession of a gun in a local school zone is in no sense an economic activity that must, through repetition elsewhere, substantially affect any sort of interstate commerce." And in *United States v. Morrison* (2000), which involved allegations of sexual assault and rape of a female student at Virginia Tech by members of the football team, the Court held unconstitutional a part of the Violence Against Women Act of 1994. Its reason: Congress lacks the power under the Commerce Clause to authorize civil suits for such cases. "Gender-motivated crimes of violence are not, in any sense of the phrase, economic activity."

One thread tying together *Wickard*, *Lopez*, and *Morrison* is the question of whether the activities alleged, growing wheat for home consumption, carrying a firearm in a school zone, committing rape and sexual assault, are properly called "commercial." In the two selections you are about to read, however, the issue is somewhat different. Purchasing health insurance is certainly a commercial activity. But the focus here is not on the purchase but the *non*-purchase of health insurance. The question is whether Congress has the power under the Commerce Clause to penalize an individual for *not* doing something. Of course, many non-activities, such as not paying federal taxes or not showing up for a federal trial, can be penalized by the federal government. But the question here is whether the federal government may penalize someone for not purchasing a certain product.

By the spring of 2011, four U.S. District Court judges had rendered decisions on the constitutionality of the ACA, two ruling in the affirmative and two in the negative. Coincidentally or not, the former were appointed by Democratic presidents and the latter by Republicans. In the following selections, George Caram Steeh, a Democrat-appointed judge for the Southern Division of Michigan, argues for the constitutionality of the "individual mandate" on grounds that, without it, individuals could refuse to buy health insurance until they were already sick, thus shifting the cost of insurance onto everyone else and driving up costs. Arguing on the other side is Henry Hudson, a Republican-appointed judge for the Eastern District of Virginia, who maintains that, by penalizing individuals for not buying health insurance, the "individual mandate" exceeds the regulatory powers granted to Congress under the Commerce Clause.

# YES ⤺

# Order Denying Plaintiff's Motion

Plaintiffs Thomas More Law Center ("TMLC"), . . . filed their complaint to challenge the constitutionality of the recently enacted federal law known as the "Patient Protection and Affordable Care Act" ("Health Care Reform Act" or "Act"), which was signed into law by President Obama on March 23, 2010. Plaintiffs seek a declaration that Congress lacked authority under the Commerce Clause to pass the Health Care Reform Act. . . .

## Factual Background

The Health Care Reform Act seeks to reduce the number of uninsured Americans and the escalating costs they impose on the health care system. In an attempt to make health insurance affordable and available, the Act provides for "health benefit exchanges," allowing individuals and small businesses to leverage their collective buying power to obtain prices competitive with group plans. It provides for incentives for expanded group plans through employers, affords tax credits for low-income individuals and families, Medicaid, and increases federal subsidies to state-run programs. The Act also prohibits insurance companies from denying coverage to those with pre-existing medical conditions, setting eligibility rules based on medical factors or claims experience, or rescinding coverage other than for fraud or misrepresentation.

Integral to the legislative effort to lower the cost of health insurance, expand coverage, and reduce uncompensated care is the so called minimum coverage provision which requires that every United States citizen, other than those falling within specified exceptions, maintain "minimum essential coverage" for health care for each month beginning in the year—. If an individual fails to comply with this requirement, the Act imposes a penalty to be included with a taxpayer's return.

Congress determined that the Individual Mandate "is an essential part of this larger regulation of economic activity," and that its absence "would undercut Federal regulation of the health insurance market." Congress found that without the Individual Mandate, the reforms in the Act, such as the ban on denying coverage based on pre-existing conditions, would increase the existing incentives for individuals to "wait to purchase health

United States District Court, October 7, 2010.

insurance until they needed care," which in turn would shift even greater costs onto third parties. Conversely, Congress found that by "significantly reducing the number of the uninsured, the requirement, together with the other provisions of this Act, will lower health insurance premiums." Congress concluded that the Individual Mandate "is essential to creating effective health insurance markets in which improved health insurance products that are guaranteed issue and do not exclude coverage of pre-existing conditions can be sold."

Plaintiff Thomas More Law Center ("TMLC") is a national public interest law firm based in Ann Arbor, Michigan. TMLC's employees receive health care through an employer health care plan sponsored and contributed to by TMLC. TMLC's health care plan is subject to the provisions and regulations of the Health Care Reform Act. The individual plaintiffs are United States citizens, Michigan residents, and federal taxpayers. None of them have private health care insurance, and each of them objects to being compelled by the federal government to purchase health care coverage. They contend that if they do not purchase health insurance and are forced to pay a tax, such tax money would go into the general fund and could go to fund abortions. Each of the individual plaintiffs objects to being forced by the federal government to contribute in any way to the funding of abortions. . . .

## Congressional Power to Regulate Interstate Commerce

The Individual Mandate requires that each "applicable individual" purchase health insurance, or be subject to a "penalty" or "Shared Responsibility Payment." The definition of "applicable individual" is "an individual other than" religious objectors who oppose health insurance in principle, non-residents or illegal residents, and incarcerated individuals. The Act, and the Individual Mandate, therefore, apply to everyone living in the United States, unless they are excepted.

The crux of plaintiffs' argument is that the federal government has never attempted to regulate inactivity, or a person's mere existence within our Nation's boundaries, under the auspices of the Commerce Clause. It is plaintiffs' position that if the Act is found constitutional, the Commerce Clause would provide Congress with the authority to regulate every aspect of our lives, including our choice to refrain from acting.

The Constitution grants Congress the authority to "regulate Commerce . . . among the several States. . . ." U.S. Const. art. I, § 8, cl. 3. In the body of jurisprudence interpreting the Commerce Clause, the Supreme Court has set out a three-prong analysis to determine if a federal law properly falls within this enumerated grant of authority. This inquiry presumes that Congress may regulate: (1) "the use of the channels of interstate commerce," such as regulations covering the interstate shipment of stolen goods; (2) to protect "the instrumentalities of interstate commerce, or persons or things in interstate commerce," such as legislation criminalizing the destruction of aircraft and theft from interstate commerce; and (3) "those activities that substantially affect interstate commerce." *United States v. Lopez* (1995); *see also, Perez v. United States* (1971). It is the last category, which deals with local activities that in themselves do not participate in interstate commerce, but which nonetheless "substantially affect" interstate commerce, which is the focus of this case.

"In assessing the scope of Congress' authority under the Commerce Clause," the court's task "is a modest one." *Gonzalez v. Raich* (2005). The court need not itself determine whether the regulated activities, "taken in the aggregate, substantially affect interstate commerce in fact, but only whether a 'rational basis' exists for so concluding."

The Supreme Court has expanded the reach of the Commerce Clause to reach purely local, non-commercial activity, simply because it is an integral part of a broader statutory scheme that permissibly regulates interstate commerce. Two cases, decided sixty years apart, demonstrate the breadth of the Commerce power and the deference accorded Congress's judgments.

In *Wickard v. Filburn* (1942), the Supreme Court upheld a penalty on wheat grown for home consumption despite the farmer's protest that he did not intend to put the commodity on the market. For purposes of Congress invoking its Commerce Clause power, the Court held it was sufficient that the existence of home-grown wheat, in the aggregate, could "suppl[y] a need of the man who grew it which would otherwise be reflected by purchases in the open market," thus undermining the efficacy of the federal price stabilization scheme. The Supreme Court's decision in *Gonzales v. Raich*, handed down in 2005, also supports the notion that the Commerce Clause affords Congress broad power to regulate even purely local matters that have substantial economic effects. There, the Supreme Court sustained Congress's authority to prohibit the possession of home-grown marijuana intended solely for personal use. The Controlled Substances Act "regulates the production, distribution, and consumption of commodities for which there is an established, and lucrative, interstate market." The restriction on home-grown marijuana for personal use was essential to the Act's broader regulatory scheme. In both *Wickard* and *Raich,* the Supreme Court sustained Congress's power to impose obligations on individuals who claimed not to participate in interstate commerce, because those obligations were components of broad schemes regulating interstate commerce.

Far from permitting the Commerce Clause to provide Congress with unlimited power to regulate, the Supreme Court has, in fact, placed limits on its reach. The Court was asked to review Congress's power to enact the Gun-Free School Zone Act of 1990 which criminalized possession of a gun within a statutorily defined school zone. *United States v. Lopez* (1995). The government argued that possession of a firearm in a school zone may result in violent crime, which can be expected to affect the national economy in several ways. First, the costs of violent crime are substantial, and via insurance those costs are spread throughout the population. Second, violent crime reduces the willingness of individuals to travel to areas that are perceived to be unsafe. Finally, the presence of guns in schools threatens the educational process, which will result in a less productive citizenry. The government concluded that these adverse effects on the nation's economic well-being gave Congress the power to pass the Gun-Free School Zone Act under the Commerce Clause. The Lopez Court held that Congress could not "pile inference upon inference" to find a link between the regulated activity and interstate commerce. Ultimately, the Court concluded that possessing a gun in a school zone was not an economic activity. Nor was the prohibition against possessing a gun "an essential part [ ] of a larger regulation of economic activity, in which the regulatory scheme could be undercut unless the intrastate activity were regulated." Clearly, the Gun-Free School Zone Act was first and foremost about providing a safe environment for students in the areas surrounding their schools, as opposed to an economic regulation.

Similarly, in *United States v. Morrison* (2000), the Court invalidated the cause of action created in the Violence Against Women Act, finding that any link between gender-motivated violence and economic activity could be established only through a chain of speculative assumptions. In declining to accept Congress's rationale for regulating under the Commerce Clause because gender-motivated violence deters "potential victims from traveling interstate, from engaging in employment in interstate business, . . . and by diminishing national productivity . . . ," the Court strove to preserve the "distinction between what is truly national and what is truly local."

In *Morrison* and *Lopez*, the Court found that the statutes at issue legislated non-commercial activities. Plaintiffs in the present case focus on the common fact that each of the regulations that survived Supreme Court scrutiny under the Commerce Clause regulated an economic "activity," as opposed to the "inactivity" they have demonstrated by merely existing and not purchasing health care insurance. The Supreme Court has always required an economic or commercial component in order to uphold an act under the Commerce Clause. The Court has never needed to address the activity/inactivity distinction advanced by plaintiffs because in every Commerce Clause case presented thus far, there has been some sort of activity. In this regard, the Health Care Reform Act arguably presents an issue of first impression. Plaintiffs contend that the court must engage in metaphysical gymnastics in order to find that "the act not to purchase insurance" is an affirmative economic activity, specifically "a choice regarding the method of payment." According to plaintiffs, this is the type of inferential chain prohibited by Lopez and its progeny.

In its legislative findings, Congress explains that it enacted the Health Care Reform Act to address a national crisis—an interstate health care market in which tens of millions of Americans are without insurance coverage and in which the cost of medical treatment has spiraled out of control. The government explains that as part of a comprehensive reform to reduce the ranks of the uninsured, the Act regulates economic decisions regarding the way in which health care services are paid for. The government contends that the Individual Mandate falls within Congress' authority under the Commerce Clause for two principal reasons. First, the economic decisions that the Act regulates as to how to pay for health care services have direct and substantial impact on the interstate health care market. Second, the minimum coverage provision is essential to the Act's larger regulation of the interstate business of health insurance.

## A. Substantial Effect on Interstate Commerce

There is a rational basis to conclude that, in the aggregate, decisions to forego insurance coverage in preference to attempting to pay for health care out of pocket drive up the cost of insurance. The costs of caring for the uninsured who prove unable to pay are shifted to health care providers, to the insured population in the form of higher premiums, to governments, and to taxpayers. The decision whether to purchase insurance or to attempt to pay for health care out of pocket, is plainly economic. These decisions, viewed in the aggregate, have clear and direct impacts on health care providers, taxpayers, and the insured population who ultimately pay for the care provided to those who go without insurance. These are the economic effects addressed by Congress in enacting the Act and the minimum coverage provision.

The health care market is unlike other markets. No one can guarantee his or her health, or ensure that he or she will never participate in the health care market. Indeed, the opposite is nearly always true. The question is how participants in the health care market pay for medical expenses—through insurance, or through an attempt to pay out of pocket with a backstop of uncompensated care funded by third parties. This phenomenon of cost-shifting is what makes the health care market unique. Far from "inactivity," by choosing to forgo insurance plaintiffs are making an economic decision to try to pay for health care services later, out of pocket, rather than now through the purchase of insurance, collectively shifting billions of dollars, $43 billion in 2008, onto other market participants. As this cost-shifting is exactly what the Health Care Reform Act was enacted to address, there is no need for metaphysical gymnastics of the sort proscribed by Lopez.

The plaintiffs have not opted out of the health care services market because, as living, breathing beings, who do not oppose medical services on religious grounds, they cannot opt out of this market. As inseparable and integral members of the health care services market, plaintiffs have made a choice regarding the method of payment for the services they expect to receive. The government makes the apropos analogy of paying by credit card rather than by check. How participants in the health care services market pay for such services has a documented impact on interstate commerce. Obviously, this market reality forms the rational basis for Congressional action designed to reduce the number of uninsureds.

The Supreme Court has consistently rejected claims that individuals who choose not to engage in commerce thereby place themselves beyond the reach of the Commerce Clause. See, e.g., Raich (rejecting the argument that plaintiffs' home-grown marijuana was "entirely separated from the market"); Wickard (home-grown wheat "competes with wheat in commerce" and "may forestall resort to the market"); Heart of Atlanta Motel v. United States (1964) (Commerce Clause allows Congress to regulate decisions not to engage in transactions with persons with whom plaintiff did not wish to deal). Similarly, plaintiffs in this case are participants in the health care services market. They are not outside the market. While plaintiffs describe the Commerce Clause power as reaching economic *activity,* the government's characterization of the Commerce Clause reaching economic *decisions* is more accurate.

## B. Essential to Broader Regulatory Scheme

The Act regulates a broader interstate market in health care services. This is not a market created by Congress, it is one created by the fundamental need for health care and the necessity of paying for such services received. The provision at issue addresses cost-shifting in those markets and operates as an essential part of a comprehensive regulatory scheme. The uninsured, like plaintiffs, benefit from the "guaranteed issue" provision in the Act, which enables them to become insured even when they are already sick. This benefit makes imposing the minimum coverage provision appropriate.

The Supreme Court recognized Congress's power to regulate wholly intrastate, wholly non-economic matters that form "an essential part of a larger regulation of economic activity, in which the regulatory scheme could be undercut unless the intrastate activity were regulated." Raich (quoting Lopez). [T]he Act will bar insurers from refusing to cover individuals with pre-existing conditions and from setting eligibility rules based on health status or claims experience. At that time, all Americans will be insurable. Without the minimum coverage provision, there would be an incentive for some individuals to wait to purchase health insurance until they needed care, knowing that insurance would be available at all times. As a result, the most costly individuals would be in the insurance system and the least costly would be outside it. In turn, this would aggravate current problems with cost-shifting and lead to even higher premiums. The prospect of driving the insurance market into extinction led Congress to find that the minimum coverage provision was essential to the larger regulatory scheme of the Act.

The minimum coverage provision, which addresses economic decisions regarding health care services that everyone eventually, and inevitably, will need, is a reasonable means of effectuating Congress's goal.

Henry Hudson

# Memorandum Opinion

In this case, the Commonwealth of Virginia (the "Commonwealth"), through its Attorney General, challenges the constitutionality of the pivotal enforcement mechanism of the health care scheme adopted by Congress in the Patient Protection and Affordable Care Act ("ACA" or "the Act"). At issue is Section 1501 of the Act, commonly known as the Minimum Essential Coverage Provision ("the Provision"). The Minimum Essential Coverage Provision requires that every United States citizen, other than those falling within specified exceptions, maintain a minimum level of health insurance coverage for each month beginning in 2014. Failure to comply will result in a penalty included with the taxpayer's annual return. . . .

Kathleek Sebelius, Secretary of the Department of Health and Human Services, in her Memorandum in Support of Defendant's Motion for Summary Judgment, aptly sets the framework of the debate: "[t]his case concerns a pure question of law, whether Congress acted within its Article I powers in enacting the ACA." At this final stage of the proceedings, with some refinement, the issues remain the same. . . .

The historically-accepted contours of Article I Commerce Clause power were restated by the Supreme Court in *Perez v. United States* (1971). The *Perez* Court divided traditional Commerce Clause powers into three distinct strands. First, Congress can regulate the channels of interstate commerce. Second, Congress has the authority to regulate and protect the instrumentalities of interstate commerce and persons or things in interstate commerce. Third, Congress has the power to regulate activities that substantially affect interstate commerce. It appears from the tenor of the debate in this case that only the third category of Commerce Clause power is presently at issue.

Critical to the Secretary's argument is the notion that an individual's decision not to purchase health insurance is in effect "economic activity." The Secretary rejects the Commonwealth's implied premise that a person can simply elect to avoid participation in the health care market. It is inevitable, in her view, that every individual—today or in the future—healthy or otherwise—will require medical care. She adds that a large segment of the population is uninsured and "consume[s] tens of billions of dollars in uncompensated care each year." The Secretary maintains that the irrefutable facts demonstrate that "[t]he conduct of the uninsured—their economic decision as to how to finance their health care needs, their actual use of the health care system, their

United States District Court, December 13, 2010.

migration in and out of coverage, and their shifting of costs on to the rest of the system when they cannot pay—plainly is economic activity."

The Secretary relies on what is commonly referred to as an aggregation theory, which is conceptually based on the hypothesis that the sum of individual decisions to participate or not in the health insurance market has a critical collective effect on interstate commerce. Congress may regulate even intrastate activities if they are within a class of activities that, in the aggregate, substantially affect interstate commerce. In support of this argument, the Secretary relies on the teachings of the Supreme Court in *Gonzales,* wherein the Court noted that "[w]hen Congress decides that the 'total incidence' of a practice poses a threat to a national market, it may regulate the entire class." *Gonzales v. Raich* (2005). In other words, her argument is premised on the theoretical effect of an aggregation or critical mass of indecision on interstate commerce.

The core of the Secretary's primary argument under the Commerce Clause is that the Minimum Essential Coverage Provision is a necessary measure to ensure the success of its larger reforms of the interstate health insurance market. The Secretary emphasizes that the ACA is a vital step in transforming a currently dysfunctional interstate health insurance market. In the Secretary's view, the key elements of health care reform are coverage of those with pre-existing conditions and prevention of discriminatory premiums on the basis of medical history. These features, the Secretary maintains, will have a material effect on the health insurance underwriting process, and inevitably, the cost of insurance coverage. Therefore, without full market participation, the financial foundation supporting the health care system will fail, in effect causing the entire health care regime to "implode." Unless everyone is required by law to purchase health insurance, or pay a penalty, the revenue base will be insufficient to underwrite the costs of insuring individuals presently considered as high risk or uninsurable. Therefore, under the Secretary's reasoning, since Congress has the power under the Commerce Clause to reform the interstate health insurance market, it also possesses, under the Necessary and Proper Clause, the power to make the regulation effective by enacting the Minimum Essential Coverage Provision. *United States v. Wrightwood Dairy Co.* (1942).

The Secretary seeks legal support for her aggregation theory in the Supreme Court's holding in *Wickard v. Filburn* (1942) and *Gonzales.* She maintains that the central question is whether there is a rational basis for concluding that the class of activities at issue, when "taken in the aggregate," substantially affects interstate commerce. In other words, "[w]here the class of activities is regulated and that class is within reach of federal power, the courts have no power 'to excise, as trivial, individual instances' of the class."

In *Wickard,* the Supreme Court upheld the power of Congress to regulate the personal cultivation and consumption of wheat on a private farm. The Court reasoned that the consumption of such non-commercially produced wheat reduced the amount of commercially produced wheat purchased and consumed nationally, thereby affecting interstate commerce. *Wickard* is generally acknowledged to be the most expansive application of the Commerce Clause by the Supreme Court, followed by *Gonzales.*

At issue in *Gonzales* was whether the aggregate effect of personal growth and consumption of marijuana for medicinal purposes under California law had a sufficient impact on interstate commerce to warrant regulation under the Commerce Clause. The Supreme Court concluded that "[l]ike the farmer in *Wickard*, respondents are cultivating, for home consumption, a fungible commodity for which there is an established, albeit illegal, interstate market. . . . Here too, Congress had a rational basis for concluding that leaving home-consumed marijuana outside federal control would similarly affect price and market conditions."

The Secretary emphasizes that the Commonwealth's challenge fails to appreciate the significance of the overall regulatory scheme and program at issue. Quoting from *Gonzales,* the Secretary notes that when "a general regulatory statute bears a substantial relation to commerce, the *de minimis* character of individual instances arising under the statute is of no consequence." Furthermore, the Secretary adds that "[f]or the provisions of '[a] complex regulatory program' to fall within [Congress's] commerce power, '[i]t is enough that the challenged provisions are an integral part of the regulatory program and that the regulatory scheme when considered as a whole satisfies this test.'"

When reviewing congressional exercise of the Commerce Clause powers, the Secretary cautions that a court "need not itself measure the impact on interstate commerce of the activities Congress sought to regulate, nor need the court calculate how integral a particular provision is to a larger regulatory program. The court's task instead is limited to determining 'whether a rational basis exists' for Congress's conclusions."

Because the Minimum Essential Coverage Provision is the linchpin which provides financial viability to the other critical elements of the overall regulatory scheme, the Secretary concludes that its adoption is within congressional Commerce Clause powers. She emphasizes that Congress "rationally found that a failure to regulate the decision to delay or forego insurance—*i.e.,* the decision to shift one's costs on to the larger health care system—would undermine the 'comprehensive regulatory regime.'" Therefore, the Secretary posits that because the guaranteed coverage and rate discrimination issues are unquestionably within the Commerce Clause powers, the mechanism chosen by Congress to effectuate those reforms, the Minimum Essential Coverage Provision, is also a proper exercise of that power—either under the Commerce Clause or the associated Necessary and Proper Clause.

The Secretary characterizes the Minimum Essential Coverage Provision as the vital kinetic link that animates Congress's overall regulatory reform of interstate health care and insurance markets. "[T]he Necessary and Proper Clause makes clear that the Constitution's grants of specific federal legislative authority are accompanied by broad power to enact laws that are 'convenient, or useful' or 'conducive' to the authority's 'beneficial exercise.'" *United States v. Comstock* (2010) (quoting *McCulloch v. Maryland* (1819)). The Secretary maintains that because Congress has rationally concluded "that the minimum coverage provision is necessary to make the other regulations in the Act effective," it is an appropriate exercise of the Necessary and Proper Clause. Again, the Secretary contends that the determination of whether the means adopted to attain its legislative goals are rationally related is reserved for Congress alone.

Although the Necessary and Proper Clause vests Congress with broad authority to exercise means, which are not themselves an enumerated power, to implement legislation, it is not without limitation. As the Secretary concedes, the means adopted must not only be rationally related to the implementation of a constitutionally-enumerated power, but it must not violate an independent constitutional prohibition. Whether the Minimum Essential Coverage Provision, which requires an individual to purchase health insurance or pay a penalty, is borne of a constitutionally-enumerated power, is the core issue in this case. As the Supreme Court noted in *Buckley v. Valeo* (1976). "Congress has plenary authority in all areas in which it has substantive legislative jurisdiction, . . . so long as the exercise of that authority does not offend some other constitutional restriction." The Commonwealth argues that the Provision offends a fundamental restriction on Commerce Clause powers.

In their opposition, the Commonwealth focuses on what it perceives to be the central element of Commerce Clause jurisdiction—economic activity. The Commonwealth distinguishes what was deemed to be "economic activity" in *Wickard* and *Gonzales,* namely a voluntary decision to grow wheat or cultivate marijuana, from the involuntary act of purchasing health insurance as required by the Provision. In *Wickard* and *Gonzales,* individuals made a conscious decision to grow wheat or cultivate marijuana, and consequently, voluntarily placed themselves within the stream of interstate commerce. Conversely, the Commonwealth maintains that the Minimum Essential Coverage Provision compels an unwilling person to perform an involuntary act and, as a result, submit to Commerce Clause regulation.

Drawing on the logic articulated in *United States v. Lopez* (1995) and *United States v. Morrison* (2000), which limited the boundaries of Commerce Clause jurisdiction to activities truly economic in nature and that actually affect interstate commerce, the Commonwealth contends that a decision not to purchase a product, such as health insurance, is not an economic *activity.* In *Morrison,* the Court noted that "[e]ven [our] modern-era precedents which have expanded congressional power under the Commerce Clause confirm that this power is subject to outer limits." The Court in *Morrison* also pointed out that "the existence of congressional findings is not sufficient, by itself, to sustain the constitutionality of Commerce Clause legislation." Finally, in *Morrison,* the Court rejected "the argument that Congress may regulate non-economic, violent criminal conduct based solely on the conduct's aggregate effect on interstate commerce." The Commonwealth urges a similar analysis in this case.

The Commonwealth does not appear to challenge the aggregate effect of the many moving parts of the ACA on interstate commerce. Its lens is narrowly focused on the enforcement mechanism to which it is hinged, the Minimum Essential Coverage Provision.

The Commonwealth argues that the Necessary and Proper Clause cannot be employed as a vehicle to enforce an unconstitutional exercise of Commerce Clause power, no matter how well intended. Although the Necessary and

Proper Clause grants Congress broad authority to pass laws in furtherance of its constitutionally-enumerated powers, its authority is not unbridled. As Chief Justice John Marshall observed in *McCulloch*, "[l]et the end be legitimate, let it be within the scope of the constitution, and all means which are appropriate, which are plainly adapted to that end, which are not prohibited, but consistent with the letter and spirit of the constitution, are constitutional."

More recently, in restating the limitations on the scope of the Necessary and Proper Clause, the Supreme Court defined the relevant inquiry, "we look to see whether the statute constitutes a means that is rationally related to the implementation of a constitutionally enumerated power." If a person's decision not to purchase health insurance at a particular point in time does not constitute the type of economic activity subject to regulation under the Commerce Clause, then logically an attempt to enforce such provision under the Necessary and Proper Clause is equally offensive to the Constitution.

The Secretary, in rebuttal, faults the Commonwealth's reasoning as overly simplistic. She argues that the Commonwealth's theory is dependent on which method a person chooses to finance their inevitable health care expenditures. If the costs are underwritten by an insurance carrier, it is activity; if the general public pays by default, it is passivity. She maintains that under the Commonwealth's reasoning, the former is subject to Commerce Clause powers, while the latter is not. The Secretary also points out that under the Commonwealth's approach, "it [is] unclear whether an individual became 'passive,' and therefore supposedly beyond the reach of the commerce power, if he dropped his policy yesterday, a week ago, or a year ago." She characterizes the Commonwealth's logic as untenable. . . .

Despite the laudable intentions of Congress in enacting a comprehensive and transformative health care regime, the legislative process must still operate within constitutional bounds. Salutatory goals and creative drafting have never been sufficient to offset an absence of enumerated powers. As the Supreme Court noted in *Morrison*, "[e]ven [our] modern-era of precedents which have expanded congressional power under the Commerce Clause confirm that this power is subject to outer limits." Congressional findings, no matter how extensive, are insufficient to enlarge the Commerce Clause powers of Congress.

In *Wickard* and *Gonzales*, the Supreme Court staked out the outer boundaries of Commerce Clause power. In both cases, the activity under review was the product of a self-directed affirmative move to cultivate and consume wheat or marijuana. This self-initialed change of position voluntarily placed the subject within the stream of commerce. Absent that step, governmental regulation could have been avoided.

In *Morrison* and *Lopez*, however, the Supreme Court tightened the reins and insisted that the perimeters of legislation enacted under Commerce Clause powers square with the historically-accepted contours of Article I authority delineated by the Supreme Court in *Perez v. United States* (1971). Pertinent to the immediate case, the Court in *Perez* stated that Congress has the power to regulate *activities* that substantially affect interstate commerce. In *Perez*, the Court upheld a federal prohibition on extortionate credit transactions, even though the specific transaction in question had not occurred in interstate commerce.

The Court in *Lopez* and *Morrison* constrained the boundaries of Commerce Clause jurisdiction to activities truly economic in nature and that had a demonstrable effect on interstate commerce. In *Lopez,* the Court found that the Gun-Free School Zones Act, which made it a federal offense for any individual knowingly to possess a firearm in a school zone, exceeded Congress's Commerce Clause authority. First, the Court held that the statute by its terms had nothing to do with commerce or any sort of economic enterprise. Second, it concluded that the act could not be sustained "under our cases upholding regulations of activities that arise out of or are connected with a commercial transaction, which viewed in the aggregate, substantially affects interstate commerce."

Later in *Morrison,* the Court concluded that the Commerce Clause did not provide Congress with the authority to impose civil remedies under the Violence Against Women Act. Despite extensive factual findings regarding the serious impact that gender-motivated violence has on victims and their families, the Court concluded that it was insufficient by itself to sustain the constitutionality of Commerce Clause legislation. The Court in *Morrison* ultimately rejected the argument that Congress may regulate noneconomic, violent criminal conduct based solely on that conduct's aggregated effect on interstate commerce.

In surveying the legal landscape, several operative elements are commonly encountered in Commerce Clause decisions. First, to survive a constitutional challenge the subject matter must be economic in nature and affect interstate commerce, and second, it must involve activity. Every application of Commerce Clause power found to be constitutionally sound by the Supreme Court involved some form of action, transaction, or deed placed in motion by an individual or legal entity. The constitutional viability of the Minimum Essential Coverage Provision in this case turns on whether or not a person's decision to refuse to purchase health care insurance is such an activity.

In her argument, the Secretary urges an expansive interpretation of the concept of activity. She posits that every individual in the United States will require health care at some point in their lifetime, if not today, perhaps next week or even next year. Her theory further postulates that because near universal participation is critical to the underwriting process, the collective effect of refusal to purchase health insurance affects the national market. Therefore, she argues, requiring advance purchase of insurance based upon a future contingency is an activity that will inevitably affect interstate commerce. Of course, the same reasoning could apply to transportation, housing, or nutritional decisions. This broad definition of the economic activity subject to congressional regulation lacks logical limitation and is unsupported by Commerce Clause jurisprudence.

The power of Congress to regulate a class of activities that in the aggregate has a substantial and direct effect on interstate commerce is well settled. This even extends to noneconomic activity closely connected to the intended market. But these regulatory powers are triggered by some type of self-initiated action. Neither the Supreme Court nor any federal circuit court of appeals has extended Commerce Clause powers to compel an individual to involuntarily enter the stream of commerce by purchasing a commodity in the private market. In doing so, enactment of the Minimum Essential Coverage Provision exceeds the Commerce Clause powers vested in Congress under Article I.

Because an individual's personal decision to purchase—or decline to purchase—health insurance from a private provider is beyond the historical reach of the Commerce Clause, the Necessary and Proper Clause does not provide a safe sanctuary. This clause grants Congress broad authority to pass laws in furtherance of its constitutionally-enumerated powers. This authority may only be constitutionally deployed when tethered to a lawful exercise of an enumerated power. As Chief Justice Marshall noted in *McCulloch,* it must be within "the letter and spirit of the constitution." The Minimum Essential Coverage Provision is neither within the letter nor the spirit of the Constitution. Therefore, the Necessary and Proper Clause may not be employed to implement this affirmative duty to engage in private commerce.

# EXPLORING THE ISSUE

## May Congress Require People to Buy Health Insurance?

## Critical Thinking and Reflection

1. What is the "commerce clause," and how can it be used to justify the requirement that people purchase health insurance?
2. Are you satisfied with the Obama administration's justification for its use? Why or why not?
3. During the confirmation hearings for Justice Elena Kagan, one of President Obama's nominees to the Supreme Court, Kagan was asked by a Senator to suppose that Congress passed a law saying "you have to eat three vegetables and three fruits each day." Would that be unconstitutional? "Sounds like a dumb law," she answered, but she didn't think it should be struck down by the courts. Do you agree? Why or why not?

## Is There Common Ground?

It is the nature of judicial proceedings that there isn't any common ground. One side wins the case and the other loses. Since this issue will be at the heart of the case now headed toward the Supreme Court on an expedited basis, we shall soon know whether Congress may require people to buy health insurance. What happens after that may indeed open up some room for compromise. If the so-called "individual mandate" is upheld, there may be room for some exemptions. (The Obama administration has already granted some.) If the mandate is struck down, other parts of Obamacare may still survive if enough Republican members of Congress find merit in them.

## Additional Resources

In the *New York Review of Books* ("Is Health Care Reform Unconstitutional?," February 24, 2011), David Cole defends the constitutionality of the ACA's individual mandate. "Absent a return to a constitutional jurisprudence that has been rejected for more than seventy years . . . the individual mandate is plainly constitutional." But in his blog, *Shameless Popery,* Joe Heschmeyer disagrees. "The absence of commerce isn't commerce. The power to regulate commerce doesn't mean the power to force commerce where none exists." See http://catholicdefense.blogspot.com/2011/02/why-obamacares-individual-mandate-is .html. Sally C. Pipes, in *The Truth About Obamacare* (Regnery, 2010), does not raise constitutional questions about the Affordable Health Care Act but denies that it will be either affordable or healthy, claiming that it makes health care more expensive and leads to deteriorating service. But in *U.S. News*'s online edition for December 22, 2009, John A. Farrell argues that "The Health Reform Bill Is a Win for the Middle Class." See  http://search.usnews.com/index_library/search ?keywords=Farrell%2C+the+health+reform+bill+is+a+win+for+the+middle+class&x= 16&y=10.

Dan T. Coenen, *Constitutional Law: The Commerce Clause* (Foundation Press, 2003), discusses the scope of the commerce power and federalism-based restrictions on that power in American jurisprudence.

# ISSUE 9

## Should the President Be Allowed "Executive Privilege"?

**YES: Mark J. Rozell**, from "Pro," in Richard J. Ellis and Michael Nelson, eds., *Debating the Presidency: Conflicting Perspectives on the American Executive* (CQ Press, 2006)

**NO: David Gray Adler**, from "Con," in Richard J. Ellis and Michael Nelson, eds., *Debating the Presidency: Conflicting Perspectives on the American Executive* (CQ Press, 2006)

### ISSUE SUMMARY

**YES:** Public policy professor Mark J. Rozell believes that executive privilege is needed for the proper functioning of the executive branch, because presidents need candid advice from their staffs.

**NO:** Political science professor David Gray Adler concludes that neither debate in the Constitutional Convention nor the text of the Constitution provide any support for the view that the Framers supported giving the president the power to conceal information from Congress.

**A**rticle II of the United States Constitution states: "The executive power shall be vested in a President of the United States of America." Apart from the president's power of appointment, Article II has little to add about the content and conduct of the executive power. (Even the president's power to veto legislation is described in Article I, under the powers of Congress.) Yet from the nation's beginning, presidents have extended their power, and sought to exempt it from oversight or overruling by Congress.

In 1792, when the House of Representatives requested documents relating to a failed military campaign, President George Washington decided that he would provide only such papers as the public good permitted. Four years later, Washington turned down a House request for documents relating to a recently adopted treaty. President Thomas Jefferson refused to allow two cabinet members to supply documents at the trial of Aaron Burr. President Andrew Jackson refused to give the Senate a paper he had read to executive department heads. President Abraham Lincoln refused to reveal his dispatches to a military commander.

President Dwight D. Eisenhower in 1953 was the first to call presidential defiance of Congress "executive privilege," when he refused to turn over to a Senate committee notes of his meetings with members of the U.S. Army, claiming that national security might be breached if administration officials were compelled to testify under oath.

President Richard Nixon cited executive privilege when he refused to turn over to a special prosecutor audiotapes of conversations in the Oval Office that were sought in connection with criminal charges that were being sought against members of his administration. The Supreme Court responded to Nixon's claim in 1974, when it acknowledged the validity of an appropriate claim of executive privilege, noting "the valid need for protection of communications between high government officials and those who advise and assist them in the performance of their manifold duties." The Court offered a defense of executive privilege that presidents have often since expressed: "Human experience teaches that those who expect public dissemination of their remarks may well temper candor with a concern for appearances and for their own interests to the detriment of the decision-making process."

But the Supreme Court went on to conclude that there can be no "absolute privilege," stating: "To read the Article II powers of the President as providing an absolute privilege as against a subpoena essential to enforcement of criminal statutes on no more than a generalized claim of the public interest in confidentiality of non-military and non-diplomatic discussions would upset the constitutional balance of 'a workable government' and gravely impair the role of the courts."

President Bill Clinton lost his claim of executive privilege in 1998 when a federal judge ruled that Clinton aides could be called to testify in the scandal involving the president's sexual relationship with Monica Lewinsky. Despite the ultimate rejection of executive privilege defenses by Presidents Nixon and Clinton, most presidential claims have been upheld by the courts or were not opposed by Congress.

The claim of executive privilege has been made for the vice president as well. The U.S. Supreme Court upheld Vice President Dick Cheney's refusal to reveal to Congress information regarding meetings he had with a taskforce regarding energy policy.

When President George W. Bush refused to allow administration officials to testify before a House committee on the circumstances relating to the firing of eight United States attorneys, who hold their posts at the pleasure of the president, the White House counsel defended "the constitutional prerogatives of the presidency." The issue of executive privilege became most controversial for the Bush presidency when it sought to defy congressional investigation over domestic surveillance and interrogation of prisoners taken in connection with the American war in Iraq.

Professors Mark J. Rozell and David Gray Adler offer opposing interpretations regarding the constitutional status, necessity, and desirability of the president's right to withhold information from Congress.

# YES ↵

# PRO

**C**ontroversies over executive privilege date back to the earliest years of the Republic. Although the phrase "executive privilege" was not a part of the nation's common language until the 1950s, almost every president has exercised some form of this presidential power.

Executive privilege is controversial because it is nowhere mentioned in the Constitution. That fact has led some observers to suggest that executive privilege does not exist and that the congressional power of inquiry is absolute. This view is mistaken. Executive privilege is an implied presidential power and is sometimes needed for the proper functioning of the executive branch. Presidents and their staffs must be able to deliberate without fear that their every utterance may be made public.

Granted, the power of executive privilege is not absolute. Like other constitutionally based powers, it is subject to a balancing test. Presidents and their advisers may require confidentiality, but Congress must have access to information from the executive branch to carry out its investigative function. Therefore, any claim of executive privilege must be weighed against Congress's legitimate need for information to carry out its own constitutional role. Yet the power of inquiry is also not absolute, whether it is wielded by Congress or by prosecutors.

Not all presidents have exercised executive privilege judiciously. Some have used it to cover up embarrassing or politically inconvenient information, or even outright wrongdoing. As it is with all other grants of authority, the power to do good things is also the power to do bad things. The only way to avoid the latter is to strip away the authority altogether and thereby eliminate the ability to do the former. Eliminating executive privilege would hamper the ability of presidents to discharge their constitutional duties effectively and to protect the public interest.

## The Need for Candid Advice

The constitutional duties of presidents require that they be able to consult with advisers without fear that the advice will be made public. If officers of the executive branch believe their confidential advice could be disclosed, the quality of that advice could be seriously damaged. Advisers cannot be completely honest and frank in their discussions if they know that their every word might be disclosed to partisan opponents or to the public. In *United States v. Nixon*

From *Debating the Presidency: Conflicting Perspectives on the American Executive* by Mark J. Rozell (CQ Press, 2006). Copyright © 2006 by CQ Press, a division of Congressional Quarterly, Inc. Reprinted by permission.

(1974), the Supreme Court recognized that the need for candid exchanges is an important basis for executive privilege:

> The valid need for protection of communications between high government officials and those who advise and assist them in the performance of their manifold duties . . . is too plain to require further discussion. Human experience teaches that those who expect public dissemination of their remarks may well temper candor with a concern for appearances and for their own interests to the detriment of the decision-making process. . . . The confidentiality of presidential communications . . . has constitutional underpinnings. . . . The privilege is fundamental to the operation of government and inextricably rooted in the separation of powers under the Constitution.

In 1979 the Court reiterated its support of executive privilege based on the need for a candid exchange of opinions among advisers. "Documents shielded by executive privilege," the Court explained, "remain privileged even after the decision to which they pertain may have been effected, since disclosure at any time could inhibit the free flow of advice, including analysis, reports and expression of opinions."

Although Congress needs access to information from the executive branch to carry out its oversight and investigative duties, it does not follow that Congress must have full access to the details of every executive branch communication. Congressional inquiry, like executive privilege, has limits. That is not to suggest that presidents can claim the need for candid advice to restrict any and all information. The president must demonstrate a need for secrecy in order to trump Congress's power of inquiry.

## Limits on Congressional Inquiry

Congress's power of inquiry, though broad, is not unlimited. A distinction must be drawn between sources of information generally and those necessary to Congress's ability to perform its legislative and investigative functions. There is a strong presumption of validity to a congressional request for information relevant to these investigative functions. The presumption weakens in the case of a congressional "fishing expedition"—a broad, sweeping quest for any and all executive branch information that might be of interest to Congress for one reason or another. Indeed, Congress itself has recognized that there are limits on its power of inquiry. For example, in 1879 the House Judiciary Committee issued a report stating that neither the legislative nor the executive branch had compulsory power over the records of the other. Congress gave the executive branch the statutory authority to withhold information when it enacted the "sources and methods proviso" of the 1947 National Security Act, the implementation provision of the 1949 CIA Act, and the 1966 Freedom of Information Act.

Nevertheless, critics of executive privilege argue that Congress has an absolute, unlimited power to compel disclosure of all executive branch information. Rep. John Dingell, D-Mich., for example, said that members of Congress "have the power under the law to receive each and every item in the hands of the government." But this expansive view of congressional inquiry is as wrong as the belief that the president has the unlimited power to withhold all information from Congress. The legitimacy of the congressional power of inquiry does not confer an absolute and unlimited right to all information. The debates at the 1787 Constitutional Convention and at the subsequent ratifying conventions provide little evidence that the framers intended to confer such authority on Congress. There are inherent constitutional limits on the powers of the respective governmental branches. The common standard for legislative inquiry is whether the requested information is vital to the Congress's law-making and oversight functions.

## The Other Branches and Confidentiality

Executive privilege can also be defended on the basis of accepted practices of secrecy in the other branches of government. In the legislative branch, members of Congress receive candid, confidential advice from committee staff and legislative assistants. Meanwhile, congressional committees meet on occasion in closed session to mark up legislation. Congress is not obligated to disclose information to another branch. A court subpoena will not be honored except by a vote of the legislative chamber concerned. Members of Congress enjoy a constitutional form of privilege that absolves them from having to account for certain official behavior, particularly speech, anywhere but in Congress. But as with the executive, this protection does not extend into the realm of criminal conduct.

Secrecy is found as well in the judicial branch. It is difficult to imagine more secretive deliberations than those that take place in Supreme Court conferences. Court observer David M. O'Brien refers to secrecy as one of the "basic institutional norms" of the Supreme Court. "Isolation from the Capitol and the close proximity of the justices' chambers within the Court promote secrecy, to a degree that is remarkable. . . . The norm of secrecy conditions the employment of the justices' staff and has become more important as the number of employees increases." Members of the judiciary claim immunity from having to respond to congressional subpoenas. The norm of judicial privilege also protects judges from having to testify about their professional conduct.

It is thus inconceivable that secrecy, so common to the legislative and judicial branches, would be uniquely excluded from the executive. Indeed, the executive branch regularly engages in activities that are secret in nature. George C. Calhoun explains that the executive branch "presents . . . matters to grand juries; assembles confidential investigative files in criminal matters; compiles files containing personal information involving such things as census, tax, and veterans information; and health, education and welfare benefits to name a few. All of these activities must, of necessity, generate a considerable amount of confidential information. And personnel in the executive branch . . . necessarily prepare many more confidential memoranda. Finally, they produce a considerable amount of classified information as a result of the activities of the intelligence community."

Legislative, judicial, and executive branch secrecy serves a common purpose: to arrive at policy decisions more prudent than those that would be made through an open process. And in each case, the end result is subject to scrutiny. Indeed, accountability is built into secretive decision-making processes, because elected public officials must justify the end result at some point.

# Giving Executive Privilege Its Due

The dilemma of executive privilege is how to permit governmental secrecy while maintaining accountability. On the surface, the dilemma is a difficult one to resolve: how can democratically elected leaders be held accountable when they are able to deliberate in secret or to make secretive decisions?

The post-Watergate period witnessed a breakdown in the proper exercise of executive privilege. Because of former president Richard Nixon's abuses, Presidents Gerald R. Ford and Jimmy Carter avoided using executive privilege. Ford and Carter still sought to preserve presidential secrecy, but they relied on other constitutional and statutory means to achieve that goal. President Ronald Reagan tried to restore executive privilege as a presidential prerogative, but he ultimately failed when congressional committees threatened administration officials with contempt citations and adopted other retaliatory actions to compel disclosure. President George Bush, like Ford and Carter before him, avoided executive privilege whenever possible and used other strategies to preserve secrecy. President Bill Clinton exercised executive privilege more often than all of the other post-Watergate presidents combined, but often improperly, such as in the investigation into his sexual relationship with White House intern Monica Lewinsky. President George W. Bush has exercised the privilege more sparingly than his predecessor, but he also has exercised this power in some questionable circumstances, such as his attempt to deny Congress access to decades-old Justice Department documents.

Thus in the post-Watergate era either presidents have avoided uttering the words "executive privilege" and have protected secrecy through other sources of authority (Ford, Carter, G. Bush), or they have tried to restore executive privilege and failed (Reagan, Clinton, G. W. Bush). Clinton's aggressive use of executive privilege in the Lewinsky scandal served to revive the national debate over this presidential power—a debate that continued into the Bush years. It is therefore an appropriate time to discuss how to restore a sense of balance to the executive privilege debate.

First, it needs to be recognized that executive privilege is a legitimate constitutional power—not a "constitutional myth." Consequently, presidents should not be devising schemes for achieving the ends of executive privilege while avoiding any mention of this principle. Furthermore, Congress (and the courts) must recognize that the executive branch—like the legislative and judicial branches—has a legitimate need to deliberate in secret and that every assertion of executive privilege is not a devious attempt to conceal wrongdoing.

Second, executive privilege is not an unlimited, unfettered presidential power. It should be exercised rarely and only for the most compelling reasons.

Congress has the right—and often the duty—to challenge presidential assertions of executive privilege.

Third, there are no clear, precise constitutional boundaries that determine, a priori, whether any particular claim of executive privilege is legitimate. The resolution to the dilemma of executive privilege is found in the political ebb and flow of the separation of powers system. Indeed, there is no need for any precise definition of the constitutional boundaries surrounding executive privilege. Such a power cannot be subject to precise definition, because it is impossible to determine in advance all of the circumstances under which presidents may have to exercise that power. The separation of powers created by the framers provides the appropriate resolution of the dilemma of executive privilege and democratic accountability.

Congress already has the institutional capability to challenge claims of executive privilege by means other than eliminating the right to withhold information or attaching statutory restrictions on the exercise of that power. For example, if members of Congress are not satisfied with the response to their demands for information, they have the option of retaliating by withholding support for the president's agenda or for the president's executive branch nominees. In one famous case during the Nixon years, a Senate committee threatened not to confirm a prominent presidential nomination until a separate access to information dispute had been resolved. That action resulted in President Nixon ceding to the senators' demands. If information can be withheld only for the most compelling reasons, it is not unreasonable for Congress to try to force the president's hand by making him weigh the importance of withholding the information against that of moving forward a nomination or piece of legislation. Presumably, information being withheld for purposes of vital national security or constitutional concerns would take precedence over pending legislation or a presidential appointment. If not, then there appears to be little justification in the first place for withholding the information.

Congress possesses many other means by which it can compel presidential compliance with requests for information. One of those is the control Congress maintains over the government's purse strings, which means that it holds formidable power over the executive branch. In addition, Congress often relies on the subpoena power and the contempt of Congress charge to compel release of withheld information. It is not merely the exercise of these powers that matters, but the threat that Congress may resort to such powers. Congress has successfully elicited information from the executive branch using both powers. During the Reagan years, for example, in several executive privilege disputes Congress prevailed and received all the information it had requested from the administration—but only after it subpoenaed documents and threatened to hold certain administration officials in contempt. The Reagan White House simply decided it was not worth the political cost to continue such battles with Congress. In these cases, the system worked as it is supposed to. Had the information in dispute been critical to national security or preserving White House candor, certainly Reagan would have taken a stronger stand to protect the documents.

In the extreme case, Congress also has the power of impeachment—the ultimate weapon with which to threaten the executive. Clearly, this congressional power cannot be routinely exercised as a means of compelling disclosure of information, and thus it will not constitute a real threat in commonplace information disputes. Nevertheless, when a scandal emerges of Watergate-like proportions and in which all other remedies have failed, Congress can threaten to exercise its ultimate power over the president. In fact, for a time in 1998 Congress considered an impeachment article against President Clinton for abuses of presidential powers, including executive privilege. Congress ultimately dropped that particular article.

In the vast majority of cases—and history verifies this point—it can be expected that the president will comply with requests for information rather than withstand retaliation from Congress. Presidential history is replete with examples of chief executives who tried to invoke privilege or threatened to do so, only to back down in the face of congressional challenges. If members of Congress believe that the executive privilege power is too formidable, the answer resides not in crippling presidential authority, but in exercising to full effect the vast array of powers already at Congress's disposal.

David Gray Adler

→ **NO**

# CON

Executive privilege—the claim that a president has the right to withhold information from Congress and the courts—has become a principal tool in the promotion of executive secrecy and deception. Executive secrecy represents a continual threat to the values and principles of the Republic. Some of the nation's darkest moments have stemmed from a presidential penchant for secrecy: the quagmire of Vietnam, the suppression of the *Pentagon Papers,* Watergate, the Iran-contra scandal, and President George W. Bush's obscurantism over the rationale for the invasion of Iraq.

The pernicious effects of executive secrecy have not deterred advocates of executive privilege from asserting its central importance to the president's performance of his constitutional responsibilities, particularly in matters of national security and foreign affairs. Yet advocates of executive privilege have been unable to document instances in which resort to executive privilege has served the interests of the nation. Nor have they been able to document any national disasters that have resulted from executive transmission of information to Congress.

Defenders of executive privilege have urged legal justifications as well, yet there is no mention of executive privilege in the Constitution. Like Topsy in *Uncle Tom's Cabin,* executive privilege "never was born. It just growed like cabbage and corn." Even if, for the sake of argument, one were to concede the occasional utility of a claim of executive privilege, that would not establish its constitutionality. As Chief Justice John Marshall wrote in *McCulloch v. Maryland,* "The peculiar circumstances of the moment may render a measure more or less wise, but cannot render it more or less constitutional."

There are a good many reasons to doubt both the constitutionality and the utility of executive privilege. When the concept of a constitutionally based executive privilege was created by the judiciary in *United States v. Nixon* (1974), it was said to be grounded in the separation of powers. Proponents of executive privilege have also sought its justification in historical precedents. In truth, both of these efforts to establish the legality of executive privilege rest on flimsy scaffolding. Moreover, whatever the legality of executive privilege it is not essential to the success of the presidency and, in fact, poses serious harms to the political system.

## Constitutional Considerations

Questions of presidential authority properly begin with constitutional analysis. Where in the Constitution—in its express provisions or implied derivations—

is provision made for executive privilege? Moreover, which of the president's constitutional assignments require resort to claims of executive privilege?

The framers of the Constitution made no provision for executive privilege, which is not surprising because of the framers' deep-seated fear of executive power. As the historian Charles Warren has pointed out, "Fear of a return of Executive authority like that exercised by the Royal Governors or by the King had been ever present in the states from the beginning of the Revolution." The founders assumed, as James Iredell stated at the North Carolina ratification convention, that "nothing is more fallible than human judgment." And so it was a cardinal principle of republicanism that the conjoined wisdom of the many was superior to the judgment of one. Accordingly, the founders embraced the doctrine of checks and balances as a check on executive unilateralism. In foreign affairs, too, the founders insisted on a structure of shared powers. For, as even Alexander Hamilton agreed, "The history of human conduct does not warrant that exalted opinion of human virtue which would make it wise in a nation to commit interests of so delicate and momentous a kind, as those which concerns its intercourse with the rest of the world, to the sole disposal of a magistrate created and circumstanced as would be a President of the United States."

The framers showed no sympathy for the notion of executive privilege. Speaking at the Pennsylvania ratifying convention, James Wilson, the delegate from Pennsylvania who was second in importance only to James Madison of Virginia as an architect of the Constitution, defended the Constitutional Convention's decision to establish a single presidency rather than a plural presidency. "Executive power," he explained, "is better to be trusted when it has no screen." Wilson noted the visibility and accountability of the president: "he cannot act improperly, and hide either his negligence or inattention," and although he possesses sufficient power, "not a *single privilege* is annexed to his character; far from being above the laws, he is amenable to them in his private character as a citizen, and in his public character by impeachment." The president was to be bound by the strictures of the Constitution, made amenable to the laws and the judicial process, and barred from hiding his activities. The framers' understanding, as Madison put it, that the executive power should be "confined and defined" affords no ground for the view that executive privilege was regarded as an attribute of executive power that might be advanced to conceal the president's "negligence or inattention."

The delegates' refusal to grant the president the authority to conceal information from Congress reflected more than just a generalized distrust of executive power. That decision also reflected the framers' belief that Congress, like the British Parliament, would need on occasion to pursue investigations as a prelude to impeachment. Wilson was one of many delegates to trumpet the role of the House of Commons as the "Grand Inquest of the Nation," which, he declared, has "checked the progress of arbitrary power. . . . The proudest ministers of the proudest monarchs . . . have appeared at the bar of the house to give an account of their conduct." In addition, the framers acted out of a belief that the powers vested in Congress—including its general oversight authority to supervise the enforcement of its laws and the implementation of its appropriations, as well as its broad informing function—required legislative access to information possessed by the executive.

The lone provision of the Constitution that addresses secrecy vests in Congress, not the president, the authority to conceal information from the public. Article I, Section 5, requires both houses of Congress to keep and publish journals, except "such parts as may in their judgment require secrecy." This provision proved divisive in the Constitutional Convention and in the state ratifying conventions. Wilson was one of those who objected. "The people," he insisted, "have a right to know what their Agents are doing or have done, and it should not lie in the option of the Legislature to conceal their proceedings." The framers preferred publicity over secrecy, and they understood that information and knowledge were critical to the preservation of liberty and the enterprise of self-governance.

In summary, neither the Constitutional Convention debates—in which the idea of executive privilege was never discussed—nor the text of the Constitution supports the notion that the founders intended to bestow upon the president the power to conceal information from Congress. Nor at the time of the framing was there either an inherent or implied executive power to conceal information from legislative inquiry. The framers knew how to grant power, confer immunities, and create exceptions to power, but there is no evidence to support the contention that they ascribed to the president an implied power to undercut the investigatory power of Congress.

In *United States v. Nixon,* the Supreme Court ignored the text and the architecture of the Constitution in creating the doctrine of a constitutionally based executive privilege. The Court, in an opinion written by Chief Justice Warren E. Burger, held that "a presumptive privilege for confidential communications . . . is fundamental to the operation of government and inextricably rooted in the separation of powers" and that "to the extent this interest relates to the effective discharge of a President's powers, it is constitutionally based." The Court's employment of a mere ipse dixit served to elevate executive privilege to the constitutional level for the first time. Before that ruling, executive privilege had been known only as an "evidentiary" or "presumptive" privilege—that is, one similar to the lawyer–client or doctor–patient relationship that must yield to the showing of a greater public need.

The Court's effort to ground executive privilege in the separation of powers is unpersuasive. Separation of powers does not create or grant power; rather, it constitutes a rough division of authority that serves to preserve the Constitution's enumeration of powers against acts of usurpation. The Court's claim that executive privilege is "inextricably rooted in the separation of powers" would have astonished Chief Justice Marshall, who faced the question of a presidential privilege to withhold information from the courts in 1807 in the treason trial of Aaron Burr. Burr had requested from President Thomas Jefferson a letter written to him by Gen. James Wilkinson. Jefferson's attorney, George Hay, offered to submit the letter to Marshall, "excepting such parts thereof as are, in my opinion, not material for the purposes of justice, for the defense of the accused, or pertinent to the issue. . . . The accuracy of this opinion, I am willing to refer to the judgment of the Court, by submitting the original letter for its inspection." When Jefferson submitted the letter, with certain deletions, he did not assert a right to withhold information from the court; indeed, he made no challenge to the authority of the court to demand from the president materials relevant to the trial.

Marshall said nothing at all about an executive privilege "rooted" in the separation of powers. The chief justice approached the question of a presidential power to withhold information as an evidentiary privilege, not as a constitutional power. To acknowledge a constitutionally based privilege would acknowledge the president's authority to draw the line and determine issues of disclosure. But Marshall made it clear that he, not the president, would determine the measure of a president's authority to withhold material from the Court.

No historical materials, English or American, would have given the framers an understanding of executive power that included the authority to conceal information from a legislative inquiry. The framers largely drew their understanding of separation of powers from Baron de Montesquieu, who found no grounds in separation of powers for an executive to resist a legislative inquiry. The legislature, Montesquieu wrote, "has a right, and ought to have the means, of examining in what manner its laws have been executed." That right is an attribute of the English system, unlike others, he noted, in which government officers give "no account of their administration." In short, for the framers the separation of powers did not imply an executive right to withhold information from the legislature. On the contrary, it entailed a strong belief that the legislature had a right to demand from the executive the information it deemed relevant to its inquiries.

The effort to ground executive privilege in the original understanding of separation of powers fails to withstand historical scrutiny. The case for executive privilege fares no better when early precedents are considered.

## Precedents

Political scientist Mark J. Rozell has contended that "President George Washington's actions established precedents for the exercise of what is now known as executive privilege." This contention rests on the slender reed of Washington's response to a House investigation in 1792 into the disastrous military campaign of Gen. Arthur St. Clair against the Indians. The House had appointed a committee to investigate the "causes of the failure" of the campaign and had vested in it the authority to call for persons and papers to assist its investigation. For his part, Washington recognized the authority of Congress to conduct an inquiry into the conduct of an executive officer, which reflected the historic practice of parliamentary inquiries into executive actions. As president, he cooperated completely.

The assertion that Washington claimed executive privilege is drawn not so much from anything he said or did, but rests, rather, on an excerpt from Secretary of State Jefferson's notes of a cabinet meeting. Jefferson wrote that the cabinet had agreed that the "house was an inquest, and therefore might institute inquiries," but determined that the president had discretion to refuse papers, "the disclosure of which would injure the public." There is no reason to doubt the accuracy of Jefferson's notes, but little precedential value can be gleaned from this episode. First, Washington complied with the committee's demand and supplied all materials and documents relevant to the failed expedition. He offered no separation of powers objection. Second, there is no evidence that Jefferson's notes were presented to Congress or filed with the government. In short, they formed no part of the official record; there was no assertion to Congress of an executive privilege and no statement or declaration of an executive power to withhold information from Congress. Finally, the incident's precedential value is vitiated by the fact that neither Washington nor Jefferson ever invoked the St. Clair "precedent" in subsequent episodes that allegedly involved their respective claims to executive privilege.

The early years of the Republic reflect widespread understanding of Congress's right to demand information relevant to the exercise of its constitutional powers and responsibilities. President Washington freely supplied information to Congress pursuant to investigations of the St. Clair disaster and accusations of impropriety brought against Secretary of the Treasury Alexander Hamilton. He refused demands from the House for information relative to the Jay Treaty, but not for reasons of executive privilege. Rather, he withheld the requested materials on grounds that the House has no part of the treaty power. During Washington's tenure, the question was not executive concealment from Congress, but disclosure to the public. As a consequence, as political scientist Daniel N. Hoffman has shown, information was supplied to Congress, "some on a public and some on a confidential basis." On some occasions, Congress disclosed information to the public; on others, Congress persuaded the executive to disclose information to the public. It was able to do so because Article I, Section 5, of the Constitution grants to Congress the exclusive authority to withhold information from the citizenry. At all events, what emerged from this early period was not a record of constitutionally based claims to executive privilege, but rather an institutional practice of comity between the president and Congress.

## Executive Privilege and a Successful Presidency

In *United States v. Nixon,* the Court declared that executive privilege is "constitutionally based" if it "relates to the effective discharge of a President's powers." This test begs the question: which of the president's constitutional powers requires resort to concealment of information from Congress in the pursuit of a successful presidency? None. The primary purpose animating the invention of the presidency was to create an executive to enforce the laws and policies of Congress. And although the "Imperial Presidency" has soared beyond the constitutional design, it remains true that the constitutional powers and roles assigned to the president do not require the use of executive privilege. The president's constitutional duty to faithfully execute the laws requires no resort to executive privilege; indeed, it was President Nixon's resort to executive privilege that obscured his failure to faithfully enforce the laws. Moreover, the exercise of the pardon and veto powers are subject to close scrutiny and demand accountability and explanation—hardly criteria for concealment. The appointment power—a shared power, it bears reminding—cannot be carried out unless the president and the Senate cooperate, a dynamic that precludes the claim of executive privilege. In none of these areas do presidents need executive privilege to successfully carry out their constitutional duties.

The argument for executive privilege in foreign policy and national security, a favorite among extollers of a strong presidency, shatters upon close analysis. The argument assumes that executive unilateralism in foreign affairs and war making is constitutionally based. It is not. The constitutional governance of American foreign policy reflects the framers' commitment to collective decision making and their fear of executive unilateralism. As a consequence, the Constitution grants to Congress the lion's share of the nation's foreign policy powers; the president's powers pale in comparison, and they require no resort to an executive privilege. The president is commander in chief of the nation's armed forces, but in this role the president is accountable to Congress and thus possesses no authority to withhold information from it. The president is assigned the duty of receiving ambassadors from other countries, but the framers viewed the performance of this duty as a routine, administrative function, exercised in most other countries by a ceremonial head of state. The lack of discretionary or policy-making authority in this duty precludes any presidential need to conceal information from Congress. Finally, in partnership with the Senate the president appoints ambassadors and makes treaties. Because neither power can be effectuated without the consent of both parties, the claim of privilege would defy not only the text and structure of the Constitution, but also the values, policy concerns, and logic that undergird the partnership.

Nothing in the creation of the commander in chief clause justifies presidential concealment of information from Congress. The war clause vests in Congress the sole and exclusive authority to initiate military hostilities, large or small, on behalf of the American people. In his role as commander in chief, the president conducts war, as Hamilton explained at the Constitutional Convention, "once war is authorized or begun." In the capacity of "first General or Admiral," the president conducts the military campaign, but the president remains accountable to congressional supervision. As Madison explained, Congress has the sole authority to determine whether "a war ought to be commenced, continued or concluded." As a consequence, Congress is entitled to complete information about the status of military activities, a need that prohibits resort to executive concealments. At bottom, no theory of executive privilege can be adduced to subvert the express grant of the war power to Congress.

It is folly as well to assert a presidential privilege to conceal information from the Senate in matters relevant to treaty making, because the Constitution conceives the treaty power as the joint province of the president and the Senate. Under the Constitution, treaties require the advice and consent of the Senate, an arrangement that urges consultation and cooperation and renders concealment unwise and inefficacious. In *Federalist* No. 64, John Jay of New York conveyed his understanding that negotiations with those who desired to "rely on the secrecy of the President" might arise, but he emphasized that such secrecy applied to "those preparatory and auxiliary measures which are not otherwise important in a national view, than as they tend to facilitate the attainment of the objects of the negotiations." The president may "initiate" the negotiations, which require secrecy, but the framers anticipated that the Senate would, consistent with the meaning of "advise," participate equally with the president throughout the negotiation of treaties.

In summary, the constitutional design for foreign affairs provides no basis for the assertion of a presidential power to withhold information from Congress. Rather, the Constitution reflects the understanding that Congress possesses in the realm of foreign policy the same interests, powers, and responsibilities that it has in domestic matters: an informing function, an interest in knowing how its laws and policies have been executed, a responsibility to determine that its appropriations have been effectuated, as well as a general oversight function and the power of inquiry, as prelude to impeachment.

## Conclusion

Little or no evidence exists to suggest that resort to executive privilege has served the national interest. Of course, the president's interests may differ from the nation's. In that event, executive concealment may be a viable option, as it was for Richard Nixon, but it is unlikely to be worthy of emulation and likely to inflict harm on the Republic. Mark Rozell has suggested that the competitive political process will provide a sufficient safeguard against the abuse of executive privilege. That is doubtful. American history has richly affirmed the framers' understanding that the integrity of government officials will not afford a sufficient bulwark against the abuse of power. That is why the founders wrote a constitution, and it is safe to say that trust in government officials was not an animating force behind the Constitutional Convention. Convention delegates did not fail to address the issue of secrecy; rather, they chose not to clothe the president with authority to withhold information from Congress. Nothing in law or history suggested to them the wisdom of an executive power to conceal information from Congress. Nothing since—either in law or in history—has offered persuasive evidence that the framers were mistaken.

# EXPLORING THE ISSUE

## Should the President Be Allowed "Executive Privilege"?

## Critical Thinking and Reflection

1. What is executive privilege and what is the constitutional basis for it?
2. Would the Framers of the Constitution have supported executive privilege for the president?
3. Can a president make a greater claim of executive privilege in his role as Commander in Chief?
4. Does executive privilege constitute a constraint on Congress's power to investigate presidential action?
5. How did President Nixon employ executive privilege and how did his critics oppose him?
6. Should a former president continue to possess an executive privilege to withhold confidential information?
7. Is a president or former president ever subject to legal inquiry into his conduct in office?
8. Does or should executive privilege apply to the vice president?

## Is There Common Ground?

Presidents and Congress are often adversaries, whether or not they represent the same party. Unlike prime ministers in some parliamentary governments, presidents have felt no responsibility for sharing their confidences with the relevant committees of Congress. Congress adopted the Presidential Record Act to compel the publication of documents years after their relevance, but presidents have been reluctant to comply. The difficulty in establishing clear limits on executive privilege may have been made more acute because one or both houses of Congress may be controlled by a party other than the president's. It is not likely that the United States will adopt any procedure similar to Great Britain's question time for the prime minister. Even after the president has left office, there has been no sustained congressional inquiry into challenges to the president's exercise of executive privilege.

## Additional Resources

The constitutional and other advantages that the president possesses in maintaining confidentiality in making executive decisions and the claims of Congress to obtain the information he needs to legislate are examined in Louis Fisher, *The Politics of Executive Privilege* (Carolina Academic Press, 2004). Fisher concludes that any fixed rules setting legislative and executive boundaries are neither realistic nor desirable, because "disputes over information invariably come with unique qualities, characteristics, and histories, both legal and political, and are not likely to be governed by past practices and understandings."

Many aspects of executive privilege are considered in Matthew Crenson and Benjamin Ginsberg, *Presidential Power: Unbridled and Unbalanced* (W. W. Norton, 2007), including whether the privilege extends to conversations between the vice president and persons other than the president. Crenson and Ginsberg maintain that the federal courts have bolstered the claims of executive power, including executive privilege, at the expense of Congress.

Further scholarly commentary and analysis in the context of the full range of presidential power can be found in Christopher S. Kelly, ed., *Executing the Constitution: Putting the President Back into the Constitution* (SUNY Press, 2006), and Katy J. Harriger, *Separation of Powers: Documents and Commentary* (CQ Press, 2003), which contains a provocative essay by Neal Devins, "Executive Privilege and Congressional and Independent Investigations."

# Internet References . . .

In addition to the Internet sites listed below, type in key words, such as "gay rights," "abortion," and "affirmative action" to find other listings.

## New American Studies Web

This eclectic site provides links to a wealth of Internet resources for research in American studies, including agriculture and rural development, government, and race and ethnicity.

**www.georgetown.edu/crossroads/asw/**

## Public Agenda Online

Public Agenda, a nonpartisan, nonprofit public opinion research and citizen education organization, provides links to policy options for issues ranging from abortion to Social Security.

**www.publicagenda.org**

## NCPA Idea House

Through this site of the National Center for Policy Analysis, access discussions on an array of topics that are of major interest in the study of American government, from regulatory policy and privatization to economy and income.

**www.ncpa.org/iss/**

## U.S. Immigration and Customs Enforcement

Created in 2003, this is the largest investigative branch of the Department of Homeland Security and targets illegal immigrants: the people, money, and materials that support terrorism and other criminal activities. The site contains some interesting information on child exploitation, counter-terrorism investigations, counter-narcotics efforts, and other topics.

**www.ice.gov**

## Policy Library

This site provides a collection of documents on social and policy issues submitted by different research organizations all over the world.

**www.policylibrary.com/US/index.html**

# Social Change and Public Policy

*E*conomic and moral issues divide Americans along an ideological spectrum from "left" to "right." The issues are exceedingly diverse; they include economic equality, social welfare, gay rights, abortion, race relations, religious freedom, drug legalization, and whether there should be limits on speech activities. Disagreements break out on the floor of Congress, in state legislatures, in the nation's courtrooms, and sometimes in the streets. These controversial issues generate intense emotions because they force us to defend our most deeply held values and explain how they can be worked out in public policy.

- Does Affirmative Action Advance Racial Equality?
- Should Abortion Be Restricted?
- Is the Welfare State Obsolete?
- Are Americans Overtaxed?
- Is America Becoming More Unequal?
- Should Same-Sex Marriage Be a Constitutional Right?
- Should There Be a "Wall of Separation" Between Church and State?
- Do Corporations Have the Same Free Speech Rights as Persons?
- Should "Recreational" Drugs Be Legalized?

# ISSUE 10

# Does Affirmative Action Advance Racial Equality?

**YES: Glenn C. Loury,** from *The Anatomy of Racial Inequality* (Harvard University Press, 2002)

**NO: Walter E. Williams,** from "Affirmative Action Can't Be Mended," in David Boaz, ed., *Toward Liberty: The Idea That Is Changing the World* (Cato Institute, 2002)

## ISSUE SUMMARY

**YES:** Political scientist Glenn Loury argues that the prudent use of "race-sighted" policies is essential to reducing the deleterious effects of race stigmatization, especially the sense of "racial otherness," which still remain in America.

**NO:** Economist Walter Williams argues that the use of racial preferences sets up a zero-sum game that reverses the gains of the civil rights movement, penalizes innocent people, and ends up harming those they are intended to help.

"**W**e didn't land on Plymouth Rock, my brothers and sisters—Plymouth Rock landed on *us!*" Malcolm X's observation is borne out by the facts of American history. Snatched from their native land, transported thousands of miles—in a nightmare of disease and death—and sold into slavery, blacks were reduced to the legal status of farm animals. Even after emancipation, blacks were segregated from whites—in some states by law, and by social practice almost everywhere. American apartheid continued for another century.

In 1954 the Supreme Court declared state-compelled segregation in schools unconstitutional, and it followed up that decision with others that struck down many forms of official segregation. Still, discrimination survived, and in most southern states blacks were either discouraged or prohibited from exercising their right to vote. Not until the 1960s was compulsory segregation finally and effectively challenged. Between 1964 and 1968 Congress passed the most sweeping civil rights legislation since the end of the Civil War.

But is that enough? Equality of condition between blacks and whites seems as elusive as ever. The black unemployment rate is double that of whites, and the percentage of black families living in poverty is nearly four times that of whites. Only a small percentage of blacks ever make it into medical school or law school.

Advocates of affirmative action have focused upon these *de facto* differences to bolster their argument that it is no longer enough just to stop discrimination. The damage done by three centuries of racism now has to be remedied, they argue, and effective remediation requires a policy of "affirmative action." At the heart of affirmative action is the use of "numerical goals." Opponents call them "racial quotas." Whatever the name, what they imply is the setting aside of a certain number of jobs or positions for blacks or other historically oppressed groups. Opponents charge that affirmative action penalizes innocent people simply because they are white, that it often results in unqualified appointments, and that it ends up harming instead of helping blacks.

Affirmative action has had an uneven history in U.S. federal courts. In *Regents of the University of California v. Allan Bakke* (1978), which marked the first time the Supreme Court directly dealt with the merits of affirmative action, a 5–4 majority ruled that a white applicant to a medical school had been wrongly excluded due to the school's affirmative action policy; yet the majority also agreed that "race-conscious" policies may be used in admitting candidates—as long as they do not amount to fixed quotas. Since *Bakke*, other Supreme Court decisions have tipped toward one side or the other, depending on the circumstances of the case and the shifting line-up of Justices. Notable among these were two cases decided by the Court on the same day in 2003, *Gratz v. Bollinger* and *Grutter v. Bollinger*. Both involved affirmative action programs at the University of Michigan, *Gratz* pertaining to undergraduate admissions and *Grutter* to the law school. The court struck down the undergraduate program in *Gratz* on grounds that it was not "narrowly tailored" enough; it awarded every black and other protected minority an extra twenty points out of a one-hundred point scale—which, the court said, amounted to a "quota." But the law school admissions criteria in *Grutter* were more flexible, using race as only one criterion among others, and so the Court refused to strike them down.

The most radical popular challenge to affirmative action was the ballot initiative endorsed by California voters in 1996. Proposition 209 banned any state program based upon racial or gender "preferences." Among the effects of this ban was a sharp decline in the numbers of non-Asian minorities admitted to the elite campuses of the state's university system, especially Berkeley and UCLA. (Asian admissions to the elite campuses either stayed the same or increased, and non-Asian minority admissions to some of the less-prestigious branches increased.)

In the following selections, political scientist Glenn Loury argues that the prudent use of "race-sighted" policies is essential to reducing the deleterious effects of race stigmatization, while economist Walter Williams contends that racial preferences reverse the gains of the civil rights movement and end up harming those they are intended to help.

# YES ↵

Glenn C. Loury

# The Anatomy of Racial Inequality

## Affirmative Action and the Poverty of Proceduralism

The current policy debate over racial preferences in higher education, while not the most significant racial justice question facing the nation today, is nonetheless worth considering here. I incline toward the view that the affirmative action debate receives too much attention in public discourses about racial inequality, obscuring as much as it clarifies. However, by exploring some aspects of this hotly contested public question, I hope to illustrate more incisively the conceptual distinctions that drive my larger argument. . . .

The deep question here are these: When should we explicitly undertake to reduce racial disparities, and what are the means most appropriately employed in pursuit of that end? My argument asserts an ordering of moral concerns, racial justice before race-blindness. I hold that departures from "blindness" undertaken to promote racial equality ought not be barred as a matter of principle. Instead, race-sighted policies should be undertaken, or not, as the result of prudential judgments made on a case-by-case basis. The broad acceptance of this view in U.S. society would have profound consequences. When prestigious institutions use affirmative action to ration access to their ranks, they tacitly and publicly confirm this ordering of moral priorities, in a salient and powerful way. This confirmation is the key civic lesson projected into American national life by these disputed policies. At bottom, what the argument over racial preference, in college admissions and elsewhere, is really about is this struggle for priority among competing public ideals. This is a struggle of crucial importance to the overall discourse on race and social justice in the United States.

Fundamentally, it is because these elite institutions are not "indifferent" to the racial effects of their policies that they have opted not to be "blind" to the racial identities of their applicants. If forced to be race-blind, they can pursue their race-egalitarian goals by other (in all likelihood, less efficient) means. Ought they to do so? Anyone interested in racial justice needs to answer this question. Liberal individualism provides little useful guidance here.

The priority of concerns I am asserting has far-reaching consequences. It implies, for example, that an end to formal discrimination against blacks in this post–civil rights era should in no way foreclose a vigorous public discussion about racial justice. More subtly, elevating racial equality above race-blindness as a normative concern inclines us to think critically, and with greater nuance, about the value of race-blindness. It reminds us that the demand for race-blindness—our moral queasiness about using race in public decisions—has arisen for historically specific reasons, namely slavery and enforced racial seg-regation over several centuries. These reasons involved the caste-like subordi-nation of blacks—a phenomenon whose effects still linger, and one that was certainly not symmetrical as between the races. As such, taking account of race while trying to mitigate the effects of this subordination, though perhaps ill-advised or unworkable in specific cases, cannot plausibly be seen as the moral equivalent of the discrimination that produced the subjugation of blacks in the first place. To see it that way would be to mire oneself in ahistorical, pro-cedural formalism.

Yet this is precisely what some critics of affirmative action have done, putting forward as their fundamental moral principle the procedural require-ment that admissions policies be race-blind. "America, A Race-Free Zone," screams the headline from a recent article by Ward Connerly, who led the successful 1996 ballot campaign against affirmative action in California and is now at the helm of a national organization working to promote similar initia-tives in other jurisdictions. Mr. Connerly wants to rid the nation of what he calls "those disgusting little boxes"—the ones applicants check to indicate their racial identities. He and his associates see the affirmative action dispute as an argument between people like themselves, who seek simply to eliminate dis-crimination, and people like the authors of *The Shape of the River*, who want permission to discriminate if doing so helps the right groups.

This way of casting the question is very misleading. *It obscures from view the most vital matter at stake in the contemporary debate on race and social equity— whether public purposes formulated explicitly in racial terms (that is, violating race-indifference) are morally legitimate, or even morally required.* Anti-preference advocates suggest not, arguing from the premise that an individual's race has no moral relevance to the race-indifferent conclusion that it is either wrong or unnecessary to formulate public purposes in racial terms. But this argument is a *non sequitur*. Moral irrelevance does not imply instrumental irrelevance. Nor does the conviction that an individual's race is irrelevant to an assessment of that individual's worth require the conclusion that patterns of unequal racial representation in important public venues are irrelevant to an assessment of the moral health of our society.

The failure to make these distinctions is dangerous, for it leads inexora-bly to doubts about the validity of discussing social justice issues in the United States in racial terms at all. Or, more precisely, it reduces such a discussion to the narrow ground of assessing whether or not certain policies are race-blind. Whatever the anti-preference crusaders may intend, and however desirable in the abstract may be their colorblind ideal, their campaign is having the effect of devaluing our collective and still unfinished efforts to achieve greater equal-ity between the races. Americans are now engaged in deciding whether the pursuit of racial equality will continue in the century ahead to be a legitimate and vitally important purpose in our public life. Increasingly, doubts are being expressed about this. *Fervency for race-blindness has left some observers simply blind to a basic fact of American public life: We have pressing moral dilemmas in our society that can be fully grasped only when viewed against the backdrop of our unlovely racial history.*

# "Figment of the Pigment" or "Enigma of the Stigma"?

Consider the stubborn social reality of race-consciousness in U.S. society. A standard concern about racial preferences in college admissions is that they promote an unhealthy fixation on racial identity among students. By classifying by race, it is said, we distance ourselves further from the goal of achieving a race-blind society. Many proponents of race-blindness as the primary moral ideal come close to equating the use of racial information in administrative practices with the continued awareness of racial identity in the broad society. They come close, that is, to collapsing the distinction between racial *information* and racial *identity*. Yet consciousness of race in the society at large is a matter of subjective states of mind, involving how people understand themselves and how they perceive others. It concerns the extent to which race is taken into account in the intimate, social lives of citizens. The implicit assumption of advocates of race-blindness is that, if we would just stop putting people into these boxes, they would oblige us by not thinking of themselves in these terms. But this assumption is patently false. Anti-preference advocates like to declare that we cannot get beyond race while taking race into account—as if someone has proven a theorem to this effect. But no such demonstration is possible.

The conservative scholars Stephen and Abigail Thernstrom, in their influential study *America in Black and White*, provide an example of this tendency of thought. They blame race-conscious public policies for what they take to be an excess of racial awareness among blacks. Affirmative action, they argue, induces blacks to seek political benefits from racial solidarity. This, in turn, encourages a belief by blacks in what they call "the figment of the pigment"—the conviction that, for African Americans, race is a trait that is inexorably and irrevocably different from European or Asian ethnicity. This gets it exactly backwards, in my view. It is not the use of race as a criterion of public action that causes blacks to nurture a sense of racial otherness. Rather, it is the historical fact and the specific nature of blacks' racial otherness that causes affirmative action—when undertaken to benefit blacks—to be so fiercely contested in contemporary American politics.

To see what I am getting at here, consider the following thought experiment. Few people, upon entering a shop with the sign "Smith and Sons" in the window to encounter a youngish proprietor at the counter, will begin to worry that they are about to be served by an unqualified beneficiary of nepotism. But I venture that a great many people, upon seeing a black as part of their treatment team at a top-flight hospital, may be led to consider the possibility that, because of affirmative action in medical school admissions, they are about to be treated by an unqualified doctor. Yet supposing that some preference had, in fact, been given in both cases and bearing in mind the incentives created by the threat of a malpractice suit, the objective probability that a customer will receive lower-quality service in the former situation is likely to be greater than the chance that a patient will receive lower-quality treatment in the latter. This difference between reality and perception has little to do with political principles, and everything to do with racial stigma.

Moreover, the ongoing experience of racial stigma is what causes many blacks to see racial solidarity as an existential necessity. Perhaps I could put it this way: It's not *the figment of the pigment,* it is *the enigma of the stigma* that causes race to be so salient for blacks today. Now mind you, I have already stipulated (in Axioms 1 and 2) that, at the most fundamental level, the "pigment" is a "figment." I have rejected racial essentialism. But I also have argued that, not withstanding the arbitrariness of racial markers, the classifying of persons on the basis of such markers is an inescapable social-cognitive activity. And I have suggested that such markers could be invested with powerful social meanings—that meaning-hungry agents could build elaborate structures of self-definition around them.

So after centuries of intensive racial classification we are now confronted with raced subjects demanding to be recognized as such. Here are selves endogenous to the historical and cultural flow, who see their social world partly through the lens of their "pigment," and the best some critics can do by way of a response is to dismiss them as deluded, confused believers in a "figment." ("Why are they so obsessed with race? Can't they see it was all a big mistake?") Would-be moralists, even some blacks, are puzzled and disturbed at the specter of African Americans being proud of the accomplishments, and ashamed of the failures, of their co-racialists. And those to whom the "wages of whiteness" flow like manna from heaven, who have a race but never have to think about it, can blithely declare, "It's time to move on."

This is simplistic social ethics and sophomoric social psychology, it seems to me. And it is an especially odd position for a liberal individualist to take. I have always supposed that the core idea of liberalism is to credit the dignity of human beings. Yet when those subjected to racial stigma, having managed to construct a more or less dignified self-concept out of the brute facts of an imposed categorization, confront us with their "true" selves—perhaps as believers in the need to carry forward a tradition of racial struggle inherited from their forebears, or as proponents of a program of racial self-help—they are written off as benighted adherents of a discredited creed. We would never tell the antagonists in a society divided by religion that the way to move forward is for the group in the minority to desist from worshiping their false god. But this, in effect, is what many critics today are saying to black Americans who simply refuse to "get over it."

The basic point needing emphasis here is this: The use of race-based instruments is typically the result, rather than the cause, of the wider awareness of racial identity in society. This is why race-blindness is such a superficial moral ideal: To forgo cognizance of race, out of fear that others will be encouraged to think in racial terms, is a bit like closing the barn door after the horses have gone. One cannot grasp the workings of the social order in which we are embedded in the United States without making use of racial categories, because these socially constructed categories are etched in the consciousness of the individuals with whom we must reckon. Because they use race to articulate their self-understandings, we must be mindful of race as we conduct our public affairs. This is a *cognitive,* not a *normative* point. One can agree with the liberal individualist claim that race is irrelevant to an individual's moral worth, that individuals and not groups are the bearers of rights, and nevertheless affirm that, to deal effectively with these autonomous individuals, account must be taken of the categories of thought in which they understand themselves.

Indeed, it is easy to produce compelling examples in which the failure to take race into account serves to exacerbate racial awareness. Consider the extent to which our public institutions are regarded as legitimate by all the people. When a public executive (like the hypothetical governor considered earlier) recognizes the link between the perceived legitimacy of institutions and their degree of racial representation, and acts on that recognition, he or she is acting so as to *inhibit,* not to *heighten,* the salience of race in public life. When the leaders of elite educational philanthropies attempt to bring a larger number of black youngsters into their ranks, so as to increase the numbers of their graduates from these communities, they are acting in a similar fashion. *To acknowledge that institutional legitimacy can turn on matters of racial representation is to recognize a basic historical fact about the American national community, not to make a moral error.* The U.S. Army has long understood this. It is absurd to hold that this situation derives from the existence of selection rules—in colleges and universities, in the military, or anywhere else—that take account of race.

So much may seem too obvious to warrant stating but, sadly, it is not. In the 5th U.S. Circuit Court of Appeals *Hopwood* opinion, Judge Smith questions the diversity rationale for using racial preferences in higher education admissions. He argues that, because a college or university exists to promote the exchange of ideas, defining diversity in racial terms necessarily entails the pernicious belief that blacks think one way, whites another. But this argument is fallacious for reasons just stated. Suppose one begins with the contrary premise, that there is no "black" or "white" way of thinking. Suppose further that conveying this view to one's students is a high pedagogic goal. The students being keenly aware of their respective racial identities, some racial diversity may be required to achieve the pedagogic goal. Teaching that "not all blacks think alike" will be much easier when there are enough blacks around to show their diversity of thought.

Walter E. Williams                                    **NO**

# Affirmative Action Can't Be Mended

For the last several decades, affirmative action has been the basic component of the civil rights agenda. But affirmative action, in the form of racial
preferences, has worn out its political welcome. In Gallup Polls, between 1987
and 1990, people were asked if they agreed with the statement: "We should
make every effort to improve the position of blacks and other minorities even
if it means giving them preferential treatment." More than 70 percent of the
respondents opposed preferential treatment while only 24 percent supported
it. Among blacks, 66 percent opposed preferential treatment and 32 percent
supported it.

The rejection of racial preferences by the broad public and increasingly
by the Supreme Court has been partially recognized by even supporters of
affirmative action. While they have not forsaken their goals, they have begun
to distance themselves from some of the language of affirmative action. Thus,
many business, government, and university affirmative action offices have
been renamed "equity offices." Racial preferences are increasingly referred to
as "diversity multiculturalism." What is it about affirmative action that gives
rise to its contentiousness?

For the most part, post-World War II America has supported civil rights
for blacks. Indeed, if we stick to the uncorrupted concept of civil rights, we can
safely say that the civil rights struggle for blacks is over and won. Civil rights
properly refer to rights, held simultaneously among individuals, to be treated
equally in the eyes of the law, make contracts, sue and be sued, give evidence,
associate and travel freely, and vote. There was a time when blacks did not
fully enjoy those rights. With the yeoman-like work of civil rights organizations and decent Americans, both black and white, who fought lengthy court,
legislative, and street battles, civil rights have been successfully secured for
blacks. No small part of that success was due to a morally compelling appeal to
America's civil libertarian tradition of private property, rule of law, and limited
government.

Today's corrupted vision of civil rights attacks that civil libertarian tradition. Principles of private property rights, rule of law, freedom of association,
and limited government are greeted with contempt. As such, the agenda of
today's civil rights organizations conceptually differs little from yesteryear's
restrictions that were the targets of the earlier civil rights struggle. Yesteryear
civil rights organizations fought *against* the use of race in hiring, access to
public schools, and university admissions. Today, civil rights organizations fight

From *Cato Journal*, vol. 17, no. 1, Spring/Summer 1997, pp. 1–9. Copyright © 1997 by Cato
Institute.

*for* the use of race in hiring, access to public schools, and university admissions. Yesteryear, civil rights organizations fought *against* restricted association in the forms of racially segregated schools, libraries, and private organizations. Today, they fight *for* restricted associations. They use state power, not unlike the racists they fought, to enforce racial associations they deem desirable. They protest that blacks should be a certain percentage of a company's workforce or clientele, a certain percentage of a student body, and even a certain percentage of an advertiser's models.

Civil rights organizations, in their successful struggle against state-sanctioned segregation, have lost sight of what it means to be truly committed to liberty, especially the freedom of association. The true test of that commitment does not come when we allow people to be free to associate in ways we deem appropriate. The true test is when we allow people to form those voluntary associations we deem offensive. It is the same principle we apply to our commitment to free speech. What tests our commitment to free speech is our willingness to permit people the freedom to say things we find offensive.

## Zero-Sum Games

The tragedy of America's civil rights movement is that it has substituted today's government-backed racial favoritism in the allocation of resources for yesterday's legal and extralegal racial favoritism. In doing so, civil rights leaders fail to realize that government allocation of resources produces the kind of conflict that does not arise with market allocation of resources. Part of the reason is that any government allocation of resources, including racial preferential treatment, is a zero-sum game.

A zero-sum game is defined as any transaction where one person's gain necessarily results in another person's loss. The simplest example of a zero-sum game is poker. A winner's gain is matched precisely by the losses of one or more persons. In this respect, the only essential difference between affirmative action and poker is that in poker participation is voluntary. Another difference is the loser is readily identifiable, a point to which I will return later.

The University of California, Berkeley's affirmative action program for blacks captures the essence of a zero-sum game. Blacks are admitted with considerably lower average SAT scores (952) than the typical white (1232) and Asian student (1254).* Between UCLA and UC Berkeley, more than 2,000 white and Asian straight A students are turned away in order to provide spaces for black and Hispanic students. The admissions gains by blacks are exactly matched by admissions losses by white and Asian students. Thus, any preferential treatment program results in a zero-sum game almost by definition.

More generally, government allocation of resources is a zero-sum game primarily because government has no resources of its very own. When government gives some citizens food stamps, crop subsidies, or disaster relief payments, the recipients of the largesse gain. Losers are identified by asking: where does

---

*This practice was outlawed in California in 1996 with the passage of proposition 209. [*Editors*]

government acquire the resources to confer the largesse? In order [to] fix government to give to some citizens, it must through intimidation, threats, and coercion take from other citizens. Those who lose the rights to their earnings, to finance government largesse, are the losers.

Government-mandated racial preferential treatment programs produce a similar result. When government creates a special advantage for one ethnic group, it necessarily comes at the expense of other ethnic groups for whom government simultaneously creates a special disadvantage in the form of reduced alternatives. If a college or employer has $X$ amount of positions, and $R$ of them have been set aside for blacks or some other group, that necessarily means there are $(X - R)$ fewer positions for which other ethnic groups might compete. At a time when there were restrictions against blacks, that operated in favor of whites, those restrictions translated into a reduced opportunity set for blacks. It is a zero-sum game independent of the race or ethnicity of the winners and losers.

Our courts have a blind-sided vision of the zero-sum game. They have upheld discriminatory racial preferences in hiring but have resisted discriminatory racial preferences in job layoffs. An example is the U.S. Supreme Court's ruling in *Wygant v. Jackson Board of Education* (1986), where a teacher union's collective-bargaining agreement protected black teachers from job layoffs in order to maintain racial balance. Subsequently, as a result of that agreement, the Jackson County School Board laid off white teachers having greater seniority while black teachers with less seniority were retained.

A lower court upheld the constitutionality of the collective bargaining agreement by finding that racial preferences in layoffs were a permissible means to remedy societal discrimination. White teachers petitioned the U.S. Supreme Court, claiming their constitutional rights under the Equal Protection clause were violated. The Court found in their favor. Justice Lewis F. Powell delivered the opinion saying, "While hiring goals impose a diffuse burden, only closing one of several opportunities, layoffs impose the entire burden of achieving racial equity on particular individuals, often resulting in serious disruption of their lives. The burden is too intrusive."

In *Wygant,* the Supreme Court recognized the illegitimacy of creating a special privilege for one citizen (a black teacher) that comes at the expense and disadvantage of another citizen (a white teacher). However, the Court made a false distinction when it stated that "hiring goals impose a diffuse burden [while] . . . layoffs impose the entire burden . . . on particular individuals."

There is no conceptual distinction in the outcome of the zero-sum game whether it is played on the layoff or the hiring side of the labor market. If a company plans to lay off $X$ amount of workers and decides that $R$ of them will have their jobs protected because of race, that means the group of workers that may be laid off have $(X - R)$ fewer job retention opportunities. The diffuseness to which Justice Powell refers is not diffuseness at all. It is simply that the victims of hiring preferencas are less visible than victims of layoff preferences as in the case of *Wygant*. The petitioners in *Wygant* were identifiable people who could not be covered up as "society." That differs from the cases of hiring and college admissions racial preferences where those who face a reduced opportunity set tend to be unidentifiable to the courts, other people, and even to themselves. Since they are invisible victims, the Supreme Court and others can blithely say racial hiring goals (and admission goals) impose a diffuse burden.

## Tentative Victim Identification

In California, voters passed the California Civil Rights Initiative of 1996 (CCRI) that says: "The state shall not discriminate against, or grant preferential treatment to, any individual or group on the basis of race, sex, color, ethnicity, or national origin in the operation of public employment, public education, or public contracting." Therefore, California public universities can no longer have preferential admission policies that include race as a factor in deciding whom to admit. As a result, the UCLA School of Law reported accepting only 21 black applicants for its fall 1997 class—a drop of 80 percent from the previous year, in which 108 black applicants were accepted. At the UC Berkeley Boalt Hall School of Law, only 14 of the 792 students accepted for the fall 1997 class are black, down from 75 the previous year. At the UCLA School of Law, white enrollment increased by 14 percent for the fall 1997 term and Asian enrollment rose by 7 percent. At UC Berkeley, enrollment of white law students increased by 12 percent and Asian law students increased by 18 percent.

For illustrative purposes, let us pretend that CCRI had not been adopted and the UCLA School of Law accepted 108 black students as it had in 1996 and UC Berkeley accepted 75. That being the case, 83 more blacks would be accepted to UCLA Law School for the 1997–98 academic year and 61 more blacks would be accepted to UC Berkeley's Law School. Clearly, the preferential admissions program, at least in terms of being accepted to these law schools, benefits blacks. However, that benefit is not without costs. With preferential admission programs in place, both UCLA and UC Berkeley law schools would have had to turn away 144 white and Asian students, with higher academic credentials, in order to have room for black students.

In the case of UC Berkeley's preferential admissions for blacks, those whites and Asians who have significantly higher SAT scores and grades than the admitted blacks are victims of reverse discrimination. However, in the eyes of the courts, others, and possibly themselves, they are invisible victims. In other words, no one can tell for sure who among those turned away would have gained entry to UC Berkeley were it not for the preferential treatment given to blacks.

The basic problem of zero-sum games (those of an involuntary nature) is that they are politically and socially unstable. In the case of UCLA and UC Berkeley, two of California's most prestigious universities, one would not expect parents to permanently tolerate seeing their children work hard to meet the university's admission standards only to be denied admission because of racial preference programs. Since the University of California is a taxpayer-subsidized system, one suspects that sooner or later parents and others would begin to register complaints and seek termination of racial preferences in admissions. That is precisely much of the political motivation behind Proposition 209.

# Affirmative Action and Supply

An important focus of affirmative action is statistical underrepresentation of different racial and ethnic groups on college and university campuses. If the percentages of blacks and Mexican-Americans, for example, are not at a level deemed appropriate by a court, administrative agency, or university administrator, racial preference programs are instituted. The inference made from the underrepresentation argument is that, in the absence of racial discrimination, groups would be represented on college campuses in proportion to their numbers in the relevant population. In making that argument, little attention is paid to the supply issue—that is, to the pool of students available that meet the standards or qualifications of the university in question.

In 1985, fewer than 1,032 blacks scored 600 and above on the verbal portion of the SAT and 1,907 scored 600 and above on the quantitative portion of the examination. There are roughly 58 elite colleges and universities with student body average composite SAT scores of 1200 and above. If blacks scoring 600 or higher on the quantitative portion of the SAT (assuming their performance on the verbal portion of the examination gave them a composite SAT score of 1200 or higher) were recruited to elite colleges and universities, there would be less than 33 black students available per university. At none of those universities would blacks be represented according to their numbers in the population.

There is no evidence that suggests that university admissions offices practice racial discrimination by turning away blacks with SAT scores of 1200 or higher. In reality, there are not enough blacks to be admitted to leading colleges and universities on the same terms as other students, such that their numbers in the campus population bear any resemblance to their numbers in the general population.

Attempts by affirmative action programs to increase the percent of blacks admitted to top schools, regardless of whether blacks match the academic characteristics of the general student body, often produce disastrous results. In order to meet affirmative action guidelines, leading colleges and universities recruit and admit black students whose academic qualifications are well below the norm for other students. For example, of the 317 black students admitted to UC Berkeley in 1985, all were admitted under affirmative action criteria rather than academic qualifications. Those students had an average SAT score of 952 compared to the national average of 900 among all students. However, their SAT scores were well below UC Berkeley's average of nearly 1200. More than 70 percent of the black students failed to graduate from UC Berkeley.

Not far from UC Berkeley is San Jose State University, not one of the top-tier colleges, but nonetheless respectable. More than 70 percent of its black students fail to graduate. The black students who might have been successful at San Jose State University have been recruited to UC Berkeley and elsewhere where they have been made artificial failures. This pattern is one of the consequences of trying to use racial preferences to make a student body reflect the relative importance of different ethnic groups in the general population. There is a mismatch between black student qualifications and those of other students when the wrong students are recruited to the wrong universities.

There is no question that preferential admissions is unjust to both white and Asian students who may be qualified but are turned away to make room for less-qualified students in the "right" ethnic group. However, viewed from a solely black self-interest point of view, the question should be asked whether such affirmative action programs serve the best interests of blacks. Is there such an abundance of black students who score above the national average on the SAT, such as those admitted to UC Berkeley, that blacks as a group can afford to have those students turned into artificial failures in the name of diversity, multiculturalism, or racial justice? The affirmative action debate needs to go beyond simply an issue of whether blacks are benefited at the expense of whites. Whites and Asians who are turned away to accommodate blacks are still better off than the blacks who were admitted. After all, graduating from the university of one's second choice is preferable to flunking out of the university of one's first choice.

To the extent racial preferences in admission produce an academic mismatch of students, the critics of California's Proposition 209 may be unnecessarily alarmed, assuming their concern is with black students actually graduating from college. If black students, who score 952 on the SAT, are not admitted to UC Berkeley, that does not mean that they cannot gain admittance to one of America's 3,000 other colleges. It means that they will gain admittance to some other college where their academic characteristics will be more similar to those of their peers. There will not be as much of an academic mismatch. To the extent this is true, we may see an *increase* in black graduation rates. Moreover, if black students find themselves more similar to their white peers in terms of college grades and graduation honors, they are less likely to feel academically isolated and harbor feelings of low self-esteem.

## Affirmative Action and Justice

Aside from any other question, we might ask what case can be made for the morality or justice of turning away more highly credentialed white and Asian students so as to be able to admit more blacks? Clearly, blacks as a group have suffered past injustices, including discrimination in college and university admissions. However, that fact does not spontaneously yield sensible policy proposals for today. The fact is that a special privilege cannot be created for one person without creating a special disadvantage for another. In the case of preferential admissions at UCLA and UC Berkeley, a special privilege for black students translates into a special disadvantage for white and Asian students. Thus, we must ask what have those individual white and Asian students done to deserve punishment? Were they at all responsible for the injustices, either in the past or present, suffered by blacks? If, as so often is the case, the justification for preferential treatment is to redress past grievances, how just is it to have a policy where a black of today is helped by punishing a white of today for what a white of yesterday did to a black of yesterday? Such an idea becomes even more questionable in light of the fact that so many whites and Asians cannot trace the American part of their ancestry back as much as two or three generations.

# Affirmative Action and Racial Resentment

In addition to the injustices that are a result of preferential treatment, such treatment has given rise to racial resentment where it otherwise might not exist. While few people support racial resentment and its manifestations, if one sees some of affirmative action's flagrant attacks on fairness and equality before the law, one can readily understand why resentment is on the rise.

In the summer of 1995, the Federal Aviation Administration (FAA) published a "diversity handbook" that said, "The merit promotion process is but one means of filling vacancies, which need not be utilized if it will not promote your diversity goals." In that spirit, one FAA job announcement said, "Applicants who meet the qualification requirements . . . cannot be considered for this position. . . . Only those applicants who do not meet the Office of Personnel Management requirements . . . will be eligible to compete."

According to a General Accounting Office report that evaluated complaints of discrimination by Asian-Americans, prestigious universities such as UCLA, UC Berkeley, MIT, and the University of Wisconsin have engaged in systematic discrimination in the failure to admit highly qualified Asian students in order to admit relatively unqualified black and Hispanic students.

In Memphis, Tennessee, a white police officer ranked 59th out of 209 applicants for 75 available positions as police sergeant, but he did not get promoted. Black officers, with lower overall test scores than he, were moved ahead of him and promoted to sergeant. Over a two-year period, 43 candidates with lower scores were moved ahead of him and made sergeant.

There is little need to recite the litany of racial preference instances that are clear violations of commonly agreed upon standards of justice and fair play. But the dangers of racial preferences go beyond matters of justice and fair play. They lead to increased group polarization ranging from political backlash to mob violence and civil war as seen in other countries. The difference between the United States and those countries is that racial preferences have not produced the same level of violence. However, they have produced polarization and resentment.

Affirmative action proponents cling to the notion that racial discrimination satisfactorily explains black/white socioeconomic differences. While every vestige of racial discrimination has not been eliminated in our society, current social discrimination cannot begin to explain all that affirmative action proponents purport it explains. Rather than focusing our attention on discrimination, a higher payoff can be realized by focusing on real factors such as fraudulent education, family disintegration, and hostile economic climates in black neighborhoods. Even if affirmative action was not a violation of justice and fair play, was not a zero-sum game, was not racially polarizing, it is a poor cover-up for the real work that needs to be done.

# EXPLORING THE ISSUE

## Does Affirmative Action Advance Racial Equality?

## Critical Thinking and Reflection

1. What is meant by "color blindness"? To what extent can our laws be color-blind?
2. In Martin Luther King's "I Have a Dream" speech, he said he dreamed of a society where people will not be judged by the "color of their skin but by the content of their character." A worthy goal? How can it be brought about? Might it require temporary color-consciousness to bring it about?
3. Is there a danger that temporary color-consciousness can turn into a permanent policy? What safeguards are there?

## Is There Common Ground?

In reacting against California's Proposition 209 banning the use of racial quotas in the admission policies of state's colleges and universities, some of those on the losing side said, in effect, "OK, we won't use strict quotas, all we're saying is that admission officers can simply *note* the race of the applicants." But that, too, is unlikely to survive when measured against the sweeping ban in Prop 209. The best sort of common ground is to make available to *all* applicants some sort of pre-testing tutoring program, and that has already begun in California. Police and fire departments in many cities have also initiated these programs.

## Additional Resources

Linda Chavez, a columnist and president of the Center for Equal Opportunity, an organization opposing affirmative action, develops her argument against it in "Promoting Racial Harmony," an essay published in George E. Curry, ed., *The Affirmative Action Debate* (Perseus, 1996); Mary Francis Berry, former chair of the U.S. Civil Rights Commission, argues for it ("Affirmative Action: Why We Need It, Why It Is Under Attack") in the same volume. An article by Richard H. Sander in the November, 2004 *Stanford Law Review* caused a stir in legal education circles. Sander argued that reduced admission standards for blacks entering law school leads to their receiving "lower grades and less learning," which in turn produce "higher attrition rates, lower pass rates on the bar," and "problems in the job market." The following spring (May 2005), the *Review* published four rebuttals to Sanders, together with Sander's reply.

Columnist Jim Sleeper's *Liberal Racism* (Viking, 1997) is critical of affirmative action and other race-based programs, as is a book by *ABC News* reporter Bob Zelnick, *Backfire: A Reporter's Look at Affirmative Action* (Regnery, 1996).

Barbara Bergmann supports affirmative action in *In Defense of Affirmative Action* (Basic Books, 1996), while Stephan Thernstrom and Abigail Thernstrom, in their comprehensive survey of racial progress in America entitled *America in Black and White: One Nation, Indivisible* (Simon & Schuster, 1997), argue that it is counterproductive. In *Collision Course: The Strange Convergence of Affirmative Action and Immigration Policy in America* (Oxford University Press, 2002), Hugh David Graham maintains that affirmative action is now at loggerheads with America's expanded immigration policies, in that employers use affirmative action to hire new immigrants at the expense of American blacks. Peter Schmidt, *Color and Money: How Rich White Kids Are Winning the War over College Affirmative Action* (Palgrave Macmillan, 2007), summarizes the history of government policy, court decisions, and politics as they affect affirmative action in America and concludes that they ill-serve poor and working-class students of all colors.

# ISSUE 11

## Should Abortion Be Restricted?

**YES: Robert P. George**, from "God's Reasons," *The Clash of Orthodoxies: Law, Religion, and Morality in Crisis* (ISI Books, 2001)

**NO: Mary Gordon**, from "A Moral Choice," *The Atlantic Monthly* (March 1990)

### ISSUE SUMMARY

**YES:** Legal philosopher Robert P. George asserts that, since each of us was a human being from conception, abortion is a form of homicide and should be banned.

**NO:** Writer Mary Gordon maintains that having an abortion is a moral choice that women are capable of making for themselves, that aborting a fetus is not killing a person, and that antiabortionists fail to understand female sexuality.

Until 1973 the laws governing abortion were set by the states, most of which barred legal abortion except where pregnancy imperiled the life of the pregnant woman. In that year, the U.S. Supreme Court decided the controversial case *Roe v. Wade*. The *Roe* decision acknowledged both a woman's "fundamental right" to terminate a pregnancy before fetal viability and the state's legitimate interest in protecting both the woman's health and the "potential life" of the fetus. It prohibited states from banning abortion to protect the fetus before the third trimester of a pregnancy, and it ruled that even during that final trimester, a woman could obtain an abortion if she could prove that her life or health would be endangered by carrying to term. (In a companion case to *Roe,* decided on the same day, the Court defined *health* broadly enough to include "all factors—physical, emotional, psychological, familial, and the woman's age—relevant to the well-being of the patient.") These holdings, together with the requirement that state regulation of abortion had to survive "strict scrutiny" and demonstrate a "compelling state interest," resulting in later decisions striking down mandatory 24-hour waiting periods, requirements that abortions be performed in hospitals, and so-called informed consent laws.

The Supreme Court did uphold state laws requiring parental notification and consent for minors (though it provided that minors could seek permission from a judge if they feared notifying their parents). And federal courts have affirmed the right of Congress not to pay for abortions. Proabortion groups, proclaiming the "right to choose," have charged that this and similar action at the state level discriminates against poor women because it does not inhibit the ability of women who are able to pay for abortions to obtain them. Efforts to adopt a constitutional amendment or federal law barring abortion have failed, but antiabortion forces have influenced legislation in many states.

Can legislatures and courts establish the existence of a scientific fact? Opponents of abortion believe that it is a fact that life begins at conception and that the law must therefore uphold and enforce this concept. They argue that the human fetus is a live human being, and they note all the familiar signs of life displayed by the fetus: a beating heart, brain waves, thumb sucking, and so on. Those who defend abortion maintain that human life does not begin before the development of specifically human characteristics and possibly not until the birth of a child. As Justice Harry A. Blackmun put it in 1973, "There has always been strong support for the view that life does not begin until live birth."

Antiabortion forces sought a court case that might lead to the overturning of *Roe v. Wade*. Proabortion forces rallied to oppose new state laws limiting or prohibiting abortion. In *Webster v. Reproductive Health Services* (1989), with four new justices, the Supreme Court upheld a Missouri law that banned abortions in public hospitals and abortions that were performed by public employees (except to save a woman's life). The law also required that tests be performed on any fetus more than 20 weeks old to determine its viability. In the later decision of *Planned Parenthood v. Casey* (1992), however, the Court affirmed what it called the "essence" of the constitutional right to abortion while permitting some state restrictions, such as a 24-hour waiting period and parental notification in the case of minors.

In 2000, a five-to-four decision of the Supreme Court in *Stenberg v. Carhart* overturned a Nebraska law that outlawed "partial birth" abortions. The law defined "partial birth abortion" as a procedure in which the doctor "partially delivers vaginally a living child before killing" the child, further defining the process as "intentionally delivering into the vagina a living unborn child, or a substantial portion thereof, for the purpose of performing a procedure that the [abortionist] knows will kill the child." The Court's stated reason for striking down the law was that it lacked a "health" exception. Critics complained that the Court has defined "health" so broadly that it includes not only physical health but also "emotional, psychological," and "familial" health, and that the person the Court has authorized to make these judgments is the attendant physician, that is, the abortionist himself.

In the following selections, Robert P. George contends that, since each of us was a human being from conception, abortion is a form of homicide and should be banned. Mary Gordon asserts that the fetus removed in most abortions may not be considered a person and that women must retain the right to make decisions regarding their sexual lives.

# YES ↵

**Robert P. George**

## God's Reasons

**I**n his contributions to the February 1996 issue of *First Things* magazine—contributions in which what he has to say (particularly in his critique of liberalism) is far more often right than wrong—Stanley Fish of Duke University cites the dispute over abortion as an example of a case in which "incompatible first assumptions [or] articles of opposing faiths"—make the resolution of the dispute (other than by sheer political power) impossible. Here is how Fish presented the pro-life and pro-choice positions and the shape of the dispute between their respective defenders:

> A pro-life advocate sees abortion as a sin against God who infuses life at the moment of conception; a pro-choice advocate sees abortion as a decision to be made in accordance with the best scientific opinion as to when the beginning of life, as we know it, occurs. No conversation between them can ever get started because each of them starts from a different place and they could never agree as to what they were conversing *about*. A pro-lifer starts from a belief in the direct agency of a personal God, and this belief, this religious conviction, is not incidental to his position; it is his position, and determines its features in all their detail. The "content of a belief" is a *function* of its source, and the critiques of one will always be the critique of the other.

It is certainly true that the overwhelming majority of pro-life Americans are religious believers and that a great many pro-choice Americans are either unbelievers or less observant or less traditional in their beliefs and practice than their fellow citizens. Indeed, although most Americans believe in God, polling data consistently show that Protestants, Catholics, and Jews who do not regularly attend church or synagogue are less likely than their more observant co-religionists to oppose abortion. And religion is plainly salient politically when it comes to the issue of abortion. The more secularized a community, the more likely that community is to elect pro-choice politicians to legislative and executive offices.

Still, I don't think that Fish's presentation of the pro-life and pro-choice positions, or of the shape of the dispute over abortion, is accurate. True, inasmuch as most pro-life advocates are traditional religious believers who, as such, see gravely unjust or otherwise immoral acts as sins—and understand sins precisely as offenses against God—"a pro-life advocate sees abortion as a sin against

God." But most pro-life advocates see abortion as a sin against God *precisely because it is the unjust taking of innocent human life*. That is their reason for opposing abortion; and that is God's reason, as they see it, for opposing abortion and requiring that human communities protect their unborn members against it. And, they believe, as I do, that this reason can be identified and acted on even independently of God's revealing it. Indeed, they typically believe, as I do, that the precise content of what God reveals on the subject ("in thy mother's womb I formed thee") cannot be known without the application of human intelligence, by way of philosophical and scientific inquiry, to the question.

Fish is mistaken, then, in *contrasting* the pro-life advocate with the pro-choice advocate by depicting (only) the latter as viewing abortion as "a decision to be made in accordance with the best scientific opinion as to when the beginning of life . . . occurs." First of all, supporters of the pro-choice position are increasingly willing to sanction the practice of abortion even where they concede that it constitutes the taking of innocent human life. Pro-choice writers from Naomi Wolfe to Judith Jarvis Thomson have advanced theories of abortion as "justifiable homicide." But, more to the point, people on the pro-life side *insist* that the central issue in the debate is the question "as to when the beginning of life occurs." And they insist with equal vigor that this question is not a "religious" or even "metaphysical" one: it is rather, as Fish says, "scientific." In response to this insistence, it is pro-choice advocates who typically want to transform the question into a "metaphysical" or "religious" one. It was Justice Harry Blackmun who claimed in his opinion for the Court legalizing abortion in *Roe v. Wade* (1973) that "at this point in man's knowledge" the scientific evidence was inconclusive and therefore could not determine the outcome of the case. And twenty years later, the influential pro-choice writer Ronald Dworkin went on record claiming that the question of abortion is inherently "religious." It is pro-choice advocates, such as Dworkin, who want to distinguish between when a human being comes into existence "in the biological sense and when a human being comes into existence" in the moral sense. It is they who want to distinguish a class of human beings "with rights" from pre- (or post-) conscious human beings who "don't have rights." And the reason for this, I submit, is that, short of defending abortion as "justifiable homicide," the pro-choice position collapses if the issue is to be settled purely on the basis of scientific inquiry into the question of when a new member of Homo sapiens comes into existence as a self-integrating organism whose unity, distinctiveness, and identity remain intact as it develops without substantial change from the point of its beginning through the various stages of its development and into adulthood.

All this was, I believe, made wonderfully clear at a debate at the 1997 meeting of the American Political Science Association between Jeffrey Reiman of American University, defending the pro-choice position, and John Finnis of Oxford and Notre Dame, defending the pro-life view. That debate was remarkable for the skill, intellectual honesty, and candor of the interlocutors. What is most relevant to our deliberations, however, is the fact that it truly was a debate, Reiman and Finnis did not talk past each other. They did not proceed from "incompatible first assumptions." They *did* manage to agree as to what they were talking *about*—and it was not about whether or when life was infused by God. It was precisely about the *rational* (i.e., scientific and philosophical) grounds, if any, available for distinguishing a class of human beings "in the moral sense" (with rights) from a class of human beings "in the (merely) biological sense" (without rights). Finnis did not claim any special revelation to the effect that no such grounds existed. Nor did Reiman claim that Finnis's arguments against his view appealed implicitly (and illicitly) to some such putative revelation. Although Finnis is a Christian and, as such, believes that the new human life that begins at conception is in each and every case created by God in His image and likeness, his argument never invoked, much less did it "start from a belief in the direct agency of a personal God." It proceeded, rather, by way of point-by-point philosophical challenge to Reiman's philosophical arguments. Finnis marshaled the scientific facts of embryogenesis and intrauterine human development and defied Reiman to identify grounds, compatible with those facts, for denying a right to life to human beings in the embryonic and fetal stages of development.

Interestingly, Reiman began his remarks with a statement that would seem to support what Fish said in *First Things*. While allowing that debates over abortion were useful in clarifying people's thinking about the issue, Reiman remarked that they "never actually cause people to change their minds." It is true, I suppose, that people who are deeply committed emotionally to one side or the other are unlikely to have a road-to-Damascus type conversion after listening to a formal philosophical debate. Still, any open-minded person who sincerely wishes to settle his mind on the question of abortion—and there continue to be many such people, I believe—would find debates such as the one between Reiman and Finnis to be extremely helpful toward that end. Anyone willing to consider the *reasons* for and against abortion and its legal prohibition or permission would benefit from reading or hearing the accounts of these reasons proposed by capable and honest thinkers on both sides. Of course, when it comes to an issue like abortion, people can have powerful motives for clinging to a particular position even if they are presented with conclusive reasons for changing their minds. But that doesn't mean that such reasons do not exist.

I believe that the pro-life position is superior to the pro-choice position precisely because the scientific evidence, considered honestly and dispassionately, fully supports it. A human being is conceived when a human sperm containing twenty-three chromosomes fuses with a human egg also containing twenty-three chromosomes (albeit of a different kind) producing a single-cell human zygote containing, in the normal case, forty-six chromosomes that are mixed differently from the forty-six chromosomes as found in the mother or father. Unlike the gametes (that is, the sperm and egg), the zygote is genetically unique and distinct from its parents. Biologically, it is a separate organism. It produces, as the gametes do not, specifically human enzymes and proteins. It possesses, as they do not, the active capacity or potency to develop itself into a human embryo, fetus, infant, child, adolescent, and adult.

Assuming that it is not conceived *in vitro*, the zygote is, of course, in a state of dependence on its mother. But independence should not be confused with distinctness. From the beginning, the newly conceived human being, not its mother, directs its integral organic functioning. It takes in nourishment and converts it to energy. Given a hospitable environment, it will, as Dianne Nutwell Irving says, "develop continuously without any biological interruptions, or gaps, throughout the embryonic, fetal, neo-natal, childhood and adulthood stages—until the death of the organism."

⋅❦⋅

Some claim to find the logical implication of these facts—that is, that life begins at conception—to be "virtually unintelligible." A leading exponent of that point of view in the legal academy is Jed Rubenfeld of Yale Law School, author of an influential article entitled "On the Legal Status of the Proposition that 'Life Begins at Conception.'" Rubenfeld argues that, like the zygote, *every* cell in the human body is "genetically complete"; yet nobody supposes that every human cell is a distinct human being with a right to life. However, Rubenfeld misses the point that there comes into being at conception, not a mere clump of human cells, but a distinct, unified, self-integrating organism, which develops itself, truly himself or herself, in accord with its own genetic "blueprint." The significance of genetic completeness for the status of newly conceived human beings is that no outside genetic material is required to enable the zygote to mature into an embryo, the embryo into a fetus, the fetus into an infant, the infant into a child, the child into an adolescent, the adolescent into an adult. What the zygote needs to function as a distinct self-integrating human organism, a human being, it already possesses.

At no point in embryogenesis, therefore, does the distinct organism that came into being when it was conceived undergo what is technically called "substantial change" (or a change of natures). It is human and will remain human. This is the point of Justice Byron White's remark in his dissenting opinion in *Thornburgh v. American College of Obstetricians & Gynecologists* that "there is no non-arbitrary line separating a fetus from a child." Rubenfeld attacks White's point, which he calls "[t]he argument based on the gradualness of gestation," by pointing out that, "[n]o non-arbitrary line separates the hues of green and red. Shall we conclude that green is red?"

White's point, however, was *not* that fetal development is "gradual," but that it is *continuous* and is the (continuous) development of a single lasting (fully human) being. The human zygote that actively develops itself is, as I have pointed out, a genetically complete organism directing its own integral organic functioning. As it matures, *in utero* and *ex utero*, it does not "become" a human being, for it is a human being *already*, albeit an immature human being, just as a newborn infant is an immature human being who will undergo quite dramatic growth and development over time.

These considerations undermine the familiar argument, recited by Rubenfeld, that "the potential" of an *unfertilized* ovum to develop into a whole human being does not make it into "a person." The fact is, though, that an ovum is not a whole human being. It is, rather, a part of another human being (the woman whose ovum it is) with merely the potential to give rise to, in interaction with a part of yet another human being (a man's sperm cell), a new and whole human being. Unlike the zygote, it lacks both genetic distinctness and completeness, as well as the active capacity to develop itself into an adult member of the human species. It is living human cellular material, but, left to itself, it will never become a human being, however hospitable its environment may be. It will "die" as a human ovum, just as countless skin cells "die" daily as nothing more than skin cells. If successfully fertilized by a human sperm, which, like the ovum (but dramatically unlike the zygote), lacks the active potential to develop into an adult member of the human species, then *substantial* change (that is, a change of *natures*) will occur. There will no longer be merely an egg, which was part of the mother, sharing her genetic composition, and a sperm, which was part of the father, sharing his genetic composition; instead, there will be a genetically complete, distinct, unified, self-integrating human organism, whose nature differs from that of the gametes—not mere human material, but a human being.

These considerations also make clear that it is incorrect to argue (as some pro-choice advocates have argued) that, just as "I" was never a week-old sperm or ovum, "I" was likewise never a week-old embryo. It truly makes no sense to say that "I" was once a sperm (or an unfertilized egg) that matured into an adult. Conception was the occasion of substantial change (that is, change from one complete individual entity to another) that brought into being a distinct self-integrating organism with a specifically human nature. By contrast, it makes every bit as much sense to say that I was once a week-old embryo as to say that I was once a week-old infant or a ten-year-old child. It was the new organism created at conception that, without itself undergoing any change of substance, matured into a week-old embryo, a fetus, an infant, a child, an adolescent, and, finally, an adult.

But Rubenfeld has another argument: "Cloning processes give to non-zygotic cells the potential for development into distinct, self-integrating human beings; thus to recognize the zygote as a human being is to recognize all human cells as human beings, which is absurd."

It is true that a distinct, self-integrating human organism that came into being by a process of cloning would be, like a human organism that comes into being as a monozygotic twin, a human being. That being, no less than human beings conceived by the union of sperm and egg, would possess a human nature and the active potential to mature as a human being. However, even assuming the possibility of cloning human beings from non-zygotic human cells, the non-zygotic cell must be activated by a process that effects substantial change and not mere development or maturation. Left to itself, apart from an activation process capable of effecting a change of substance or natures, the cell will mature and die as a human cell, not as a human being.

❧⦿❧

The scientific evidence establishes the fact that each of us was, from conception, a human being. Science, not religion, vindicates this crucial premise of the pro-life claim. From it, there is no avoiding the conclusion that deliberate feticide is a form of homicide. The only real questions remaining are moral and political, not scientific: Although I will not go into the matter here, I do not see how direct abortion can even be considered a matter of "justified homicide." It is important to recognize, however, as traditional moralists always have recognized, that not all procedures that foreseeably result in fetal death are, properly speaking, abortions. Although any procedure whose precise objective is the destruction of fetal life is certainly an abortion, and cannot be justified, some procedures result in fetal death as an unintended, albeit foreseen and accepted, side effect. Where procedures of the latter sort are done for very grave reasons, they may be justifiable. For example, traditional morality recognizes that a surgical operation to remove a life-threateningly cancerous uterus, even in a woman whose pregnancy is not far enough along to enable the child to be removed from her womb and sustained by a life support system, is ordinarily morally permissible. Of course, there are in this area of moral reflection, as in others, "borderline" cases that are difficult to classify and evaluate. Mercifully, modern medical technology has made such cases exceptionally rare in real life. Only in the most extraordinary circumstances today do women and their families and physicians find it necessary to consider a procedure that will result in fetal death as the only way of preserving maternal life. In any event, the political debate about abortion is not, in reality, about cases of this sort; it is about "elective" or "social indication" abortions, viz., the deliberate destruction of unborn human life for non-therapeutic reasons.

A final point: In my own experience, conversion from the pro-choice to the pro-life cause is often (though certainly not always) a partial cause of religious conversion rather than an effect. Frequently, people who are not religious, or who are only weakly so, begin to have doubts about the moral defensibility of deliberate feticide. Although most of their friends are pro-choice, they find that position increasingly difficult to defend or live with. They perceive practical inconsistencies in their, and their friends', attitudes toward the unborn depending on whether the child is "wanted" or not. Perhaps they find themselves arrested by sonographic (or other even more sophisticated) images of the child's life in the womb. So the doubts begin creeping in. For the first time, they are really prepared to listen to the pro-life argument (often despite their negative attitude toward people—or "the kind of people"—who are pro-life); and somehow, it sounds more compelling than it did before. Gradually, as they become firmly pro-life, they find themselves questioning the whole philosophy of life—in a word, secularism—associated with their former view. They begin to understand the reasons that led them out of the pro-choice and into the pro-life camp as God's reasons, too.

**Mary Gordon**  **NO**

# A Moral Choice

**I** am having lunch with six women. What is unusual is that four of them are in their seventies, two of them widowed, the other two living with husbands beside whom they've lived for decades. All of them have had children. Had they been men, they would have published books and hung their paintings on the walls of important galleries. But they are women of a certain generation, and their lives were shaped around their families and personal relations. They are women you go to for help and support. We begin talking about the latest legislative act that makes abortion more difficult for poor women to obtain. An extraordinary thing happens. Each of them talks about the illegal abortions she had during her young womanhood. Not one of them was spared the experience. Any of them could have died on the table of whatever person (not a doctor in any case) she was forced to approach, in secrecy and in terror, to end a pregnancy that she felt would blight her life.

I mention this incident for two reasons: first as a reminder that all kinds of women have always had abortions; second because it is essential that we remember that an abortion is performed on a living woman who has a life in which a terminated pregnancy is only a small part. Morally speaking, the decision to have an abortion doesn't take place in a vacuum. It is connected to other choices that a woman makes in the course of an adult life.

Anti-choice propagandists paint pictures of women who choose to have abortions as types of moral callousness, selfishness, or irresponsibility. The woman choosing to abort is the dressed-for-success yuppie who gets rid of her baby so that she won't miss her Caribbean vacation or her chance for promotion. Or she is the feckless, promiscuous ghetto teenager who couldn't bring herself to just say no to sex. A third, purportedly kinder, gentler picture has recently begun to be drawn. The woman in the abortion clinic is there because she is misinformed about the nature of the world. She is having an abortion because society does not provide for mothers and their children, and she mistakenly thinks that another mouth to feed will be the ruin of her family, not understanding that the temporary truth of family unhappiness doesn't stack up beside the eternal verity that abortion is murder. Or she is the dupe of her husband or boyfriend, who talks her into having an abortion because a child will be a drag on his life-style. None of these pictures created by the anti-choice movement assumes that the decision to have an abortion is made responsibly, in the context of a morally lived life, by a free and responsible moral agent.

# The Ontology of the Fetus

How would a woman who habitually makes choices in moral terms come to the decision to have an abortion? The moral discussion of abortion centers on the issue of whether or not abortion is an act of murder. At first glance it would seem that the answer should follow directly upon two questions: Is the fetus human? and Is it alive? It would be absurd to deny that a fetus is alive or that it is human. What would our other options be—to say that it is inanimate or belongs to another species? But we habitually use the terms "human" and "live" to refer to parts of our body—"human hair," for example, or "live red-blood cells"—and we are clear in our understanding that the nature of these objects does not rank equally with an entire personal existence. It then seems important to consider whether the fetus, this alive human thing, is a *person,* to whom the term "murder" could sensibly be applied. How would anyone come to a decision about something so impalpable as personhood? Philosophers have struggled with the issue of personhood, but in language that is so abstract that it is unhelpful to ordinary people making decisions in the course of their lives. It might be more productive to begin thinking about the status of the fetus by examining the language and customs that surround it. This approach will encourage us to focus on the choosing, acting woman, rather than the act of abortion—as if the act were performed by abstract forces without bodies, histories, attachments.

This focus on the acting woman is useful because a pregnant woman has an identifiable, consistent ontology, and a fetus takes on different ontological identities over time. But common sense, experience, and linguistic usage point clearly to the fact that we habitually consider, for example, a seven-week-old fetus to be different from a seven-month-old one. We can tell this by the way we respond to the involuntary loss of one as against the other. We have different language for the experience of the involuntary expulsion of the fetus from the womb depending upon the point of gestation at which the experience occurs. If it occurs early in the pregnancy, we call it a miscarriage; if late, we call it a stillbirth.

We would have an extreme reaction to the reversal of those terms. If a woman referred to a miscarriage at seven weeks as a stillbirth, we would be alarmed. It would shock our sense of propriety; it would make us uneasy; we would find it disturbing, misplaced—as we do when a bag lady sits down in a restaurant and starts shouting, or an octogenarian arrives at our door in a sailor suit. In short, we would suspect that the speaker was mad. Similarly, if a doctor or a nurse referred to the loss of a seven-month-old fetus as a miscarriage, we would be shocked by that person's insensitivity: could she or he not understand that a fetus that age is not what it was months before?

Our ritual and religious practices underscore the fact that we make distinctions among fetuses. If a woman took the bloody matter—indistinguishable from a heavy period—of an early miscarriage and insisted upon putting it in a tiny coffin and marking its grave, we would have serious concerns about her mental health. By the same token, we would feel squeamish about flushing a seven-month-old fetus down the toilet—something we would quite normally do with an early miscarriage. There are no prayers for the matter of a miscarriage, nor do we feel there should be. Even a Catholic priest would not baptize the issue of an early miscarriage.

The difficulties stem, of course, from the odd situation of a fetus's ontology: a complicated, differentiated, and nuanced response is required when we are dealing with an entity that changes over time. Yet we are in the habit of making distinctions like this. At one point we know that a child is no longer a child but an adult. That this question is vexed and problematic is clear from our difficulty in determining who is a juvenile offender and who is an adult criminal and at what age sexual intercourse ceases to be known as statutory rape. So at what point, if any, do we on the pro-choice side say that the developing fetus is a person, with rights equal to its mother's?

The anti-choice people have one advantage over us; their monolithic position gives them unity on this question. For myself, I am made uneasy by third-trimester abortions, which take place when the fetus could live outside the mother's body, but I also know that these are extremely rare and often performed on very young girls who have had difficulty comprehending the realities of pregnancy. It seems to me that the question of late abortions should be decided case by case, and that fixation on this issue is a deflection from what is most important: keeping early abortions, which are in the majority by far, safe and legal. I am also politically realistic enough to suspect that bills restricting late abortions are not good-faith attempts to make distinctions about the nature of fetal life. They are, rather, the cynical embodiments of the hope among anti-choice partisans that technology will be on their side and that medical science's ability to create situations in which younger fetuses are viable outside their mothers' bodies will increase dramatically in the next few years. Ironically, medical science will probably make the issue of abortion a minor one in the near future. The RU-486 pill, which can induce abortion early on, exists, and whether or not it is legally available (it is not on the market here, because of pressure from anti-choice groups), women will begin to obtain it. If abortion can occur through chemical rather than physical means, in the privacy of one's home, most people not directly involved will lose interest in it. As abortion is transformed from a public into a private issue, it will cease to be perceived as political; it will be called personal instead.

## An Equivocal Good

But because abortion will always deal with what it is to create and sustain life, it will always be a moral issue. And whether we like it or not, our moral thinking about abortion is rooted in the shifting soil of perception. In an age in which much of our perception is manipulated by media that specialize in the sound bite and the photo op, the anti-choice partisans have a twofold advantage over us on the pro-choice side. The pro-choice moral position is more complex, and the experience we defend is physically repellent to contemplate. None of us in the pro-choice movement would suggest that abortion is not a regrettable occurrence. Anti-choice proponents can offer pastel photographs of babies in buntings, their eyes peaceful in the camera's gaze. In answer, we can't offer the material of an early abortion, bloody, amorphous in a paper cup, to prove that what has just been removed from the woman's body is not a child, not in the same category of being as the adorable bundle in an adoptive mother's arms. It is not a pleasure to look at the physical evidence of abortion, and most of us don't get the opportunity to do so.

The theologian Daniel Maguire, uncomfortable with the fact that most theological arguments about the nature of abortion are made by men who have never been anywhere near an actual abortion, decided to visit a clinic and observe abortions being performed. He didn't find the experience easy, but he knew that before he could in good conscience make a moral judgment on abortion, he needed to experience through his senses what an aborted fetus is like: he needed to look at and touch the controversial entity. He held in his hand the bloody fetal stuff; the eight-week-old fetus fit in the palm of his hand, and it certainly bore no resemblance to either of his two children when he had held them moments after their birth. He knew at that point what women who have experienced early abortions and miscarriages know: that some event occurred, possibly even a dramatic one, but it was not the death of a child.

Because issues of pregnancy and birth are both physical and metaphorical, we must constantly step back and forth between ways of perceiving the world. When we speak of gestation, we are often talking in terms of potential, about events and objects to which we attach our hopes, fears, dreams, and ideals. A mother can speak to the fetus in her uterus and name it; she and her mate may decorate a nursery according to their vision of the good life; they may choose for an embryo a college, a profession, a dwelling. But those of us who are trying to think morally about pregnancy and birth must remember that these feelings are our own projections onto what is in reality an inappropriate object. However charmed we may be by an expectant father's buying a little football for something inside his wife's belly, we shouldn't make public policy based on such actions, nor should we force others to live their lives conforming to our fantasies.

As a society, we are making decisions that pit the complicated future of a complex adult against the fate of a mass of cells lacking cortical development. The moral pressure should be on distinguishing the true from the false, the real suffering of living persons from our individual and often idiosyncratic dreams and fears. We must make decisions on abortion based on an understanding of how people really do live. We must be able to say that poverty is worse than not being poor, that having dignified and meaningful work is better than working in conditions of degradation, that raising a child one loves and has desired is better than raising a child in resentment and rage, that it is better for a twelve-year-old not to endure the trauma of having a child when she is herself a child.

When we put these ideas against the ideas of "child" or "baby," we seem to be making a horrifying choice of life-style over life. But in fact we are telling the truth of what it means to bear a child, and what the experience of abortion really is. This is extremely difficult, for the object of the discussion is hidden, changing, potential. We make our decisions on the basis of approximate and inadequate language, often on the basis of fantasies and fears. It will always be crucial to try to separate genuine moral concern from phobia, punitiveness, superstition, anxiety, a desperate search for certainty in an uncertain world.

One of the certainties that is removed if we accept the consequences of the pro-choice position is the belief that the birth of a child is an unequivocal good. In real life we act knowing that the birth of a child is not always a good thing: people are sometimes depressed, angry, rejecting, at the birth of a child. But this is a difficult truth to tell; we don't like to say it, and one of the fears preyed on by anti-choice proponents is that if we cannot look at the birth of a child as an unequivocal good, then there is nothing to look toward. The desire for security of the imagination, for typological fixity, particularly in the area of "the good," is an understandable desire. It must seem to some anti-choice people that we on the pro-choice side are not only murdering innocent children but also murdering hope. Those of us who have experienced the birth of a desired child and felt the joy of that moment can be tempted into believing that it was the physical experience of the birth itself that was the joy. But it is crucial to remember that the birth of a child itself is a neutral occurrence emotionally: the charge it takes on is invested in it by the people experiencing or observing it.

## The Fear of Sexual Autonomy

These uncertainties can lead to another set of fears, not only about abortion but about its implications. Many anti-choice people fear that to support abortion is to cast one's lot with the cold and technological rather than with the warm and natural, to head down the slippery slope toward a brave new world where handicapped children are left on mountains to starve and the old are put out in the snow. But if we look at the history of abortion, we don't see the embodiment of what the anti-choice proponents fear. On the contrary, excepting the grotesque counterexample of the People's Republic of China (which practices forced abortion), there seems to be a real link between repressive anti-abortion stances and repressive governments. Abortion was banned in Fascist Italy and Nazi Germany; it is illegal in South Africa and in Chile. It is paid for by the governments of Denmark, England, and the Netherlands, which have national health and welfare systems that foster the health and well-being of mothers, children, the old, and the handicapped.

Advocates of outlawing abortion often refer to women seeking abortion as self-indulgent and materialistic. In fact these accusations mask a discomfort with female sexuality, sexual pleasure, and sexual autonomy. It is possible for a woman to have a sexual life unriddled by fear only if she can be confident that she need not pay for a failure of technology or judgment (and who among us has never once been swept away in the heat of a sexual moment?) by taking upon herself the crushing burden of unchosen motherhood.

It is no accident, therefore, that the increased appeal of measures to restrict maternal conduct during pregnancy—and a new focus on the physical autonomy of the pregnant woman—have come into public discourse at precisely the time when women are achieving unprecedented levels of economic and political autonomy. What has surprised me is that some of this new anti-autonomy talk comes to us from the left. An example of this new discourse is an article by Christopher Hitchens that appeared in *The Nation* last April, in which the author asserts his discomfort with abortion. Hitchens's tone is impeccably British: arch, light, we're men of the left.

> Anyone who has ever seen a sonogram or has spent even an hour with a textbook on embryology knows that the emotions are not the deciding factor. In order to terminate a pregnancy, you have to still a heartbeat, switch off a developing brain, and whatever the method, break some bones and rupture some organs. As to whether this involves pain on the "Silent Scream" scale, I have no idea. The "right to life" leadership, again, has cheapened everything it touches. ["Silent Scream" refers to Dr. Bernard Nathanson's widely debated antiabortion film *The Silent Scream*, in which an abortion on a 12-week-old fetus is shown from inside the uterus.—Eds.]

"It is a pity," Hitchens goes on to say, "that . . . the majority of feminists and their allies have stuck to the dead ground of 'Me Decade' possessive individualism, an ideology that has more in common than it admits with the prehistoric right, which it claims to oppose but has in fact encouraged." Hitchens proposes, as an alternative, a program of social reform that would make contraception free and support a national adoption service. In his opinion, it would seem, women have abortions for only two reasons: because they are selfish or because they are poor. If the state will take care of the economic problems and the bureaucratic messiness around adoption, it remains only for the possessive individualists to get their act together and walk with their babies into the communal utopia of the future. Hitchens would allow victims of rape or incest to have free abortions, on the grounds that since they didn't choose to have sex, the women should not be forced to have the babies. This would seem to put the issue of volition in a wrong and telling place. To Hitchens's mind, it would appear, if a woman chooses to have sex, she can't choose whether or not to have a baby. The implications of this are clear. If a woman is consciously and volitionally sexual, she should be prepared to take her medicine. And what medicine must the consciously sexual male take? Does Hitchens really believe, or want us to believe, that every male who has unintentionally impregnated a woman will be involved in the lifelong responsibility for the upbringing of the engendered child? Can he honestly say that he has observed this behavior—or, indeed, would want to see it observed—in the world in which he lives?

## Real Choices

It is essential for a moral decision about abortion to be made in an atmosphere of open, critical thinking. We on the pro-choice side must accept that there are indeed anti-choice activists who take their position in good faith. I believe, however, that they are people for whom childbirth is an emotionally overladen topic, people who are susceptible to unclear thinking because of their unrealistic hopes and fears. It is important for us in the pro-choice movement to be open in discussing those areas involving abortion which are nebulous and unclear. But we must not forget that there are some things that we know to be undeniably true. There are some undeniable bad consequences of a woman's being forced to bear a child against her will. First is the trauma of going through a pregnancy and giving birth to a child who is not desired, a trauma more long-lasting than that experienced by some (only some) women who experience an early abortion. The grief of giving up a child at its birth—and at nine months it is a child whom one has felt move inside one's body—is underestimated both by anti-choice partisans and by those for whom access to adoptable children is important. This grief should not be forced on any woman—or, indeed, encouraged by public policy.

We must be realistic about the impact on society of millions of unwanted children in an overpopulated world. Most of the time, human beings have sex not because they want to make babies. Yet throughout history sex has resulted in unwanted pregnancies. And women have always aborted. One thing that is not hidden, mysterious, or debatable is that making abortion illegal will result in the deaths of women, as it has always done. Is our historical memory so short that none of us remember aunts, sisters, friends, or mothers who were killed or rendered sterile by septic abortions? Does no one in the anti-choice movement remember stories or actual experiences of midnight drives to filthy rooms from which aborted women were sent out, bleeding, to their fate? Can anyone genuinely say that it would be a moral good for us as a society to return to those conditions?

Thinking about abortion, then, forces us to take moral positions as adults who understand the complexities of the world and the realities of human suffering, to make decisions based on how people actually live and choose, and not on our fears, prejudices, and anxieties about sex and society, life and death.

# EXPLORING THE ISSUE

## Should Abortion Be Restricted?

### Critical Thinking and Reflection

1. Is being a "person" different from being "a human being"? Gordon seems to think so, but George considers the distinction an arbitrary one, based more on emotion than reason. How do you come out on the question?
2. When does human life begin? Is an 8-month fetus essentially different from a 2-minute old baby? If so, how so? If not, should late-term abortions be banned?
3. What is the point of Gordon's story about her conversation with older women who had had abortions?

### Is There Common Ground?

There are some areas where common ground can be found. They include help for women who decide not to abort, such as medical assistance during pregnancy and after birth, care for their babies, assistance in housing, and job searches for the mothers. Pro-lifers would also like greater information about child development in the womb, so that women can make a more informed decision about whether to abort. Pro-choicers would like more information to be given young people about methods of birth control, to which pro-lifers would rejoin that information about the advantages of "waiting until marriage" would be better. If *Roe v. Wade* is ever overturned, still other areas of common ground might be found in various states, such as banning late-term abortions, favored by large majorities of Americans.

### Additional Resources

Barbara Hinkson Craig and David M. O'Brien, *Abortion and American Politics* (Chatham House, 1993), is a historical treatment of the abortion controversy in America. An interesting examination of the political factors that have influenced the abortion debate can be found in William Saletan, *Bearing Right: How Conservatives Won the Abortion War* (University of California Press, 2000). Saletan concludes that although abortion remains legal, antiabortion forces have largely won by eliminating most public financing of anything related to abortion or family planning. Peter Charles Hoffer, ed., *The Abortion Rights Controversy in America: A Legal Reader* (University of North Carolina Press, 2004), brings together a wide variety of legal briefs, oral arguments, court opinions, newspaper reports, and contemporary essays. In *What* Roe v. Wade *Should Have Said,* edited by Jack M. Balkin (New York University Press, 2005), eleven leading constitutional scholars of varying viewpoints have rewritten the opinions in *Roe v. Wade* with the insights acquired by three decades of experience. Francis J. Beckwith, *Defending Life: A Moral and Legal Case Against Abortion Choice* (Cambridge University Press, 2007), offers a comprehensive philosophical defense of the pro-life position; in the process, it takes on *Roe v. Wade* and its leading defenders, offering rebuttals to their arguments.

# ISSUE 12

# Is the Welfare State Obsolete?

**YES: Yuval Levin,** from "Beyond the Welfare State," *National Affairs* (Spring 2011)

**NO: Irwin Garfinkel, Lee Rainwater, and Timothy Smeeding,** from *Wealth & Welfare States: Is America a Laggard or Leader?* (Oxford University Press, 2010)

### ISSUE SUMMARY

**YES:** Yuval Levin, a Fellow at the Ethics and Public Policy Center in Washington, DC argues that democratic capitalism provides a compelling contrast to the shortcomings of the socialist welfare state.

**NO:** Social scientists Irwin Garfinkel, Lee Rainwater, and Timothy Smeeding believe that the welfare state enriches nations and should be maintained.

"The Welfare State" is an idea that has been defended and condemned, but rarely given an agreed-upon definition. Broadly conceived by its supporters, the welfare state is optimistically viewed as a network of benefits that enable all members of society to fulfill their capacities as individuals and members of society. Except for absolutist libertarians and anarchists, nearly all Americans accept the desirability of police to protect individuals, the military to protect the nation, and certain other services that only the government can provide.

But what Americans mean by the welfare state involves much more government involvement in the lives of its citizens. There has always been widespread support for government's provision of the police and military to safeguard individuals and the nation, the building of roads and other public projects beyond the capacity or financial interest of private individuals and corporations, and the most basic areas requiring universal agreement (ranging from patent laws to traffic laws). More controversially, Congress and the states had adopted legislation in the early twentieth century to establish childhood education, product safety, and other social policies. Still more controversial was the adoption of federal regulation of banking and food safety.

Despite all of this government regulation, Americans are likely to identify the beginning of the American welfare state with the adoption by Congress of public policies to safeguard Americans, as President Franklin Delano Roosevelt put it in 1934, "against misfortunes which cannot be wholly eliminated in this man-made world of ours." Roosevelt called this the New Deal. Spurred by the president, Congress adopted unprecedented programs such as government regulation as far-reaching as Aid to Dependent Children, unemployment insurance, and a federal pension scheme for older retired citizens.

That pension system was part of the Social Security Act of 1935 that covered workers in commerce and industry, and was financed by compulsory payroll taxes imposed upon both employees and employers. The Act has been amended many times to expand coverage to new groups of workers, add benefits for survivors and dependents, adjust benefits to reflect inflation, add disability, hospital and medical insurance, and numerous other changes.

Opponents objected that the Social Security Act imposed a tax on workers and employers that would overburden industry, reduce the purchasing power of workers, and could be diverted to other uses, leading to an increase in the national debt. The harshest criticism of Social Security and of later welfare state regulation is that these laws endorse the proposition that "big brother (that is, the government) knows best," and people are not to be trusted to look out for their own best interests. Opponents believed, and still believe, that the fundamental flaw of the welfare state is that it imposes socialistic state paternalism at the price of the loss of freedom and personal responsibility. It is, conservatives believe, too high a price to pay.

Defenders of Social Security argued that the tax meant that retiring workers were not being promised a reward that a future Congress could withdraw, but earning a retirement pension that could not be denied because it represented not an ordinary Act of Congress, but a contract to which the beneficiaries had contributed. The debate has been renewed recently by those who would allow younger workers to opt out of the retirement system.

The three decades following the Second World War have been hailed as a "golden age" for the welfare state. In some European countries this resulted in the adoption of government-sponsored child care, health insurance, university education, and extended employment benefits. Great Britain adopted the Beveridge Plan for cradle-to-grave insurance. Industrial nations raised taxes in order to pay tor these new programs. The United States never went this far, yet President Lyndon Johnson's vision of the Great Society led to the adoption of unprecedented social programs that greatly expanded the welfare state in America.

These programs include the Elementary and Secondary Education Act, committing the federal government for the first time to helping local school districts; Head Start, a program to provide pre-school education; Medicare, providing health insurance for older Americans; Medicaid, providing similar coverage for poorer Americans; environmental laws to promote clean air, clean water, air pollution, and solid-waste disposal; the Civil Rights Act that eliminated "whites only" in employment and public accommodations, and the Voting Rights Act to eliminate racial discrimination in elections. More recent welfare state measures have included the Earned Income Tax Credit, the Family and Medical Leave Act, the Child Tax Credit, and the Americans with Disabilities Act.

A major intent of many of these measures was to reduce poverty and inequality. Whether as a result of these laws or as a consequence of the prosperity that followed the Second World War, poverty and inequality declined. But this has not occurred in the past three decades. Social and financial conditions beyond the law have had a negative influence. Millions of jobs have been lost in the United States because businesses have failed or merged (resulting in the dismissal of surplus employees) or have moved overseas, as we witness every day in the near-absence of "made-in-U.S.A." tags on so many consumer products. Well-paid men and women are more likely to marry each other, concentrating wealth still more. Better-financed schools in higher income communities are likely to equip young people better to qualify for new types of employment. Some young people, partly because of economic or social handicap, lack the will, ability, or opportunity to succeed in this new economy.

This decline has been evident for a generation, and particularly since the beginning of the great recession that began in 2007–2008. Neither the federal nor the state governments can afford the massive costs of welfare programs, and they are inclined to reduce those programs that are most costly, or most controversial, or fail to achieve their objectives. States, obliged to balance their budgets (unlike the national government) have sharply cut their expenditures for public education and civil services, and are unwilling or unable to meet the costs of federal welfare programs. The normal Social Security retirement age has been raised from 65 to 67, reducing the number of years that people can collect benefits. In the 1980s, it became more difficult to qualify for disability insurance.

At one time, the term "welfare" had so positive an attachment that *The Saturday Evening Post*, the most popular magazine in America in the early twentieth century, warned critics of welfare to avoid using the term: "Who's against welfare: Nobody. . . . Fighting an election by opposing welfare is on a par with taunting an opponent for having been born in a log cabin." Times have changed, and "welfare" has acquired a negative connotation associated with what many view as the people who expect "handouts" with no effort to work required of them, welfare cheats, freeloaders, illegal immigrants, and other members of the "undeserving poor."

When President Bill Clinton, in signing the 1996 welfare reform bill, promised to "end welfare as we know it," the national government was adopting large cuts to food stamps for low-income families, ending the entitlement to public assistance, placing time limits on benefits, tying aid to work, transferring programs from the federal government to the states, and reducing or eliminating the eligibility of immigrants and the disabled. Nearly two decades after the welfare reform bill, the challenge that confronts public policy is that the new program's work requirements cannot be met when there are few jobs for unemployed workers to fill. It is ironic, but nevertheless true, that governments are likely to curtail welfare programs when more people are experiencing economic need, because governments are also running out of money.

The United States devotes about one-fifth of its gross domestic product to financing the welfare state, including direct spending and tax breaks for social purposes. One of the challenges for the future is the expectation that their will be greater social needs because the number of aged people is growing and the proportion of employable people is declining.

Yuval Levin, an authority on health care and bioethics, argues that democratic capitalism provides a compelling contrast to the shortcomings of the socialist welfare state. Social scientists Garfinkel, Rainwater, and Smeeding believe that the welfare state enriches nations and should be maintained.

# YES ↵

Yuval Levin

## Beyond the Welfare State

It is becoming increasingly clear that we in America are living through a period of transition. One chapter of our national life is closing, and another is about to begin. We can sense this in the tense volatility of our electoral politics, as dramatic "change elections" follow closely upon one another. We can feel it in the unseemly mood of decline that has infected our public life—leaving our usually cheerful nation fretful about global competition and unsure if the next generation will be able to live as well as the present one. Perhaps above all, we can discern it in an overwhelming sense of exhaustion emanating from many of our public institutions—our creaking mid-century transportation infrastructure, our overburdened regulatory agencies struggling to keep pace with a dynamic economy, our massive entitlement system edging toward insolvency.

But these are mostly symptoms of our mounting unease. The most significant cause runs deeper. We have the feeling that profound and unsettling change is afoot because the vision that has dominated our political imagination for a century—the vision of the social-democratic welfare state—is drained and growing bankrupt, and it is not yet clear just what will take its place.

That vision was an answer to a question America must still confront: How shall we balance the competing aspirations of our society—aspirations to both wealth and virtue, dynamism and compassion? How can we fulfill our simultaneous desires to race ahead yet leave no one behind? The answer offered by the social-democratic ideal was a technocratic welfare state that would balance these aspirations through all-encompassing programs of social insurance. We would retain a private economy, but it would be carefully managed in order to curb its ill effects, and a large portion of its output would be used by the government to address large social problems, lessen inequality, and thus also build greater social solidarity.

Of course, this vision has never been implemented in full. But it has offered a model, for good and for ill. For the left, it provided long-term goals, criteria for distinguishing progress from retreat in making short-term compromises, and a kind of definition of the just society. For the right, it was a foil to be combated and averted—an archetype of soulless, stifling bureaucratic hubris—and it helped put objections to seemingly modest individual leftward steps into a broader, more coherent context. But both ends of our politics seemed implicitly to agree that, left to its own momentum, this is where our country was headed—where history would take us if no one stood athwart it yelling stop.

It is no longer really possible to think so. All over the developed world, nations are coming to terms with the fact that the social-democratic welfare state is turning out to be untenable. The reason is partly institutional: The administrative state is dismally inefficient and unresponsive, and therefore ill-suited to our age of endless choice and variety. The reason is also partly cultural and moral: The attempt to rescue the citizen from the burdens of responsibility has undermined the family, self-reliance, and self-government. But, in practice, it is above all fiscal: The welfare state has turned out to be unaffordable, dependent as it is upon dubious economics and the demographic model of a bygone era. Sustaining existing programs of social insurance, let alone continuing to build new ones on the social-democratic model, has become increasingly difficult in recent years, and projections for the coming decades paint an impossibly grim and baleful picture. There is simply no way that Europe, Japan, or America can actually go where the economists' long-term charts now point—to debts that utterly overwhelm their productive capacities, governments that do almost nothing but support the elderly, and economies with no room for dynamism, for growth, or for youth. Some change must come, and so it will. . . .

The fact is that we do not face a choice between the liberal welfare state on one hand and austerity on the other. Those are two sides of the same coin: Austerity and decline are what will come if we do not reform the welfare state. . . .

Conservatives must produce . . . a vision that emphasizes the pursuit of economic growth, republican virtues, and social mobility over economic security, value-neutral welfare, and material equality; that redefines the safety net as a means of making the poor more independent rather than making the middle class less so; and that translates these ideals into institutional forms that suit our modern, dynamic society. . . . The events of the past few years forced many Americans to wonder whether we were not headed toward an abyss. . . .

The fiscal crisis we face *is* an extended and expanded version of our deficit problem; the recession from which we are emerging *was* a preview of life under suffocating debt; the Obama agenda *does* seek incrementally to advance the larger social-democratic vision—especially on the health-care front, where that vision has seen its greatest fiscal failures. In each case, we have become more powerfully aware of the grave troubles that await us if we do not reform our welfare state—as though the frog in the pot got a glimpse of just how hot the water was about to get. This has made a growing number of Americans (though surely still not a majority) open to changing our ways while there remains a little time to do so, and has raised the possibility of gradually putting not only one program or another but the broad vision at the heart of our politics on the table.

That vision begins with the belief that capitalism, while capable of producing great prosperity, leaves a great many people profoundly insecure, and so must be both strictly controlled by a system of robust regulations and balanced off by a system of robust social insurance. From birth to death, citizens should be ensconced in a series of protections and benefits intended to shield them from the harsh edges of the market and allow them to pursue dignified, fulfilling lives: universal child care, universal health care, universal public schooling and higher education, welfare benefits for the poor, generous labor protections for workers, dexterous management of the levers of the economy to ease the cycles of boom and bust, skillful direction of public funds to spur private productivity and efficiency, and, finally, pensions for the elderly. Each component would be overseen by a competent and rational bureaucracy, and the whole would make for a system that is not only beneficent but unifying and dignifying, and that enables the pursuit of common national goals and ideals.

This system would encompass all citizens, not only the poor, in an effort to overcome some of the social consequences of the iniquities inherent in a capitalist economy. . . . The inequality, dislocation, and isolation caused by capitalism could be remedied together, and in a way that would also help to get the middle class invested in the system (not to say dependent on it) and help society to grow increasingly rational and enlightened under the guidance of an educated and benevolent governing class. This kind of welfare state aims not just at keeping the poor above a certain minimum level of subsistence and helping them rise, but at a new arrangement of society to be achieved by the redistribution of resources and responsibilities. . . .

Ours may be the only government to arise out of a distrust of government. Again and again in our history, passionate waves of resistance to authority have rattled our politics, while periods of trust in the state have been rare. The left has sought to use those rare moments—particularly the emergency of the Great Depression and the unique stretch of relative peace and prosperity of the early 1960s—to advance the welfare state where it could. Even then, however, it always faced staunch resistance, and proceeded by fits and starts—enacting one program or another in the hope of coming back for more when circumstances allowed it.

This has left us with a somewhat disjointed arrangement of welfare-state programs, tilted disproportionately toward the elderly—who are the foremost beneficiaries of our two largest entitlement programs (Social Security and Medicare) and receive more than a quarter of the benefits provided by the third largest (Medicaid). The other elements of our welfare state have taken the form of the many dozens of smaller, more targeted programs—from Head Start to public housing to the Children's Health Insurance Program—that fill out the federal government's massive entitlement and domestic discretionary budgets. All of these individual programs, large and small, fit into a broader pattern and trajectory defined by the social-democratic ideal. . . .

While the enactment of the two massive health-care entitlements of the Great Society period may have represented the peak of social-democratic activism in America, those two entitlements now also represent the failure of the social-democratic vision in practice. They have grown so unwieldy and expensive as to be thoroughly unsustainable, and in the process have helped inflate costs in the broader health-care sector in ways that now imperil the nation's fiscal future. The new health-care entitlement . . . promises to do more of the same, and thus to place even further stress on the crumbling foundations of our welfare state. . . .

The three key arguments in favor of this vision of the welfare state—its rationality and efficiency, its morality and capacity for unifying society, and its economic benefits—all turn out in reality to be among its foremost failings. First, the welfare state functions in practice through the administrative state—the network of public agencies that employ technical expertise and bureaucratic management to enforce rules and provide benefits and services. . . .

In our everyday experience, the bureaucratic state presents itself not as a benevolent provider and protector but as a corpulent behemoth—flabby, slow, and expressionless, unmoved by our concerns, demanding compliance with arcane and seemingly meaningless rules as it breathes musty air in our faces and sends us to the back of the line. . . .

Unresponsive ineptitude is not merely an annoyance. The sluggishness of the welfare state drains it of its moral force. The crushing weight of bureaucracy permits neither efficiency nor idealism. . . .

Worse yet, because the institutions of the welfare state are intended to be partial substitutes for traditional familial, social, religious, and cultural mediating institutions, their growth weakens the very structures that might balance our society's restless quest for prosperity and novelty and might replenish our supply of idealism.

This is the second major failing of this vision of society—a kind of spiritual failing. Under the rules of the modern welfare state, we give up a portion of the capacity to provide for ourselves and in return are freed from a portion of the obligation to discipline ourselves. Increasing economic collectivism enables increasing moral individualism, both of which leave us with less responsibility, and therefore with less grounded and meaningful lives.

Moreover, because all citizens—not only the poor—become recipients of benefits, people in the middle class come to approach their government as claimants, not as self-governing citizens, and to approach the social safety net not as a great majority of givers eager to make sure that a small minority of recipients are spared from devastating poverty but as a mass of dependents demanding what they are owed. It is hard to imagine an ethic better suited to undermining the moral basis of a free society. . . . Rather than strengthening social bonds, the rise of the welfare state has precipitated the collapse of family and community, especially among the poor. . . .

The failure of the social-democratic vision is . . . fundamentally a failure of moral wisdom. That is not to say, of course, that it did not produce positive benefits along the way. Indeed, the era in which the social-democratic vision has dominated our politics has hardly been an age of decline for America—it has been, if anything, the American century. And it has been a time of diminishing poverty and rising standards of living. But it is now becoming apparent that this was achieved by our spending our capital (economic, moral, and human) without replenishing it, and that this failure, too, is a defining characteristic of the social-democratic vision.

America's unchallenged economic prowess in the wake of the Second World War, and the resulting surge of growth and prosperity, were essential to enabling the flurry of social-democratic activism we know as the Great Society, and which continues to define the basic shape of our domestic policy. Flush with revenue and stirred by the promise of technocratic mastery, our government took on immense entitlement commitments and major social reforms in that era, and these have certainly had some of their intended consequences. But they have also struck at the roots (economic and especially moral) of our ability to sustain our strength. The collapse of the family among the poor—powerfully propelled by the ethic of social democracy and by a horrendously designed welfare system that was not improved until the mid-1990s—has vastly worsened social and economic inequality in America, and the capacity of generations to rise out of poverty. Our entitlement commitments, particularly those of the massive health-care entitlements enacted in the 1960s, stand to make ever-greater demands on our economic strength, and so to sap our potential to sustain that strength. And our system of age-based wealth transfers relies upon a demographic model that the welfare state seriously undermines, and that now bears no relation to the reality of American life. In the age of social democracy, we have failed to think generationally, and so have failed to think of the prerequisites for renewal.

These trends all come together in the third major failing of our welfare state, and the one that, more than any other, may yet bring about real change: its economic breakdown. Simply put, we cannot afford to preserve our welfare state in anything like its present form.

The heart of the problem is the heart of our welfare state: our entitlement system. Age-based wealth transfers in an aging society are obviously problematic. As Americans are living longer and having fewer children (and as the Baby Boomers retire at a rate of 10,000 people per day over the next 20 years), the ratio of workers paying taxes to retirees collecting benefits is falling precipitously—from 16 workers per retiree in 1950 to just three today, and closer to two in the coming decades. This means that even the simplest and least troubled of our age-based transfer programs—the Social Security program—is facing serious problems: Social Security ran a deficit for the first time last year, and the Congressional Budget Office estimates it will continue to do so from now on unless its structure is reformed. Add to that our exploding health-care costs—which the design of our health-care entitlements severely exacerbates—and you will begin to get a sense of the problem we confront. . . . The CBO estimates that, by 2025, Medicare, Medicaid, Social Security, and interest payments on the debt alone will consume every last cent of federal revenues, leaving all discretionary spending to be funded by borrowing. And that spending, too, has been growing by leaps and bounds recently—domestic discretionary spending has increased by 25% in just the past three years.

That explosion in discretionary spending is why our immediate budget picture is so bleak, but the fact that an entitlement crisis waits just around the corner means that there is no clear boundary any longer between our short-term and our longer-term fiscal problems. Our debt has begun to balloon, and absent major reforms, it will not stop. CBO figures show that, if current policies remain in place, the national debt will grow much faster than the economy in the coming years: A decade from now, the United States will owe nearly $20 trillion—more than three times what we owed in 2008. At that point, interest payments alone will consume about $800 billion a year—more than four times as much as they did in 2008. And the entitlement crisis will only just be getting underway.

This explosion of both discretionary and entitlement spending is like nothing our country has ever experienced, and it is why our welfare state is unsustainable. . . . If we do not change course, by 2030, America's national debt will be nearly twice the size of the economy; by 2050, it will be roughly three times the size of the economy and will continue to grow from there. Such massive and unprecedented debt will make it impossible for America to experience anything like the growth and prosperity that marked the post-war era. Simply paying interest on this debt, let alone funding the activities of government, will require more and more borrowing, as well as cuts in other areas and major tax increases. It will also leave us exposed to tremendous risk of inflation and dependent on the goodwill of our lenders. It will leave future generations saddled with an immense burden but unable to enjoy the benefits of much of what they will be paying for, since it will make it impossible to sustain our welfare state in anything like its current form.

Japan and the nations of Western Europe are looking at similar projections. And in our country, many state governments are facing their own dire fiscal prospects as a result of similarly unsustainable retirement commitments and spending patterns. This is where the social-democratic project has gotten us. If we simply follow this trajectory, then future generations considering this chart will have no doubt as to just when the turning point came, and just which generation failed to keep its charge.

It is unimaginable that the world's foremost economic power would do this to itself by choice. And we will not. We will change course. Changing course . . . will require extraordinary sacrifices from today's young Americans, who will need to continue paying the taxes necessary to support the retirements of their parents and grandparents while denying themselves the same level of benefits so their children and grandchildren can thrive. To persuade them to make such sacrifices, our political leaders will need to offer them a plausible program of reform, and an appealing vision of American life beyond the dream of social democracy.

That vision . . . must be a serious answer . . . to the same question that motivated the social-democratic ideal: How do we balance our aspirations to prosperity and virtue and build a thriving society that makes its wealth and promise accessible to all?

In their struggle with the left these past 60 years, conservatives . . . have focused on the size and scope of government, but not on its proper purposes— on yelling stop, but not on where to go instead. Now, as the social-democratic dream grows truly bankrupt and untenable, America finds itself governed by a reactionary party and a conservative party. The reactionary party, the Democratic Party, its head in the sand and its mind adrift in false nostalgia, insists that nothing is wrong, and that the welfare state requires little more than tinkering at the edges, and indeed further expansions. It lives always with the model of the Great Society in mind, and fails to grasp the ruin it threatens to bring upon the rising generation. It cannot imagine a different approach.

The conservative party, the Republican Party, still struggles for a vocabulary of resistance, and so has not taken up in earnest the vocabulary of alternatives. It calls on the spirit of the founders, but not on their genius for designing institutions; it shadowboxes Progressives who no longer exist (and whose successors, running on fumes and inertia, have nowhere near the intellectual depth to take up their case); it insists that our problem is just too much government.

But if the Republican Party is to be a truly conservative party, it will need to think its way to an agenda of conservative reform. Conservatism is reformist at its core, combining, as Edmund Burke put it, "a disposition to preserve and an ability to improve," and so responding to the changing world by means that seek to strengthen what is most essential. A conservative vision would be driven not by a desire to "fundamentally transform America" (as Barack Obama promised to do in 2008), but rather by an idea of what we want to be that is the best form of what we are. It would look to make our institutions suit us better, and so to make them serve us better and more effectively help us improve ourselves.

Our welfare state is very poorly suited to the kind of society we are—an aging society in which older people are, on the whole, wealthier than younger people. And it is very poorly suited to the kind of society we want to be—enterprising and vibrant, with a free economy, devoted to social mobility and eager to offer a hand up to the poor. A successful reform agenda would have to take account of both. . . .

It would begin with a simple and predictable tax system, with a broad base and low rates, free of most of today's deductions and exclusions. The only three worth keeping in the individual tax code are the tax exemption for retirement savings (which are far preferable to universal cash benefits to retirees), a unified child tax credit (to encourage parenthood and to offset the mistreatment of parents in the tax code), and the charitable-giving deduction (since a reduction in government's role in social welfare must be met with an increase in the role of civil society, which should be encouraged).

Second, essentially all government benefits—including benefits for the elderly—should be means-tested so that those in greater need receive more help and those who are not needy do not become dependent on public support. . . . Means-testing should, to the extent possible, be designed to avoid discouraging saving and work. And private retirement savings should be strongly encouraged and incentivized, so that people who have the means would build private nest eggs with less reliance on government.

Third, we should advance a consumer-based health-care system. . . .

Fourth, we should gradually but significantly reduce domestic discretionary spending, ending most of the discretionary Great Society programs and folding others into block grants to the states. The federal government's role in the provision of social services should be minimal, and largely limited to helping the states and the institutions of civil society better carry out their missions. . . .

Fifth, we should reduce the reach of the administrative state, paring back all but essential regulations and protections and adopting over time an ethic of keeping the playing field level rather than micromanaging market forces, and of preferring set rules (in regulation, in monetary policy, and elsewhere) to administrative discretion.

Obviously, these are only general principles and aims. And at least as important as what they contain is what they do not—what is left to the sphere of the family, religion, and civil society. Government must see itself as an ally and supporter of these crucial mediating institutions, not as a substitute for them. Its role is to sustain the preconditions for social, cultural, and economic vitality. . . .

Champions of our welfare state view democratic capitalism as the grim reality to be overcome and social democracy as the elevated ideal to be realized. But this has it backwards. The vision of social democracy has dominated our political life for many decades, but it is failing us. Real democratic capitalism—a free society with a free economy and a commitment to help every citizen enjoy the benefits of both—is the ideal that must guide the work of American domestic policy in the coming years. . . .

Irwin Garfinkel, Lee Rainwater, and Timothy Smeeding

→ **NO**

# The Future of the American Welfare State

...**T**he most general challenge to welfare states can be posed as reducing poverty and inequality, while at the same time increasing efficiency and growth. Although this exercise cannot be value free, scientific evidence plays a central role in our analysis. We place high value on achieving the traditional objectives of welfare state programs—economic security, poverty prevention and amelioration, opportunity and equality. At the same time, we believe that priority should be given to welfare state reforms that promote these objectives in ways that increase efficiency, economic growth and well-being. This priority points to investments in children, which is why the third challenge is the most important. But it also points to other reforms that are likely to improve both equity and efficiency. Though the specific proposals examined are limited to the United States, the challenges faced by our nation are not unique and therefore our analyses have implications for the welfare states of all rich nations.

## Balancing Taxes and Benefits in Old-Age Insurance

The Old Age, Survivors,' and Disability Insurance (OASDI) program—popularly known as Social Security—once again faces financial difficulties. [T]he 1983 Greenspan Commission recommended and Congress legislated to restore fiscal balance through a combination of benefit cuts and tax increases—increasing the age of retirement, taxing benefits, and increasing tax rates on workers. OASDI is financed primarily on a pay-as-you-go basis, with payroll taxes from current workers financing the benefits paid to current retirees. The payroll tax in 2009 equals 12.4 percent of the first $106,800 of earnings. An additional 2.9 percent of payroll tax on all earnings finances the Medicare program (which we deal with separately below). Since 1983, payroll taxes have exceeded benefits paid so that future benefits for both programs could be financed from the accumulated trust funds. Payments to beneficiaries are projected to exceed payroll tax revenues, starting in 2017 for Social Security, and requiring redemption of trust fund bonds to support payments. The Medicare system began to draw down its reserves in 2007. Without a change in policy, the OASDI trust fund is projected to be depleted by 2040. At that point, payroll taxes are projected to equal only 74 percent of benefit obligations. . . .

From *Wealth and Welfare States: Is America a Laggard or Leader?* (Oxford University Press, 2010). Copyright © 2010 by Irwin Garfinkel, Lee Rainwater, and Timothy Smeeding. Reprinted by permission of Oxford University Press.

## Adding Security and Efficiency to the System

President Bush proposed in 2003 to divert Social Security revenues to finance private savings accounts that would be invested in the stock market. Diverted contributions would reduce the guaranteed benefit that participants receive from Social Security, thereby decreasing benefit payments and reducing costs in the long term. Although increasing wealth and inheritances among the lower classes through private savings accounts is an attractive idea, doing so at the expense of the economic security achieved by social insurance is not a good idea, as the huge stock market decline in 2008 has clearly borne out. In practice, the Bush proposal would have led to little inheritable wealth among low earners as they would have been required to convert their private accounts into annuities. Moreover, the diversion of payroll taxes to private accounts would have exacerbated the Social Security revenue shortfall because the revenue diverted to private accounts would not be available to pay current benefits and would have to be raised from another source. President Bush never explained how he would finance the increased deficit. For all these reasons, the proposal was deservedly a non-starter in Congress.

While private accounts as a substitute for Social Security are not desirable, private accounts as an *add-on* to Social Security may be desirable. The United States could go a long way toward helping low- and moderate-income families achieve a higher living standard in retirement by enacting a new 1.5–2 percent private retirement account administered by a Federal Reserve-like Board of Directors. These accounts, equivalent to a national mandatory IRA or 401k retirement plan, would be an "add on" to OASDI and would require new financing. They would have no effect on people with adequate private pensions, who would reduce contributions to current plans to compensate for the new OASDI add-on. But they would provide private retirement accounts to the 40 percent of Americans now lacking them, thus giving every family another leg to stand on besides OASDI when they reach retirement age, while also cushioning against any further reductions in OASDI benefits. Furthermore, private accounts as an add-on rather than a substitute for Social Security had bi-partisan support. The precipitous drop in the stock market in 2008, however, is likely to diminish the attractiveness of private accounts even as an add-on to Social Security. Private accounts will contribute to security only if they can guarantee a safe investment vehicle, such as indexed government bonds. . . .

## Achieving Equal Access and Restraining the Growth of Health-Care Costs

The US health-care system stands out from that of other rich nations in two negative respects. It has the largest inequalities in access to health care and is, by far, the most expensive system. On the positive side, it provides high-quality care for the most fortunate and best-insured segment of its population. . . .

## Equal Access and Universal Coverage

Health care, like education, is a fundamental determinant of human capital and well-being. At the most fundamental level, health care is often a matter of life and death. At a slightly less, but still fundamental, level, it is an essential ingredient to the productivity and quality of life. Because of vaccinations, children no longer die from or become crippled by chicken pox, diphtheria, measles, mumps, rubella, polio, smallpox, and tetanus. Eyeglasses allow children and adults with weak vision to see very well. Steroids, nasal sprays, and consistent care allow children and adults with asthma to control the disease and lead normal lives. Without hip replacement surgery, those who need it experience ever-increasing pain and disability. With hip replacement surgery, older citizens in all the rich nations lead normal pain-free lives. Equal access to personal health care is, in this sense, an aspect of equality of opportunity. R. H. Tawney, the Fabian socialist, made this point eloquently nearly 80 years ago in his classic book *Equality*. Nobel Prize-winning economist, Amartya Sen makes essentially the same argument in his book *Inequality Re-examined* (1992). Virtually everyone in rich countries recognizes that health care is an essential ingredient to the productivity and quality of life and frequently to life itself. That conviction helps explain why large majorities in all countries favor equal access to health care and, along with the efficiency of community-provided health insurance, why medical care is largely socialized in all rich countries. Even in the United States, most adults believe in equal access to health care, and . . . health-care consumption is largely socialized.

But US practice diverges substantially from the ideal—not that the ideal has been achieved in many nations. In Great Britain, for example, where personal health care has been socialized since 1949, upper-class British citizens make better use of the National Health Service than do their lower-income compatriots. In the real world, perfection is unattainable. Elites will always find a way to secure better-than-average care. But other rich countries more closely approach equal access to health care. Britain comes closer. So do the Netherlands and Switzerland—which are viewed by some as possible models for the United States, and where privatized but heavily regulated insurers manage with government support to cover nearly all citizens. While the rich (the top 10–15 percent of the populations) in Europe can and do "buy up" with unsubsidized insurance to provide private rooms and quicker access to specialists, the "floor level" of health care is usually very high. . . .

## Constraining Costs

### Why Are Costs So High and Growing Rapidly?

Constraining the growth in health-care costs is at least as important as achieving universal coverage. For the last 30 years, per capita health-care costs in the US have grown a bit more than twice as rapidly as the growth in per capita GDP—4.3 percent versus 2.0 percent. The Congressional Budget Office (CBO) has projected the consequences for the federal costs of Medicare and Medicaid as a percentage of GDP if health-care costs continue to grow so rapidly compared to GDP. Currently, Social Security, Medicare, and Medicaid amount to under 10 percent of GDP. By 2074, all three are projected to amount to over 25 percent of GDP. . . .

### Short- and Long-Run Solutions

The twin goals of achieving equal access and restraining the growth of health-care costs create a very strong case for a publicly financed National Health Insurance system. Two other arguments strengthen that case. First, research-ers have found that increases in health-care spending are crowding out other public spending. Most recently, a study by Thomas Kane and Peter Orszag indicates that increased spending on Medicaid has displaced spending on higher education and other benefits, such as early childhood education, at both the federal and [the] state level. Restraining health-care spending is a prerequisite for shifting from ever increasing spending on the elderly to more productive spending on children. Second, a publicly financed system of National Health Insurance can help reverse the seemingly inexorable trend to increased inequality. Employer-provided health insurance, for the most part, assures that each employee pays for his or her own health insurance. If health insurance costs $5,000 per person, under employer-provided insurance, then each employee pays $5,000, in the form of reduced wages. By way of contrast, if health insurance were publicly financed by a proportional tax, the richest fifth of the population which earns about 60 percent of total income would pay for 60 percent of the cost or about $15,000 per person, while the poorest fifth which earns only about 5 percent of total income would pay only about $1,500 per person.

A publicly financed universal National Health Insurance program, even with private insurers as agents, would promote opportunity by equal-izing access to health care, reduce inequality by increasing the progressivity of financing, and increase economic efficiency by restraining the growth in health-care costs. . . .

# Restoring American Pre-Eminence in Education

Welfare state programs in all rich nations transfer substantial resources from the working-age population to the elderly population. As populations have grown older in all rich nations, old-age pensions and medical care have become the biggest welfare state programs. As the populations of rich countries continue to age, the costs of these programs will grow larger. The economic demographer Sam Preston, in his famous presidential address to the Population Association of America, called attention to the danger that the increasing burden of cash and in-kind transfers to the aged would crowd out investments in children.

Investing in children now will increase their future productivity, thereby increasing future earnings and the tax base and allowing the same level of support at lower tax rates. Conversely, investing inadequately now in children will lower future productivity, reduce incomes and the tax base, and require higher tax rates. Thus, ironically, perhaps, nations with aging populations must invest all the more in children in order to make the future burden of sup-porting the aged more tolerable. In this section, we discuss investments that would restore American pre-eminence in education. In the following section, we discuss other complementary investments in children.

## Universal Pre-School for Three and Four Year Olds

Extending the age of compulsory schooling downward to age three by enacting universal pre-school programs would increase productivity and reduce poverty and inequality. A 2003 National Academy of Sciences study estimated the cost of such a program at $25–35 billion above and beyond the $25–30 billion in public funds which we now spend on various public and non-profit pre-school programs.

Children who begin school at age three are more likely to enjoy learning and do better not only in school but also in adult life. Of children age three to five whose mothers are college-educated, 70 percent already attend pre-school. Only 38 percent of children whose mothers did not complete high school attend pre-school. Children whose mothers are high school drop-outs have the most to gain from pre-school, and the broader society will benefit the most from educating these children in high-quality public schools beginning at age three. But, more generally, because of the public benefits of education, everyone will benefit from universal pre-school.

Researchers have gathered very strong evidence that the benefits of high-quality early childhood education exceed the costs, especially for disadvantaged children. The strongest evidence comes from the Perry pre-school experiment initiated more than 30 years ago in Ypsilanti, Michigan, where children from disadvantaged families were randomly selected to be in either the experimental group or a control group. Children in the experimental group were eligible to participate in a very high-quality pre-school program. As the children grew older, those in the experimental group outperformed those in the control group in many ways. They did better in school, needed less remedial assistance, completed more years of schooling, committed fewer crimes, were less likely to be dependent upon welfare, earned more money, and paid more taxes. Even though high-quality pre-school is quite expensive—more than $16,000 for a two-year half-day program in 2004 dollars—and though most of the benefits come much later than costs are incurred and therefore get discounted, James Heckman reports in *Science* that the present discounted value of the benefits was nearly nine times the costs—or about $144,000! Evaluations of other good pre-school programs, including Head Start, also find positive effects. . . .

## Higher Education

Higher education graduation rates for children from low-income families are very low. Only 8 percent of all children born into the lowest-income quartile in 1966–70 graduated from college (within six years of finishing high school), as against 50 percent of top-quartile children. A study of elite colleges finds that, among all enrollees, 44 percent of lower-quartile children and 78 percent of higher-quartile enrollees now graduate. In fact, most disadvantaged kids, and especially minority kids, first enroll in two-year community colleges, from which only about a third go on to four-year colleges and universities. Because Americans are committed to greater social mobility, we hope that once these facts are widely known and understood, we will see a number of modest but important changes in United States higher education policy, at both federal and state levels, to address these inequities.

Achieving greater success in higher education for low-income children will require several changes. Students must be better prepared in high school, by taking the right courses, by developing better study habits, by taking standardized examinations, and by applying for admission to colleges. Secondary schools must take the lead here, especially with better career counseling, monitoring, and better information on the true costs of college (not the daunting "sticker prices" at very selective schools). State and federal governments need to expand need-based financial aid. Researchers have now amassed good evidence that higher tuition subsidies and direct grants increase both college attendance and completion.

Moreover, though zero-cost tuition reduces dropout rates in higher education by nearly 50 percent, it does not eliminate them. Recent evidence from Turner and Pallais and Turner suggests that college-going is an ever-lengthening process that is stretching itself out beyond five to six years after secondary school graduation. To reduce the time it takes them to earn a degree, students must not only become better prepared when they first enter college, but polices to retain students who are at risk of dropping out for non-academic reasons must be expanded. Thus, in addition to zero-cost tuition for students from low-income families, higher education policy should increasingly turn to the important issue of enrollment management and persistence to degree by instituting strategies that produce higher rates of graduation for those who enter post-secondary education.

Finally, a major policy focus for low-income youth will be community and two-year colleges, where the majority of both black and Latino children first enter higher education. These schools will need to provide remedial education for four-year college-bound students who are not well enough prepared, and to provide direct skill-based technical education for those who do not want to pursue a four-year degree.

None of these steps by themselves are very costly, but none is costless. The costs of all of the steps add up and mustering political support for them will not be easy. Once again, however, the Obama administration is taking steps in the right direction, instituting polices to lower costs for student loans, to increase Pell grants, and to influence high school and college graduation rates. . . .

## Summary and Conclusion: Laggard or Leader?

. . . Will the United States be a leader or laggard in the future? The American welfare state faces three major challenges: (1) making the old-age insurance program fiscally sound; (2) achieving universal health insurance and restraining the growth in health-care costs; and (3) restoring American pre-eminence in education and making other productive and complementary investments in children. The overarching challenge is to increase opportunity and security and reduce poverty and inequality in ways that enhance productivity. Minor tinkering with the existing system—a mix of small benefit cuts and small increases in taxes—will restore fiscal balance in the old-age insurance system. The second challenge is far more difficult. Achieving universality in health care will increase costs. Aging of the population and, more important, costly improvements in medical care also drive up health-care costs. Restraining health-care costs is probably the more daunting of the twin health-care challenges. The third challenge may be the most difficult of all because, in the face of an aging population, the first two must be resolved to free up the resources to adequately invest in American children. Restoring American pre-eminence in education and other public investments in children is the most important challenge not just in terms of the US being true to its historical self, but also in terms of future American wealth and productivity.

The United States, like every other nation, has responded both poorly and well to past challenges, but, on balance, the record is pretty good. Despite serious, fundamental flaws in its social, economic, and political framework[s], throughout most of its history, the United States of America has been a beacon of hope, inspiration, and leadership in the struggle for democracy and equality. The victory of the Democratic Party candidate Barack Obama in the 2008 presidential election indicates that the long swing right in American politics has come to an end. Americans and citizens of other nations, rich and poor, are excited by the prospect that the United States of America has elected a black man as president. As a foreign friend said to one of us with much admiration, as the saying goes, "Only in America." No one knows for sure what the future portends. We are hopeful.

# EXPLORING THE ISSUE

## Is the Welfare State Obsolete?

## Critical Thinking and Reflection

Is the welfare state in America growing or declining? Are Garfinkel, Rainwater, and Smeeding correct in their belief that education is the most important expenditure of the welfare state? Has the United States kept pace with other welfare states? Has the gap between economic classes contracted or expanded in recent decades? What factors account for the change? Which welfare state measures in the United States principally serve the interests of the poorest Americans? Which principally serve the interests of middle-class Americans? Is it possible that some measures principally benefit the most prosperous Americans? How have European industrial societies created more extensive welfare state policies? How does Levin distinguish between his proposals and welfare state policies? How are Tea Party conservatives likely to be critical of Levin's proposals? Do you benefit more from the welfare state or would you gain more without it?

## Is There Common Ground?

Yuval Levin presents a nuanced position that categorically rejects the welfare state and at the same time embraces specific welfare proposals. It comes closer to some conservative positions of the recent past than to the laissez-faire stance adopted by some contemporary conservatives. Some possible reconciliation seems possible in the recognition by Garfinkel et al. that the American welfare state is falling far short of its objectives. Garfinkel et al. conclude that the lead that the United States once had in education has vanished. This surely would contribute to what other welfare state adherents deplore as the widening gap between income and wealth. Neither of the essays represents the most extreme pro- and anti-welfare states, and it remains to be seen whether some reconciliation of these views is possible.

## Additional Resources

The classic critique of the welfare state is Friedrich von Hayek, *The Road to Serfdom* (University of Chicago Press, 1944). No book has had a greater influence on American critics of paternalistic government. Opponents of the welfare state are also influenced by Milton Friedman, whose *Capitalism and Freedom* (University of Chicago Press, 1962) provides a useful introduction to American laissez-faire capitalism opposed to the welfare state. More contemporary in analyzing the American welfare state is Christopher Howard, *The Welfare*

*State Nobody Knows: Debunking Myths About U.S. Social Policy* (Princeton; 2009). Howard argues that the welfare state is both larger and less successful than many Americans believe. His challenge to the welfare state is that it is doing more and achieving less. The consequence is that American inequality has increased both in income and wealth.

Michael B. Katz, *The Price of Citizenship: Redefining the American Welfare State* (revised edition, University of Pennsylvania Press, 2008), offers an optimistic defense of the welfare state and its provision of economic security for all persons, against what he deems to be its greatest threats: a war against dependence, the devolution of authority, and the application of market models to social policy.

How the preferences of citizens influence welfare politics is examined in Clem Brooks and Jeff Manza, *Why Welfare States Persist: The Importance of Public Opinion in Democracies* (University of Chicago Press, 2007). Brooks and Manza seek to explain why social democracies create stronger welfare states than the United States. Contemporary political conflicts regarding the welfare state are examined in a number of periodicals, ranging from the anti-welfare state views of *National Review* to the pro-welfare state positions of *The Nation*.

# ISSUE 13

## Are Americans Overtaxed?

**YES: Curtis S. Dubay,** from "Seven Myths About Taxing the Rich," *Backgrounder, The American Heritage Foundation* (August 3, 2009)

**NO: Steve Brouwer,** "If We Decided to Tax the Rich," from *Sharing the Pie: A Citizen's Guide to Wealth and Power* (Holt Paperbacks, 1998)

### ISSUE SUMMARY

**YES:** Economist Curtis S. Dubay believes that raising the already high taxes on high incomes would stifle job creation, slow the growth of already stagnant wages, and lead to larger deficits.

**NO:** Author Steve Brouwer maintains that higher and more progressive taxes on high incomes would enable the government to finance health care, higher education, and the rebuilding of the nation's infrastructure.

**B**enjamin Franklin is credited with having first said, "In this world nothing is certain but death and taxes." That does not mean that we have to look forward to either one. When the American colonists confronted the collection of taxes by Great Britain, they moved toward revolution and the creation of the United States when they proclaimed "No taxation without representation." A cynic has since expressed the popular opinion that "taxation with representation ain't so great either."

In 1912 the Sixteenth Amendment to the Constitution was adopted, enabling the federal government to levy taxes directly on income. The following year Congress adopted a graduated income tax, ranging from a 1 percent tax on individuals and businesses earning over $4,000 in a year (most Americans did not earn that much) up to 6 percent on incomes over $500,000. Since then, tax rates have gone up and sometimes down, but some measure of progressivity—higher rates for higher incomes—has been retained. Against progressive rates, supporters of a flat tax (the same rate for all persons) believe that this would be simpler, fairer, and least prone to creating special advantages.

By contrast, every change in the tax code has produced new deductions, concessions, and loopholes that benefit some groups to the disadvantage of others, lengthen and complicate the law, and stimulate a major tax-filing occupation for accountants and tax lawyers. Warren Buffett, the second-richest person in the United States, said that in 2007 he was taxed at 17.7 percent of his taxable income, without taking advantage of any tax shelters. By contrast, his receptionist was taxed at about 30 percent. The consequence was that the gap between their incomes was even greater after taxation than it was before. The simple fact is that every tax system is redistributive, in that it results in some individuals and groups gaining and others losing in relative wealth.

No one likes taxes, but upon reflection most Americans are likely to agree with Supreme Court Justice Oliver Wendell Holmes, Jr., that "taxes are what we pay for a civilized society." No other way has been devised to pay for such essential services as public education, police and fire protection, roads and public transportation, and the military defense of the nation. So the question is not whether Americans should be taxed but how much and how—that is, by what method of taxation.

Most other industrial nations have higher rates of taxation. Sweden and Denmark levy taxes approximately equal to one-half of their GDP (gross domestic product), with which they provide health, education, and other benefits that exceed those in the United States. Other European democracies also pay higher rates of taxation. By contrast, all taxes by all governments in the United States amount to less than 30 percent of the nation's gross domestic product.

Nevertheless, Americans appear to respond more favorably than the citizens of other countries to proposals of lower taxes. When presidential candidate George H.W. Bush in 1988 said, "Read my lips: No new taxes," he enhanced his prospects for election. But when then-president Bush ran for reelection in 1992, his broken promise (he obtained a tax raise) contributed to his defeat. President George W. Bush secured the enactment of substantial tax cuts in his first term as president. Bush argued that these would result in new investments that would revive a declining economy after the end of the Internet boom of the 1990s. His critics maintained that the tax cuts were of significant benefit only for the wealthiest Americans and blamed them, in part, for the nation's escalating deficit.

Upon taking office, President Barack Obama proposed raising the income tax paid by individuals earning more than $200,000 and by married couples earning more than $250,000. Obama has pledged that increases in federal spending must be accompanied by corresponding increases in tax revenue. The president's critics argue that raising taxes will result in prolonging the recession that began in 2007.

In a free society, almost everyone agrees that most decisions regarding how we spend our money are personal and not subject to government intervention. Apart from anarchists who oppose all government and extreme libertarians who oppose *almost* all government, everyone acknowledges that government can tax and spend our money to protect national security and continue specific long-established social welfare policies such as Social Security. Disagreement arises over how much government should do, how much it should tax, and how the tax burden should be shared.

Economist Curtis S. Dubay believes that wealthy Americans already pay a disproportionately high percentage of the revenue, and to raise their taxes will increase the deficit and badly damage the economy. Author Steve Brouwer argues that higher taxes on wealthy Americans would provide the financial resources to pay for many public services that the nation does not now provide, as well as result in more egalitarian economic outcomes.

# YES ↵

**Curtis S. Dubay**

## Seven Myths About Taxing the Rich

**P**resident Barack Obama plans to raise the top two income tax rates from their current 33 and 35 percent levels to 36 and 39.6 percent, respectively. This would undo the 2001 and 2003 tax cuts for Americans earning more than $250,000 ($200,000 for singles) and return the top rates to the levels of 1993 to 2000 during the Clinton Administration.

In addition to these tax hikes, the House of Representatives' Ways and Means Committee, led by Chairman Charlie Rangel (D–NY), favors another tax to fund the government takeover of the health care system. The "Rangel plan" would levy a 1 percent surtax for married couples earning between $350,000 and $500,000 a year, a 1.5 percent surtax on couple incomes between $500,000 and $1,000,000, and a 5.4 percent surtax for couples earning more than $1,000,000. For singles, the surtax would kick in for earners making more than $280,000 a year, $400,000, and $800,000, respectively. It would be phased in beginning in 2011 and could rise higher in future years if Congress decides it needs more revenue to fund its government-run health care system. Contrary to arguments made by proponents of these tax hikes, tax increases in the early 1990s did not lift the economy to the highs experienced later in the decade.

President Obama's and Chairman Rangel's tax hikes would increase the progressivity of the already highly progressive tax code. High-income earners pay substantially higher tax rates than do lower-income earners. If passed, this increased progressivity will damage economic growth by lowering the incentives to work, save, and invest. This will stifle job creation, further slowing the growth of already stagnant wages.

Those who support this tax increase point to several arguments to boost their case. But when these arguments are scrutinized, it is clear they do not hold up. Tax hikes on the rich will not balance the budget or close deficits. High earners already have a vast majority of the federal income tax burden, and the proposed tax hikes will badly damage the economy at a time when it cannot absorb any new negative shocks.

The President should scrap his plan to hike the top two income tax rates and Chairman Rangel his plan to pile additional tax hikes on high earners. Instead, they should propose to immediately cut spending, including reforming entitlement programs, and extending the 2001 and 2003 tax cuts for all taxpayers. Additionally, they should propose further *cutting* tax rates to help the ailing economy.

From *The Heritage Foundation Backgrounder,* no. 2306, August 3, 2009, pp. 1–4 (notes omitted).

# What Taxing the Rich Does to the Budget

**Myth 1:** *Raising taxes on the rich will close budget deficits.*

**Truth:** *Increasing the progressivity of the income tax code by raising the top two rates will not close the deficit. In fact, it will lead to more revenue volatility, which will lead to larger future deficits.*

A progressive income tax system collects increasing amounts of revenue during periods of economic growth and decreasing revenue during downturns. It does so mostly because of the volatility of high earners' incomes. During periods of economic growth, their incomes rise sharply and they pay increasingly higher taxes. But because much of high earners' income stems from volatile sources, such as capital gains, dividends, business income, and bonuses, their incomes fall just as sharply during economic downturns as they rose during good economic times and they have less income to be taxed.

Unless Congress suddenly develops spending restraint, increasing the progressivity of the tax code will only amplify the volatility of revenue fluctuations and increase future deficits. When revenue increases, mostly from high earners, during periods of economic growth, spending would increase because Congress cannot resist spending additional money. But, as history shows, when economic growth slows and revenues fall, Congress does not cut back on its spending largesse. Larger deficits would occur because the gap between spending and revenue would grow compared to previous recessionary periods.

Even if Congress ignores the long-term implications of more volatility and decides to close the deficits by raising taxes instead of borrowing as it is doing currently, it still cannot do it just by taxing more of high earners' income. Congress would have to decide to raise top rates to levels most Americans would consider confiscatory. In 2006, the latest year of available data, there was $2.2 trillion of taxable income for taxpayers earning more than $200,000. Assuming the amount of income at that level is similar this year, Congress would need to tax 80 percent of that income in order to close the projected $1.8 trillion deficit. Tax rates at such levels would significantly decrease economic activity and taxpayers would likely avoid or evade paying them so the revenue gains would likely never materialize.

# Who Pays the Largest Chunk of Taxes?

**Myth 2:** *The rich do not pay their fair share.*

**Truth:** *The top 20 percent of income earners pay almost all federal taxes.*

The top 20 percent of all income earners pay a substantial majority of all federal taxes. According to the Congressional Budget Office (CBO), in 2006, the latest year of available data, the top 20 percent of income earners paid almost 70 percent of all federal taxes. This share was 4 percent higher than in 2000, before the 2001 and 2003 tax cuts.

When only looking at income taxes, the share of the top 20 percent increases even further. In 2006, the top 20 percent paid 86.3 percent of all income taxes. This was an increase of 6 percent from 2000.

**Myth 3:** *The income tax code favors the rich and well-connected.*

**Truth:** *The bottom 50 percent of income earners pay almost no income taxes and the poor and middle-income earners benefit greatly from the tax code.*

This widely propagated myth has found its way to the White House Web site's tax page: "For too long, the U.S. tax code has benefited the wealthy and well-connected at the expense of the vast majority of Americans."

As shown in myth number 2, the top 20 percent pay almost 70 percent of all federal taxes and over 86 percent of all income taxes. It is hard to see how the rich benefit from a tax code they pay almost exclusively.

The bottom 40 percent of all income earners benefit greatly from the income tax code. In fact, they actually pay negative income tax rates because refundable credits, such as the Child Tax Credit and the Earned Income Tax Credit (EITC), wipe out their tax liability and pay out more money to them than they ever paid in.

Because of refundable credits, a family of four in the bottom 20 percent of income earners paid an effective income tax rate of –6.6 percent in 2006. As a result, such a family received $1,300 through the tax code. A family of four in the second-lowest 20 percent of income earners paid an effective tax rate of –0.8 percent and received $408 of income through the tax code.

The stimulus bill created a new refundable credit and expanded three others. This will further reduce the income tax burden of low-income earners, to the extent they can pay less, and increase the income they receive through the tax code.

The income tax burden of low-income earners has trended down for years. In 2006, the bottom 50 percent of all income tax filers paid only 2.99 percent of all income taxes. This was down 57 percent from 1980 levels, when the bottom 50 percent paid 7 percent.

Altogether, historical trends and the recent tax policies in the stimulus likely mean that when the data for recent years is released, the bottom 50 percent of all taxpayers will have paid no income taxes whatsoever.

**Myth 4:** *It is all right to raise tax rates on the rich—they can afford it.*

**Truth:** *Just because someone can afford to pay higher taxes does not mean he should be forced to do so.*

The faulty principle of "ability to pay" holds that those who earn more should pay proportionally more taxes because they can afford to do so. Such thinking can be a slippery slope because, technically, virtually anyone can afford to pay more taxes. The ability-to-pay principle has no grounding in economics, as it relies on a completely subjective judgment of fairness.

The tax code should collect revenue in the least economically damaging way possible. Raising rates on the rich damages economic growth because it reduces the incentives to work, save, invest, and accept economic risk—the ingredients necessary for economic growth.

Raising taxes on the rich hurts workers at all income levels—especially low- and middle-income earners. The rich are the most likely to invest. Their investment allows new businesses to get off the ground or existing businesses to expand. This creates new jobs and raises wages for Americans at all income levels. Taxing more of their income transfers money to Congress that they could otherwise have invested. This means the economy forgoes new jobs and higher wages that the investment would have created for less effective government spending.

There is a tax code that can collect more from the high earners than from the lower earners without being a barrier to economic growth: Under a flat tax, a taxpayer who earns 100 percent more than another taxpayer pays 100 percent more taxes, but faces no disincentive to earn more since he will pay the same rate on every additional dollar earned.

## The Economic Impact of Higher Tax Rates

**Myth 5:** *Higher tax rates in the 1990s did not hurt economic growth, so it is all right to raise them to those levels again.*

**Truth:** *High tax rates in the 1990s were a contributing factor to the 2001 recession and returning to those rates will damage the already severely weakened economy.*

The economy boomed during the 1990s for a number of reasons. One key factor was an advance in information technology. Computers, cell phones, the Internet, and other technological advances made businesses more efficient. This increased profits and wages and created numerous new jobs.

The 1997 tax cut that lowered tax rates on dividends and capital gains from 28 to 20 percent was also a major factor helping fuel the economic growth of this period. It strengthened the already strong gains from the technology boom. The impressive growth of the S&P 500 index after its passage is testimony to that fact. In the year before the tax cut, the S&P 500 index increased by 22 percent. In the following year, it increased by more than 40 percent.

The economic benefits of the technological advances and lower taxes on investment were strong enough to overcome the negative impact of the higher income tax rates and the economy exhibited impressive growth—initially. Even though the economy overcame high income tax rates temporarily, it was not strong enough to resist their negative pull forever:

> A contributing factor to the 2001 recession was the oppressively high levels of federal tax extracted from the economy. In the 40 years prior to 2000, federal tax receipts averaged about 18.2 percent of gross domestic product (GDP). In 1998 and 1999, the tax share stood at 20.0 percent, and in 2000, it shot up to tie the previous record of 20.9 percent set in 1944.

Taxes were high because the top income tax rates were 39.6 percent and 36 percent—the same rates President Obama and Congress now target.

The economy is in a much more precarious position now than it was in the 1990s. In June 2009 alone the economy lost 467,000 jobs. With no new innovations like those that created economic growth in the 1990s on the horizon to jump-start growth today, the economy simply cannot afford tax policies that will destroy more jobs and make it more difficult for the economy to recover.

**Myth 6:** *The 2001 and 2003 tax cuts did not generate strong economic growth.*

**Truth:** *The tax cuts generated strong economic growth.*

The 2001 and 2003 tax cuts generated strong economic growth. The 2003 cuts, however, were more effective at creating economic growth because Congress designed them expressly for that purpose. They worked better because they increased the incentives to generate new income by accelerating the phase-in of the 2001 reduction in marginal income tax rates, and by reducing rates on capital gains and dividends, lowering the cost of capital which is critical for economic recovery and growth.

Lower income tax rates generally promote growth, but since the 2001 cuts were phased in over several years, they did not kick in quickly enough to change the behavior of workers, businesses, and investors to help boost the ailing economy, so growth remained sluggish. The 2001 cuts also increased the Child Tax Credit from $500 to $1,000 a child. Although a large tax cut from a revenue perspective, the increase in the Child Tax Credit did nothing to increase growth-promoting incentives. Recognizing that the slow phase-in of rate reductions was not generating economic growth, Congress accelerated the rate reductions to increase the incentives to work, save, and invest during the 2003 cuts.

The 2003 tax cuts also lowered rates on capital gains and dividends, generating strong growth by decreasing the cost of capital, which caused investment to increase. More investment meant that more money was available for start-up capital for new businesses and for existing businesses to expand operations and add new jobs. The rate cuts on capital gains and dividends also unlocked capital trapped in investments that paid lower returns than otherwise could have been earned if the tax did not exist. This generated economic growth by allowing capital to flow freely to its most efficient use.

The increased incentives to save and invest, coupled with an acceleration of the cuts on marginal income tax rates, were a major reason economic growth picked up steam almost immediately after the 2003 tax cuts:

> The passage of [the 2003 tax cuts] started a different story. In the first quarter of that year, real GDP grew at a pedestrian 1.2 percent. In the second quarter, during which [the 2003 cuts were] signed into law, economic growth jumped to 3.5 percent, the fastest growth since the previous decade. In the third quarter, the rate of growth jumped again to an astounding 7.5 percent.

Unfortunately, President Obama and Congress plan to increase the income tax rates and taxes on capital gains and dividends. This would reverse the beneficial effects of the 2001 and 2003 cuts and further slow economic growth during this severe recession.

**Myth 7:** *Raising the top two income tax rates will not negatively impact small businesses because only 2 percent of them pay rates at that level.*

**Truth:** *Raising the top two income tax rates will negatively impact almost three-fourths of all economic activity created by small businesses.*

Small businesses are a vital component of the economy. They create jobs for millions of Americans and are a major factor driving economic growth.

Evaluating tax policy on the number of small businesses that pay the top two rates is not the proper way to determine the impact of raising those rates. What is important is how much small-business income is subject to the top two rates. This measures the extent to which the top two rates affect the economic activity that small businesses create.

Using this more accurate metric, it is clear that the top two rates have an enormous impact on small businesses. According to the Treasury Department, 72 percent of small business income is subject to those rates.

The amount of small business income subject to the top two rates is high in relation to the number of businesses that pay the rates because these businesses are the most successful. As a result they employ the most people and generate the most economic activity.

Raising rates on these successful businesses would damage the economy at any time, but doing so now will only cost more people their jobs. Highly successful small businesses faced with higher tax rates will cut back on plans to expand, hire fewer workers, and lower wages for current workers at a time when the economy desperately needs them to expand and create more jobs.

Higher rates also discourage would-be entrepreneurs from entering the market. This will negatively affect long-term economic growth because businesses that otherwise would have been created and added jobs to the economy will never get off the starting blocks.

# Conclusion

The many arguments used by proponents of higher taxes ignore basic economic facts and distort the positive benefits of the 2001 and 2003 tax cuts.

The truth is that the 2001 and 2003 tax cuts were a major factor behind robust economic growth between 2003 and 2007. Undoing those tax cuts now for any taxpayers would inflict unnecessary damage to a struggling economy and needlessly cost many more Americans their jobs.

Adding additional higher surtaxes on high earners to fund a government takeover of the health care system would only do more damage to the economy and lead to more lost jobs and lower economic growth.

Instead of imposing these economy-injuring tax hikes, Congress should close budget deficits and spur economic growth by:

- Immediately cutting spending, including reforming the Social Security Medicare, and Medicaid entitlement programs, in order to get long-term budget deficits under control;
- Making the 2001 and 2003 tax cuts permanent for all taxpayers; and
- Further cutting tax rates on workers and investors.

Raising taxes on the rich will hurt the economy at a time when the U.S. can least afford further damage.

**Steve Brouwer**　　　　　　　　　　　　　　　➡ **NO**

# If We Decided to Tax the Rich

**C**an the people of the United States retake control, once again taxing the richest citizens at a progressive rate and creating a fair society for all? If we had a Congress and a president who were willing to promote the interests of the vast majority of Americans, we could recapture some of the accumulated wealth that has been transferred to the rich over the last two decades. A reallocation of our resources could serve working people in the following ways:

- by creating full employment, with a higher minimum wage and shorter workweek
- by supporting quality day care for all who need it
- by providing for federally funded health care that serves everyone
- by rebuilding the nation's schools, roads, bridges, sewers, and parks
- by offering free higher education and other training to all citizens

Measures such as this will certainly cost hundreds of billions of dollars. Where can we get this kind of money while keeping the budget deficit reasonably low? There are several places to start:

- We must reestablish upper-bracket federal income tax rates comparable to those imposed during the prosperous decades of the 1950s and 1960s. The current effective rate on the richest 1 percent, whose income is at least $900 billion per year, is about 25 percent. An effective tax rate of 50 percent on the very richest 1 percent of Americans would raise an extra $225 billion.
- Raise the effective tax rate on corporate profits to 50 percent, the approximate rate of the 1950s. Profits have risen dramatically, to over $600 billion per year, while taxes have remained at an effective rate of about 25 percent, so this increase would yield another $150 billion.
- Institute an annual wealth tax of 3 percent on the richest 1 percent of Americans; this will yield $250 billion per year.
- Cut defense spending on new weaponry by $100 billion to stay in line with the diminished military budgets of the rest of the world.

These proposals, and the $725 billion they would raise, might outrage the corporations and the rich, as well as the politicians whom they have so carefully cultivated; but it would hardly be a case of impoverishing the well-to-do. The $625 billion in increased taxation would simply restore the more equitable (but hardly equal) distribution of income and wealth enjoyed by Americans three decades ago. The exact fiscal measures used to achieve more egalitarian economic outcomes are not all that important; the ones listed above could be modified or partially replaced by others. (For instance, Social Security taxes could be made less regressive by assessing them on the highest salaries, and on all forms of property and financial income as well.) Other worthy forms of taxation could be reestablished, such as the once progressive but now largely eviscerated inheritance tax.

## Big Problems Require Big Solutions

A class war, waged by the rich with very little opposition from the working class, has already taken place. The size of economic transfers recommended here would enable us to redress the imbalance of power in appropriate proportion to the inequality that has been imposed over the past twenty years. The money is there, and its redistribution back to working people would establish the balance that exists in most of the other highly industrialized countries.

Righting the imbalance between the rich and the working class is not just a matter of tinkering with budget deficit rules or massaging the Consumer Price Index or the measures of productivity. It is a battle for political and economic power, a matter of control over the political economy. Sharing our economic resources more equitably again will require ordinary citizens to exercise their democratic rights in a determined and unified manner. This fundamental shift cannot be accomplished by a quick swing of voters in one election, but only through a lengthy process of education and organization that convinces the American people that major changes are both desirable and possible.

## Labor and Work

Even though labor unions in the United States threw $35 million into targeted congressional races in 1996, there is little merit in the conservative claim that organized labor has the same kind of power in the Democratic Party as big business interests have in the Republican Party. Unions have resources that are minuscule compared with those of business interests: in 1996, all labor associations together collected $6 billion in dues, as compared with the $4 trillion in revenues and $360 billion in profits gathered by corporations. Labor can gain politically only when millions of working people, unionized and non-unionized, are engaged in the political process.

There are reasons for optimism. Despite the fact that the percentage of organized workers has been more than cut in half in the past forty years, from 35 percent to less than 15 percent, unions have made recent gains in organizing women, Hispanics, and African-Americans as members. In making an effort to organize the working poor and to alleviate the exploitation of part-time and contingent workers, unions are reviving the universal goals that once gave life to the labor movement. The emphasis on raising the wages of those at the bottom is crucial in two ways: it stresses the equal status due to all those who are willing to work, and it protects the wages and benefits of those already organized.

A distinct turnaround in public perceptions of the labor movement became evident in August of 1997 during the strike by drivers and package handlers at United Parcel Service. Opinion polls showed that Americans backed the Teamsters over UPS management by a margin of 2 to 1. This was a bit surprising given the Teamsters' well-publicized history of corruption and the fact that UPS was generally regarded as a good company. Two beliefs seemed most compelling to average Americans: first, that a company making billions in profits should be able to share them with hardworking employees; and second, that a company which had increased its number of part-timers to over 60 percent of its workforce, then paid them only half the wages of full-time workers, was trying to screw people over. This resonated with many average Americans who had either experienced downsizing themselves or who clearly understood that many companies felt free to throw loyal and competent workers aside.

The shift in public attitudes was having an effect on some voices emanating from the business press. *Business Week,* which had celebrated corporate CEOs as "stars" who deserved the 30 percent raises they received in 1995, did an about-face in April of 1997 when it reviewed the 54 percent increase in CEO compensation for 1996: "Call it Executive Over-Compensation," read the headline of their editorial, which concluded, "Compensation is running riot in many corner offices of corporate America. This simply has to stop." More surprising still was the magazine's reaction when it uncovered a tiny increase in wages of working Americans (about 1 percent) that had occurred between the summer of 1996 and the summer of 1997: "The prosperity of recent years is finally being shared by those in the lower tier of the economy—and that is cause for celebration, not despair." While *Business Week* was obviously premature in announcing that prosperity was being shared, its sentiments suggested that American concerns with inequality were finally being heard.

While the destruction of the social safety net has been a defeat for labor, welfare itself can be redefined by a progressive, labor-backed political program. Welfare should represent part of a universal social contract that can be extended to anyone who meets with severe economic hardships. The contract would make only one demand: that every capable citizen be willing to work. In return each citizen would receive good wages, quality education, and job training, with the added benefits of universal health care and day care. This kind of practical social democracy, grounded in the culture of working people, would quickly deflate the false claims of the right, that the poor are "lazy," "shiftless," and worse. The vast majority of the unemployed and underemployed poor, of whatever race, would be happy to claim membership in a newly dignified working class.

The power of labor has been unfairly curtailed in recent decades, so it is necessary to fight the legal restrictions and management policies that prevent union activity among the poorly paid and unorganized. But this alone is not sufficient. The more challenging task is convincing a good portion of the middle class that it too benefits from working-class mobilization. New kinds of political and social organizations must be formed—not necessarily traditional labor unions—to articulate the goals that middle-class employees share with lower-paid workers. Political solutions will require a very broad solidarity among working Americans, a solidarity that can bridge class, racial, and ethnic lines. This should not be too difficult at a time when working conditions, benefits, and job security are deteriorating even among privileged salaried workers, and when many in the so-called middle class are being subjected to "working-class" treatment by senior management.

# Conclusion

. . . Not all of our economic and social problems began in the last two decades of the twentieth century, but the policies pursued during the Reagan-Bush-Clinton era have made things considerably worse. Working people have suffered so that a small elite could enlarge its fortunes. In turn, this accumulated money has been wasted on speculative trading, widespread fraud, and nonproductive sectors of the economy, as well as corporate investment in countries where labor is provided by desperately poor people.

The old structures of capital accumulation have brought us regular cycles of poverty and depression in the past. Today things are worse, for capital has lost whatever productive drive and capability it once possessed; the glorification of entrepreneurship in the 1980s brought on the destruction, not the multiplication, of our national assets. The upper class tried to regenerate itself through money games that were far removed from real economic production: the plunder of the banking system, the privatization of public savings, and the paper trade in corporate assets.

It seemed, only a few years back, that if the United States failed to break these habits we would keep sinking in relation to other highly industrialized countries. The ascent of the economies of Japan, Germany, and the rest of Western Europe from 1950 to 1990 was remarkable. They seemed poised to leave us behind precisely because they were taking much better care of their people at the same time that their societies were becoming more productive.

Today something more frightening is happening. The United States, in concert with the corporate engines of globalization, may well bring the rest of the industrialized world down to its level. Once that has happened, the forces unleashed by international finance capital will keep pushing living standards downward. It is uncertain whether the kinds of social democracy set up in Western Europe can survive the current trends that have internationalized capital. Now, as capital moves quickly from continent to continent, often searching for cheap labor disciplined by authoritarian regimes, the capitalists are becoming more internationalized, too (whether they know it or not). They cannot possibly show loyalty, whether feigned or real, to the working and middle classes in their own countries.

Without a sharp turnaround toward democracy and equality in the United States, Europe will be virtually alone in its commitment to social democracy. The pressures of low-wage immigrant labor, cheap imports from Eastern Europe and Asia, and free-market practices of governments are already threatening once secure areas of employment and causing right-wing populism to pop up in various Western European countries. Surprising numbers of middle-class and working-class voters have supported ultra-nationalist, neo-fascist parties throughout Europe because, like white male workers in the United States, they see their status slipping.

Europe's weakened remnants of social democracy may survive for a while, but are unlikely to do very well if the American, Japanese, and other international investors (including Europeans) keep filling the world's markets with cheaper products produced by mainland Chinese, Indonesians, Thais, Vietnamese, Filipinos, and others in the vast new workhouse of Asia. In this chaotic world mess, the authoritarian/austerity regimes based on the Taiwanese and South Korean experience will be the model for modern development; their kinds of management teams are exportable, as are their long hours and brutal working conditions. These factors are rapidly turning China, the ultimate labor resource, into a giant replica of the Asian Tiger economy.

In the United States few mainstream commentators are paying attention to the ways that "free-trade" ideology is undermining real freedom. They have failed, for instance, to see the dark portents behind President Clinton's willingness to seek campaign contributions from Indonesian billionaires and Chinese corporations. Conservative columnist and former Nixon speechwriter William Safire was one of the few to see the situation clearly when he described "the central point of the ideo-economic struggle going on in today's world. On one side are governments that put 'order' above all, and offer an under-the-table partnership to managers who like arranged outcomes and a docile work force."

If Arkansas, which looks suspiciously like a center of third world development within the United States, is the economic and political model stuck inside our President's head, then we are already in trouble. And if Singapore is the model state for globalizing high-tech development in the eyes of the world's investing class, then we are drifting toward something worse: an illusion of democracy called "authoritarian democracy."

Nearly one hundred and seventy years ago, Alexis de Tocqueville wrote that "the manufacturing aristocracy which is growing up before our eyes is one of the harshest that ever existed in the world. . . . If ever a permanent inequality of conditions and aristocracy again penetrate the world, it may be predicted that this is the gate by which they will enter." The new corporate aristocracy—controlling not just transnational manufacturing but also worldwide finance and services—is more powerful than anything de Tocqueville could have imagined, and it has diminished the prospects for democracy in America.

The citizens of the United States need to restrain the single-minded accumulation of private capital, invest in strong public institutions, and give human values some room to thrive. Real democracy requires that the people find ways to share wealth and power.

As the repositories of immense wealth and technical expertise, the rich nations of the North ought to promote peaceful and fair development rather than unleash free-market chaos throughout the rest of the world. At home, the productive forces of the United States and the other advanced industrialized countries are easily sufficient to enhance equality and democratic values, as well as provide a comfortable standard of living for all.

# EXPLORING THE ISSUE

## Are Americans Overtaxed?

### Critical Thinking and Reflection

1. How much should Americans be taxed? What activities or functions do we want to support with taxes?
2. Who should be taxed? Should poor people pay any taxes, or should there be at least a token tax for "skin in the game"?
3. What kind of taxes should we have—a sharply graduated tax or a flatter tax? What about sales tax or a VAT tax?
4. What is the purpose of taxes—merely to raise income or also to redistribute income?

### Is There Common Ground?

Common ground between liberal Democrats and conservative Republicans on the tax issue was found in 1986, when President Ronald Reagan met with Democratic leaders of Congress and worked out a tax plan that reduced the highest tax bracket from 32 percent to 28 percent, yet also eliminated a number of tax loopholes traditionally used by the rich to avoid paying tax. Much depends on an atmosphere of interparty goodwill, which existed to some extent in 1986 but no longer does.

### Additional Resources

John O. Fox, author of *If Americans Really Understood the Income Tax: Uncovering Our Most Expensive Ignorance* (Westview Press, 2001), without endorsing more or less taxation, urges tax reform by eliminating special tax benefits and consequently instituting lower tax rates across the board. Conservative economists believe that lower rates of taxation encourage higher rates of income and a greater amount of tax revenue for government, whereas lower rates of income discourage higher rates of wealth and reduce the amount of taxation that will be paid. This came to be known as supply-side economics.

A recent defense of this theory of taxation is *The End of Prosperity: How Higher Taxes Will Doom the Economy—If We Let It Happen* (Threshold Editions, 2008), by Arthur B. Laffer, Stephen Moore, and Peter J. Tanous. Conservative economists are not of one mind. Bruce Bartlett, who championed supply-side economics in the presidency of Ronald Reagan, has written *Imposter: How George W. Bush Bankrupted America and Betrayed the Reagan Legacy* (Doubleday, 2006), arguing that coupling the Bush tax cuts with unrestricted spending will result in very much higher taxes in the future. The liberal rejection of conservative tax policy is found in David Cay Johnston, *Perfectly Legal: The Covert Campaign to Rig Our Tax System to Benefit the Super Rich—and Cheat Everyone Else* (Portfolio, 2003). Johnston believes that the tax code extends a widening gulf between the superrich and everyone else.

# ISSUE 14

## Is America Becoming More Unequal?

**YES: Robert Greenstein,** from *Testimony before the Subcommittee on Workforce Protections of the House Committee on Education and Labor* (July 31, 2008)

**NO: Christopher C. DeMuth,** from "The New Wealth of Nations," *Commentary* (October 1997)

### ISSUE SUMMARY

**YES:** Center on Budget and Policy Priorities Executive Director Robert Greenstein maintains that the long-term trend of inequality of income in the United States continues to grow greater as a consequence of public policy.

**NO:** American Enterprise Institute president Christopher C. DeMuth asserts that Americans have achieved an impressive level of wealth and equality and that a changing economy ensures even more opportunities.

There has always been a wide range in real income in the United States. In the first three decades after the end of World War II, family incomes doubled, income inequality narrowed slightly, and poverty rates declined. Prosperity declined in the mid-1970s, when back-to-back recessions produced falling average incomes, greater inequality, and higher poverty levels. Between the mid-1980s and the late 1990s, sustained economic recovery resulted in a modest average growth in income, but high poverty rates continued.

Defenders of the social system maintain that, over the long run, poverty has declined. Many improvements in social conditions benefit virtually all people and, thus, make us more equal. The increase in longevity (attributable in large measure to advances in medicine, nutrition, and sanitation) affects all social classes. In a significant sense, the U.S. economy is far fairer now than at any time in the past. In the preindustrial era, when land was the primary measure of wealth, those without land had no way to improve their circumstances. In the industrial era, when people of modest means needed physical strength and stamina to engage in difficult and hazardous labor in mines, mills, and factories, those who were too weak, handicapped, or too old stood little chance of gaining or keeping reasonable jobs.

In the postindustrial era, many of the manufactured goods that were once "Made in U.S.A.," ranging from clothing to electronics, are now made by cheaper foreign labor. Despite this loss, America achieved virtually full employment in the 1990s, largely because of the enormous growth of the information and service industries. Intelligence, ambition, and hard work—qualities that cut across social classes—are likely to be the determinants of success.

In the view of the defenders of the American economic system, the sharp increase in the nation's gross domestic product has resulted in greater prosperity for most Americans. Although the number of superrich has grown, so has the number of prosperous small business owners, middle-level executives, engineers, computer programmers, lawyers, doctors, entertainers, sports stars, and others who have gained greatly from the longest sustained economic growth in American history. For example, successful young pioneers in the new technology and the entrepreneurs whose capital supported their ventures have prospered, and so have the technicians and other workers whom they hired. Any change that mandated more nearly equal income would greatly diminish the incentives for invention, discovery, and risk-taking enterprises. As a result, the standard of living would be much lower and rise much more slowly, and individual freedom would be curtailed by the degree of state interference in people's private lives.

None of these objections will satisfy those who deplore what they see as an increasing disparity in the distribution of income and wealth. In 2008 the first full year since the recession that began in 2007, the wealthiest 10 percent of Americans, those making more than $138,000 a year, earned 11.4 times the $12,000 earned by those living near or below the poverty line in 2008. Poverty jumped to 13.2 percent, an eleven-year high. Nearly ten million households used food stamps. There has been a long-term acceleration of a gap between rich and poor in the United States. Between 1979 and 2005 (the latest year for which the non-partisan Congressional Budget Office has complete statistics), the average after-tax income of the top one percent of households, after adjusting for inflation, increased by $745,000, or 228 percent; that of the 20 percent of Americans in the middle of the income spectrum grew an average of $8,700, or 21 percent; by contrast, that of the poorest 20 percent of Americans grew by $900, or 6 percent.

The financial wealth of the top one percent of households exceeds the combined household financial wealth of the bottom 98 percent. Contrary to popular cliché, a rising tide does not lift all boats; it does not lift leaky boats or those who have no boats. Advocates of more nearly equal income argue that this would produce less social conflict and crime as well as more and better social services. They maintain that more egalitarian nations (Scandinavia and Western Europe are often cited) offer more nearly equal access to education, medical treatment, and legal defense. Is democracy diminished if those who have much more also enjoy greater political power than those who have much less?

In the following selections, Robert Greenstein explores the public policies that he believes lead to high levels of income and wealth inequality and discusses the policies that can narrow the gap, while Christopher DeMuth examines the social and scientific forces that he concludes have led to widespread wealth and increasing equality.

# YES ↵   Robert Greenstein

# Testimony Before the Subcommittee on Workforce Protections, Committee on Education and Labor

Thank you for the invitation to testify about widening income inequality in the United States. As former Federal Reserve chairman Alan Greenspan has said, "This is not the type of thing which a democratic society—a capitalist democratic society—can really accept without addressing," and I commend the subcommittee for holding this hearing. . . .

Income inequality in the United States has risen to historically high levels. This is not because of the current slump in the economy—the economic downturn is too recent to be reflected in the data, which only go through 2005 or 2006. And it is not a new development. Inequality has been increasing for more than 30 years.

There is, however, something different about the increase in inequality since 2001 that I want to comment on before examining the longer-run trends. Usually, concerns about inequality move to the back burner, at least in the public discourse, during economic expansions when most people see their standard of living rise and feel good about their economic prospects. That happened, for example, during the second half of the long economic expansion of the 1990s. But those good feelings have been noticeably absent in recent years, even though economic statisticians would characterize the economy's performance from the end of 2001 through most of last year as a business-cycle recovery and expansion following the 2001 recession.

The disconnect in recent years between how the overall economy is doing statistically and how most people living in that economy are doing has puzzled some pundits and some elected officials and their advisors. But it really is not very complicated. First, the post-2001 period was the weakest of all economic expansions since World War II by almost every economic measure. Second, to an unprecedented degree, the gains from economic growth after 2001 accrued to a narrow slice of the population at the top of the income distribution.

When I said the recovery was weak by *almost* every measure, I was alluding to the fact that there is one important exception—corporate profits. While aggregate wages and salaries grew *less than half* as fast after 2001 as they did in the average postwar economic expansion, corporate profits grew almost 30 percent

U.S. House of Representatives, July 31, 2008.

faster. Both employment growth and wage and salary growth were weaker in the most recent expansion than in any prior expansion since the end of World War II; growth in corporate profits was stronger than the average of all post World War II expansions.

What have been the consequences for income inequality of that weak and unbalanced economic recovery? First, the share of pre-tax income flowing to the top 1 percent of households is at its highest level since 1928. Second, the gap between the after-tax income of people at the top of the income distribution and the after-tax income of people in the middle or at the bottom has continued to widen. So now that the economy is stumbling, the labor market is weakening, and household budgets are being strained by higher food and energy prices, it should be no surprise that people are even more pessimistic about their prospects. It is not just in their heads.

Let me turn now to a discussion of the data on income inequality and what they show about longer-term trends. There are two primary sources of annual data on household income and its distribution. The first is Census Bureau data on poverty and income based on the Current Population Survey, and the second is income tax data from the IRS. Neither alone can give a complete picture of trends in income inequality. The tax data provide good coverage of people who pay income taxes, including people with very high incomes, but they omit people with low incomes who are not required to file an income tax return. The Census data have good coverage of that low-income population but for various reasons do not have good coverage of people with very high incomes. . . .

What do these data tell us about long-term trends in inequality? First, the CBO data in Figure 1, which shows the percentage increase in after-tax

*Figure 1*

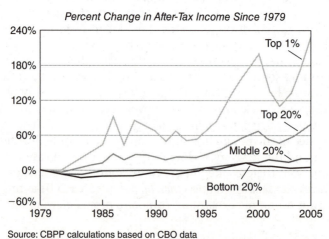

**Highest Income Households Have Seen Far Greater Income Growth Than Others**

*Percent Change in After-Tax Income Since 1979*

Source: CBPP calculations based on CBO data

*Table 1*

### Change in After-Tax Income, 1976–2005, by Income Group

| | Bottom 20 percent | Second 20 percent | Middle 20 percent | Fourth 20 percent | Top 20 percent | Top 1 percent |
|---|---|---|---|---|---|---|
| Increase in 2005 dollars | 900 | 4,600 | 8,700 | 16,000 | 76,500 | 745,100 |
| Percentage increase | 6.3% | 15.8% | 21.0% | 29.5% | 79.9% | 228.3% |

income at different points on the income scale since 1979, portray a widening gap between income at the top and income in the middle and at the bottom, with the largest income gains accruing at the very top. As Table 1 shows, after adjusting for inflation, income in the bottom fifth of the population was only 6 percent—or $900—higher in 2005 than it was twenty-six years earlier in 1979, and income in the middle fifth of the population was 21 percent—or $8,700— higher. In contrast, income in the top fifth of the distribution rose 80 percent— or $76,500 per household—from 1979 to 2005, and income in the top 1 percent more than tripled, rising 228 percent—or $745,100 per household.

While these CBO data show a strong upward trend in inequality over the past 25 years, it would be a mistake to think that rising inequality and increasing concentration of income at the very top of the income scale have been an inevitable feature of the American economy. As Figure 2 shows, the pattern of growth in household income over the past three decades is distinctly different from the pattern over the first three decades after the end of World War II. . . .

From 1946 to 1976, the increase in the average income of the bottom 90 percent of households closely matched the growth of per capita national income, while income at the very top grew more slowly. In other words, the gap between the average income of the very richest households and that of the bottom 90 percent of households narrowed over this period. Over the next three decades, in contrast, growth in the average income of the bottom 90 percent of households fell far short of growth in per-capita national income, while growth in the average income of the top 1 percent of households soared. If we had a figure like Figure 1 for this longer period, we would see the incomes of the top, middle, and bottom fifths trending upward together at roughly the same rate from 1946 to sometime in the 1970s, followed by a sharp divergence in the years since 1976 like that depicted in Figure 1. . . .

## How Do Government Policies Affect Inequality?

Government policies affect the distribution of income most directly through taxes and benefit programs, and federal taxes are, on balance, progressive. As a result, there is modestly less inequality in the after-tax distribution of

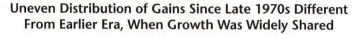

*Figure 2*

Uneven Distribution of Gains Since Late 1970s Different
From Earlier Era, When Growth Was Widely Shared

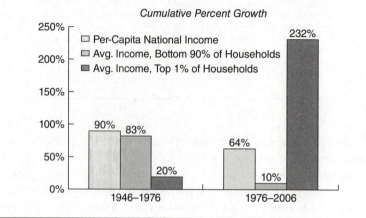

income than in the before-tax distribution. But while this difference is real, it should not be exaggerated. Furthermore, the large tax cuts enacted in 2001 and 2003 favored higher income groups that were already benefiting from disproportionate gains in pre-tax income. As a result, federal taxes, while still progressive, are less progressive today than they were before the 2001–2003 tax cuts.

    . . . In 2005, households in the bottom fifth of the income scale paid an average of 4.3 percent of their income in federal taxes, those in the middle paid 14.2 percent, those in the top fifth paid 25.5 percent, and those in the top 1 percent paid 31.2 percent. The bottom fifth of households received 4.0 percent of before-tax income and 4.8 percent of after-tax income. For the middle fifth, those percentages were 13.3 percent of before-tax income and 14.4 percent of after-tax income. The top fifth of households, in contrast, received a larger share of before-tax income (55.1 percent) than of after-tax income (51.6 percent) as did the top 1 percent (18.1 percent of pre-tax income compared with 15.6 percent of after-tax income). Nevertheless, both before-tax and after-tax income distributions reveal a high degree of inequality. Moreover, the shares of after-tax income going to the top 20 percent and to the top 1 percent—like their shares of before-tax income—are now the highest on record in the CBO data, which go back to 1979. . . .

    . . . As these data show, there is a great deal of inequality in the distribution of income in the United States. But that inequality pales in comparison to the inequality in the distribution of wealth. Our main source of data about wealth inequality comes from the Federal Reserve's Survey of Consumer Finances. Those data show that roughly a third of household wealth is held by the top 1 percent of households, another third is held by the next affluent 9 percent, and the remaining third of wealth is held by the remaining 90 percent of households. . . .

# Implications for Policy

The United States faces a number of tough challenges ahead, including an unsustainable long-term deficit, the need for health care reform, fundamental tax reform, and the need to address climate change. The problem of widening income inequality is exceedingly unlikely to go away on its own. But how we address these other critical challenges also will have important implications for whether policymakers make inequality worse or better through their policy actions. In this section of the testimony, I will discuss some broad policy implications and offer some specific recommendations.

Addressing our long-term budget imbalance is important to achieving strong sustainable growth over the long term. But the distributional implications are vastly different if we address the challenge by slashing promised benefits in programs like Social Security, Medicare, and Medicaid to preserve the tax cuts we have enacted and add new regressive tax cuts on top, or if we instead pursue a more balanced approach that puts everything on the table. Similar distributional differences attach to alternative ways of approaching health care reform and fundamental tax reform.

Climate change legislation poses a similar challenge. Reducing greenhouse gas emissions, through either a cap-and-trade system or a carbon tax, works by raising the price of energy and energy-related products. Because low- and moderate-income households spend a disproportionate amount of their income on these products, they will experience the largest relative hits to their purchasing power from such legislation.

At the same time, however, either a cap-and-trade system in which most of the emissions allowances are auctioned off or a carbon tax has the potential to raise substantial revenues. If a portion of those revenues are used for well-designed climate rebates to offset the impacts of higher energy prices on low- and moderate-income households, we can achieve the benefits of reduced greenhouse gas emissions while protecting the purchasing power of vulnerable households and avoiding regressive effects. In contrast, if we give away a large percentage of the allowances to existing industrial emitters or we use the proceeds to cut income tax rates, we would provide tax relief benefits to high-income households that are larger than the increase in their energy costs while leaving low- and moderate-income households worse off. Inequality would effectively be widened further.

I believe that if we are to take the problem of increasing inequality seriously, we need to keep these distributional considerations in mind as we address the big challenges that lie ahead. At the same time, strong economic growth and rising productivity are a necessary condition for achieving widespread prosperity. Sound investments in education, worker training, infrastructure, and basic research are necessary to complement private investment in generating that growth and productivity.

Having a strong economy is a necessary condition for achieving widespread prosperity. But as we have seen for more than 30 years, the outcomes determined by market forces alone seem to be aggravating inequality, especially during periods when the political environment is tilted toward skepticism about or outright hostility toward policies that provide an effective safety net for those struggling to keep their heads above water and policies aimed at ensuring that the gains from economic growth are shared more equally, as they were in the 1946–1976 period.

One important place we need to start to achieve that goal is a focused effort to reduce poverty. The poverty rate rose for four straight years from 2000 to 2004, peaking at 12.7 percent in 2004. In 2006, the rate was still stubbornly high at 12.3 percent, and over 36 million people were poor. Poverty is higher in the United States than in many other developed countries, and it is costly to the economy to have so many adults with limited skills and earnings and to perpetuate that situation through the damaging effects of persistent child poverty. We can do better. An effort that deserves attention here is the Half in Ten campaign, which is calling on policymakers to adopt the goal of cutting poverty in half over the next ten years.

Let me conclude with some concrete steps to address the problem of widening inequality. I'll start with the tax code, which includes provisions worth hundreds of billions of dollars a year to encourage a wide variety of activities from saving for retirement to acquiring more education. From the standpoint of equal treatment of people with different incomes, there is a fundamental flaw in most of these incentives: they are provided in the form of deductions, exemptions, and exclusions rather than in the form of refundable tax credits. That means that the size of the tax break is higher for taxpayers in higher income brackets. For many of the activities that the tax incentive is meant to promote, there is no obvious reason why lower-income taxpayers or people who do not file income taxes should get smaller incentives (or no tax incentives at all).

But it is even worse than that: the central structure of these tax breaks also makes them economically inefficient. Because a large number of taxpayers will not have incomes high enough to benefit fully from current non-refundable incentives, society will get less of the activity it is trying to encourage; people with smaller income-tax liabilities will have a smaller incentive, and people with no income-tax liability will have no additional incentive to engage in the activity. Moreover, high-income taxpayers are likely to save for retirement and to invest in their children's education with or without the tax breaks; the tax breaks do not appear to have a large effect on their behavior. As a result, the current tax deduction structure used for these tax breaks is inefficient. Providing more modest tax breaks to high-income taxpayers and using the savings to provide refundable credits to lower-income taxpayers would increase the amount of desirable economic activity that the tax break is meant to encourage, at no additional cost. . . .

If a system of refundable credits were in place, it also would have the virtue of providing a form of stabilization to the economy when the economic picture darkened, since people who lost their jobs or experienced a sharp drop in income during an economic downturn would continue to receive the full value of tax credits for which they qualified, rather than losing the value of the credits or seeing them reduced as is the case now. We could begin next year to take steps toward such a reform of the tax code by making the higher-education and savers' tax credits refundable and making improvements in the EITC. Moving to refundable tax credits for promoting socially worth-while activities would be an important step toward enhancing progressivity in the tax code in a way that would improve economic efficiency and perform-ance at the same time.

Other steps we could take that would contribute to reducing poverty and expanding educational opportunities include: increased investment in pre-school education and decent-quality child care for low- and moderate-income families. Such steps would both enable more low-income mothers to work (or enable those already working to work more) and increase the educational attainment and skills of the children.

In the area of health care, the lion's share of those without health insurance are low- or moderate-income. So legislation to achieve universal health insur-ance coverage and begin to put mechanisms in place to slow health care cost growth are important—both to improve the health and alleviate the squeeze on the uninsured *and* to ease the pressure on wages and salaries more broadly that rising health care costs impose. . . .

Christopher C. DeMuth

➜ **NO**

# The New Wealth of Nations

The Nations of North America, Western Europe, Australia, and Japan are wealthier today than they have ever been, wealthier than any others on the planet, wealthier by far than any societies in human history. Yet their governments appear to be impoverished—saddled with large accumulated debts and facing annual deficits that will grow explosively over the coming decades. As a result, government spending programs, especially the big social-insurance programs like Social Security and Medicare in the United States, are facing drastic cuts in order to avert looming insolvency (and, in France and some other European nations, in order to meet the Maastricht treaty's criteria of fiscal rectitude). American politics has been dominated for several years now by contentious negotiations over deficit reduction between the Clinton administration and the Republican Congress. This past June, first at the European Community summit in Amsterdam and then at the Group of Eight meeting in Denver, most of the talk was of hardship and constraint and the need for governmental austerity ("Economic Unease Looms Over Talks at Denver Summit," read the *New York Times* headline).

These bloodless problems of governmental accounting are said, moreover, to reflect real social ills: growing economic inequality in the United States; high unemployment in Europe; an aging, burdensome, and medically needy population everywhere; and the globalization of commerce, which is destroying jobs and national autonomy and forcing bitter measures to keep up with the bruising demands of international competitiveness.

How can it be that societies so surpassingly wealthy have governments whose core domestic-welfare programs are on the verge of bankruptcy? The answer is as paradoxical as the question. We have become not only the richest but also the freest and most egalitarian societies that have ever existed, and it is our very wealth, freedom, and equality that are causing the welfare state to unravel.

❧

That we have become very rich is clear enough in the aggregate. That we have become very equal in the enjoyment of our riches is an idea strongly resisted by many. Certainly there has been a profusion of reports in the media and political speeches about increasing income inequality: the rich, it is said, are getting richer, the poor are getting poorer, and the middle and working classes are under the relentless pressure of disappearing jobs in manufacturing and middle management.

Although these claims have been greatly exaggerated, and some have been disproved by events, it is true that, by some measures, there has been a recent increase in income inequality in the United States. But it is a very small tick in the massive and unprecedented leveling of material circumstances that has been proceeding now for almost three centuries and in this century has accelerated dramatically. In fact, the much-noticed increase in measured-income inequality is in part a result of the increase in real social equality. Here are a few pieces of this important but neglected story.

• First, progress in agriculture, construction, manufacturing, and other key sectors of economic production has made the material necessities of life—food, shelter, and clothing—available to essentially everyone. To be sure, many people, including the seriously handicapped and the mentally incompetent, remain dependent on the public purse for their necessities. And many people continue to live in terrible squalor. But the problem of poverty, defined as material scarcity, has been solved. If poverty today remains a serious problem, it is a problem of individual behavior, social organization, and public policy. This was not so 50 years ago, or ever before.

• Second, progress in public health, in nutrition, and in the biological sciences and medical arts has produced dramatic improvements in longevity, health, and physical well-being. Many of these improvements—resulting, for example, from better public sanitation and water supplies, the conquest of dread diseases, and the abundance of nutritious food—have affected entire populations, producing an equalization of real personal welfare more powerful than any government redistribution of income.

The Nobel prize-winning economist Robert Fogel has focused on our improved mastery of the biological environment—leading over the past 300 years to a doubling of the average human life span and to large gains in physical stature, strength, and energy—as the key to what he calls "the egalitarian revolution of the 20th century." He considers this so profound an advance as to constitute a distinct new level of human evolution. Gains in stature, health, and longevity are continuing today and even accelerating. Their outward effects may be observed, in evolutionary fast-forward, in the booming nations of Asia (where, for example, the physical difference between older and younger South Koreans is strikingly evident on the streets of Seoul).

• Third, the critical *source* of social wealth has shifted over the last few hundred years from land (at the end of the 18th century) to physical capital (at the end of the 19th) to, today, human capital—education and cognitive ability. This development is not an unmixed gain from the standpoint of economic equality. The ability to acquire and deploy human capital is a function of intelligence, and intelligence is not only unequally distributed but also, to a significant degree, heritable. As Charles Murray and the late Richard J. Herrnstein argue in *The Bell Curve,* an economy that rewards sheer brainpower replaces one old source of inequality, socioeconomic advantage with a new one, cognitive advantage.

But an economy that rewards human capital also tears down far more artificial barriers than it erects. For most people who inhabit the vast middle range of the bell curve, intelligence is much more equally distributed than land or physical capital ever was. Most people, that is, possess ample intelligence to pursue all but a handful of specialized callings. If in the past many were held back by lack of education and closed social institutions, the opportunities to use one's human capital have blossomed with the advent of universal education and the erosion of social barriers.

Furthermore, the material benefits of the knowledge-based economy are by no means limited to those whom Murray and Herrnstein call the cognitive elite. Many of the newest industries, from fast food to finance to communications, have succeeded in part by opening up employment opportunities for those of modest ability and training—occupations much less arduous and physically much less risky than those they have replaced. And these new industries have created enormous, widely shared economic benefits in consumption; I will return to this subject below.

• Fourth, recent decades have seen a dramatic reduction in one of the greatest historical sources of inequality: the social and economic inequality of the sexes. Today, younger cohorts of working men and women with comparable education and job tenure earn essentially the same incomes. The popular view would have it that the entry of women into the workforce has been driven by falling male earnings and the need "to make ends meet" in middle-class families. But the popular view is largely mistaken. Among married women (as the economist Chinhui Juhn has demonstrated), it is wives of men with high incomes who have been responsible for most of the recent growth in employment.

• Fifth, in the wealthy Western democracies, material needs and desires have been so thoroughly fulfilled for so many people that, for the first time in history, we are seeing large-scale voluntary reductions in the amount of time spent at paid employment. This development manifests itself in different forms: longer periods of education and training for the young; earlier retirement despite longer life spans; and, in between, many more hours devoted to leisure, recreation, entertainment, family, community and religious activities, charitable and other nonremunerative pursuits, and so forth. The dramatic growth of the sports, entertainment, and travel industries captures only a small slice of what has happened. In Fogel's estimation, the time devoted to nonwork activities by the average male head of household has grown from 10.5 hours per week in 1880 to 40 hours today, while time per week at work has fallen from 61.6 hours to 33.6 hours. Among women, the reduction in work (including not only outside employment but also household work, food preparation, childbearing and attendant health problems, and child rearing) and the growth in nonwork have been still greater.

There is a tendency to overlook these momentous developments because of the often frenetic pace of modern life. But our busy-ness actually demonstrates the point: time, and not material things, has become the scarce and valued commodity in modern society.

ಀಁ಄

One implication of these trends is that in very wealthy societies, income has become a less useful gauge of economic welfare and hence of economic equality. When income becomes to some degree discretionary, and when many peoples' incomes change from year to year for reasons unrelated to their life circumstances, *consumption* becomes a better measure of material welfare. And by this measure, welfare appears much more evenly distributed: people of higher income spend progressively smaller shares on consumption, while in the bottom ranges, annual consumption often exceeds income. (In fact, government statistics suggest that in the bottom 20 percent of the income scale, average annual consumption is about twice annual income—probably a reflection of a substantial underreporting of earnings in this group.) According to the economist Daniel Slesnick, the distribution of consumption, unlike the distribution of reported income, has become measurably *more* equal in recent decades.

If we include leisure-time pursuits as a form of consumption, the distribution of material welfare appears flatter still. Many such activities, being informal by definition, are difficult to track, but Dora Costa of MIT has recently studied one measurable aspect—expenditures on recreation—and found that these have become strikingly more equal as people of lower income have increased the amount of time and money they devote to entertainment, reading, sports, and related enjoyments.

Television, videocassettes, CD's, and home computers have brought musical, theatrical, and other entertainments (both high and low) to everyone, and have enormously narrowed the differences in cultural opportunities between wealthy urban centers and everywhere else. Formerly upper-crust sports like golf, tennis, skiing, and boating have become mass pursuits (boosted by increased public spending on parks and other recreational facilities as well as on environmental quality), and health clubs and full-line book stores have become as plentiful as gas stations. As some of the best things in life become free or nearly so, the price of pursuing them becomes, to that extent, the "opportunity cost" of time itself.

The substitution of leisure activities for income-producing work even appears to have become significant enough to be contributing to the recently much-lamented increase in inequality in measured income. In a new AEI study, Robert Haveman finds that most of the increase in earnings inequality among U.S. males since the mid-1970's can be attributed not to changing labor-market opportunities but to voluntary choice—to the free pursuit of nonwork activities at the expense of income-producing work.

Most of us can see this trend in our own families and communities. A major factor in income inequality in a wealthy knowledge economy is age—many people whose earnings put them at the top of the income curve in their late fifties were well down the curve in their twenties, when they were just getting out of school and beginning their working careers. Fogel again: today the average household in the top 10 percent might consist of a professor or accountant married to a nurse or secretary, both in their peak years of earning. As for the stratospheric top 1 percent, it includes not only very rich people like

Bill Cosby but also people like Cosby's fictional Huxtable family: an obstetrician married to a corporate lawyer. All these individuals would have appeared well down the income distribution as young singles, and that is where their young counterparts appear today.

That more young people are spending more time in college or graduate school, taking time off for travel and "finding themselves," and pursuing interesting but low- or non-paying jobs or apprenticeships before knuckling down to lifelong careers is a significant factor in "income inequality" measured in the aggregate. But this form of economic inequality is in fact the social equality of the modern age. It is progress, not regress, to be cherished and celebrated, not feared and fretted over.

❧

Which brings me back to my contention that it is our very wealth and equality that are the undoing of the welfare state. Western government today largely consists of two functions. One is income transfers from the wages of those who are working to those who are not working: mainly social-security payments to older people who have chosen to retire rather than go on working and education subsidies for younger people who have chosen to extend their schooling before beginning work. The other is direct and indirect expenditures on medical care, also financed by levies on the wages of those who are working. It is precisely these aspects of life—nonwork and expenditures on medical care and physical well-being—that are the booming sectors of modern, wealthy, technologically advanced society.

When the Social Security program began in America in the 1930's, retirement was still a novel idea: most men worked until they dropped, and they dropped much earlier than they do today. Even in the face of our approaching demographic crunch, produced by the baby boom followed by the baby bust, we could solve the financial problems of the Social Security program in a flash by returning to the days when people worked longer and died younger. Similarly, a world without elaborate diagnostic techniques, replaceable body parts, and potent pharmaceutical and other means of curing or ameliorating disease—a world where medical care consisted largely of bed rest and hand-holding—would present scant fiscal challenge to government as a provider of health insurance.

Our big government-entitlement programs truly are, as conservatives like to call them, obsolete. They are obsolete not because they were terrible ideas to begin with, though some of them were, but because of the astounding growth in social wealth and equality and because of the technological and economic developments which have propelled that growth. When Social Security was introduced, not only was retirement a tiny part of most people's lives but people of modest means had limited ability to save and invest for the future. Today, anyone can mail off a few hundred dollars to a good mutual fund and hire the best investment management American finance has to offer.

In these circumstances it is preposterous to argue, as President Clinton has done, that privatizing Social Security (replacing the current system of income transfers from workers to retirees with one of individually invested retirement savings) would be good for Warren Buffett but bad for the little guy. Private savings—through pension plans, mutual funds, and personal investments in housing and other durables—are *already* a larger source of retirement income than Social Security transfers. Moreover, although there is much talk nowadays about the riskiness of tying retirement income to the performance of financial markets, the social developments I have described suggest that the greater risk lies in the opposite direction. The current Social Security program ties retirement income to the growth of wage earners' payrolls; that growth is bound to be less than the growth of the economy as a whole, as reflected in the financial markets.

Similarly, Medicare is today a backwater of old-fashioned fee-for-service medicine, hopelessly distorted by a profusion of inefficient and self-defeating price-and-service controls. Over the past dozen years, a revolution has been carried out in the private financing and organization of medical care. The changes have not been unmixed blessings; nor could they be, so long as the tax code encourages people to overinsure for routine medical care. Yet substantial improvements in cost control and quality of service are now evident throughout the health-care sector—except under Medicare. These innovations have not been greeted by riots or strikes at the thousands of private organizations that have introduced them. Nor will there be riots in the streets if, in place of the lame-brained proposals for Medicare "spending cuts" and still more ineffective price controls currently in fashion in Washington, similar market-based innovations are introduced to Medicare.

&c~@~&

In sum, George Bush's famous statement in his inaugural address that "we have more will than wallet" was exactly backward. Our wallets are bulging; the problems we face are increasingly problems not of necessity, but of will. The political class in Washington is still marching to the tune of economic redistribution and, to a degree, "class warfare." But Washington is a lagging indicator of social change. In time, the progress of technology and the growth of private markets and private wealth will generate the political will to transform radically the redistributive welfare state we have inherited from an earlier and more socially balkanized age.

There are signs, indeed, that the Progressive-era and New Deal programs of social insurance, economic regulation, and subsidies and protections for farming, banking, labor organization, and other activities are already crumbling, with salutary effects along every point of the economic spectrum. Anyone who has been a business traveler since the late 1970's, for example, has seen firsthand how deregulation has democratized air travel. Low fares and mass marketing have brought such luxuries as foreign travel, weekend getaways to remote locales, and reunions of far-flung families—just twenty years ago, pursuits of the wealthy—to people of relatively modest means. Coming reforms, including the privatization of Social Security and, most of all, the dismantling of the public-school monopoly in elementary and secondary education, will similarly benefit the less well-off disproportionately, providing them with opportunities enjoyed today primarily by those with high incomes.

I venture a prediction: just as airline deregulation was championed by Edward Kennedy and Jimmy Carter before Ronald Reagan finished the job, so the coming reforms will be a bipartisan enterprise. When the political class catches on (as Prime Minister Tony Blair has already done in England), the Left will compete vigorously and often successfully with the Right for the allegiance of the vast new privileged middle class. This may sound implausible at a moment when the Clinton administration has become an energetic agent of traditional unionism and has secured the enactment of several new redistributive tax provisions and spending programs. But the watershed event of the Clinton years will almost certainly be seen to be not any of these things but rather the defeat of the President's national health-insurance plan in the face of widespread popular opposition.

The lesson of that episode is that Americans no longer wish to have the things they care about socialized. What has traditionally attracted voters to government as a provider of insurance and other services is not that government does the job better or more efficiently or at a lower cost than private markets; it is the prospect of securing those services through taxes paid by others. That is why today's advocates of expanding the welfare state are still trying to convince voters to think of themselves as members of distinct groups that are net beneficiaries of government: students, teachers, women, racial minorities, union members, struggling young families, retirees, and so forth. But as the material circumstances of the majority become more equal, and as the proficiency and social reach of private markets increasingly outstrip what government can provide, the possibilities for effective redistribution diminish. The members of an egalitarian, middle-class electorate cannot improve their lot by subsidizing one another, and they know it.

With the prospects dimming for further, broad-based socialization along the lines of the Clinton health-care plan, the private supply of important social services will continue to exist and, in general, to flourish alongside government programs. Defenders of the welfare state will thus likely be reduced to asserting that private markets and personal choice may be fine for the well-off, but government services are more appropriate for those of modest means. This is the essence of President Clinton's objection to privatizing Social Security and of the arguments against school choice for parents of students in public elementary and high schools. But "capitalism for the rich, socialism for the poor" is a highly unpromising banner for liberals to be marching under in an era in which capitalism has itself become a profound egalitarian force.

❧

Where, then, will the battlegrounds be for the political allegiance of the new middle class? Increasingly, that allegiance will turn on policies involving little or no redistributive cachet but rather society-wide benefits in the form of personal amenity, autonomy, and safety: environmental quality and parks, medical and other scientific research, transportation and communications infrastructure, defense against terrorism, and the like. The old welfare-state debates between Left and Right will be transformed into debates over piece-meal incursions into private markets that compete with or replace government services. Should private insurers be required to cover annual mammograms for women in their forties? Should retirement accounts be permitted to invest in tobacco companies? Should parents be permitted to use vouchers to send their children to religious schools? Thus transformed, these debates, too, will tend to turn on considerations of general social advantage rather than on the considerations of social justice and economic desert that animated the growth of the welfare state.

Political allegiance will also turn increasingly on issues that are entirely nonmaterial. I recently bumped into a colleague, a noted political analyst, just after I had read the morning papers, and asked him to confirm my impression that at least half the major political stories of the past few years had something to do with sex. He smiled and replied, "Peace and prosperity."

What my colleague may have had in mind is that grave crises make all other issues secondary: President Roosevelt's private life received less scrutiny than has President Clinton's, and General Eisenhower's private life received less scrutiny than did that of General Ralston (whose nomination to become chairman of the Joint Chiefs of Staff was torpedoed by allegations of an extra-marital affair). There is, however, another, deeper truth in his observation. The stupendous wealth, technological mastery, and autonomy of modern life have freed man not just for worthy, admirable, and self-improving pursuits but also for idleness and unworthy and self-destructive pursuits that are no less a part of his nature.

And so we live in an age of astounding rates of divorce and family breakup, of illegitimacy, of single teenage motherhood, of drug use and crime, of violent and degrading popular entertainments, and of the "culture of narcissism"—and also in an age of vibrant religiosity, of elite universities where madrigal singing and ballroom dancing are all the rage and rampant student careerism is a major faculty concern, and of the Promise Keepers, over a million men of all incomes and races who have packed sports stadiums around the United States to declare their determination to be better husbands, fathers, citizens, and Christians. Ours is an age in which obesity has become a serious public-health problem—and in which dieting, fitness, environmentalism, and self-improvement have become major industries.

It is true, of course, that the heartening developments are in part responses to the disheartening ones. But it is also true that *both* are the results of the economic trends I have described here. In a society as rich and therefore as free as ours has become, the big question, in our personal lives and also in our politics, is: what is our freedom for?

# EXPLORING THE ISSUE

## Is America Becoming More Unequal?

## Critical Thinking and Reflection

1. What factors contribute to increased inequality of income and wealth in the United States?
2. Under what conditions does economic inequality increase?
3. What circumstances tend to reduce economic inequality in the United States?
4. Is economic inequality in America increasing or decreasing? Why? Is this process reversible?
5. How does the United States compare with other democracies regarding economic inequality?
6. What do European democracies do that makes their economic outcomes different?
7. What are the desirable and undesirable consequences of economic inequality in the United States?
8. What are the major policies that Robert Greenstein would adopt to reduce economic inequality?
9. Why does Christopher DeMuth believe that Social Security and Medicare are obsolete policies?

## Is There Common Ground?

Both those who deplore increasing inequality and those who believe that Americans have achieved an impressive level of equality agree that equality of opportunity is critical. They disagree as to how much opportunity is necessary and whether American society has achieved it. Where Robert Greenstein and other critics of American inequality advocate much greater public investment in education, health, and other areas as the most effective means of equalizing opportunity, Christopher DeMuth concludes that economic freedom has produced both the challenge of social ills and the development of social solutions. The divide is between those who approach equal justice in public policies that reduce sharp areas of inequality and those who seek it in the social forces of a free society.

A study released October 27, 2011 by the Bertelsmann Stiftung Foundation in Germany comparing poverty rates, income inequality, pre-primary education, and health rating in 32 member countries of the Organization for Economic Co-operation and Development ranked the United States 27 among 31 countries overall in what it characterized as social justice, with the United States among the bottom five in poverty prevention, overall poverty rate, child poverty rate, and income inequality; among the bottom 10 in senior citizen poverty rate, pre-primary education and health rating, and in the bottom 15 in intergenerational justice, which includes family and pension policies, environmental policies, and assessment of political-economic being established for future generations. In none of the eight categories did the United States place in the top half of the 31 nations. [Bertelsmann Stiftung Foundation, "Social Justice in the OECD—How Do the Member States Compare?"]

## Additional Resources

In an effort to deal with educational inequality and its later economic and social consequences, the No Child Left Behind Act of 2001 required that every public school abolish social class differences in achievement, but that hope was contradicted by a U.S. Department of Education study that saw a close correlation between socioeconomic status and educational achievement in most countries including the United States, according to Richard Rothstein, *Class and Schools: Using Social, Economic, and Educational Reform to Close the Black-White Educational Gap* (The Economic Policy Institute and Teachers College Press, 2004). A "culture of underachievement" is fostered and enforced by the absence of a literate and conversational family environment, peer pressure, and discrimination in school and the workplace.

Will Wilkinson, in *Thinking Clearly About Economic Inequality* (Cato Institute, 2009), argues that income inequality is a dangerous distraction from the real problems of poverty, lack of economic opportunity, and systematic injustice. Representative Ron Paul presents a libertarian defense of natural inequality in *The Revolution: A Manifesto* (Grand Central Publishing, 2009). Both conservative and libertarian positions are rejected in *Inequality Matters: The Growing Economic Divide in America with Its Poisonous Consequences,* a collection of essays edited by James Lardner and David A. Smith (The New Press, 2006). Larry M. Bartels, in *Unequal Democracy: The Political Economic of the New Gilded Age* (Princeton University Press, 2008), sees a close association between which party is in power and the extent of economic inequality. These books and essays reflect the continuing debate as to whether economic equality is consistent with the existence and strengthening of American democracy.

# ISSUE 15

## Should Same-Sex Marriage Be a Constitutional Right?

**YES: Theodore B. Olson,** from "The Conservative Case for Gay Marriage: Why Same-Sex Marriage Is an American Value," *The Daily Beast* (January 8, 2010)

**NO: Sam Shulman,** from "Gay Marriage—and Marriage," *Commentary* (November 2003)

### ISSUE SUMMARY

**YES:** Attorney Theodore B. Olson argues that the right of homosexual people to marry, is the logical extension of the equality proclaimed in the Declaration of Independence and guaranteed by the Fourteenth Amendment.

**NO:** Columnist Sam Shulman sees gay marriage as a burlesque of marriage that will harm the interests of women.

Fifty years ago, talk of "gay marriage" would more likely to be found in a comedy sketch than in a courtroom or a legislative chamber. Until 1961 all 50 states outlawed homosexual behavior. It was condemned by the clergy of all denominations, barely hinted at in Hollywood movies, and could hardly be spoken of in middle-class homes. The image of an official ceremony legitimizing and celebrating the sexual union of two men or two women would have been beyond shocking; it would have been farcical.

But times change, sometimes very quickly. In 2003, the Supreme Court, overturning its own ruling from two years earlier, struck down as unconstitutional the sodomy laws that still remained in 24 states. In dissent, Justice Antonin Scalia posed a rhetorical question intended as a kind of *reductio ad absurdum*: With this case as a precedent, Scalia wrote, "[W]hat [remaining] justification could there possibly be for denying the benefits of marriage to homosexual couples. . . .?" Some of the members of the Court's majority went to pains to show that the decision could not possibly become a precedent for gay marriage, but within a decade Scalia's words had become prophetic.

Hawaii had blazed the trail in 1996 when its highest court ruled that the state must present a compelling public reason for prohibiting gay marriage. The ruling set off widespread alarms, because Article IV, Section 1 of the Constitution stipulates that "Full Faith and Credit shall be given in each state to the public Acts, Records, and judicial Proceedings of every other State." Thus, if a gay couple got married in Hawaii, they could go back to their home state or to any other state and force it to recognize the validity of their marriage, permitting them to enjoy all the same benefits and rights accorded to other married couples in that state—effectively nationalizing gay marriage.

To prevent that from happening, Congress passed the Defense of Marriage Act (DOMA) in 1996. It stipulated that "the word 'marriage' means only a legal union between one man and one woman" and protects states against having to grant legal recognition to out-of-state unions between people of the same sex. That seemed at least to be a kind of fail-safe. If a state actually were to legitimize gay marriage (Hawaii's 1998 court ruling was reversed by an amendment to the state's constitution), DOMA would keep it limited to that one state.

But events were now moving quickly in various states. In 1999, the Vermont Supreme Court held that denying same-sex couples the rights that come with civil marriage violates the state's equality guarantee, and the Vermont legislature followed it up in 2000 with a "civil union" statute for gays, the first in the nation. Later that year San Francisco became the first city to compel private businesses to extend the benefits accorded to married couples to cohabiting couples regardless of sex. Still, full–fledged gay marriage had not yet arrived. That changed in 2004, when the Massachusetts Supreme Court ruled unconstitutional the state's ban on gay marriage.

As of this writing, 6 of the 50 states and the District of Columbia now allow same-sex marriage: Iowa, Connecticut, Massachusetts, New Hampshire, Vermont and New York. Four states—Delaware, Hawaii, Illinois, and New Jersey—have approved gay civil unions. But gay marriage is banned in 39 states, and popular votes have consistently opposed it. A case in point is California, where in 2000 the voters overturned a decision by the California Supreme Court legitimating gay marriage. That is now being contested in federal court and may soon reach the U.S. Supreme Court. The 1996 DOMA is also being challenged in the lower courts, and if the Supreme Court strikes it down, every state in the Union would have to give "full faith and credit" to a gay marriage ceremony conducted in any single state. Although DOMA is a federal law, in February 2010 the Obama administration's Attorney General refused to defend it in the federal court.

Opponents of gay marriage often emphasize the novelty of it. The practice has never existed in recorded history of any people on earth. Its supporters argue that time-honored practices or taboos is a shaky way to make a case.

Yet change has its own problems. Once we start down its road, how do we know when to get off? Once we allow marriage between two people of the same sex, how can we object to a threesome or beyond? And what about Polygamy or marriage between brother and sister?

Can we draw limits when we're on a slippery slope? Yet drawing limits is a task any lawmaker has to face, especially when breaking new ground, and the difficulty in doing so is not a good argument for stifling needed reforms. Whether gay marriage *is* a needed reform, or a reform at all, is a question that divides the two discussants in this section.

# YES ↵

**Theodore B. Olson**

# The Conservative Case for Gay Marriage: Why Same-Sex Marriage Is an American Value

Together with my good friend and occasional courtroom adversary David Boies, I am attempting to persuade a federal court to invalidate California's Proposition 8—the voter-approved measure that overturned California's constitutional right to marry a person of the same sex.

My involvement in this case has generated a certain degree of consternation among conservatives. How could a politically active, lifelong Republican, a veteran of the Ronald Reagan and George W. Bush administrations, challenge the "traditional" definition of marriage and press for an "activist" interpretation of the Constitution to create another "new" constitutional right?

My answer to this seeming conundrum rests on a lifetime of exposure to persons of different backgrounds, histories, viewpoints, and intrinsic characteristics, and on my rejection of what I see as superficially appealing but ultimately false perceptions about our Constitution and its protection of equality and fundamental rights.

Many of my fellow conservatives have an almost knee-jerk hostility toward gay marriage. This does not make sense, because same-sex unions promote the values conservatives prize. Marriage is one of the basic building blocks of our neighborhoods and our nation. At its best, it is a stable bond between two individuals who work to create a loving household and a social and economic partnership. We encourage couples to marry because the commitments they make to one another provide benefits not only to themselves but also to their families and communities. Marriage requires thinking beyond one's own needs. It transforms two individuals into a union based on shared aspirations, and in doing so establishes a formal investment in the well-being of society. The fact that individuals who happen to be gay want to share in this vital social institution is evidence that conservative ideals enjoy widespread acceptance. Conservatives should celebrate this, rather than lament it.

Legalizing same-sex marriage would also be a recognition of basic American principles, and would represent the culmination of our nation's commitment to equal rights. It is, some have said, the last major civil-rights milestone yet to be surpassed in our two-century struggle to attain the goals we set for this nation at its formation.

From *The Daily Beast*, January 8, 2010. Copyright © 2010 by Newsweek. Reprinted by permission via PARS International.

This bedrock American principle of equality is central to the political and legal convictions of Republicans, Democrats, liberals, and conservatives alike. The dream that became America began with the revolutionary concept expressed in the Declaration of Independence in words that are among the most noble and elegant ever written: "We hold these truths to be self-evident, that all men are created equal, that they are endowed by their Creator with certain unalienable Rights, that among these are Life, Liberty and the pursuit of Happiness."

Sadly, our nation has taken a long time to live up to the promise of equality. In 1857, the Supreme Court held that an African-American could not be a citizen. During the ensuing Civil War, Abraham Lincoln eloquently reminded the nation of its founding principle: "our fathers brought forth on this continent, a new nation, conceived in liberty and dedicated to the proposition that all men are created equal."

At the end of the Civil War, to make the elusive promise of equality a reality, the 14th Amendment to the Constitution added the command that "no State shall deprive any person of life, liberty or property, without due process of law; nor deny to any person the equal protection of the laws."

Subsequent laws and court decisions have made clear that equality under the law extends to persons of all races, religions, and places of origin. What better way to make this national aspiration complete than to apply the same protection to men and women who differ from others only on the basis of their sexual orientation? I cannot think of a single reason—and have not heard one since I undertook this venture—for continued discrimination against decent, hardworking members of our society on that basis.

Various federal and state laws have accorded certain rights and privileges to gay and lesbian couples, but these protections vary dramatically at the state level, and nearly universally deny true equality to gays and lesbians who wish to marry. The very idea of marriage is basic to recognition as equals in our society; any status short of that is inferior, unjust, and unconstitutional.

The United States Supreme Court has repeatedly held that marriage is one of the most fundamental rights that we have as Americans under our Constitution. It is an expression of our desire to create a social partnership, to live and share life's joys and burdens with the person we love, and to form a lasting bond and a social identity. The Supreme Court has said that marriage is a part of the Constitution's protections of liberty, privacy, freedom of association, and spiritual identification. In short, the right to marry helps us to define ourselves and our place in a community. Without it, there can be no true equality under the law.

It is true that marriage in this nation traditionally has been regarded as a relationship exclusively between a man and a woman, and many of our nation's multiple religions define marriage in precisely those terms. But while the Supreme Court has always previously considered marriage in that context, the underlying rights and liberties that marriage embodies are not in any way confined to heterosexuals.

Marriage is a civil bond in this country as well as, in some (but hardly all) cases, a religious sacrament. It is a relationship recognized by governments as providing a privileged and respected status, entitled to the state's support and benefits. The California Supreme Court described marriage as a "union unreservedly approved and favored by the community." Where the state has accorded official sanction to a relationship and provided special benefits to those who enter into that relationship, our courts have insisted that with-holding that status requires powerful justifications and may not be arbitrarily denied.

What, then, are the justifications for California's decision in Proposition 8 to withdraw access to the institution of marriage for some of its citizens on the basis of their sexual orientation? The reasons I have heard are not very persuasive.

The explanation mentioned most often is tradition. But simply because something has always been done a certain way does not mean that it must always remain that way. Otherwise we would still have segregated schools and debtors' prisons. Gays and lesbians have always been among us, forming a part of our society, and they have lived as couples in our neighborhoods and communities. For a long time, they have experienced discrimination and even persecution; but we, as a society, are starting to become more tolerant, accept-ing, and understanding. California and many other states have allowed gays and lesbians to form domestic partnerships (or civil unions) with most of the rights of married heterosexuals. Thus, gay and lesbian individuals are now permitted to live together in state-sanctioned relationships. It therefore seems anomalous to cite "tradition" as a justification for withholding the status of marriage and thus to continue to label those relationships as less worthy, less sanctioned, or less legitimate.

The second argument I often hear is that traditional marriage furthers the state's interest in procreation—and that opening marriage to same-sex couples would dilute, diminish, and devalue this goal. But that is plainly not the case. Preventing lesbians and gays from marrying does not cause more heterosexuals to marry and conceive more children. Likewise, allowing gays and lesbians to marry someone of the same sex will not discourage heterosex-uals from marrying a person of the opposite sex. How, then, would allowing same-sex marriages reduce the number of children that heterosexual couples conceive?

This procreation argument cannot be taken seriously. We do not inquire whether heterosexual couples intend to bear children, or have the capacity to have children, before we allow them to marry. We permit marriage by the elderly, by prison inmates, and by persons who have no intention of having children. What's more, it is pernicious to think marriage should be limited to heterosexuals because of the state's desire to promote procreation. We would surely not accept as constitutional a ban on marriage if a state were to decide, as China has done, to discourage procreation.

Another argument, vaguer and even less persuasive, is that gay marriage somehow does harm to heterosexual marriage. I have yet to meet anyone who can explain to me what this means. In what way would allowing same-sex partners to marry diminish the marriages of heterosexual couples? Tell-ingly, when the judge in our case asked our opponent to identify the ways in which same-sex marriage would harm heterosexual marriage, to his credit he answered honestly: he could not think of any.

The simple fact is that there is no good reason why we should deny marriage to same-sex partners. On the other hand, there are many reasons why we should formally recognize these relationships and embrace the rights of gays and lesbians to marry and become full and equal members of our society.

No matter what you think of homosexuality, it is a fact that gays and lesbians are members of our families, clubs, and workplaces. They are our doctors, our teachers, our soldiers (whether we admit it or not), and our friends. They yearn for acceptance, stable relationships, and success in their lives, just like the rest of us.

Conservatives and liberals alike need to come together on principles that surely unite us. Certainly, we can agree on the value of strong families, lasting domestic relationships, and communities populated by persons with recognized and sanctioned bonds to one another. Confining some of our neighbors and friends who share these same values to an outlaw or second-class status undermines their sense of belonging and weakens their ties with the rest of us and what should be our common aspirations. Even those whose religious convictions preclude endorsement of what they may perceive as an unacceptable "lifestyle" should recognize that disapproval should not warrant stigmatization and unequal treatment.

When we refuse to accord this status to gays and lesbians, we discourage them from forming the same relationships we encourage for others. And we are also telling them, those who love them, and society as a whole that their relationships are less worthy, less legitimate, less permanent, and less valued. We demean their relationships and we demean them as individuals. I cannot imagine how we benefit as a society by doing so.

I understand, but reject, certain religious teachings that denounce homosexuality as morally wrong, illegitimate, or unnatural; and I take strong exception to those who argue that same-sex relationships should be discouraged by society and law. Science has taught us, even if history has not, that gays and lesbians do not choose to be homosexual any more than the rest of us choose to be heterosexual. To a very large extent, these characteristics are immutable, like being left-handed. And, while our Constitution guarantees the freedom to exercise our individual religious convictions, it equally prohibits us from forcing our beliefs on others. I do not believe that our society can ever live up to the promise of equality, and the fundamental rights to life, liberty, and the pursuit of happiness, until we stop invidious discrimination on the basis of sexual orientation.

If we are born heterosexual, it is not unusual for us to perceive those who are born homosexual as aberrational and threatening. Many religions and much of our social culture have reinforced those impulses. Too often, that has led to prejudice, hostility, and discrimination. The antidote is understanding, and reason. We once tolerated laws throughout this nation that prohibited marriage between persons of different races. California's Supreme Court was the first to find that discrimination unconstitutional. The U.S. Supreme Court unanimously agreed 20 years later, in 1967, in a case called *Loving v. Virginia*.

It seems inconceivable today that only 40 years ago there were places in this country where a black woman could not legally marry a white man. And it was only 50 years ago that 17 states mandated segregated public education—until the Supreme Court unanimously struck down that practice in *Brown v. Board of Education*. Most Americans are proud of these decisions and the fact that the discriminatory state laws that spawned them have been discredited. I am convinced that Americans will be equally proud when we no longer discriminate against gays and lesbians and welcome them into our society.

Reactions to our lawsuit have reinforced for me these essential truths. I have certainly heard anger, resentment, and hostility, and words like "betrayal" and other pointedly graphic criticism. But mostly I have been overwhelmed by expressions of gratitude and goodwill from persons in all walks of life, including, I might add, from many conservatives and libertarians whose names might surprise. I have been particularly moved by many personal renditions of how lonely and personally destructive it is to be treated as an outcast and how meaningful it will be to be respected by our laws and civil institutions as an American, entitled to equality and dignity. I have no doubt that we are on the right side of this battle, the right side of the law, and the right side of history.

Some have suggested that we have brought this case too soon, and that neither the country nor the courts are "ready" to tackle this issue and remove this stigma. We disagree. We represent real clients—two wonderful couples in California who have longtime relationships. Our lesbian clients are raising four fine children who could not ask for better parents. Our clients wish to be married. They believe that they have that constitutional right. They wish to be represented in court to seek vindication of that right by mounting a challenge under the United States Constitution to the validity of Proposition 8 under the equal-protection and due-process clauses of the 14th Amendment. In fact, the California attorney general has conceded the unconstitutionality of Proposition 8, and the city of San Francisco has joined our case to defend the rights of gays and lesbians to be married. We do not tell persons who have a legitimate claim to wait until the time is "right" and the populace is "ready" to recognize their equality and equal dignity under the law.

Citizens who have been denied equality are invariably told to "wait their turn" and to "be patient." Yet veterans of past civil-rights battles found that it was the act of insisting on equal rights that ultimately sped acceptance of those rights. As to whether the courts are "ready" for this case, just a few years ago, in *Romer v. Evans*, the United States Supreme Court struck down a popularly adopted Colorado constitutional amendment that withdrew the rights of gays and lesbians in that state to the protection of anti-discrimination laws. And seven years ago, in *Lawrence v. Texas*, the Supreme Court struck down, as lacking any rational basis, Texas laws prohibiting private, intimate sexual practices between persons of the same sex, overruling a contrary decision just 20 years earlier.

These decisions have generated controversy, of course, but they are decisions of the nation's highest court on which our clients are entitled to rely. If all citizens have a constitutional right to marry, if state laws that withdraw legal protections of gays and lesbians as a class are unconstitutional, and if private, intimate sexual conduct between persons of the same sex is protected by the Constitution, there is very little left on which opponents of same-sex marriage can rely. As Justice Antonin Scalia, who dissented in the Lawrence case, pointed out, "[W]hat [remaining] justification could there possibly be for denying the benefits of marriage to homosexual couples exercising '[t]he liberty protected by the Constitution'?" He is right, of course. One might agree or not with these decisions, but even Justice Scalia has acknowledged that they lead in only one direction.

California's Proposition 8 is particularly vulnerable to constitutional challenge, because that state has now enacted a crazy-quilt of marriage regulation that makes no sense to anyone. California recognizes marriage between men and women, including persons on death row, child abusers, and wife beaters. At the same time, California prohibits marriage by loving, caring, stable partners of the same sex, but tries to make up for it by giving them the alternative of "domestic partnerships" with virtually all of the rights of married persons except the official, state-approved status of marriage. Finally, California recognizes 18,000 same-sex marriages that took place in the months between the state Supreme Court's ruling that upheld gay-marriage rights and the decision of California's citizens to withdraw those rights by enacting Proposition 8.

So there are now three classes of Californians: heterosexual couples who can get married, divorced, and remarried, if they wish; same-sex couples who cannot get married but can live together in domestic partnerships; and same-sex couples who are now married but who, if they divorce, cannot remarry. This is an irrational system, it is discriminatory, and it cannot stand.

Americans who believe in the words of the Declaration of Independence, in Lincoln's Gettysburg Address, in the 14th Amendment, and in the Constitution's guarantees of equal protection and equal dignity before the law cannot sit by while this wrong continues. This is not a conservative or liberal issue; it is an American one, and it is time that we, as Americans, embraced it.

→ **NO**

# Gay Marriage—and Marriage

"... **t**ampering with the unwritten and unfailing laws."

The feeling seems to be growing that gay marriage is inevitably coming our way in the U.S., perhaps through a combination of judicial fiat and legislation in individual states. Growing, too, is the sense of a shift in the climate of opinion. The American public seems to be in the process of changing its mind—not actually in favor of gay marriage, but toward a position of slightly revolted tolerance for the idea. Survey results suggest that people have forgotten why they were so opposed to the notion even as recently as a few years ago.

It is curious that this has happened so quickly. With honorable exceptions, most of those who are passionately on the side of the traditional understanding of marriage appear to be at a loss for words to justify their passion; as for the rest, many seem to wish gay marriage had never been proposed in the first place, but also to have resigned themselves to whatever happens. In this respect, the gay-marriage debate is very different from the abortion debate, in which few with an opinion on either side have been so disengaged.

I think I understand why this is the case: as someone passionately and instinctively opposed to the idea of homosexual marriage, I have found myself disappointed by the arguments I have seen advanced against it. The strongest of these arguments predict measurable harm to the family and to our arrangements for the upbringing and well-being of children. I do not doubt the accuracy of those arguments. But they do not seem to get at the heart of the matter.

To me, what is at stake in this debate is not only the potential unhappiness of children, grave as that is; it is our ability to maintain the most basic components of our humanity. I believe, in fact, that we are at an "Antigone moment." Some of our fellow citizens wish to impose a radically new understanding upon laws and institutions that are both very old and fundamental to our organization as individuals and as a society. As Antigone said to Creon, we are being asked to tamper with "unwritten and unfailing laws, not of now, nor of yesterday; they always live, and no one knows their origin in time." I suspect, moreover, that everyone knows this is the case, and that, paradoxically, this very awareness of just how much is at stake is what may have induced, in defenders of those same "unwritten and unfailing laws," a kind of paralysis.

Admittedly, it is very difficult to defend that which is both ancient and "unwritten"—the arguments do not resolve themselves into a neat parade of

From *Commentary*, November 2003, pp. 35–40. Copyright © 2003 by Commentary, Inc. Reprinted by permission of Commentary. All rights reserved.

documentary evidence, research results, or citations from the legal literature. Admittedly, too, proponents of this radical new understanding have been uncommonly effective in presenting their program as something that is not radical at all but as requiring merely a slight and painless adjustment in our customary arrangements. Finally, we have all learned to practice a certain deference to the pleas of minorities with a grievance, and in recent years no group has benefited more from this society-wide dispensation than homosexuals. Nevertheless, in the somewhat fragmentary notes that follow, I hope to re-articulate what I am persuaded everyone knows to be the case about marriage, and perhaps thereby encourage others with stronger arguments than mine to help break the general paralysis.

Let us begin by admiring the case for gay marriage. Unlike the case for completely unrestricted abortion, which has come to be something of an embarrassment even to those who advance it, the case for gay marriage enjoys the decided advantage of appealing to our better moral natures as well as to our reason. It deploys two arguments. The first centers on principles of justice and fairness and may be thought of as the civil-rights argument. The second is at once more personal and more utilitarian, emphasizing the degradation and unhappiness attendant upon the denial of gay marriage and, conversely, the human and social happiness that will flow from its legal establishment.

Both arguments have been set forth most persuasively by two gifted writers, Bruce Bawer and Andrew Sullivan, each of whom describes himself as a social conservative. In their separate ways, they have been campaigning for gay marriage for over a decade. Bawer's take on the subject is succinctly summarized in his 1993 book, *A Place at the Table;* Sullivan has held forth on the desirability of legalizing gay marriage in numerous articles, on his website (andrewsullivan.com), and in an influential book, *Virtually Normal* (1995).

The civil-rights argument goes like this. Marriage is a legal state conferring real, tangible benefits on those who participate in it: specifically, tax breaks as well as other advantages when it comes to inheritance, property ownership, and employment benefits. But family law, since it limits marriage to heterosexual couples over the age of consent, clearly discriminates against a segment of the population. It is thus a matter of simple justice that, in Sullivan's words, "all public (as opposed to private) discrimination against homosexuals be ended and that every right and responsibility that heterosexuals enjoy as public citizens be extended to those who grow up and find themselves emotionally different." Not to grant such rights, Sullivan maintains, is to impose on homosexuals a civil deprivation akin to that suffered by black Americans under Jim Crow.

The utilitarian argument is more subtle; just as the rights argument seems aimed mainly at liberals, this one seems mostly to have in mind the concerns of conservatives. In light of the disruptive, anarchic, violence-prone behavior of many homosexuals (the argument runs), why should we not encourage the formation of stable, long-term, monogamous relationships that will redound to the health of society as a whole? . . .

Bawer, for his part, has come close to saying that the inability of many male homosexuals to remain faithful in long-term relationships is a consequence of the lack of marriage rights—a burning sign of the more general stigma under which gays labor in our society and which can be redressed by changes in law. . . .

The case is elegant, and it is compelling. But it is not unanswerable. And answers have indeed been forthcoming, even if, as I indicated at the outset, many of them have tended to be couched somewhat defensively. Thus, rather than repudiating the very idea of an abstract "right" to marry, many upholders of the traditional definition of marriage tacitly concede such a right, only going on to suggest that denying it to a minority amounts to a lesser hurt than conferring it would impose on the majority, and especially on children, the weakest members of our society.

Others, to be sure, have attacked the Bawer/Sullivan line more forthrightly. In a September 2000 article in Commentary, "What Is Wrong with Gay Marriage," Stanley Kurtz challenged the central contention that marriage would do for gay men what it does for straights—i.e., "domesticate" their natural male impulse to promiscuity. Citing a number of academic "queer theorists" and radical gays, Kurtz wrote:

> In contrast to moderates and "conservatives" like Andrew Sullivan, who consistently play down [the] difference [between gays and straights] in order to promote their vision of gays as monogamists-in-the-making, radical gays have argued—more knowledgeably, more powerfully, and more vocally than any opponent of same-sex marriage would dare to do—that homosexuality, and particularly male homosexuality, is by its very nature incompatible with the norms of traditional monogamous marriage.

True, Kurtz went on, such radical gays nevertheless support same-sex marriage. But what motivates them is the hope of "eventually undoing the institution [of marriage] altogether," by delegitimizing age-old understandings of the family and thus (in the words of one such radical) "striking at the heart of the organization of Western culture and societies.". . .

James Q. Wilson, Maggie Gallagher, Stanley Kurtz, and others—including William J. Bennett in *The Broken Hearth* (2001)—are right to point to the deleterious private and public consequences of instituting gay marriage. Why, then, do their arguments fail to satisfy completely? Partly, no doubt, it is because the damage they describe is largely prospective and to that degree hypothetical; partly, as I remarked early on, the defensive tone that invariably enters into these polemics may rob them of the force they would otherwise have. I hardly mean to deprecate that tone: anyone with homosexual friends or relatives, especially those participating in longstanding romantic relationships, must feel abashed to find himself saying, in effect, "You gentlemen, you ladies, are at one and the same time a fine example of fidelity and mutual attachment—and the thin edge of the wedge." Nevertheless, in demanding the right to marry, that is exactly what they are.

To grasp what is at the other edge of that wedge—that is, what stands to be undone by gay marriage—we have to distinguish marriage itself from a variety of other goods and values with which it is regularly associated by its defenders and its aspirants alike. Those values—love and monogamous sex and establishing a home, fidelity, childbearing and childrearing, stability, inheritance, tax breaks, and all the rest—are not the same as marriage. True, a good marriage generally contains them, a bad marriage is generally deficient in them, and in law, religion, and custom, even under the strictest of moral regimes, their absence can be grounds for ending the union. But the essence of marriage resides elsewhere, and those who seek to arrange a kind of marriage for the inherently unmarriageable are looking for those things in the wrong place.

The largest fallacy of all arises from the emphasis on romantic love. In a book published last year, Tipper and Al Gore defined a family as those who are "joined at the heart"—"getting beyond words, legal formalities, and even blood ties." The distinction the Gores draw in this sentimental and offhand way is crucial, but they utterly misconstrue it. Hearts can indeed love, and stop loving. But what exactly does this have to do with marriage, which can follow, precede, or remain wholly independent of that condition?

It is a truism that many married people feel little sexual or romantic attraction to each other—perhaps because they have been married too long, or perhaps, as some men have always claimed, because the death of sexual desire is coincident with the wedding ceremony. ("All comedies are ended by a marriage," Byron wittily and sadly remarked.) Many people—in ages past, certainly most people—have married for reasons other than sexual or romantic attraction. So what? I could marry a woman I did not love, a woman I did not feel sexually attracted to or want to sleep with, and our marriage would still be a marriage, not just legally but in its essence.

The truth is banal, circular, but finally unavoidable: by definition, the essence of marriage is to sanction and solemnize that connection of opposites which alone creates new life. (Whether or not a given married couple does in fact create new life is immaterial.) Men and women can marry only because they belong to different, opposite, sexes. In marriage, they surrender those separate and different sexual allegiances, coming together to form a new entity. Their union is not a formalizing of romantic love but represents a certain idea—a construction, an abstract thought—about how best to formalize the human condition. This thought, embodied in a promise or a contract, is what holds marriage together, and the creation of this idea of marriage marks a key moment in the history of human development, a triumph over the alternative idea, which is concubinage.

Let me try to be more precise. Marriage can only concern my connection to a woman (and not to a man) because, as my reference to concubinage suggests, marriage is an institution that is built around female sexuality and female procreativity. (The very word "marriage" comes from the Latin word for mother, mater.) It exists for the gathering-in of a woman's sexuality under the protective net of the human or divine order, or both. This was so in the past and it is so even now, in our supposedly liberated times, when a woman who is in a sexual relationship without being married is, and is perceived to be, in a different state of being (not just a different legal state) from a woman who is married.

Circumstances have, admittedly, changed. Thanks to contraception, the decision to marry no longer precedes sexual intercourse as commonly as it did 50 years ago, when, for most people, a fully sexual relationship could begin only with marriage (and, when, as my mother constantly reminds me, one married for sex). Now the decision can come later; but come it almost certainly must. Even with contraception, even with feminism and women's liberation, the feeling would appear to be nearly as strong as ever that, for a woman, a sexual relationship must either end in marriage, or end.

This is surely understandable, for marriage benefits women, again not just in law but essentially. A woman can control who is the father of her children only insofar as there is a civil and private order that protects her from rape; marriage is the bulwark of that order. The 1960's feminists had the right idea: the essential thing for a woman is to control her own body. But they were wrong that this is what abortion is for; it is, rather, what marriage is for. It is humanity's way of enabling a woman to control her own body and to know (if she cares to) who is the father of her children.

Yes, marriage tends to regulate or channel the sexual appetite of men, and this is undoubtedly a good thing for women. But it is not the ultimate good. A husband, no matter how unfaithful, cannot introduce a child who is not his wife's own into a marriage without her knowledge; she alone has the power to do such a thing. For a woman, the fundamental advantage of marriage is thus not to regulate her husband but to empower herself—to regulate who has access to her person, and to marshal the resources of her husband and of the wider community to help her raise her children.

Every human relationship can be described as an enslavement, but for women the alternative to marriage is a much worse enslavement—which is why marriage, for women, is often associated as much with sexual freedom as with sexual constraint. In the traditional Roman Catholic cultures of the Mediterranean and South America, where virginity is fiercely protected and adolescent girls are hardly permitted to "date," marriage gives a woman the double luxury of controlling her sexuality and, if she wishes, extending it.

For men, by contrast, the same phenomenon—needing to be married in order to feel safe and free in a sexual relationship—simply does not exist. Men may wish to marry, but for more particular reasons: because they want to have children, or because they want to make a woman they love happy, or because they fear they will otherwise lose the woman they love. But it is rare for a man to feel essentially incomplete, or unprotected, in a sexual relationship that has not been solemnized by marriage. In fact, a man desperate to marry is often considered to have something wrong with him—to be unusually controlling or needy.

Because marriage is an arrangement built around female sexuality, because the institution has to do with women far more than it has to do with men, women will be the victims of its destruction. Those analysts who have focused on how children will suffer from the legalization of gay marriage are undoubtedly correct—but this will not be the first time that social developments perceived as advances for one group or another have harmed children. After all, the two most important (if effortless) achievements of the women's movement of the late 1960's were the right to abort and the right—in some social classes, the commandment—to join the professional workforce, both manifestly harmful to the interests of children.

But with the success of the gay-liberation movement, it is women themselves, all women, who will be hurt. The reason is that gay marriage takes something that belongs essentially to women, is crucial to their very freedom, and empties it of meaning.

Why should I not be able to marry a man? The question addresses a class of human phenomena that can be described in sentences but nonetheless cannot be. However much I might wish to, I cannot be a father to a pebble—I cannot be a brother to a puppy—I cannot make my horse my consul. Just so, I cannot, and should not be able to, marry a man. If I want to be a brother to a puppy, are you abridging my rights by not permitting it? I may say what I please; saying it does not mean that it can be.

In a gay marriage, one of two men must play the woman, or one of two women must play the man. "Play" here means travesty—burlesque. Not that their love is a travesty; but their participation in a ceremony that apes the marriage bond, with all that goes into it, is a travesty. Their taking-over of the form of this crucial and fragile connection of opposites is a travesty of marriage's purpose of protecting, actually and symbolically, the woman who enters into marriage with a man. To burlesque that purpose weakens those protections, and is essentially and profoundly anti-female.

Radical feminists were right, to an extent, in insisting that men's and women's sexuality is so different as to be inimical. Catharine MacKinnon has proclaimed that in a "patriarchal" society, all sexual intercourse is rape. Repellent as her view is, it is formed around a kernel of truth. There is something inherently violative about sexual intercourse—and there is something dangerous about being a woman in a sexual relationship with a man to whom she is not yet married. Among the now-aging feminists of my generation, no less than among their mothers, such a woman is commonly thought to be a victim.

Marriage is a sign that the ever-so-slight violation that is involved in a heterosexual relationship has been sanctioned by some recognized authority. That sanction is also what makes divorce a scandal—for divorce cannot truly undo the sanction of sexual intercourse, which is to say the sanction to create life, with one's original partner. Even in the Jewish tradition, which regards marriage (but not love) in a completely unsacralized way, divorce, though perfectly legal, does not erase the ontological status of the earlier marriage. (The Talmud records that God weeps when a man puts aside his first wife.) This sanction does not exist for homosexual couples. They are not opposites; they are the same. They live in a world of innocence, and neither their union nor their disunion partakes of the act of creation.

This brings us back to the incest ban, with which marriage is intimately and intricately connected. Indeed, marriage exists for the same reason that incest must not: because in our darker, inhuman moments we are driven toward that which is the same as ourselves and away from that which is fundamentally different from ourselves. Therefore we are enjoined from committing incest, negatively, and commanded to join with our opposite, positively—so that humanity may endure. . . .

Marriage, to say it for the last time, is what connects us with our nature and with our animal origins, with how all of us, heterosexual and homosexual alike, came to be. It exists not because of custom, or because of a conspiracy (whether patriarchal or matriarchal), but because, through marriage, the world exists. Marriage is how we are connected backward in time, through the generations, to our Creator (or, if you insist, to the primal soup), and forward to the future beyond the scope of our own lifespan. It is, to say the least, bigger than two hearts beating as one.

Severing this connection by defining it out of existence—cutting it down to size, transforming it into a mere contract between chums—sunders the natural laws that prevent concubinage and incest. Unless we resist, we will find ourselves entering on the path to the abolition of the human. The gods move very fast when they bring ruin on misguided men.

# EXPLORING THE ISSUE

## Should Same-Sex Marriage Be a Constitutional Right?

## Critical Thinking and Reflection

The reader may wish to revisit some of the questions we posed in our introcruction to this issue. What role should tradition and precedent play in the argument over same sex marriage? Can the radical novelty of same-sex marriage in human history be a valid argument against beginning the practice today? And what about the "slippery slope" argument that, once we start legitimizing gay marriage, what is to stop us from doing the same with polygamy and incest? And what are we to make of Sam Shulman's argument that marriage protects women against violation? Does that argument still hold up today? Is it any more strained than Theodore Olson's assumption that if Thomas Jefferson were rigorously to pursue his own logic in the Declaration of Independence, he would be led to recognize the propriety of gay marriage?

## Is There Common Ground

The common ground that might once have appealed to both sides in this controversy no longer does so. The common ground was the "civil union" compromise, once favored by moderates and many liberals. Enacted in a number of states, civil unions provide virtually all the benefits granted to married couples, but without the full title of marriage. The gay rights movement rejects this as an anemic halfway measure, insisting that it fails to achieve real equality between gays and straights. The fight over gay marriage, then, can no longer be compromised: one side will win and the other side will lose. Gay marriage advocates, convinced that they are on the winning side, tend to the view that the losers will eventually come to terms with defeat, much as racial segregationists have come to accept the end of Jim Crow. But, just as the parallel to the civil rights struggle may not be as obvious to others as it is to them, so the outcome of the struggle may not emerge in quite the same way.

## Additional Resources

In *Virtually Normal: An Argument About Homosexuality* (Alfred A. Knopf, 1995), Andrew Sullivan contends that legalizing gay marriage would be a humanizing step because such marriages would promote social stability and teach valuable lessons even to "straights." Criticizing that view is James Q. Wilson ("Against Homosexual Marriage," *Commentary*, March 1996). Sullivan himself provides some essays against gay marriage in an edited work, *Same-Sex Marriage: Pro and*

*Con* (Vintage, rev. ed., 2004). Jonathan Rauch supports gay marriage, but his *Gay Marriage: Why It Is Good for Gays, Good for Straights, and Good for America* (Times Books, 2004), takes a cautious approach, since he believes that "same sex marriage will work best when people accept and understand it, whereas a sudden national enactment, were it suddenly to happen, might spark a culture war on the order of the abortion battle." The legal aspects of same-sex marriage are examined by Mark Strasser in *The Challenge of Same-Sex Marriages: Federalist Principles and Constitutional Protections* (Praeger, 1999). Peter Sprigg's *Outrage: How Gay Activists and Liberal Judges are trashing Democracy to Redefine Marriage* (Regnery, 2004) charges that liberal judges are cooperating with homosexual activists to overturn the will of the people on the definition of marriage. But Anthony Verona, in an article in the *Columbia Journal of Gender and Law* ("Taking Initiatives: Reconciling Race, Religion, Media and Democracy in the Quest for Marriage Equality," May 9, 2011), worries about legal assaults from the other side, citing initiatives passed in various states in 2008 and 2009 prohibiting gays from marrying, adopting children, or serving as foster parents.

# ISSUE 16

## Should There Be a "Wall of Separation" Between Church and State?

**YES: John Paul Stevens,** from Dissenting Opinion in *Van Orden v. Perry*, 545 U.S. 677 (June 27, 2005)

**NO: Antonin Scalia,** from Dissenting Opinion in *McCreary County, et al., v. American Civil Liberties Union of Kentucky, et al.*, 545 U.S. 844 (June 27, 2005)

### ISSUE SUMMARY

**YES:** United States Supreme Court Justice John Paul Stevens believes that the Constitution creates "a wall of separation" between church and state that can be rarely broached and only insofar as the state recognition of religion does not express a bias in support of particular religious doctrines.

**NO:** United States Supreme Court Justice Antonin Scalia believes that both the Constitution and American history support the sympathetic acknowledgement of the nearly universal American belief in monotheistic religion as reflected in presidential proclamations, public oaths, public monuments, and other displays.

T he first words of the First Amendment to the United States Constitution are "Congress shall make no law respecting an establishment of religion." (This prohibition was later extended to the states by the Fourteenth Amendment to the Constitution.) It has proved to be one of the most controversial clauses, and as shown in the extracts from the two cases considered here, its meaning has never been clearly resolved.

In Virginia, opposition to the established Anglican Church owed less to abstract belief in tolerance than to the increasing number of members of dissenting faiths. Virginia's disestablishment in 1786 was echoed in Article VI of the U.S. Constitution written the following year that "no religious test shall ever be required as a qualification" for any public office. Other states soon abolished their religious establishments and tests.

It may seem a contradiction to some, but not to most Americans, that a nation that disestablished religion may also be the most religious democratic nation, as measured by its high proportion of believers in God and attendance at church services. Because of such deep feelings, sharp disagreement exists as to the meaning of the establishment clause when considering laws *regarding* an establishment of religion.

Government proclamations regarding religion have tended to be general. Presidents have often invoked a Supreme Being, with modern presidents often concluding a public address with "God bless America." In 1864, Congress passed a law to allow "In God We Trust" to appear on coins, and it has appeared on all U.S. coins since 1938. In 1956, "In God We Trust" became the official national motto of the United States. A similar phrase ("And this be our motto, 'In God is our trust'") is in the fourth stanza of "The Star-Spangled Banner," adopted as the national anthem in 1931. The Ninth U.S. Circuit Court of Appeals concluded in 1970 that the spiritual, psychological, and inspirational value of the phrase "has nothing whatsoever to do with the establishment of religion."

The closest the Supreme Court has come to creating a standard for permissible state acknowledgment of and support for religion was when, in 1971 in *Lemon v. Kurtzman,* it established a three-pronged test to escape invalidation under the Establishment Clause: Governmental action must (1) have a secular purpose that neither endorses nor disapproves of religion, (2) have an effect that neither advances nor inhibits religions, and (3) avoid creating a relationship between religion and government that entangles either in the internal affair of the other. The *Lemon* criteria have been interpreted to reach contradictory conclusions, and often have been ignored.

The division is best illustrated by the two cases considered here that were decided on the same day in 2005. In *McCreary County,* a 5-4 majority rejected a courthouse display of the Ten Commandments as "an unmistakably religious statement." In *Van Orden,* a 5-4 majority concluded that a Ten Commandments monument on the Texas capitol grounds served "a mixed but primarily nonreligious purpose." The differences between the two cases are considered in the dissenting opinions excerpted here, but they served only to affect the decision of Justice Stephen Breyer, who in one case voted with the four justices who are most supportive of state acknowledgment of religious influence and in the other voted with the four justices who are most hostile to such state support. His switch was motivated by a conclusion he alone held, that the display had a primarily religious purpose in one case, but not in the other. The other justices divided 4-4, but none was moved by the different circumstances that influenced Breyer.

The selections that follow are from the dissenting opinion of Justice John Paul Stevens in *Van Orden v. Perry*, in which he endorses Jefferson's "wall of separation" as an expression of the constitutional principle and the dissenting opinion of Justice Antonin Scalia in *McCreary County v. American Civil Liberties Union of Kentucky*, in which he rejects Jefferson's wall as a misleading metaphor that contradicts the intention of the Framers.

# YES ⬅

# Dissenting Opinion

The sole function of the monument on the grounds of Texas' State Capitol is to display the full text of one version of the Ten Commandments. The monument is not a work of art and does not refer to any event in the history of the State. It is significant because, and only because, it communicates the following message:

"I AM the LORD thy God.
"Thou shalt have no other gods before me.
"Thou shalt not make to thyself any graven images.
"Thou shalt not take the Name of the Lord thy God in vain.
"Remember the Sabbath day, to keep it holy.
"Honor thy father and thy mother, that thy days may be long upon the land which the Lord thy God giveth thee.
"Thou shalt not kill.
"Thou shalt not commit adultery.
"Thou shalt not steal.
"Thou shalt not bear false witness against thy neighbor.
"Thou shalt not covet thy neighbor's house.
"Thou shalt not covet thy neighbor's wife, nor his manservant, nor his maidservant, nor his cattle, nor anything that is thy neighbor's."

Viewed on its face, Texas' display has no purported connection to God's role in the formation of Texas or the founding of our Nation; nor does it provide the reasonable observer with any basis to guess that it was erected to honor any individual or organization. The message transmitted by Texas' chosen display is quite plain: This State endorses the divine code of the "Judeo-Christian" God.

For those of us who learned to recite the King James version of the text long before we understood the meaning of some of its words, God's Commandments may seem like wise counsel. The question before this Court, however, is whether it is counsel that the State of Texas may proclaim without violating the Establishment Clause of the Constitution. If any fragment of Jefferson's metaphorical "wall of separation between church and State" is to be preserved—if there remains any meaning to the "wholesome 'neutrality' of which this Court's [Establishment Clause] cases speak"—a negative answer to that question is mandatory.

Van Orden v. Perry, 545 U.S. 677 (2005), Justice John Paul Stevens, dissenting.

# I

In my judgment, at the very least, the Establishment Clause has created a strong presumption against the display of religious symbols on public property. The adornment of our public spaces with displays of religious symbols and messages undoubtedly provides comfort, even inspiration, to many individuals who subscribe to particular faiths. Unfortunately, the practice also runs the risk of "offend[ing] nonmembers of the faith being advertised as well as adherents who consider the particular advertisement disrespectful."

Government's obligation to avoid divisiveness and exclusion in the religious sphere is compelled by the Establishment and Free Exercise Clauses, which together erect a wall of separation between church and state. This metaphorical wall protects principles long recognized and often recited in this Court's cases. The first and most fundamental of these principles, one that a majority of this Court today affirms, is that the Establishment Clause demands religious neutrality—government may not exercise a preference for one religious faith over another. This essential command, however, is not merely a prohibition against the government's differentiation among religious sects. We have repeatedly reaffirmed that neither a State nor the Federal Government "can constitutionally pass laws or impose requirements which aid all religions as against non-believers, and neither can aid those religions based on a belief in the existence of God as against those religions founded on different beliefs." This principle is based on the straightforward notion that governmental promotion of orthodoxy is not saved by the aggregation of several orthodoxies under the State's banner.

Acknowledgments of this broad understanding of the neutrality principle are legion in our cases. Strong arguments to the contrary have been raised from time to time. Powerful as [Chief Justice Rehnquist's] argument was, we squarely rejected it and thereby reaffirmed the principle that the Establishment Clause requires the same respect for the atheist as it does for the adherent of a Christian faith. As we wrote, "the Court has unambiguously concluded that the individual freedom of conscience protected by the Constitution embodies the right to select any religious faith or none at all."

In restating this principle, I do not discount the importance of avoiding an overly strict interpretation of the metaphor so often used to define the reach of the Establishment Clause. The plurality is correct to note that "religion and religious traditions" have played a "strong role . . . throughout our nation's history." This Court has often recognized "an unbroken history of official acknowledgment . . . of the role of religion in American life." Given this history, it is unsurprising that a religious symbol may at times become an important feature of a familiar landscape or a reminder of an important event in the history of a community. The wall that separates the church from the State does not prohibit the government from acknowledging the religious beliefs and practices of the American people, nor does it require governments to hide works of art or historic memorabilia from public view just because they also have religious significance.

This case, however, is not about historic preservation or the mere recognition of religion. The issue is obfuscated rather than clarified by simplistic commentary on the various ways in which religion has played a role in American life, and by the recitation of the many extant governmental "acknowledgments" of the role the Ten Commandments played in our Nation's heritage. Surely, the mere compilation of religious symbols, none of which includes the full text of the Commandments and all of which are exhibited in different settings, has only marginal relevance to the question presented in this case. . . .

# II

The State may admonish its citizens not to lie, cheat or steal, to honor their parents and to respect their neighbors' property; and it may do so by printed words, in television commercials, or on granite monuments in front of its public buildings. Moreover, the State may provide its schoolchildren and adult citizens with educational materials that explain the important role that our forebears' faith in God played in their decisions to select America as a refuge from religious persecution, to declare their independence from the British Crown, and to conceive a new Nation. The message at issue in this case, however, is fundamentally different from either a bland admonition to observe generally accepted rules of behavior or a general history lesson.

The reason this message stands apart is that the Decalogue is a venerable religious text. As we held 25 years ago, it is beyond dispute that "[t]he Ten Commandments are undeniably a sacred text in the Jewish and Christian faiths." For many followers, the Commandments represent the literal word of God as spoken to Moses and repeated to his followers after descending from Mount Sinai. The message conveyed by the Ten Commandments thus cannot be analogized to an appendage to a common article of commerce ("In God we Trust") or an incidental part of a familiar recital ("God save the United States and this honorable Court"). Thankfully, the plurality does not attempt to minimize the religious significance of the Ten Commandments. . . . Attempts to secularize what is unquestionably a sacred text defy credibility and disserve people of faith.

The profoundly sacred message embodied by the text inscribed on the Texas monument is emphasized by the especially large letters that identify its author: "I AM the LORD thy God." It commands present worship of Him and no other deity. It directs us to be guided by His teaching in the current and future conduct of all of our affairs. It instructs us to follow a code of divine law, some of which has informed and been integrated into our secular legal code ("Thou shalt not kill"), but much of which has not ("Thou shalt not make to thyself any graven images. . . . Thou shalt not covet"). . . .

The Establishment Clause, if nothing else, forbids government from "specifying details upon which men and women who believe in a benevolent, omnipotent Creator and Ruler of the world are known to differ." . . . Given that the chosen text inscribed on the Ten Commandments monument invariably places the State at the center of a serious sectarian dispute, the display is unquestionably unconstitutional under our case law. . . .

Even if, however, the message of the monument, despite the inscribed text, fairly could be said to represent the belief system of all Judeo-Christians, it would still run afoul of the Establishment Clause by prescribing a compelled code of conduct from one God, namely a Judeo-Christian God, that is rejected by prominent polytheistic sects, such as Hinduism, as well as nontheistic religions, such as Buddhism. . . . And, at the very least, the text of the Ten Commandments impermissibly commands a preference for religion over irreligion. . . . Any of those bases, in my judgment, would be sufficient to conclude that the message should not be proclaimed by the State of Texas on a permanent monument at the seat of its government.

I do not doubt that some Texans, including those elected to the Texas Legislature, may believe that the statues displayed on the Texas Capitol grounds, including the Ten Commandments monument, reflect the "ideals . . . that compose Texan identity." . . . Texas, like our entire country, is now a much more diversified community than it was when it became a part of the United States or even when the monument was erected. Today there are many Texans who do not believe in the God whose Commandments are displayed at their seat of government. Many of them worship a different god or no god at all. Some may believe that the account of the creation in the Book of Genesis is less reliable than the views of men like Darwin and Einstein. The monument is no more an expression of the views of every true Texan than was the "Live Free or Die" motto that the State of New Hampshire placed on its license plates in 1969 an accurate expression of the views of every citizen of New Hampshire. . . .

Recognizing the diversity of religious and secular beliefs held by Texans and by all Americans, it seems beyond peradventure that allowing the seat of government to serve as a stage for the propagation of an unmistakably Judeo-Christian message of piety would have the tendency to make nonmonotheists and nonbelievers "feel like [outsiders] in matters of faith, and [strangers] in the political community." . . .

Even more than the display of a religious symbol on government property, . . . displaying this sectarian text at the state capitol should invoke a powerful presumption of invalidity. . . . The physical setting in which the Texas monument is displayed—far from rebutting that presumption—actually enhances the religious content of its message. . . . The monument's permanent fixture at the seat of Texas government is of immense significance. The fact that a monument: "is installed on public property implies official recognition and reinforcement of its message. That implication is especially strong when the sign stands in front of the seat of government itself. The 'reasonable observer' of any symbol placed unattended in front of any capitol in the world will normally assume that the sovereign—which is not only the owner of that parcel of real estate but also the lawgiver for the surrounding territory—has sponsored and facilitated its message." . . .

Critical examination of the Decalogue's prominent display at the seat of Texas government, rather than generic citation to the role of religion in American life, unmistakably reveals on which side of the "slippery slope," . . . this display must fall. God, as the author of its message, the Eagles, as the donor of the monument, and the State of Texas, as its proud owner, speak with one voice for a common purpose—to encourage Texans to abide by the divine code of a "Judeo-Christian" God. If this message is permissible, then the shining principle of neutrality to which we have long adhered is nothing more than mere shadow.

# III

The plurality relies heavily on the fact that our Republic was founded, and has been governed since its nascence, by leaders who spoke then (and speak still) in plainly religious rhetoric. The Chief Justice cites, for instance, George Washington's 1789 Thanksgiving Proclamation in support of the proposition that the Establishment Clause does not proscribe official recognition of God's role in our Nation's heritage. . . . Further, the plurality emphatically endorses the seemingly timeless recognition that our "institutions presuppose a Supreme Being." . . . Many of the submissions made to this Court by the parties and *amici*, in accord with the plurality's opinion, have relied on the ubiquity of references to God throughout our history.

The speeches and rhetoric characteristic of the founding era, however, do not answer the question before us. I have already explained why Texas' display of the full text of the Ten Commandments, given the content of the actual display and the context in which it is situated, sets this case apart from the countless examples of benign government recognitions of religion. But there is another crucial difference. Our leaders, when delivering public addresses, often express their blessings simultaneously in the service of God and their constituents. Thus, when public officials deliver public speeches, we recognize that their words are not exclusively a transmission from *the* government because those oratories have embedded within them the inherently personal views of the speaker as an individual member of the polity. The permanent placement of a textual religious display on state property is different in kind; it amalgamates otherwise discordant individual views into a collective statement of government approval. Moreover, the message never ceases to transmit itself to objecting viewers whose only choices are to accept the message or to ignore the offense by averting their gaze. . . . In this sense, although Thanksgiving Day proclamations and inaugural speeches undoubtedly seem official, in most circumstances they will not constitute the sort of governmental endorsement of religion at which the separation of church and state is aimed.

The plurality's reliance on early religious statements and proclamations made by the Founders is also problematic because those views were not espoused at the Constitutional Convention in 1787 nor enshrined in the Constitution's text. Thus, the presentation of these religious statements as a unified historical narrative is bound to paint a misleading picture. It does so here. In according deference to the statements of George Washington and John Adams, The Chief Justice and Justice Scalia . . . fail to account for the acts and publicly espoused views of other influential leaders of that time. Notably absent from their historical snapshot is the fact that Thomas Jefferson refused to issue the Thanksgiving proclamations that Washington had so readily embraced based on the argument that to do so would violate the Establishment Clause. The Chief Justice and Justice Scalia disregard the substantial debates that took place regarding the constitutionality of the early proclamations and acts they cite, . . . and paper over the fact that Madison more than once repudiated the views attributed to him by many, stating unequivocally that with respect to government's involvement with religion, the "'tendency to a usurpation on one side, or the other, or to a corrupting coalition or alliance between them, will be best guarded against by an entire abstinence of the Government from interference, in any way whatever, beyond the necessity of preserving public order, & protecting each sect against trespasses on its legal rights by others.'"

These seemingly nonconforming sentiments should come as no surprise. Not insignificant numbers of colonists came to this country with memories of religious persecution by monarchs on the other side of the Atlantic. Others experienced religious intolerance at the hands of colonial Puritans, who regrettably failed to practice the tolerance that some of their contemporaries preached. . . . The Chief Justice and Justice Scalia ignore the separationist impulses—in accord with the principle of "neutrality"—that these individuals brought to the debates surrounding the adoption of the Establishment Clause.

Ardent separationists aside, there is another critical nuance lost in the plurality's portrayal of history. Simply put, many of the Founders who are often cited as authoritative expositors of the Constitution's original meaning understood the Establishment Clause to stand for a *narrower* proposition than the plurality, for whatever reason, is willing to accept. Namely, many of the Framers understood the word "religion" in the Establishment Clause to encompass only the various sects of Christianity.

The evidence is compelling. Prior to the Philadelphia Convention, the States had begun to protect "religious freedom" in their various constitutions. Many of those provisions, however, restricted "equal protection" and "free exercise" to Christians, and invocations of the divine were commonly understood to refer to Christ. That historical background likely informed the Framers' understanding of the First Amendment. Accordingly, one influential thinker wrote of the First Amendment that " '[t]he meaning of the term "establishment" in this amendment unquestionably is, the preference and establishment given by law to one sect of Christians over every other.' " Jasper Adams, The Relation of Christianity to Civil Government in the United States (Feb. 13, 1833) (quoted in Dreisbach 16). That definition tracked the understanding of the text Justice Story adopted in his famous Commentaries, in which he wrote that the "real object" of the Clause was:

> "not to countenance, much less to advance Mahometanism, or Judaism, or infidelity, by prostrating Christianity; but to exclude all rivalry among Christian sects, and to prevent any national ecclesiastical establishment, which should give to an hierarchy the exclusive patronage of the national government. It thus sought to cut off the means of religious persecution, (the vice and pest of former ages,) and the power of subverting the rights of conscience in matters of religion, which had been trampled upon almost from the days of the Apostles to the present age." . . .

Along these lines, for nearly a century after the Founding, many accepted the idea that America was not just a *religious* nation, but "a Christian nation." . . . The original understanding of the type of "religion" that qualified for constitutional protection under the Establishment Clause likely did not include those followers of Judaism and Islam who are among the preferred "monotheistic" religions Justice Scalia has embraced in his *McCreary County* opinion. The inclusion of Jews and Muslims inside the category of constitutionally favored religions surely would have shocked Chief Justice Marshall and Justice Story. Indeed, Justice Scalia is unable to point to any persuasive historical evidence or entrenched traditions in support of his decision to give specially preferred constitutional status to all monotheistic religions. Perhaps this is because the history of the Establishment Clause's original meaning just as strongly supports a preference for Christianity as it does a preference for monotheism. Generic references to "God" hardly constitute evidence that those who spoke the word meant to be inclusive of all monotheistic believers; nor do such references demonstrate that those who heard the word spoken understood it broadly to include all monotheistic faiths. Justice Scalia's inclusion of Judaism and Islam is a laudable act of religious tolerance, but it is one that is unmoored from the Constitution's history and text, and moreover one that is patently arbitrary in its inclusion of some, but exclusion of other (*e.g.*, Buddhism), widely practiced non-Christian religions. Given the original understanding of the men who championed our "Christian nation"—men who had no cause to view anti-Semitism or contempt for atheists as problems worthy of civic concern—one must ask whether Justice Scalia "has not had the courage (or the foolhardiness) to apply [his originalism] principle consistently."

Indeed, to constrict narrowly the reach of the Establishment Clause to the views of the Founders would lead to more than this unpalatable result; it would also leave us with an unincorporated constitutional provision—in other words, one that limits only the *federal* establishment of "a national religion." Under this view, not only could a State constitutionally adorn all of its public spaces with crucifixes or passages from the New Testament, it would also have full authority to prescribe the teachings of Martin Luther or Joseph Smith as *the* official state religion. Only the Federal Government would be prohibited from taking sides, (and only then as between Christian sects).

A reading of the First Amendment dependent on either of the purported original meanings expressed above would eviscerate the heart of the Establishment Clause. It would replace Jefferson's "wall of separation" with a perverse wall of exclusion—Christians inside, non-Christians out. It would permit States to construct walls of their own choosing—Baptists inside, Mormons out; Jewish Orthodox inside, Jewish Reform out. A Clause so understood might be faithful to the expectations of some of our Founders, but it is plainly not worthy of a society whose enviable hallmark over the course of two centuries has been the continuing expansion of religious pluralism and tolerance. . . .

Unless one is willing to renounce over 65 years of Establishment Clause jurisprudence and cross back over the incorporation bridge, appeals to the religiosity of the Framers ring hollow. But even if there were a coherent way to embrace incorporation with one hand while steadfastly abiding by the Founders' purported religious views on the other, the problem of the selective use of history remains. As the widely divergent views espoused by the leaders of our founding era plainly reveal, the historical record of the preincorporation Establishment Clause is too indeterminate to serve as an interpretive North Star.

It is our duty, therefore, to interpret the First Amendment's command that "Congress shall make no law respecting an establishment of religion" not by merely asking what those words meant to observers at the time of the founding, but instead by deriving from the Clause's text and history the broad principles that remain valid today. As we have said in the context of statutory interpretation, legislation "often [goes] beyond the principal evil [at which the statute was aimed] to cover reasonably comparable evils, and it is ultimately the provisions of our laws rather than the principal concerns of our legislators by which we are governed." In similar fashion, we have construed the Equal Protection Clause of the Fourteenth Amendment to prohibit segregated schools, even though those who drafted that Amendment evidently thought that separate was not unequal. We have held that the same Amendment prohibits discrimination against individuals on account of their gender, despite the fact that the contemporaries of the Amendment "doubt[ed] very much whether any action of a State not directed by way of discrimination against the negroes as a class, or on account of their race, will ever be held to come within the purview of this provision." And we have construed "evolving standards of decency" to make impermissible practices that were not considered "cruel and unusual" at the founding. . . .

To reason from the broad principles contained in the Constitution does not, as Justice Scalia suggests, require us to abandon our heritage in favor of unprincipled expressions of personal preference. The task of applying the broad principles that the Framers wrote into the text of the First Amendment is, in any event, no more a matter of personal preference than is one's selection between two (or more) sides in a heated historical debate. We serve our constitutional mandate by expounding the meaning of constitutional provisions with one eye towards our Nation's history and the other fixed on its democratic aspirations. Constitutions, after all,

> "are not ephemeral enactments, designed to meet passing occasions. They are, to use the words of Chief Justice Marshall, 'designed to approach immortality as nearly as human institutions can approach it.' The future is their care and provision for events of good and bad tendencies of which no prophecy can be made. In the application of a constitution, therefore, our contemplation cannot be only of what has been but of what may be. Under any other rule a constitution would indeed be as easy of application as it would be deficient in efficacy and power. Its general principles would have little value and be converted by precedent into impotent and lifeless formulas." . . .

The principle that guides my analysis is neutrality. The basis for that principle is firmly rooted in our Nation's history and our Constitution's text. I recognize that the requirement that government must remain neutral between religion and irreligion would have seemed foreign to some of the Framers; so too would a requirement of neutrality between Jews and Christians. Fortunately, we are not bound by the Framers' expectations—we are bound by the legal principles they enshrined in our Constitution. Story's vision that States should not discriminate between Christian sects has as its foundation the principle that government must remain neutral between valid systems of belief. As religious pluralism has expanded, so has our acceptance of what constitutes valid belief systems. The evil of discriminating today against atheists, "polytheists[,] and believers in unconcerned deities," (Scalia, dissenting), is in my view a direct descendent of the evil of discriminating among Christian sects. The Establishment Clause thus forbids it and, in turn, forbids Texas from displaying the Ten Commandments monument the plurality so casually affirms.

# IV

. . . The judgment of the Court in this case stands for the proposition that the Constitution permits governmental displays of sacred religious texts. This makes a mockery of the constitutional ideal that government must remain neutral between religion and irreligion. If a State may endorse a particular deity's command to "have no other gods before me," it is difficult to conceive of any textual display that would run afoul of the Establishment Clause.

The disconnect between this Court's approval of Texas's monument and the constitutional prohibition against preferring religion to irreligion cannot be reduced to the exercise of plotting two adjacent locations on a slippery slope. Rather, it is the difference between the shelter of a fortress and exposure to "the winds that would blow" if the wall were allowed to crumble. . . . That wall, however imperfect, remains worth preserving.

 **NO**

# Dissenting Opinion

I shall discuss first, why the Court's oft repeated assertion that the government cannot favor religious practice is false; second, why today's opinion extends the scope of that falsehood even beyond prior cases; and third, why even on the basis of the Court's false assumptions the judgment here is wrong.

## I

[In] a model spread across Europe by the armies of Napoleon, . . . [r]eligion is to be strictly excluded from the public forum. This is not, and never was, the model adopted by America. George Washington added to the form of Presidential oath prescribed by Art. II, § 1, cl. 8, of the Constitution, the concluding words "so help me God." . . . The Supreme Court under John Marshall opened its sessions with the prayer, "God save the United States and this Honorable Court." . . . The First Congress instituted the practice of beginning its legislative sessions with a prayer. The same week that Congress submitted the Establishment Clause as part of the Bill of Rights for ratification by the States, it enacted legislation providing for paid chaplains in the House and Senate. The day after the First Amendment was proposed, the same Congress that had proposed it requested the President to proclaim "a day of public thanksgiving and prayer, to be observed, by acknowledging, with grateful hearts, the many and signal favours of Almighty God." President Washington offered the first Thanksgiving Proclamation shortly thereafter, devoting November 26, 1789 on behalf of the American people " 'to the service of that great and glorious Being who is the beneficent author of all the good that is, that was, or that will be,'" . . . thus beginning a tradition of offering gratitude to God that continues today. The same Congress also reenacted the Northwest Territory Ordinance of 1787, . . . Article III of which provided: "Religion, morality, and knowledge, being necessary to good government and the happiness of mankind, schools and the means of education shall forever be encouraged." And of course the First Amendment itself accords religion (and no other manner of belief) special constitutional protection.

These actions of our First President and Congress and the Marshall Court were not idiosyncratic; they reflected the beliefs of the period. Those who wrote the Constitution believed that morality was essential to the well-being of society and that encouragement of religion was the best way to foster morality. . . . President Washington opened his Presidency with a prayer, and

McCreary County, Kentucky v. American Civil Liberties Union of Kentucky, 545 U.S. 844 (2005), Justice Antonin Scalia, dissenting.

reminded his fellow citizens at the conclusion of it that "reason and experience both forbid us to expect that National morality can prevail in exclusion of religious principle." . . . President John Adams wrote to the Massachusetts Militia, "we have no government armed with power capable of contending with human passions unbridled by morality and religion. . . . Our Constitution was made only for a moral and religious people. It is wholly inadequate to the government of any other." . . . Thomas Jefferson concluded his second inaugural address by inviting his audience to pray: "I shall need, too, the favor of that Being in whose hands we are, who led our fathers, as Israel of old, from their native land and planted them in a country flowing with all the necessaries and comforts of life; who has covered our infancy with His providence and our riper years with His wisdom and power and to whose goodness I ask you to join in supplications with me that He will so enlighten the minds of your servants, guide their councils, and prosper their measures that whatsoever they do shall result in your good, and shall secure to you the peace, friendship, and approbation of all nations."

James Madison, in his first inaugural address, likewise placed his confidence "in the guardianship and guidance of that Almighty Being whose power regulates the destiny of nations, whose blessings have been so conspicuously dispensed to this rising Republic, and to whom we are bound to address our devout gratitude for the past, as well as our fervent supplications and best hopes for the future."

Nor have the views of our people on this matter significantly changed. Presidents continue to conclude the Presidential oath with the words "so help me God." Our legislatures, state and national, continue to open their sessions with prayer led by official chaplains. The sessions of this Court continue to open with the prayer "God save the United States and this Honorable Court." Invocation of the Almighty by our public figures, at all levels of government, remains commonplace. Our coinage bears the motto "IN GOD WE TRUST." And our Pledge of Allegiance contains the acknowledgment that we are a Nation "under God." As one of our Supreme Court opinions rightly observed, "We are a religious people whose institutions presuppose a Supreme Being." . . .

With all of this reality (and much more) staring it in the face, how can the Court *possibly* assert that "'the First Amendment mandates governmental neutrality between . . . religion and nonreligion,'" and that "[m]anifesting a purpose to favor . . . adherence to religion generally" is unconstitutional? Who says so? Surely not the words of the Constitution. Surely not the history and traditions that reflect our society's constant understanding of those words. Surely not even the current sense of our society, recently reflected in an Act of Congress adopted *unanimously* by the Senate and with only 5 nays in the House of Representatives, criticizing a Court of Appeals opinion that had held "under God" in the Pledge of Allegiance unconstitutional. . . . Nothing stands behind the Court's assertion that governmental affirmation of the society's belief in God is unconstitutional except the Court's own say-so, citing as support only the unsubstantiated say-so of earlier Courts going back no farther than the mid-20th century. . . . And it is, moreover, a thoroughly discredited say-so. It is discredited, to begin with, because a majority of the Justices on the current

Court (including at least one Member of today's majority) have, in separate opinions, repudiated the brain-spun *"Lemon* test" that embodies the supposed principle of neutrality between religion and irreligion. . . . And it is discredited because the Court has not had the courage (or the foolhardiness) to apply the neutrality principle consistently.

What distinguishes the rule of law from the dictatorship of a shifting Supreme Court majority is the absolutely indispensable requirement that judicial opinions be grounded in consistently applied principle. That is what prevents judges from ruling now this way, now that—thumbs up or thumbs down—as their personal preferences dictate. Today's opinion forthrightly (or actually, somewhat less than forthrightly) admits that it does not rest upon consistently applied principle. In a revealing footnote, the Court acknowledges that the "Establishment Clause doctrine" it purports to be applying "lacks the comfort of categorical absolutes." What the Court means by this lovely euphemism is that sometimes the Court chooses to decide cases on the principle that government cannot favor religion, and sometimes it does not. The footnote goes on to say that "[i]n special instances we have found good reason" to dispense with the principle, but "[n]o such reasons present themselves here." . . . It does not identify all of those "special instances," much less identify the "good reason" for their existence.

I have cataloged elsewhere the variety of circumstances in which this Court—even *after* its embrace of *Lemon*'s stated prohibition of such behavior—has approved government action "undertaken with the specific intention of improving the position of religion." . . . Suffice it to say here that when the government relieves churches from the obligation to pay property taxes, when it allows students to absent themselves from public school to take religious classes, and when it exempts religious organizations from generally applicable prohibitions of religious discrimination, it surely means to bestow a benefit on religious practice—but we have approved it. . . . Indeed, we have even approved (post-*Lemon*) government-led prayer to God. In *Marsh v. Chambers,* the Court upheld the Nebraska State Legislature's practice of paying a chaplain to lead it in prayer at the opening of legislative sessions. The Court explained that "[t]o invoke Divine guidance on a public body entrusted with making the laws is not . . . an 'establishment' of religion or a step toward establishment; it is simply a tolerable acknowledgment of beliefs widely held among the people of this country." (Why, one wonders, is not respect for the Ten Commandments a tolerable acknowledgment of beliefs widely held among the people of this country?) . . .

Besides appealing to the demonstrably false principle that the government cannot favor religion over irreligion, today's opinion suggests that the posting of the Ten Commandments violates the principle that the government cannot favor one religion over another. That is indeed a valid principle where public aid or assistance to religion is concerned, or where the free exercise of religion is at issue, but it necessarily applies in a more limited sense to public acknowledgment of the Creator. If religion in the public forum had to be entirely nondenominational, there could be no religion in the public forum at all. One cannot say the word "God," or "the Almighty," one cannot offer public supplication or thanksgiving, without contradicting the beliefs of some people that there are many gods, or that God or the gods pay no attention to human affairs. With respect to public acknowledgment of religious belief, it is entirely clear from our Nation's historical practices that the Establishment Clause permits this disregard of polytheists and believers in unconcerned deities, just as it permits the disregard of devout atheists. The Thanksgiving Proclamation issued by George Washington at the instance of the First Congress was scrupulously nondenominational—but it was monotheistic. . . .

Historical practices thus demonstrate that there is a distance between the acknowledgment of a single Creator and the establishment of a religion. . . . The three most popular religions in the United States, Christianity, Judaism, and Islam—which combined account for 97.7% of all believers—are monotheistic. All of them, moreover (Islam included), believe that the Ten Commandments were given by God to Moses, and are divine prescriptions for a virtuous life. Publicly honoring the Ten Commandments is thus indistinguishable, insofar as discriminating against other religions is concerned, from publicly honoring God. Both practices are recognized across such a broad and diverse range of the population—from Christians to Muslims—that they cannot be reasonably understood as a government endorsement of a particular religious viewpoint. . . .

I have relied primarily upon official acts and official proclamations of the United States or of the component branches of its Government, including the First Congress' beginning of the tradition of legislative prayer to God, its appointment of congressional chaplains, its legislative proposal of a Thanksgiving Proclamation, and its reenactment of the Northwest Territory Ordinance; our first President's issuance of a Thanksgiving Proclamation; and invocation of God at the opening of sessions of the Supreme Court. The only mere "proclamations and statements" of the Founders I have relied upon were statements of Founders who occupied federal office, and spoke in at least a quasi-official capacity—Washington's prayer at the opening of his Presidency and his Farewell Address, President John Adams' letter to the Massachusetts Militia, and Jefferson's and Madison's inaugural addresses. The Court and Justice Stevens, by contrast, appeal to no official or even quasi-official action in support of their view of the Establishment Clause—only James Madison's Memorial and Remonstrance Against Religious Assessments, written before the federal Constitution had even been proposed, two letters, written by Madison long after he was President, and the quasi-official *inaction* of Thomas Jefferson in refusing to issue a Thanksgiving Proclamation. The Madison Memorial and Remonstrance, dealing as it does with enforced contribution to religion rather than public acknowledgment of God, is irrelevant; one of the letters is utterly ambiguous as to the point at issue here, and should not be read to contradict Madison's statements in his first inaugural address, quoted earlier; even the other letter does not disapprove public acknowledgment of God, unless one posits (what Madison's own actions as President would contradict) that reference to God contradicts "the equality of *all* religious sects." And as to Jefferson: the notoriously self-contradicting Jefferson did not choose to have his nonauthorship of a Thanksgiving Proclamation inscribed on his tombstone.

What he did have inscribed was his authorship of the Virginia Statute for Religious Freedom, a governmental act which begins "Whereas Almighty God hath created the mind free. . . ."

It is no answer for Justice Stevens to say that the understanding that these official and quasi-official actions reflect was not "enshrined in the Constitution's text." The Establishment Clause, upon which Justice Stevens would rely, *was* enshrined in the Constitution's text, and these official actions show *what it meant*. There were doubtless some who thought it should have a broader meaning, but those views were plainly rejected. Justice Stevens says that reliance on these actions is "bound to paint a misleading picture," but it is hard to see why. What is more probative of the meaning of the Establishment Clause than the actions of the very Congress that proposed it, and of the first President charged with observing it?

Justice Stevens also appeals to the undoubted fact that some in the founding generation thought that the Religion Clauses of the First Amendment should have a *narrower* meaning, protecting only the Christian religion or perhaps only Protestantism. I am at a loss to see how this helps his case, except by providing a cloud of obfuscating smoke. (Since most thought the Clause permitted government invocation of monotheism, and some others thought it permitted government invocation of Christianity, he proposes that it be construed not to permit any government invocation of religion at all.) At any rate, those narrower views of the Establishment Clause were as clearly rejected as the more expansive ones. Washington's First Thanksgiving Proclamation is merely an example. *All* of the actions of Washington and the First Congress upon which I have relied, virtually all Thanksgiving Proclamations throughout our history, and *all* the other examples of our Government's favoring religion that I have cited, have invoked God, but not Jesus Christ. Rather than relying upon Justice Stevens' assurance that "[t]he original understanding of the type of 'religion' that qualified for constitutional protection under the First amendment certainly did not include . . . followers of Judaism and Islam," . . . I would prefer to take the word of George Washington, who, in his famous Letter to the Hebrew Congregation of Newport, Rhode Island, wrote that, "All possess alike liberty of conscience and immunities of citizenship. It is now no more that toleration is spoken of, as if it was by the indulgence of one class of people, that another enjoyed the exercise of their inherent natural rights." The letter concluded, by the way, with an invocation of the one God: "May the father of all mercies scatter light and not darkness in our paths, and make us all in our several vocations useful here, and in his own due time and way everlastingly happy." . . .

Justice Stevens argues that original meaning should not be the touchstone anyway, but that we should rather "expoun[d] the meaning of constitutional provisions with one eye toward our Nation's history and the other fixed on its democratic aspirations." This is not the place to debate the merits of the "living Constitution," though I must observe that Justice Stevens' quotation from *McCulloch v. Maryland* (1819), refutes rather than supports that approach. Even assuming, however, that the meaning of the Constitution ought to change according to "democratic aspirations," why are those aspirations to be found in Justices' notions of what the Establishment Clause ought to mean, rather than in the democratically adopted dispositions of our current society? As I have observed above, numerous provisions of our laws and numerous continuing practices of our people demonstrate that the government's invocation of God (and hence the government's invocation of the Ten Commandments) is unobjectionable—including a statute enacted by Congress almost unanimously less than three years ago, stating that "under God" in the Pledge of Allegiance is constitutional. To ignore all this is not to give effect to "democratic aspirations" but to frustrate them.

Finally, I must respond to Justice Stevens' assertion that I would "marginaliz[e] the belief systems of more than 7 million Americans" who adhere to religions that are not monotheistic. Surely that is a gross exaggeration. The beliefs of those citizens are entirely protected by the Free Exercise Clause, and by those aspects of the Establishment Clause that do not relate to government acknowledgment of the Creator. Invocation of God despite their beliefs is permitted not because nonmonotheistic religions cease to be religions recognized by the religion clauses of the First Amendment, but because governmental invocation of God is not an establishment. Justice Stevens fails to recognize that in the context of public acknowledgments of God there are legitimate *competing* interests: On the one hand, the interest of that minority in not feeling "excluded"; but on the other, the interest of the overwhelming majority of religious believers in being able to give God thanks and supplication *as a people*, and with respect to our national endeavors. Our national tradition has resolved that conflict in favor of the majority. It is not for this Court to change a disposition that accounts, many Americans think, for the phenomenon remarked upon in a quotation attributed to various authors, including Bismarck, but which I prefer to associate with Charles de Gaulle: "God watches over little children, drunkards, and the United States of America."

# II

As bad as the *Lemon* test is, it is worse for the fact that, since its inception, its seemingly simple mandates have been manipulated to fit whatever result the Court aimed to achieve. Today's opinion is no different. In two respects it modifies *Lemon* to ratchet up the Court's hostility to religion. First, the Court justifies inquiry into legislative purpose, not as an end itself, but as a means to ascertain the appearance of the government action to an " 'objective observer.'" Because in the Court's view the true danger to be guarded against is that the objective observer would feel like an "outside[r]" or "not [a] full membe[r] of the political community," its inquiry focuses not on the *actual purpose* of government action, but the "purpose apparent from government action." Under this approach, even if a government could show that its actual purpose was not to advance religion, it would presumably violate the Constitution as long as the Court's objective observer would think otherwise. . . .

I have remarked before that it is an odd jurisprudence that bases the unconstitutionality of a government practice that does not *actually* advance religion on the hopes of the government that it *would* do so. But that oddity pales in comparison to the one invited by today's analysis: the legitimacy of a government action with a wholly secular effect would turn on the *misperception* of an imaginary observer that the government officials behind the action had the intent to advance religion.

Second, the Court replaces *Lemon*'s requirement that the government have "*a* secular . . . purpose," with the heightened requirement that the secular purpose "predominate" over any purpose to advance religion. The Court treats this extension as a natural outgrowth of the longstanding requirement that the government's secular purpose not be a sham, but simple logic shows the two to be unrelated. If the government's proffered secular purpose is not genuine, then the government has no secular purpose at all. The new demand that secular purpose predominate contradicts *Lemon*'s more limited requirement, and finds no support in our cases. In all but one of the five cases in which this Court has invalidated a government practice on the basis of its purpose to benefit religion, it has first declared that the statute was motivated entirely by the desire to advance religion. . . .

I have urged that *Lemon*'s purpose prong be abandoned, because . . . even an *exclusive* purpose to foster or assist religious practice is not necessarily invalidating. But today's extension makes things even worse. By shifting the focus of *Lemon*'s purpose prong from the search for a genuine, secular motivation to the hunt for a predominantly religious purpose, the Court converts what has in the past been a fairly limited inquiry into a rigorous review of the full record. Those responsible for the adoption of the Religion Clauses would surely regard it as a bitter irony that the religious values they designed those Clauses to *protect* have now become so distasteful to this Court that if they constitute anything more than a subordinate motive for government action they will invalidate it.

## III

Even accepting the Court's *Lemon*-based premises, the displays at issue here were constitutional.

. . . . [W]hen the Ten Commandments appear alongside other documents of secular significance in a display devoted to the foundations of American law and government, the context communicates that the Ten Commandments are included, not to teach their binding nature as a religious text, but to show their unique contribution to the development of the legal system. This is doubly true when the display is introduced by a document that informs passersby that it "contains documents that played a significant role in the foundation of our system of law and government."

The same result follows if the Ten Commandments display is viewed in light of the government practices that this Court has countenanced in the past. The acknowledgment of the contribution that religion in general, and the Ten Commandments in particular, have made to our Nation's legal and governmental heritage is surely no more of a step towards establishment of religion than was the practice of legislative prayer we approved in *Marsh v. Chambers*, 463 U. S. 783 (1983), and it seems to be on par with the inclusion of a créche or a menorah in a "Holiday" display that incorporates other secular symbols, see *Lynch*. The parallels between this case and *Marsh* and *Lynch* are sufficiently compelling that they ought to decide this case, even under the Court's misguided Establishment Clause jurisprudence.

Acknowledgment of the contribution that religion has made to our Nation's legal and governmental heritage partakes of a centuries-old tradition. Members of this Court have themselves often detailed the degree to which religious belief pervaded the National Government during the founding era. Display of the Ten Commandments is well within the mainstream of this practice of acknowledgment. Federal, State, and local governments across the Nation have engaged in such display. The Supreme Court Building itself includes depictions of Moses with the Ten Commandments in the Courtroom and on the east pediment of the building, and symbols of the Ten Commandments "adorn the metal gates lining the north and south sides of the Courtroom as well as the doors leading into the Courtroom." Similar depictions of the Decalogue appear on public buildings and monuments throughout our Nation's Capital. The frequency of these displays testifies to the popular understanding that the Ten Commandments are a foundation of the rule of law, and a symbol of the role that religion played, and continues to play, in our system of government.

Perhaps in recognition of the centrality of the Ten Commandments as a widely recognized symbol of religion in public life, the Court is at pains to dispel the impression that its decision will require governments across the country to sandblast the Ten Commandments from the public square. The constitutional problem, the Court says, is with the Counties' *purpose* in erecting the Foundations Displays, not the displays themselves. The Court adds in a footnote: "One consequence of taking account of the purpose underlying past actions is that the same government action may be constitutional if taken in the first instance and unconstitutional if it has a sectarian heritage."

. . . Displays erected in silence (and under the direction of good legal advice) are permissible, while those hung after discussion and debate are deemed unconstitutional. Reduction of the Establishment Clause to such minutiae trivializes the Clause's protection against religious establishment; indeed, it may inflame religious passions by making the passing comments of every government official the subject of endless litigation. . . .

The Court has in the past prohibited government actions that "proselytize or advance any one, or . . . disparage any other, faith or belief," or that apply some level of coercion (though I and others have disagreed about the form that coercion must take). The passive display of the Ten Commandments, even standing alone, does not begin to do either. . . .

Nor is it the case that a solo display of the Ten Commandments advances any one faith. They are assuredly a religious symbol, but they are not so closely associated with a single religious belief that their display can reasonably be understood as preferring one religious sect over another. The Ten Commandments are recognized by Judaism, Christianity, and Islam alike as divinely given. . . .

Turning at last to the displays actually at issue in this case, the Court faults the Counties for not *repealing* the resolution expressing what the Court believes to be an impermissible intent. Under these circumstances, the Court says, "no reasonable observer could swallow the claim that the Counties had cast off the objective so unmistakable in the earlier displays." Even were I to accept all that the Court has said before, I would not agree with that assessment. To begin with, of course, it is unlikely that a reasonable observer *would even have been aware* of the resolutions, so there would be nothing to "cast off." The Court implies that the Counties may have been able to remedy the "taint" from the old resolutions by enacting a new one. But that action would have been wholly unnecessary in light of the explanation that the Counties included *with the displays themselves*: A plaque next to the documents informed all who passed by that each display "contains documents that played a significant role in the foundation of our system of law and government." Additionally, there was no reason for the Counties to repeal or repudiate the resolutions adopted with the hanging of the second displays, since they related *only to the second displays*. After complying with the District Court's order to remove the second displays "immediately," and erecting new displays that in content and by express assertion reflected a *different* purpose from that identified in the resolutions, the Counties had no reason to believe that their previous resolutions would be deemed to be the basis for their actions. After the Counties discovered that the sentiments expressed in the resolutions could be attributed to their most recent displays (in oral argument before this Court), they repudiated them immediately.

In sum: The first displays did not necessarily evidence an intent to further religious practice; nor did the second displays, or the resolutions authorizing them; and there is in any event no basis for attributing whatever intent motivated the first and second displays to the third. Given the presumption of regularity that always accompanies our review of official action, the Court has identified no evidence of a purpose to advance religion in a way that is inconsistent with our cases. The Court may well be correct in identifying the third displays as the fruit of a desire to display the Ten Commandments, but neither our cases nor our history support its assertion that such a desire renders the fruit poisonous.

# EXPLORING THE ISSUE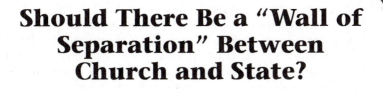

## Should There Be a "Wall of Separation" Between Church and State?

### Critical Thinking and Reflection

1. Does the First Amendment bar any law dealing with religion or religious institutions?
2. How does the word "establishment" limit the law in dealing with religion?
3. Are any restrictions on religious exercise permissible under the First Amendment?
4. Can religions engage in practices that are contrary to law in other areas?
5. Does the First Amendment's religion clauses apply equally to the states?
6. Is the phrase "under God" consistent with the original intent of the First Amendment?
7. What is the basic constitutional area of disagreement between Justices Stevens and Scalia?
8. Does "wall of separation" mean that neither government nor church can interfere with the other?
9. Why does Justice Scalia believe that the separation of church and state has been carried too far?

### Is There Common Ground?

Given the passionate commitments of those holding opposed positions, compromise often seems impossible in disputes about faith-based social services, public money for religious schools, the Pledge of Allegiance, Ten Commandments, monuments, the theory of evolution, abortion rights, stem cell research, and many other topics. Like the subject of religious preferences, discussion of church–state relations appears to be off-limits in polite society. Non-sectarian schools shy away from any serious discussion of religion for fear of giving offense. Teachers, including those who may be qualified to explain different religions and irreligion, are wary of risking unemployment or worse, and prudently avoid offending the sensitivities of others. Thoughtful explanation of the belief systems held by others is rare, and when it takes place it is open to charges of bias. The consequence is that most Americans have acquired little knowledge of religious beliefs other than their own, and are ill-equipped to deal sympathetically with other positions.

# Additional Resources

David Limbaugh charges that judicial interpretation of the establishment clause has led to bias against religion, especially Christianity. In *Persecution: How Liberals Are Waging War Against Christianity* (Regnery, 2003), he writes: "Christian expression is treated as profanity and worse in many public schools and certain federal courts across the nation." In justifying this harsh criticism, Limbaugh cites barring children from praying before football games, Hollywood caricatures of Christians as fanatics, and the suppression of criticism of Darwinian evolution in colleges. Susan Jacoby takes an opposing view, arguing in *Freethinkers: A History of American Secularism* (Metropolitan Books, 2004) that the United States was founded by secularists and is neutral, not hostile, toward all religions.

Christopher L. Eisgruber and Lawrence G. Sager, in *Religious Freedom and the Constitution* (Harvard University Press, 2007), create a principle of "equal liberty" to reconcile opposing views. Donald L. Drakeman comes close to providing an objective account of leading church–state cases in *Church-State Constitutional Issues: Making Sense of the Establishment Clause* (Greenwood Press, 1991). Drakeman concludes that the intentions of the Founding Fathers provide inadequate guidance for understanding the establishment clause. He concludes that the fairest balance is a religiously nonprofessional endorsement doctrine in which religion is not given special treatment by the government, nor is it singled out as a type of charitable organization ineligible for government benefits. In *The Founding Fathers and the Place of Religion in America* (Princeton University Press, 2006), Frank Lambert provides an overview of how America's Founders thought religion should be treated in the new nation.

# ISSUE 17

# Do Corporations Have the Same Free Speech Rights as Persons?

**YES: Anthony Kennedy,** from Opinion of the Court in *Citizens United v. Federal Election Commission* (2010)

**NO: John Paul Stevens,** from Dissenting Opinion in *Citizens United v. Federal Election Commission* (2010)

### ISSUE SUMMARY

**YES:** Supreme Court Justice Anthony Kennedy, for the majority, hold the view that corporations have all the rights and privileges of citizens under the Constitution, so their free speech rights are not to be violated.

**NO:** Supreme Court Justice John Paul Stevens insists that corporations are not citizens under the Constitution, so Congress may restrict their political speech prior to an election.

**C**itizens United is an independent conservative political organization founded in 1988. Early in 2008, when it appeared likely that Senator Hillary Clinton would be the Democratic presidential nominee, it produced "Hillary: The Movie," a motion picture that was highly critical of her candidacy. When the Federal Election Commission, in accord with existing law, sought to bar the telecast of that film during the 60 days prior to the presidential election, the United States Supreme Court, in a 5-4 decision, denied the right of the federal government to restrict the free speech rights of an independent organization.

When the Supreme Court several months later, with the same 5-4 division, rejected the imposition of contribution limits to an independent political organization, the non partisan Congressional Research Service concluded that these judicial opinions "arguably represent the most fundamental changes to campaign finance law in decades." Most conservatives and some liberals who favor unrestrained free speech were delighted; most liberals and some conservatives who deplore unlimited campaign spending were dismayed.

For four decades, Congress has sought, with limited success, to constrain the role of unlimited financial expenditures in federal elections. After the Watergate affair in which President Richard Nixon and members of his administration were accused of illegal efforts to influence the outcome of a presidential election, Congress adopted the Federal Election Campaign Act to limit contributions to and spending on federal elections. In 1976, after further revisions of the law, the Supreme Court upheld both limits on individual contributions and public financing for candidates who chose to accept it instead of raising private campaign funds. At the same time, the Court held that limits on campaign expenditures are unconstitutional restrictions on protected expression and association, whether they are by individuals or groups or by a candidate from personal funds.

Congress continued to adopt laws to reduce campaign expenses. In 2003, the Supreme Court upheld major campaign law revisions on radio and television advertisements that mentioned a candidate's name within 30 days of a primary election or 60 days of a general election, and restrictions on "soft money" donations to political parties. "Soft money" refers to contributions to a political party or other organization, as distinct from "hard money" contributions that go directly to a candidate. Since then, Congress had debated but not adopted proposals to prohibit foreign influence in federal elections and bar businesses that receive government contracts from making political contributions.

What made *Citizens United v. Federal Election Commission* different from the earlier decisions on campaign contributions was Congress's effort to impose and the Supreme Court's decision to bar any limits on expenditures by corporations. Even before considering the question of campaign limits, the majority had to assume that corporations possessed the right of freedom of speech and the minority had to deny the existence of that right. The constitutional question is whether corporations enjoy First Amendment rights and other rights of persons. If that question is answered affirmatively, corporations possess the same right of political participation as persons, and any restriction on showing a political film shortly before an election would have to be answered as it would be for an individual person. The answer would clearly be no. But if corporations do not enjoy the constitutional rights of persons, Congress may exercise its legislative discretion to impose narrow limits on the corporation's speech. The issue has been defined as "corporate personhood."

Do corporations have the same free speech and other constitutional rights of persons? It did not seem so when the United States was formed. Corporations are not mentioned in the Constitution; the American Revolution was prompted by colonial opposition to the tax on tea imposed by Britain's East India Company, and the charters of early corporations contained precise restrictions on their operation and duration. Despite these inhibitions, the wealth and power of corporations grew in the nation's first century, and so did their judicial influence. A corporation chartered under the laws of one state is able to do business in all states. Lawyers began to refer to corporations as "artificial persons." In business transactions, corporations were treated as if they were individual entities.

In the late nineteenth century, the Supreme Court assumed that corporations have the constitutional rights of persons, applying this not only to the First Amendment's grant of freedom of speech, but in later cases to the Fourth Amendment right of unreasonable searches, the Fifth Amendment right against being tried twice for the same offense, and the Seventh Amendment right to a jury trial in a civil case. The Supreme Court saw no difference between the constitutional rights accorded to persons and those given to corporations.

Critics resist the Court's conclusion because they claim that corporations are impersonal organizations whose sole purpose is the financial profit of its investors and management. They argue that the corporation has no intrinsic altruistic motive. It has no need to do good; it needs only to make money. Against this moral distinction, defenders of corporate personhood point out that, without the unique attributes of corporations, Andrew Carnegie could not have created the American free library system, Bill Gates could not have organized vast resources to combat preventable diseases, and countless good works would have gone undone by non profit foundations created in the name of—and with the wealth created by—Rockefeller, Ford, Pew, and other individuals who derived their wealth from corporations.

As a consequence of the *Citizens United* decision, Super PACs (Political Action Committees) permitted to receive unlimited political contributions have been created. At least nominally independent of the political parties, but often close to nonprofit organizations that do not have to disclose their donors, they are typically closely aligned with individual candidates. Experience will demonstrate their impact on American elections and politics.

In 2011, the Supreme Court once again returned to examine the constitutional status of campaign finance law. A 5-4 majority (the same five as in *Citizens United*) struck down an Arizona law that provided escalating matching funds to candidates who accepted public financing, and agreed to limit their personal spending to $500. The Supreme Court majority objected to Arizona's providing additional support for the publicly funded candidate in response to increasing expenditures by privately financed candidates and the independent groups that are supporting them. Chief Justice John Roberts wrote that such laws "inhibit robust and wide-open debate." Justice Elena Kagan, writing for the four dissenters, argued that "what the law does—all the law does—is fund more speech."

Justice Anthony Kennedy and Justice John Paul Stevens provide opposing eloquent arguments on the constitutional status and free speech rights of corporations in their majority and dissenting opinions in *Citizens United v. Federal Election Commission*.

# YES ⬅

Anthony Kennedy

# Opinion of the Court

Federal law prohibits corporations and unions from using their general treasury funds to make independent expenditures for speech defined as an "electioneering communication" or for speech expressly advocating the election or defeat of a candidate. . . . The Government may regulate corporate political speech through disclaimer and disclosure requirements, but it may not suppress that speech altogether. . . .

In January 2008, Citizens United released a film entitled *Hillary: The Movie*. We refer to the film as *Hillary*. It is a 90-minute documentary about then-Senator Hillary Clinton, who was a candidate in the Democratic Party's 2008 Presidential primary elections. *Hillary* mentions Senator Clinton by name and depicts interviews with political commentators and other persons, most of them quite critical of Senator Clinton. *Hillary* was released in theaters and on DVD, but Citizens United wanted to increase distribution by making it available through video-on-demand. . . .

Before the Bipartisan Campaign Reform Act of 2002(BCRA), federal law prohibited—and still does prohibit—corporations and unions from using general treasury funds to make direct contributions to candidates or independent expenditures that expressly advocate the election or defeat of a candidate, through any form of media, in connection with certain qualified federal elections. . . .

The movie, in essence, is a feature-length negative advertisement that urges viewers to vote against Senator Clinton for President. In light of historical footage, interviews with persons critical of her, and voiceover narration, the film would be understood by most viewers as an extended criticism of Senator Clinton's character and her fitness for the office of the Presidency. The narrative may contain more suggestions and arguments than facts, but there is little doubt that the thesis of the film is that she is unfit for the Presidency. The movie concentrates on alleged wrongdoing during the Clinton administration, Senator Clinton's qualifications and fitness for office, and policies the commentators predict she would pursue if elected President. . . .

Courts, too, are bound by the First Amendment. We must decline to draw, and then redraw, constitutional lines based on the particular media or technology used to disseminate political speech from a particular speaker. It must be noted, moreover, that this undertaking would require substantial litigation over an extended time, all to interpret a law that beyond doubt

Supreme Court of the United States, 2010.

discloses serious First Amendment flaws. The interpretive process itself would create an inevitable, pervasive, and serious risk of chilling protected speech pending the drawing of fine distinctions that, in the end, would themselves be questionable. . . .

Throughout the litigation, Citizens United has asserted a claim that the FEC has violated its First Amendment right to free speech. All concede that this claim is properly before us. And "'[o]nce a federal claim is properly presented, a party can make any argument in support of that claim; parties are not limited to the precise arguments they made below.'". . .

It is well known that the public begins to concentrate on elections only in the weeks immediately before they are held. There are short timeframes in which speech can have influence. The need or relevance of the speech will often first be apparent at this stage in the campaign. The decision to speak is made in the heat of political campaigns, when speakers react to messages conveyed by others. A speaker's ability to engage in political speech that could have a chance of persuading voters is stifled if the speaker must first commence a protracted lawsuit. By the time the lawsuit concludes, the election will be over and the litigants in most cases will have neither the incentive nor, perhaps, the resources to carry on, even if they could establish that the case is not moot because the issue is "capable of repetition, yet evading review.". . . Here, Citizens United decided to litigate its case to the end. Today, Citizens United finally learns, two years after the fact, whether it could have spoken during the 2008 Presidential primary—long after the opportunity to persuade primary voters has passed. . . .

When the FEC issues advisory opinions that prohibit speech, "[m]any persons, rather than undertake the considerable burden (and sometimes risk) of vindicating their rights through case-by-case litigation, will choose simply to abstain from protected speech—harming not only themselves but society as a whole, which is deprived of an uninhibited marketplace of ideas.". . .

The FEC has created a regime that allows it to select what political speech is safe for public consumption by applying ambiguous tests. If parties want to avoid litigation and the possibility of civil and criminal penalties, they must either refrain from speaking or ask the FEC to issue an advisory opinion approving of the political speech in question. Government officials pore over each word of a text to see if, in their judgment, it accords with the 11factor test they have promulgated. This is an unprecedented governmental intervention into the realm of speech. The ongoing chill upon speech that is beyond all doubt protected makes it necessary in this case to invoke the earlier precedents that a statute which chills speech can and must be invalidated where its facial invalidity has been demonstrated. . . .

The law before us is an outright ban, backed by criminal sanctions. [It] makes it a felony for all corporations—including nonprofit advocacy corporations—either to expressly advocate the election or defeat of candidates or to broadcast electioneering communications within 30 days of a primary election and 60 days of a general election. Thus, the following acts would all be felonies under §441b: The Sierra Club runs an ad, within the crucial phase of 60 days before the general election, that exhorts the public to disapprove of a Congressman who favors logging in national forests; the National Rifle Association publishes a book urging the public to vote for the challenger because the incumbent U. S. Senator supports a handgun ban; and the American Civil Liberties Union creates a Web site telling the public to vote for a Presidential candidate in light of that candidate's defense of free speech. These prohibitions are classic examples of censorship. [It] is a ban on corporate speech notwithstanding the fact that a PAC created by a corporation can still speak. . . .

Section 441b's prohibition on corporate independent expenditures is thus a ban on speech. As a "restriction on the amount of money a person or group can spend on political communication during a campaign," that statute "necessarily reduces the quantity of expression by restricting the number of issues discussed, the depth of their exploration, and the size of the audience reached." Were the Court to uphold these restrictions, the Government could repress speech by silencing certain voices at any of the various points in the speech process. . . .

The right of citizens to inquire, to hear, to speak, and to use information to reach consensus is a precondition to enlightened self-government and a necessary means to protect it. The First Amendment "'has its fullest and most urgent application' to speech uttered during a campaign for political office." . . . For these reasons, political speech must prevail against laws that would suppress it, whether by design or inadvertence. Laws that burden political speech are "subject to strict scrutiny," which requires the Government to prove that the restriction "furthers a compelling interest and is narrowly tailored to achieve that interest." . . . By taking the right to speak from some and giving it to others, the Government deprives the disadvantaged person or class of the right to use speech to strive to establish worth, standing, and respect for the speaker's voice. The Government may not by these means deprive the public of the right and privilege to determine for itself what speech and speakers are worthy of consideration. . . .

The Court has upheld a narrow class of speech restrictions that operate to the disadvantage of certain persons, but these rulings were based on an interest in allowing governmental entities to perform their functions: . . . protecting the "function of public school education"; furthering "the legitimate penological objectives of the corrections system," . . . ensuring "the capacity of the Government to discharge its [military] responsibilities." . . . The corporate independent expenditures at issue in this case, however, would not interfere with governmental functions, so these cases are inapposite. These precedents stand only for the proposition that there are certain governmental functions that cannot operate without some restrictions on particular kinds of speech. By contrast, it is inherent in the nature of the political process that voters must be free to obtain information from diverse sources in order to determine how to cast their votes. . . . We find no basis for the proposition that, in the context of political speech, the Government may impose restrictions on certain disfavored speakers. Both history and logic lead to this conclusion.

The Court has recognized that First Amendment protection extends to corporations. . . . This protection has been extended by explicit holdings to the context of political speech. . . . Corporations and other associations, like individuals, contribute to the discussion, debate, and the dissemination of information and ideas' that the First Amendment seeks to foster." . . . The Court has thus rejected the argument that political speech of corporations or other associations should be treated differently under the First Amendment simply because such associations are not "natural persons." . . .

At least since the latter part of the 19th century, the laws of some States and of the United States imposed a ban on corporate direct contributions to candidates. . . . Yet not until 1947 did Congress first prohibit independent expenditures by corporations and prohibit independent expenditures by corporations and labor unions. . . . In passing this Act Congress overrode the veto of President Truman, who warned that the expenditure ban was a "dangerous intrusion on free speech." . . .

If the First Amendment has any force, it prohibits Congress from fining or jailing citizens, or associations of citizens, for simply engaging in political speech. . . . Political speech is "indispensable to decisionmaking in a democracy, and this is no less true because the speech comes from a corporation rather than an individual."

It is irrelevant for purposes of the First Amendment that corporate funds may "have little or no correlation to the public's support for the corporation's political ideas." All speakers, including individuals and the media, use money amassed from the economic marketplace to fund their speech. The First Amendment protects the resulting speech, even if it was enabled by economic transactions with persons or entities who disagree with the speaker's ideas. . . .

There is no precedent supporting laws that attempt to distinguish between corporations which are deemed to be exempt as media corporations and those which are not. "We have consistently rejected the proposition that the institutional press has any constitutional privilege beyond that of other speakers." . . . Even assuming the most doubtful proposition that a news organization has a right to speak when others do not, the exemption would allow a conglomerate that owns both a media business and an unrelated business to influence or control the media in order to advance its overall business interest. At the same time, some other corporation, with an identical business interest but no media outlet in its ownership structure, would be forbidden to speak or inform the public about the same issue. This differential treatment cannot be squared with the First Amendment.

There is simply no support for the view that the First Amendment, as originally understood, would permit the suppression of political speech by media corporations. The Framers may not have anticipated modern business and media corporations. . . . Yet television networks and major newspapers owned by media corporations have become the most important means of mass communication in modern times. The First Amendment was certainly not understood to condone the suppression of political speech in society's most salient media. It was understood as a response to the repression of speech and the press that had existed in England and the heavy taxes on the press that were imposed in the colonies. . . . The great debates between the Federalists and the Anti-Federalists over our founding document were published and expressed in the most important means of mass communication of that era—newspapers owned by individuals. . . . At the founding, speech was open, comprehensive, and vital to society's definition of itself; there were no limits on the sources of speech and knowledge. . . .

Corporations, like individuals, do not have monolithic views. On certain topics corporations may possess valuable expertise, leaving them the best equipped to point out errors or fallacies in speech of all sorts, including the speech of candidates and elected officials. . . . The Government may not suppress political speech on the basis of the speaker's corporate identity. No sufficient governmental interest justifies limits on the political speech of nonprofit or for-profit corporations. . . .

The Framers may have been unaware of certain types of speakers or forms of communication, but that does not mean that those speakers and media are entitled to less First Amendment protection than those types of speakers and media that provided the means of communicating political ideas when the Bill of Rights was adopted. . . .

The purpose and effect of this law is to prevent corporations, including small and nonprofit corporations, from presenting both facts and opinions to the public. . . . When Government seeks to use its full power, including the criminal law, to command where a person may get his or her information or what distrusted source he or she may not hear, it uses censorship to control thought. This is unlawful. The First Amendment confirms the freedom to think for ourselves. . . .

The appearance of influence or access, furthermore, will not cause the electorate to lose faith in our democracy. By definition, an independent expenditure is political speech presented to the electorate that is not coordinated with a candidate. . . . The fact that a corporation, or any other speaker, is willing to spend money to try to persuade voters presupposes that the people have the ultimate influence over elected officials. . . . This is inconsistent with any suggestion that the electorate will refuse "'to take part in democratic governance'" because of additional political speech made by a corporation or any other speaker. . . .

When Congress finds that a problem exists, we must give that finding due deference; but Congress may not choose an unconstitutional remedy. If elected officials succumb to improper influences from independent expenditures; if they surrender their best judgment; and if they put expediency before principle, then surely there is cause for concern. We must give weight to attempts by Congress to seek to dispel either the appearance or the reality of these influences. The remedies enacted by law, however, must comply with the First Amendment; and, it is our law and our tradition that more speech, not less, is the governing rule. An outright ban on corporate political speech during the critical pre-election period is not a permissible remedy. . . .

Corporations, like individuals, do not have monolithic views. On certain topics corporations may possess valuable expertise, leaving them the best equipped to point out errors or fallacies in speech of all sorts, including the speech of candidates and elected officials. . . . The Government may not suppress political speech on the basis of the speaker's corporate identity. No sufficient governmental interest justifies limits on the political speech of non-profit or for-profit corporations. . . .

When word concerning the plot of the movie *Mr. Smith Goes to Washington* reached the circles of Government, some officials sought, by persuasion, to discourage its distribution. . . . After all, it, like *Hillary*, was speech funded by a corporation that was critical of Members of Congress. *Mr. Smith Goes to Washington* may be fiction and caricature; but fiction and caricature can be a powerful force.

Modern day movies, television comedies, or skits on Youtube.com might portray public officials or public policies in unflattering ways. Yet if a covered transmission during the blackout period creates the background for candidate endorsement or opposition, a felony occurs solely because a corporation, other than an exempt media corporation, has made the "purchase, payment, distribution, loan, advance, deposit, or gift of money or anything of value" in order to engage in political speech. . . . Speech would be suppressed in the realm where its necessity is most evident: in the public dialogue preceding a real election. Governments are often hostile to speech, but under our law and our tradition it seems stranger than fiction for our Government to make this political speech a crime. Yet this is the statute's purpose and design.

Some members of the public might consider *Hillary* to be insightful and instructive; some might find it to be neither high art nor a fair discussion on how to set the Nation's course; still others simply might suspend judgment on these points but decide to think more about issues and candidates. Those choices and assessments, however, are not for the Government to make. "The First Amendment underwrites the freedom to experiment and to create in the realm of thought and speech. Citizens must be free to use new forms, and new forums, for the expression of ideas. The civic discourse belongs to the people, and the Government may not prescribe the means used to conduct it."

# John Paul Stevens

**→ NO**

# Dissenting Opinion

**T**he real issue in this case concerns how, not if, the appellant may finance its electioneering. Citizens United is a wealthy nonprofit corporation that runs a political action committee (PAC) with millions of dollars in assets. Under the Bipartisan Campaign Reform Act of 2002 (BCRA), it could have used those assets to televise and promote Hillary: The Movie wherever and whenever it wanted to. It also could have spent unrestricted sums to broadcast Hillary at any time other than the 30 days before the last primary election. Neither Citizens United's nor any other corporation's speech has been "banned." . . . All that the parties dispute is whether Citizens United had a right to use the funds in its general treasury to pay for broadcasts during the 30-day period. The notion that the First Amendment dictates an affirmative answer to that question is, in my judgment, profoundly misguided. Even more misguided is the notion that the Court must rewrite the law relating to campaign expenditures by for-profit corporations and unions to decide this case.

The basic premise underlying the Court's ruling is its iteration, and constant reiteration, of the proposition that the First Amendment bars regulatory distinctions based on a speaker's identity, including its "identity" as a corporation. While that glittering generality has rhetorical appeal, it is not a correct statement of the law. Nor does it tell us when a corporation may engage in electioneering that some of its shareholders oppose. It does not even resolve the specific question whether Citizens United may be required to finance some of its messages with the money in its PAC. The conceit that corporations must be treated identically to natural persons in the political sphere is not only inaccurate but also inadequate to justify the Court's disposition of this case.

In the context of election to public office, the distinction between corporate and human speakers is significant. Although they make enormous contributions to our society, corporations are not actually members of it. They cannot vote or run for office. Because they may be managed and controlled by nonresidents, their interests may conflict in fundamental respects with the interests of eligible voters. The financial resources, legal structure, and instrumental orientation of corporations raise legitimate concerns about their role in the electoral process. Our lawmakers have a compelling constitutional basis, if not also a democratic duty, to take measures designed to guard against the potentially deleterious effects of corporate spending in local and national races. The majority's approach to corporate electioneering marks a dramatic break from our past. Congress has placed special limitations on campaign spending by corporations ever since the passage of the Tillman Act in 1907. . . .

Supreme Court of the United States, 2010.

S203's prohibition on certain uses of general treasury funds . . . applies in a viewpoint-neutral fashion to a narrow subset of advocacy messages about clearly identified candidates for federal office, made during discrete time periods through discrete channels. In the case at hand, all Citizens United needed to do to broadcast Hillary right before the primary was to abjure business contributions or use the funds in its PAC, which by its own account is "one of the most active PACs in America." . . .

The election context is distinctive in many ways, and the Court, of course, is right that the First Amendment closely guards political speech. But in this context, too, the authority of legislatures to enact viewpoint-neutral regulations based on content and identity is well settled. We have, for example, allowed state-run broadcasters to exclude independent candidates from televised debates. . . . We have upheld statutes that prohibit the distribution or display of campaign materials near a polling place. . . . Although we have not reviewed them directly, we have never cast doubt on laws that place special restrictions on campaign spending by foreign nationals. And we have consistently approved laws that bar Government employees, but not others, from contributing to or participating in political activities. These statutes burden the political expression of one class of speakers, namely, civil servants. Yet we have sustained them on the basis of longstanding practice and Congress' reasoned judgment that certain regulations which leave "untouched full participation . . . in political decisions at the ballot box," help ensure that public officials are "sufficiently free from improper influences," id., at 564, and that "confidence in the system of representative Government is not . . . eroded to a disastrous extent." . . .

The same logic applies to this case with additional force because it is the identity of corporations, rather than individuals, that the Legislature has taken into account. As we have unanimously observed, legislatures are entitled to decide "that the special characteristics of the corporate structure require particularly careful regulation" in an electoral context. NRWC, 459 U.S., at 209–210.50 Not only has the distinctive potential of corporations to corrupt the electoral process long been recognized, but within the area of campaign finance, corporate spending is also "furthest from the core of political expression, since corporations' First Amendment speech and association interests are derived largely from those of their members and of the public in receiving information." . . . Campaign finance distinctions based on corporate identity tend to be less worrisome, in other words, because the "speakers" are not natural persons, much less members of our political community, and the governmental interests are of the highest order. Furthermore, when corporations, as a class, are distinguished from noncorporations, as a class, there is a lesser risk that regulatory distinctions will reflect invidious discrimination or political favoritism.

If taken seriously, our colleagues' assumption that the identity of a speaker has no relevance to the Government's ability to regulate political speech would lead to some remarkable conclusions. Such an assumption would have accorded the propaganda broadcasts to our troops by "Tokyo Rose" during World War II the same protection as speech by Allied commanders. More pertinently, it would appear to afford the same protection to multinational corporations controlled by foreigners as to individual Americans. Under the majority's view, I suppose it may be a First Amendment problem that corporations are not permitted to vote, given that voting is, among other things, a form of speech. . . .

The Court invokes "ancient First Amendment principles," and original understandings . . . to defend today's ruling, yet it makes only a perfunctory attempt to ground its analysis in the principles or understandings of those who drafted and ratified the Amendment. Perhaps this is because there is not a scintilla of evidence to support the notion that anyone believed it would preclude regulatory distinctions based on the corporate form. To the extent that the Framers' views are discernible and relevant to the disposition of this case, they would appear to cut strongly against the majority's position.

This is not only because the Framers and their contemporaries conceived of speech more narrowly than we now think of it, . . . but also because they held very different views about the nature of the First Amendment right and the role of corporations in society. Those few corporations that existed at the founding were authorized by grant of a special legislative charter. . . .

The individualized charter mode of incorporation reflected the "cloud of disfavor under which corporations labored" in the early years of this Nation. . . . Thomas Jefferson famously fretted that corporations would subvert the Republic. General incorporation statutes, and widespread acceptance of business corporations as socially useful actors, did not emerge until the 1800's. . . .

The Framers thus took it as a given that corporations could be comprehensively regulated in the service of the public welfare. Unlike our colleagues, they had little trouble distinguishing corporations from human beings, and when they constitutionalized the right to free speech in the First Amendment, it was the free speech of individual Americans that they had in mind. While individuals might join together to exercise their speech rights, business corporations, at least, were plainly not seen as facilitating such associational or expressive ends. Even "the notion that business corporations could invoke the First Amendment would probably have been quite a novelty," given that "at the time, the legitimacy of every corporate activity was thought to rest entirely in a concession of the sovereign.". . .

A century of more recent history puts to rest any notion that today's ruling is faithful to our First Amendment tradition. At the federal level, the express distinction between corporate and individual political spending on elections stretches back to 1907, when Congress passed the Tillman Act, . . . banning all corporate contributions to candidates. The Senate Report on the legislation observed that "[t]he evils of the use of [corporate] money in connection with political elections are so generally recognized that the committee deems it unnecessary to make any argument in favor of the general purpose of this measure. It is in the interest of good government and calculated to promote purity in the selection of public officials." . . . President Roosevelt, in his 1905 annual message to Congress, declared: "'All contributions by corporations to any political committee or for any political purpose should be forbidden by law; directors should not be permitted to use stockholders' money for such purposes; and, moreover, a prohibition of this kind would be, as far as it went, an effective method of stopping the evils aimed at in corrupt practices acts.'" . . .

[The Tillman Act] was primarily driven by two pressing concerns: first, the enormous power corporations had come to wield in federal elections, with the accompanying threat of both actual corruption and a public perception of corruption; and second, a respect for the interest of shareholders and members in preventing the use of their money to support candidates they opposed. . . .

Over the course of the past century Congress has demonstrated a recurrent need to regulate corporate participation in candidate elections to "'[p]reserv[e] the integrity of the electoral process, preven[t] corruption, . . . sustai[n] the active, alert responsibility of the individual citizen,'" government.'" . . . Time and again, we have recognized these realities in approving measures that Congress and the States have taken. . . .

On numerous occasions we have recognized Congress' legitimate interest in preventing the money that is spent on elections from exerting an "'undue influence on an officeholder's judgment'" and from creating "'the appearance of such influence,'" beyond the sphere of quid pro quo relationships. . . . Corruption can take many forms. Bribery may be the paradigm case. But the difference between selling a vote and selling access is a matter of degree, not kind. And selling access is not qualitatively different from giving special preference to those who spent money on one's behalf. Corruption operates along a spectrum, and the majority's apparent belief that quid pro quo arrangements can be neatly demarcated from other improper influences does not accord with the theory or reality of politics. . . .

Corporations, as a class, tend to be more attuned to the complexities of the legislative process and more directly affected by tax and appropriations measures that receive little public scrutiny; they also have vastly more money with which to try to buy access and votes. . . . Business corporations must engage the political process in instrumental terms if they are to maximize shareholder value. The unparalleled resources, professional lobbyists, and single-minded focus they bring to this effort, I believe, make quid pro quo corruption and its appearance inherently more likely when they (or their conduits or trade groups) spend unrestricted sums on elections.

It is with regret rather than satisfaction that I can now say that time has borne out my concerns. The legislative and judicial proceedings relating to BCRA generated a substantial body of evidence suggesting that, as corporations grew more and more adept at crafting "issue ads" to help or harm a particular candidate, these nominally independent expenditures began to corrupt the political process in a very direct sense. The sponsors of these ads were routinely granted special access after the campaign was over; "candidates and officials knew who their friends were." . . . Many corporate independent expenditures, it seemed, had become essentially interchangeable with direct contributions in their capacity to generate quid pro quo arrangements. In an age in which money and television ads are the coin of the campaign realm, it is hardly surprising that corporations deployed these ads to curry favor with, and to gain influence over, public officials.

The majority appears to think it decisive that the BCRA record does not contain "direct examples of votes being exchanged for . . . expenditures." It would have been quite remarkable if Congress had created a record detailing such behavior by its own Members. Proving that a specific vote was exchanged for a specific expenditure has always been next to impossible. . . .

Starting today, corporations with large war chests to deploy on election-eering may find democratically elected bodies becoming much more attuned to their interests. The majority both misreads the facts and draws the wrong conclusions when it suggests that the BCRA record provides "only scant evidence that independent expenditures . . . ingratiate," and that, "in any event," none of it matters. . . .

In America, incumbent legislators pass the laws that govern campaign finance, just like all other laws. To apply a level of scrutiny that effectively bars them from regulating electioneering whenever there is the faintest whiff of self-interest, is to deprive them of the ability to regulate electioneering. . . .

The fact that corporations are different from human beings might seem to need no elaboration, except that the majority opinion almost completely elides it. . . . Unlike natural persons, corporations have "limited liability" for their owners and managers, "perpetual life," separation of ownership and control, "and favorable treatment of the accumulation and distribution of assets . . . that enhance their ability to attract capital and to deploy their resources in ways that maximize the return on their shareholders' investments." . . . Unlike voters in U.S. elections, corporations may be foreign controlled. Unlike other interest groups, business corporations have been "effectively delegated responsibility for ensuring society's economic welfare"; they inescapably structure the life of every citizen. "'[T]he resources in the treasury of a business corporation,'" furthermore, "'are not an indication of popular support for the corporation's political ideas.'" . . . "'They reflect instead the economically motivated decisions of investors and customers. The availability of these resources may make a corporation a formidable political presence, even though the power of the corporation may be no reflection of the power of its ideas.'" . . .

It might also be added that corporations have no consciences, no beliefs, no feelings, no thoughts, no desires. Corporations help structure and facilitate the activities of human beings, to be sure, and their "personhood" often serves as a useful legal fiction. But they are not themselves members of "We the People" by whom and for whom our Constitution was established. . . .

It is an interesting question "who" is even speaking when a business corporation places an advertisement that endorses or attacks a particular candidate. Presumably it is not the customers or employees, who typically have no say in such matters. It cannot realistically be said to be the shareholders, who tend to be far removed from the day-to-day decisions of the firm and whose political preferences may be opaque to management. Perhaps the officers or directors of the corporation have the best claim to be the ones speaking, except their fiduciary duties generally prohibit them from using corporate funds for personal ends. Some individuals associated with the corporation must make the decision to place the ad, but the idea that these individuals are thereby fostering their self-expression or cultivating their critical faculties is fanciful. It is entirely possible that the corporation's electoral message will conflict with their personal convictions. Take away the ability to use general treasury funds for some of those ads, and no one's autonomy, dignity, or political equality has been impinged upon in the least. . . .

The marketplace of ideas is not actually a place where items—or laws— are meant to be bought and sold, and when we move from the realm of economics to the realm of corporate electioneering, there may be no "reason to think the market ordering is intrinsically good at all." . . .

The Court's blinkered and aphoristic approach to the First Amendment may well promote corporate power at the cost of the individual and collective self-expression the Amendment was meant to serve. It will undoubtedly cripple the ability of ordinary citizens, Congress, and the States to adopt even limited measures to protect against corporate domination of the electoral process. Americans may be forgiven if they do not feel the Court has advanced the cause of self-government today. . . .

When corporations use general treasury funds to praise or attack particular candidate for office, it is the shareholders, as the residual claimants, who are effectively footing the bill. Those shareholders who disagree with the corporation's electoral message may find their financial investments being used to undermine their political convictions. The PAC mechanism, by contrast, helps assure that those who pay for an electioneering communication actually support its content and that managers do not use general treasuries to advance personal agendas. . . .

Today's decision is backwards in many senses. It elevates the majority's agenda over the litigants' submissions, facial attacks over as-applied claims, broad constitutional theories over narrow statutory grounds, individual dissenting opinions over precedential holdings, assertion over tradition, absolutism over empiricism, rhetoric over reality. . . . Their conclusion that the societal interest in avoiding corruption and the appearance of corruption does not provide an adequate justification for regulating corporate expenditures on candidate elections relies on an incorrect description of that interest, along with a failure to acknowledge the relevance of established facts and the considered judgments of state and federal legislatures over many decades.

In a democratic society, the longstanding consensus on the need to limit corporate campaign spending should outweigh the wooden application of judge-made rules. The majority's rejection of this principle "elevate[s] corporations to a level of deference which has not been seen at least since the days when substantive due process was regularly used to invalidate regulatory legislation thought to unfairly impinge upon established economic interests." . . . At bottom, the Court's opinion is thus a rejection of the common sense of the American people, who have recognized a need to prevent corporations from undermining self-government since the founding, and who have fought against the distinctive corrupting potential of corporate electioneering since the days of Theodore Roosevelt. It is a strange time to repudiate that common sense. While American democracy is imperfect, few outside the majority of this Court would have thought its flaws included a dearth of corporate money in politics.

# EXPLORING THE ISSUE

## Do Corporations Have the Same Free Speech Rights as Persons?

### Critical Thinking and Reflection

1. How does the Supreme Court distinguish between campaign contributions and campaign expenditures?
2. How does the Supreme Court distinguish between public and private financing of election campaigns?
3. What would be the likely constitutional and political consequences of public financing of national elections?
4. Should Congress limit the campaign period (as in Great Britain)? What would be the possible constitutional objections? How important is political advertising in influencing voter behavior?
5. Which elements of an election campaign are likely to have the greatest impact on you?
6. How does the high cost of campaigning influence the choice of candidates?
7. Should corporations possess the constitutional rights of persons?
8. What restrictions, if any, should be placed on political activity by corporations?
9. Should all contributions to candidates and office-holders be made public?
10. Do other groups have the same rights as corporations? Should they?
11. Should the status of corporations as participants in the political process be changed by constitutional amendment?

### Is There Common Ground?

If the long-standing division on the U.S. Supreme Court is a guide, the answer must be that there is little or no common ground on the question of the constitutional rights of corporations, and specifically on the question of whether they enjoy an uninhibited First Amendment right to free speech in American elections. The five jurists who have rendered the decisions discussed here are Chief Justice John Roberts and Justices Antonin Scalia, Anthony Kennedy, Clarence Thomas, and Samuel Alito. The four Justices who have dissented in the most recent cases are Justices Ruth Bader Ginsburg, Stephen Breyer, Sonia Sotomayor, and Elena Kagan (who succeeded Justice John Paul Stevens, who retired in 2010). Similarly, sharp and seemingly irreconcilable divisions have existed on the Supreme Court in the past, sometimes broken by a shift in sentiment by a member of the Court, but more often by a change in the Court's composition.

The conduct of elections since *Citizens United* is likely to provoke more congressional consideration of election reform, and it may be influenced by public reaction to what is likely to be greater amounts of money being spent on behalf of candidates by the new Super PACs. Public reaction to the anticipated increase in political advertising is likely to influence future congressional action on the length and financing of national election campaigns.

## Additional Resources

The Supreme Court's decision in *Citizens United v. Federal Election Commission* receives vigorous support from Richard A. Epstein, *"Citizens United v. FEC*: The Constitutional Right That Big Corporations Should Have But Do Not Want,*"* in *Harvard Journal of Law & Public Policy*, v. 34 (2011). Thomas Hartmann has written several books attacking the idea of corporation personhood. The title of his *Unequal Protection: The Rise of Corporate Dominance and the Theft of Human Rights* (Rodale Books, 2004) expresses his belief that the Supreme Court has distorted the meaning of the Constitution. Several recent books examine the role of corporations in American life. Two studies that explain their influence are David A. Westbrook, *Between Citizen and State: An Introduction to the Corporation* (Paradigm Publishers, 2008), a sympathetic analysis, and David C. Korten, *When Corporations Rule the World* (Berrett-Koehler, 2001), a highly critical examination.

The political influence of corporate, union or other interest group money could be curtailed by public financing of elections, in the judgment of David Donnelly, Janice Fine, and Ellen S. Miller, *Money and Politics: Financing Our Elections Democratically* (Beacon Press, 1999). Up-to-date information on the role of corporate, union, and independent expenditures in state politics, including the congressional district in which you live, can be obtained without charge from followthemoney.org. Other sources of interest group contributions and influence include OpenSecrets.org and MapLight.org.

# ISSUE 18

## Should "Recreational" Drugs Be Legalized?

**YES: Bryan Stevenson**, from "Drug Policy, Criminal Justice, and Mass Imprisonment," paper presented to the Global Commission on Drug Policies (January 2011)

**NO: Theodore Dalrymple**, from "Don't Legalize Drugs," *City Journal*, (Spring 1997)

### ISSUE SUMMARY

**YES:** Law professor Bryan Stevenson focuses on how the criminalization of drugs has led to mass imprisonment with negative consequences for law enforcement.

**NO:** Theodore Dalrymple, a writer for the Manhattan Institute, describes the consequences of illegal drug use and the potential for further illness and crime if drugs are legalized.

$\mathbf{P}$rohibition is a word Americans associate with the prohibition of liquor, which was adopted as a national policy with the ratification of the Eighteenth Amendment to the U.S. Constitution in 1920 and repealed with the adoption of the Twenty-first Amendment in 1933. Many states had earlier banned whiskey and other intoxicating beverages, and some states have had various restrictions since repeal.

Similarly, certain categories of illicit drugs were banned in some states prior to the passage of the Controlled Substance Act in 1970, which made the prohibition a national policy. Unlike the Prohibition Amendment, this was achieved by an Act of Congress. Many claimed then, and many still do today, that to do this in the absence of a constitutional amendment exceeds the power of the national government. Nevertheless, it has been upheld by the federal courts and has continued to function for more than four decades.

The principal substances that are banned include opium, heroin, cocaine, and marijuana. Marijuana is also known as cannabis (the plant from which it is obtained) and by a variety of informal names, most familiarly "pot." Its use dates back several thousand years, sometimes for religious or medical purposes. However, it is a so-called recreational drug that a United Nations committee characterized as "the most widely used illicit substance in the world." Because opium, heroin, and cocaine are more powerful, more addictive, and less prevalent, advocates of legalization often restrict their appeal to removing the ban on marijuana.

In the 50 years following an international convention in 1912 that urged the restriction of dangerous drugs, the use in the United States of illicit drugs other than marijuana was consistently below one-half of 1 percent of the population, with cocaine rising somewhat in the counter culture climate that began in the late 1950s. Illicit drug use was widely promoted as mind-expanding and relatively harmless. It is estimated that its use peaked in the 1970s. Present estimates for drugs other than marijuana suggest that between 5 and 10 percent of the population at least occasionally engages in the use of some illicit drugs.

In 2006, there were approximately 1.9 million drug arrests in the United States. Of these, 829,625 (44 percent of the total) were marijuana arrests. During the past two decades, the price of marijuana has gone down, its potency has increased, and it has become more readily available.

Studies, principally conducted in Sweden, Holland, and other nations with more tolerant drug policies, conclude that social factors influence drug use. Apart from peer pressure, particularly in the use of marijuana, hard drugs generally become more common in times of higher unemployment and lower income. Apart from cannabis, which is easily grown, the illicit character of hard drugs makes them expensive, but the profit motive induces growers, distributors, and "pushers" to risk arrest and punishment. It has been estimated that as many as one-sixth of all persons in federal prisons have been convicted of selling, possessing, or using marijuana.

The movement to legalize these drugs, often with a focus on marijuana, has existed as long as their prohibition, but in recent years has won recruits from both liberal and conservative ranks. As with the prohibition of alcohol, experience with the unintended consequences of prohibition of drugs led some to wonder whether this has not only failed to eliminate their use but has increased public health problems. Under the Prohibition Amendment, people drank unlicensed alcohol often adulterated by the addition of poisonous substances. Illicit drug prohibition has led to the sale of toxic ingredients added to the drugs resulting in impurer and more dangerous products. Drug users injecting the drugs employ dirty reused needles that spread HIV and hepatitis B and C. While illicit drug use has never rivaled the widespread public acceptance of alcohol, their use has been extensive enough to spawn new networks of organized crime, violence related to the drug market, and the corruption of law enforcement and governments. We have recently witnessed this in the drug gang wars in Mexico that have slipped over into the American southwest.

Milton Friedman, who was America's most influential conservative economist, reached the interesting conclusion that drug prohibition has led to the rise of drug cartels. His reasoning was that only major retailers can handle massive shipments, own aircraft fleets, have armed troops, and employ lawyers and methods of eluding and bribing the police. Consquently, law enforcement as well as competition drives out smaller, less ruthless and less efficient drug dealers.

The economic cost of legislating and attempting to enforce drug prohibition is very high. When the national policy went to effect, the federal cost was $350 million in 1971. Thirty-five years later in 2006, the cost was $30 billion. To this should be added the revenue that could be obtained if marijuana were subject to taxation. If it were taxed at the same rate as alcohol or tobacco, it has been estimated that it would yield as much as $7.7 billion. It may be, as advocates of legalization suggest, that the financial costs exceed the damages that the drugs themselves cause.

Against these arguments for repeal, those who support the war on drugs claim that prohibitive drug laws suppress drug use. Compare the large majority of Americans who consume legal alcohol with the very much smaller proportion who use illicit drugs. The Drug Enforcement Administration (DEA) has demonstrated that people under the influence of drugs are more than six times more likely to commit homicides than people looking for money to buy drugs. Drug use changes behavior and causes criminal activity. Cocaine-related paranoia frequently results in assaults, drugged driving, and domestic violence. These crimes are likely to increase when drugs are more readily available.

The point that liberalization advocates miss is that the illicit drugs are inherently harmful. In the short term, illicit drugs cause memory loss, distorted perception, a decline of motor skills, and an increased heart rate and anxiety. Particularly for young people, drug use produces a decline in mental development and motivation, as well as a reduced ability to concentrate in school.

The United States Centers for Disease Control and Prevention has concluded that although there are more than seven times more Americans who use alcohol than drugs, during a single year alone (2000), there were almost as many drug-induced deaths (15,8520) as alcohol-induced (18, 539). The DEA concludes that drugs are "far more deadly than alcohol." This is true even for marijuana, which is deemed more potent than it was a generation ago. It contains more than four hundred chemicals (the toxicity of some is clear and of many others is unknown) and one marijuana cigarette deposits four times more tar than a filtered tobacco cigarette.

In the following selections, Bryan Stevenson, executive director of the Equal Justice Initiative, focuses on how the criminalization of drugs has led to mass imprisonment with negative consequences for law enforcement. Theodore Dalrymple, a writer who worked as a doctor with prisoners convicted of illegal drug use, describes the consequences of illegal use and the potential for further illness and crime if drugs are legalized.

# YES ↵

**Bryan Stevenson**

# Drug Policy, Criminal Justice, and Mass Imprisonment

The last three decades have witnessed a global increase in the criminalization of improper drug use. Criminalization has resulted in increased use of harsh punitive sanctions imposed on drug offenders and dramatic increases in rates of incarceration. These policies have had limited impact on eliminating or reducing illegal drug use and may have resulted in adverse consequences for social and community health. The criminal justice system has proved to be an ineffective forum for managing or controlling many aspects of the drug trade or the problem of illegal drug usage. In recent years, some progress has been reported when governing bodies have managed drug use and addiction as a public health problem which requires treatment, counseling and medical interventions rather than incarceration. Primarily as a result of drug policy, the number of people currently incarcerated worldwide is at an all time high of ten million.

In the United States, the prison population has increased from 300,000 in 1972 to 2.3 million people today. One in 31 adults in the United States is in jail, prison, on probation or parole. The American government currently spends over 68 billion dollars a year on incarceration. Drug Policy and the incarceration of low-level drug offenders is the primary cause of mass incarceration in the United States. [Forty percent] of drug arrests are for simple possession of marijuana. There is also evidence that drug enforcement has diverted resources from law enforcement of violent crimes and other threats to public safety.

Incarceration of low-level drug offenders has criminogenic effects that increase the likelihood of recidivism and additional criminal behavior. Enforcement of drug policy against low-level users and small scale trafficking has been racially biased and fueled social and political antagonisms that have undermined support of drug policy.

Growing evidence indicates that drug treatment and counseling programs are far more effective in reducing drug addiction and abuse than is incarceration. Needle exchange, compulsory treatment, education, counseling, drug substitutes like Methadone or Naxolene have proved highly effective in reducing addiction, overdose and the spread of HIV and Hepatitis C.

The last three decades have witnessed a global increase in the criminalization of improper drug use. Criminalization has resulted in increased use of harsh punitive sanctions imposed on drug offenders and dramatic increases in rates of incarceration. These policies have had limited impact on eliminating or reducing illegal drug use and may have resulted in adverse consequences for social and community health. The criminal justice system has proved to be an ineffective forum for managing or controlling many aspects of the drug trade or the problem of illegal drug usage. In recent years, some progress has been reported when governing bodies have managed drug use and addiction as a public health problem which requires treatment, counseling and medical interventions rather than incarceration. Most experts agree that drug-related HIV infection, the spread of infectious diseases like Hepatitis C and related public health concerns cannot be meaningfully addressed through jail and imprisonment and are often aggravated by policies which are primarily punitive. This paper briefly reviews this issue and identifies some of the costs of over-reliance on incarceration and outlines new strategies.

# Criminal Justice Policy and Increased Use of Sanctions and Incarceration for Low-Level Drug Offenders

## The Criminalization of Drugs and the Legacy of Mass Imprisonment

Criminalization of possession and illegal use of drugs compounded by mandatory sentencing and lengthy prison sanctions for low-level drug use has become the primary cause of mass incarceration. The global prison population has skyrocketed in the last three decades with ten million people worldwide now in jails and prisons. The extraordinary increase in the number of people now incarcerated has had tremendous implications for state and national governments dealing with global recession and a range of economic, social and political challenges. Research indicates that resources that would otherwise be spent on development, infrastructure, education and health care have been redirected over the last two decades to incarcerating drug offenders, many of whom are low-level users. The trend toward mass incarceration has been especially troubling in the United States. In the last thirty-five years, the number of U.S. residents in prison has increased from 330,000 people in jails and prisons in 1972 to almost 2.3 million imprisoned people today. The United States now has the highest rate of incarceration in the world.

Over five million people are on probation and parole in America. Currently, one out of 100 adults is in jail or prison and one out of 31 adults is in jail, prison on probation or parole. The consequences of increased incarceration and penal control strategies have been dramatic and costly. Many states spend in excess of $50,000 a year to incarcerate each prisoner in a state prison or facility, including non-violent, low-level drug offenders. Corrections spending by state and federal governments has risen from $6.9 billion in 1980 to $68 billion in 2006 in America. During the ten year period between 1985 and 1995, prisons were constructed at a pace of one new prison opening each week.

The economic toll of expansive imprisonment policies has been accompanied by socio-political consequences as well. Mass incarceration has had discernible impacts in poor and minority communities which have been disproportionately impacted by drug enforcement strategies. Collateral consequences of drug prosecutions of low-level offenders have included felon disenfranchisement laws, where in some states drug offenders permanently lose the right to vote. Sociologists have also recently observed that the widespread incarceration of men in low-income communities has had a profound negative impact on social and cultural norms relating to family and opportunity. Increases in the imprisonment of poor and minority women with children have now been linked with rising numbers of displaced children and dependents. Drug policy and the over-reliance on incarceration is seen by many experts as contributing to increased rates of chronic unemployment, destabilization of families and increased risk of reincarceration for the formerly incarcerated.

There are unquestionably serious consequences for community and public health when illegal use of drugs is widespread. Addiction and other behavioral issues triggered by drug abuse have well known consequences for individuals, families, communities and governing bodies trying to protect public safety. Governing bodies are clearly justified in pursuing policies and strategies that disrupt the drug trade and the violence frequently associated with high-level drug trafficking. Similarly, drug abuse is a serious problem within communities that threatens public health and merits serious attention. However, some interventions to address drug abuse are now emerging as clearly more effective than others. Consequently, interventions that reduce drug dependence and improve the prospects for eliminating drug addiction and abuse are essential if measurable improvements on this issue are to be achieved in the coming years.

## Drug Policy and the Criminal Justice System

Many countries have employed the rhetoric of war to combat the drug trade. While there are countries where violent drug kingpens have created large militias that have necessitated more militarized responses from law enforcement, most drug arrests are directed at low-level users who have been the primary targets in the "war on drugs." States have criminalized simple possession of drugs like marijuana and imposed harsh and lengthy sentences on people arrested. Small amounts of narcotics, unauthorized prescription medicines and other drugs have triggered trafficking charges that impose even lengthier prison sentences. The introduction of habitual felony offender laws has exacerbated drug policy as it is not uncommon for illegal drug users to accumulate multiple charges in a very short period of time. Under the notorious "three strikes laws" that have become popular in America, drug offenders with no history of violence may face mandatory minimum sentences in excess of 25 years in prison. Thousands of low-level drug offenders have been sentenced to life imprisonment with no chance of parole as a result of these sentencing laws.

In the United States, drug arrests have tripled in the last 25 years, however most of these arrests have been for simple possession of low-level drugs. In 2005, nearly 43% of all drug arrests were for marijuana offenses. Marijuana possession arrests accounted for 79% of the growth in drug arrests in the 1990s. Nearly a half million people are in state or federal prisons or a local jail for a drug offense, compared to 41,000 in 1980. Most of these people have no history of violence or high-level drug selling activity.

The "war on drugs" has also generated indirect costs that many researchers contend have undermined public safety. The federal government has prioritized spending and grants for drug task forces and widespread drug interdiction efforts that often target low-level drug dealing. These highly organized and coordinated efforts have been very labor intensive for local law enforcement agencies with some unanticipated consequences for investigation of other crimes. The focus on drugs is believed to have redirected law enforcement resources that have resulted in more drunk driving, and decreased investigation and enforcement of violent crime laws. In Illinois, a 47% increase in drug arrests corresponded with a 22% decrease in arrests for drunk driving. Florida researchers have similarly linked the focus on low level drug arrests with an increase in the serious crime index.

In prison, as a result of the increased costs of incarceration, most drug addicts are less likely to receive drug treatment and therapy. The increasing costs of mass imprisonment have eliminated funds for treatment and counseling services even though some of these services have proved to be very effective. In 1991, one in three prison inmates was receiving treatment while incarcerated, today the rate is down to one in seven. The decline of treatment and counseling services makes re-offending once released much more likely. This is one of the ways in which incarceration and criminal justice intervention has proved costly and less effective than other models of managing illegal drug use.

## Racially Discriminatory Enforcement of Drug Laws

In the United States, considerable evidence demonstrates that enforcement of drug policy has proved to be racially discriminatory and very biased against the poor. America's criminal justice system is very wealth sensitive which makes it difficult for low-income residents to obtain equally favorable outcomes as more wealthy residents when they are charged with drug crimes. Targeting communities of color for enforcement of drug laws has added to the problems of racial bias in American society and generated some of the fiercest debates about the continuing legacy of racial discrimination. Illegal use of drugs is not unique to communities of color and rates of offending are not higher in these communities than they are in nonminority communities. African Americans comprise 14% of regular drug users in the United States, yet are 37% of those arrested for drug offenses and 56% of those incarcerated for drug crimes. Black people in the United States serve almost as much time in federal prison for a drug offense (58.7 months) as whites serve for a violent crime (61.7 months), primarily as a result of the racially disparate sentencing laws such as the 100-1 crack powder cocaine disparity. For years, the sentences for illegal possession or use of crack cocaine, which is more prevalent in communities of color, were 100 times greater than possession or use of equivalent amounts of powder cocaine, leading to dramatically longer prison sentences for African Americans. In 2010, Congress amended this law and reduced the disparity from 100-1 to 12-1. However, the failure to make the law retroactive has left the costly and troubling racial disparities uncorrected. Hispanic people are also disproportionately at much greater risk of arrest and prosecution for drug crimes than are whites in the United States.

Discriminatory enforcement of drug laws against communities of color has seriously undermined the integrity of drug policy initiatives and frequently these policies are perceived as unfair, unjust and targeted at racial minorities. Enforcement of drug laws tends to be directed at low-income communities or residential and social centers where residents have less political power to resist aggressive policing and engagement. Even some reforms aimed at shielding low-level drug offenders from incarceration have been skewed against the poor and people of color. Some data show that people of color are more likely to be redirected back to the criminal courts if drug court personnel have discretion. Similarly, many community-based programs that permit drug offenders to avoid jail or prison have significant admission fees and costs that many poor people simply cannot afford. Discriminatory enforcement of drug policy has undermined its effectiveness and legitimacy and contributed to continuing dysfunction in the administration of criminal justice.

## There Is Growing Evidence that Drug Treatment is More Cost Effective than Incarceration and Incapacitation Strategies

One of the clear consequences of mass incarceration directed at low level drug offenders has been to acculturate and socialize illegal drug users into criminality through extended incarceration. This criminogenic effect has been seen in studies that examined rates of recidivism among drug offenders who are given probation and not sent to jail or prison and drug offenders who are incarcerated for the same offenses. In purely human terms, these findings reveal that incarceration may be dramatically more costly than other approaches.

However, the economic analysis of approaches to low level drug offending that avoid incarceration are even more compelling. Whatever the measure, data indicates that drug treatment is more cost effective than incarceration. In California, a study has recently shown that spending on drug treatment is eight times more likely to reduce drug consumption than spending on incarceration. Corresponding decreases in drug-related crime were also documented when comparing drug treatment programs with incarceration. In a RAND analysis study, treatment was estimated to reduce crime associated with drug use and the drug trade up to 15 times as much as incarceration. These findings have been reflected in other studies that have also found that drug treatment is more cost effective in controlling drug abuse and crime than continued expansion of the prison system when looking at low level drug offenders.

Consequently, many states have now started to shift their management of drug offenders to drug courts that have discretion to redirect people who illegally use drugs away from jail or prison and into community-based treatment, counseling and therapeutic interventions. The early signs suggest that these innovations are saving states millions of dollars and accomplishing improved public safety. For the first time in 38 years, 2010 saw a slight decrease in the national state prison population in the United States. Significant reductions will need to continue to deal with a global recession and decreasing resources available for incarceration.

# New and More Effective Strategies for Managing Low-Level Drug Offenders Are Emerging

Proponents of "Harm Reduction" have long argued that a more effective way to combat illegal drug use is to spend more on public education, treatment and interventions that view illegal drug use as a public health problem rather than continued spending on incarceration and harsh sanctions. Supporters of harm reduction acknowledge that the use of incarceration and sanctions will be necessary when illegal drug trafficking or distribution threatens public safety, however, they contend that most drug arrests don't directly implicate public safety. States are beginning to recognize the benefits associated with harm reduction and in recent years have begun to reallocate resources with surprisingly good outcomes.

## Sentencing Reform

In recent years, states have begun to retreat from mandatory sentences and other harsh strategies for enforcing drug laws and moved to alternative models that involve probation, treatment, counseling and education. Between 2004 and 2006, at least 13 states expanded drug treatment or programs which divert drug offenders away from jail or prison into community-based programs. States like Michigan have recently amended statutes that required a mandatory sentence of life imprisonment without parole for distribution of cocaine or heroin. With over 5 million people on probation or parole in the United States, drug use on parole or probation has become the primary basis by which thousands of people are returned to prison. These technical violations of parole or probation account for as many as 40% of new prison admissions in some jurisdictions. In recent years, states have restricted the length of incarceration imposed when formerly incarcerated people test positive for recent drug use. These new statues . . . incarcerated drug users into drug therapy and counseling programs.

The federal government has amended mandatory sentencing laws for drug offenders and seen a dramatic reduction in the number of people facing long-term incarceration for low-level drug use. These sentencing reforms are considered critical to containing the costs of mass imprisonment in the United States and for generating resources necessary to approach drug addiction and abuse as a public health problem.

Drug courts have also emerged in the last decade to play a critical role in redirecting low-level drug offenders away from traditional, punitive models of intervention for illegal drug use. Drug courts have been set up in hundreds of communities. Court personnel have discretion to order drug treatment and community-based programs where offenders must receive counseling and treatment and receive education concerning drug addiction and abuse. By shielding thousands of drug offenders from incarceration and transfer to overcrowded prisons, drug courts have reduced the collateral consequences of illegal drug use, saved millions of dollars and had more favorable outcomes for people who have been identified as illegally using drugs. Drug court participants can avoid a criminal record and all the disabling collateral consequences associated with a criminal record.

Reducing the penalties for some low-level drug crimes, giving judges more discretion to avoid unwarranted and lengthy mandatory sentences and retreating from the rhetoric of war and unscientific policy analysis could substantially reduce incarceration rates and provide additional resources for treatment options that are more effective at eliminating drug abuse.

## Medical and Public Health Models for Drug Abuse Intervention

The risk of criminal prosecution has had many unintended consequences, especially for people with addiction problems who also have critical medical issues that require treatment and intervention. HIV infection and AIDS continue to threaten many countries with tragic and devastating effect. Intravenous drug users are primary targets for infection and have extremely elevated risks of illness from sharing needles. Rather than facilitating less hazardous practices for this community, criminal justice interventions have forced people with addiction underground and infection rates have spiraled. Providing clean needles and other strategies associated with needle exchange have had a significant impact on reducing the rate of HIV infection and offering people with addiction issues an opportunity for treatment. Creating safe zones where people struggling with drug addiction can safely come has also greatly increased the ability of public health officials to provide education, counseling and treatment opportunities that are scientifically proven to be effective to the population with the greatest needs. For example, where needle-exchange has been implemented, the results have been extremely promising for controlling illegal drug use and reducing public health threats.

Policies that make it permissible for people to safely admit to drug addiction problems are well established to be more effective at managing drug addiction. In 2006, there were 26,000 deaths in the United States from accidental drug overdose, the highest level ever recorded by the Centers for Disease Control. Accidental death through overdose is currently the leading cause of injury-related death for people between the ages of 35–54. This extraordinarily high level of death through overdose can only be meaningfully confronted with public education efforts and improving treatment options for people who are abusing drugs.

Criminalization has created huge and complex obstacles for people motivated to eliminate their drug dependence to seek or obtain necessary health care and support. When public health options are made available, studies have reported dramatic declines in drug dependence, mortality and overdose. Medical developments have proved extremely effective in reducing drug dependence and addiction. A range of maintenance therapies are available for people with addiction problems. Methadone maintenance has been cited as the primary intervention strategy for people with heroin addiction. Drugs like Naloxone have been utilized in an extremely effective manner to save lives when people ingest too many opiates. However, these very cost effective treatments are not possible without providing safe opportunities to report drug and overdose issues to health care providers who are free to treat rather than arrest people with addiction and drug dependence.

Mass imprisonment, the high economic and social costs of incarcerating low-level drug offenders and the ineffectiveness of criminalization and punitive approaches to drug addiction have had poor outcomes in many countries. Governing bodies have available dozens of new, scientifically tested interventions which have been proved to lower rates of drug abuse and addiction without incarceration. Reducing illegal drug use and disrupting the sometimes violent drug trade will require new and more effective strategies in the 21st century. The politics of fear and anger that have generated many of these policies must be resisted and adoption of scientifically established treatment protocols that have been found effective and successful should be pursued vigorously.

**Theodore Dalrymple**     ➡ **NO**

# Don't Legalize Drugs

There is a progression in the minds of men: first the unthinkable becomes thinkable, and then it becomes an orthodoxy whose truth seems so obvious that no one remembers that anyone ever thought differently. This is just what is happening with the idea of legalizing drugs: it has reached the stage when millions of thinking men are agreed that allowing people to take whatever they like is the obvious, indeed only, solution to the social problems that arise from the consumption of drugs.

Man's desire to take mind-altering substances is as old as society itself— as are attempts to regulate their consumption. If intoxication in one form or another is inevitable, then so is customary or legal restraint upon that intoxication. But no society until our own has had to contend with the ready availability of so many different mind-altering drugs, combined with a citizenry jealous of its right to pursue its own pleasures in its own way.

The arguments in favor of legalizing the use of all narcotic and stimulant drugs are twofold: philosophical and pragmatic. Neither argument is negligible, but both are mistaken, I believe, and both miss the point.

The philosophic argument is that, in a free society, adults should be permitted to do whatever they please, always provided that they are prepared to take the consequences of their own choices and that they cause no direct harm to others. The locus classicus for this point of view is John Stuart Mill's famous essay On Liberty: "The only purpose for which power can be rightfully exercised over any member of the community, against his will, is to prevent harm to others," Mill wrote. "His own good, either physical or moral, is not a sufficient warrant." This radical individualism allows society no part whatever in shaping, determining, or enforcing a moral code: in short, we have nothing in common but our contractual agreement not to interfere with one another as we go about seeking our private pleasures.

In practice, of course, it is exceedingly difficult to make people take all the consequences of their own actions—as they must, if Mill's great principle is to serve as a philosophical guide to policy. Addiction to, or regular use of, most currently prohibited drugs cannot affect only the person who takes them—and not his spouse, children, neighbors, or employers. No man, except possibly a hermit, is an island; and so it is virtually impossible for Mill's principle to apply to any human action whatever, let alone shooting up heroin or smoking crack. Such a principle is virtually useless in determining what should or should not be permitted.

Perhaps we ought not be too harsh on Mill's principle: it's not clear that anyone has ever thought of a better one. But that is precisely the point. Human affairs cannot be decided by an appeal to an infallible rule, expressible in a few words, whose simple application can decide all cases, including whether drugs should be freely available to the entire adult population. Philosophical fundamentalism is not preferable to the religious variety; and because the desiderata of human life are many, and often in conflict with one another, mere philosophical inconsistency in policy—such as permitting the consumption of alcohol while outlawing cocaine—is not a sufficient argument against that policy. We all value freedom, and we all value order; sometimes we sacrifice freedom for order, and sometimes order for freedom. But once a prohibition has been removed, it is hard to restore, even when the newfound freedom proves to have been ill-conceived and socially disastrous.

Even Mill came to see the limitations of his own principle as a guide for policy and to deny that all pleasures were of equal significance for human existence. It was better, he said, to be Socrates discontented than a fool satisfied. Mill acknowledged that some goals were intrinsically worthier of pursuit than others.

This being the case, not all freedoms are equal, and neither are all limitations of freedom: some are serious and some trivial. The freedom we cherish—or should cherish—is not merely that of satisfying our appetites, whatever they happen to be. We are not Dickensian Harold Skimpoles, exclaiming in protest that "Even the butterflies are free!" We are not children who chafe at restrictions because they are restrictions. And we even recognize the apparent paradox that some limitations to our freedoms have the consequence of making us freer overall. The freest man is not the one who slavishly follows his appetites and desires throughout his life—as all too many of my patients have discovered to their cost. . . .

The idea that freedom is merely the ability to act upon one's whims is surely very thin and hardly begins to capture the complexities of human existence; a man whose appetite is his law strikes us not as liberated but enslaved. And when such a narrowly conceived freedom is made the touchstone of public policy, a dissolution of society is bound to follow. No culture that makes publicly sanctioned self-indulgence its highest good can long survive: a radical egotism is bound to ensue, in which any limitations upon personal behavior are experienced as infringements of basic rights. Distinctions between the important and the trivial, between the freedom to criticize received ideas and the freedom to take LSD, are precisely the standards that keep societies from barbarism.

So the legalization of drugs cannot be supported by philosophical principle. But if the pragmatic argument in favor of legalization were strong enough, it might overwhelm other objections. It is upon this argument that proponents of legalization rest the larger part of their case.

The argument is that the overwhelming majority of the harm done to society by the consumption of currently illicit drugs is caused not by their pharmacological properties but by their prohibition and the resultant criminal activity that prohibition always calls into being. Simple reflection tells us that a supply invariably grows up to meet a demand; and when the demand is widespread, suppression is useless. Indeed, it is harmful, since—by raising the price of the commodity in question—it raises the profits of middlemen, which gives them an even more powerful incentive to stimulate demand further. The vast profits to be made from cocaine and heroin—which, were it not for their illegality, would be cheap and easily affordable even by the poorest in affluent societies—exert a deeply corrupting effect on producers, distributors, consumers, and law enforcers alike. Besides, it is well known that illegality in itself has attractions for youth already inclined to disaffection. Even many of the harmful physical effects of illicit drugs stem from their illegal status: for example, fluctuations in the purity of heroin bought on the street are responsible for many of the deaths by overdose. If the sale and consumption of such drugs were legalized, consumers would know how much they were taking and thus avoid overdoses.

Moreover, since society already permits the use of some mind-altering substances known to be both addictive and harmful, such as alcohol and nicotine, in prohibiting others it appears hypocritical, arbitrary, and dictatorial. Its hypocrisy, as well as its patent failure to enforce its prohibitions successfully, leads inevitably to a decline in respect for the law as a whole. Thus things fall apart, and the center cannot hold.

It stands to reason, therefore, that all these problems would be resolved at a stroke if everyone were permitted to smoke, swallow, or inject anything he chose. The corruption of the police, the luring of children of 11 and 12 into illegal activities, the making of such vast sums of money by drug dealing that legitimate work seems pointless and silly by comparison, and the turf wars that make poor neighborhoods so exceedingly violent and dangerous, would all cease at once were drug taking to be decriminalized and the supply regulated in the same way as alcohol.

But a certain modesty in the face of an inherently unknowable future is surely advisable. That is why prudence is a political virtue: what stands to reason should happen does not necessarily happen in practice. As Goethe said, all theory (even of the monetarist or free-market variety) is gray, but green springs the golden tree of life. If drugs were legalized, I suspect that the golden tree of life might spring some unpleasant surprises.

It is of course true, but only trivially so, that the present illegality of drugs is the cause of the criminality surrounding their distribution. Likewise, it is the illegality of stealing cars that creates car thieves. In fact, the ultimate cause of all criminality is law. As far as I am aware, no one has ever suggested that law should therefore be abandoned. Moreover, the impossibility of winning the "war" against theft, burglary, robbery, and fraud has never been used as an argument that these categories of crime should be abandoned. And so long as the demand for material goods outstrips supply, people will be tempted to commit criminal acts against the owners of property. This is not an argument, in my view, against private property or in favor of the common ownership of all goods. It does suggest, however, that we shall need a police force for a long time to come.

In any case, there are reasons to doubt whether the crime rate would fall quite as dramatically as advocates of legalization have suggested. Amsterdam, where access to drugs is relatively unproblematic, is among the most violent and squalid cities in Europe. The idea behind crime—of getting rich, or at least richer, quickly and without much effort—is unlikely to disappear once drugs are freely available to all who want them. And it may be that officially sanctioned antisocial behavior—the official lifting of taboos—breeds yet more antisocial behavior, as the "broken windows" theory would suggest.

Having met large numbers of drug dealers in prison, I doubt that they would return to respectable life if the principal article of their commerce were to be legalized. Far from evincing a desire to be reincorporated into the world of regular work, they express a deep contempt for it and regard those who accept the bargain of a fair day's work for a fair day's pay as cowards and fools. A life of crime has its attractions for many who would otherwise lead a mundane existence. So long as there is the possibility of a lucrative racket or illegal traffic, such people will find it and extend its scope. Therefore, since even legalizers would hesitate to allow children to take drugs, decriminalization might easily result in dealers turning their attentions to younger and younger children, who—in the permissive atmosphere that even now prevails—have already been inducted into the drug subculture in alarmingly high numbers. . . .

For the proposed legalization of drugs to have its much vaunted beneficial effect on the rate of criminality, such drugs would have to be both cheap and readily available. The legalizers assume that there is a natural limit to the demand for these drugs, and that if their consumption were legalized, the demand would not increase substantially. Those psychologically unstable persons currently taking drugs would continue to do so, with the necessity to commit crimes removed, while psychologically stabler people (such as you and I and our children) would not be enticed to take drugs by their new legal status and cheapness. But price and availability, I need hardly say, exert a profound effect on consumption: the cheaper alcohol becomes, for example, the more of it is consumed, at least within quite wide limits.

I have personal experience of this effect. I once worked as a doctor on a British government aid project to Africa. We were building a road through remote African bush. The contract stipulated that the construction company could import, free of all taxes, alcoholic drinks from the United Kingdom. These drinks the company then sold to its British workers at cost, in the local currency at the official exchange rate, which was approximately one-sixth the black-market rate. A liter bottle of gin thus cost less than a dollar and could be sold on the open market for almost ten dollars. So it was theoretically possible to remain dead drunk for several years for an initial outlay of less than a dollar.

Of course, the necessity to go to work somewhat limited the workers' consumption of alcohol. Nevertheless, drunkenness among them far outstripped anything I have ever seen, before or since. I discovered that, when alcohol is effectively free of charge, a fifth of British construction workers will regularly go to bed so drunk that they are incontinent both of urine and feces. I remember one man who very rarely got as far as his bed at night: he fell asleep in the lavatory, where he was usually found the next morning. Half the men shook in the mornings and resorted to the hair of the dog to steady their hands before they drove their bulldozers and other heavy machines (which they frequently wrecked, at enormous expense to the British taxpayer); hangovers were universal. The men were either drunk or hung over for months on end.

Sure, construction workers are notoriously liable to drink heavily, but in these circumstances even formerly moderate drinkers turned alcoholic and eventually suffered from delirium tremens. The heavy drinking occurred not because of the isolation of the African bush: not only did the company provide sports facilities for its workers, but there were many other ways to occupy oneself there. Other groups of workers in the bush whom I visited, who did not have the same rights of importation of alcoholic drink but had to purchase it at normal prices, were not nearly as drunk. And when the company asked its workers what it could do to improve their conditions, they unanimously asked for a further reduction in the price of alcohol, because they could think of nothing else to ask for.

The conclusion was inescapable: that a susceptible population had responded to the low price of alcohol, and the lack of other effective restraints upon its consumption, by drinking destructively large quantities of it. The health of many men suffered as a consequence, as did their capacity for work; and they gained a well-deserved local reputation for reprehensible, violent, antisocial behavior.

It is therefore perfectly possible that the demand for drugs, including opiates, would rise dramatically were their price to fall and their availability to increase. And if it is true that the consumption of these drugs in itself predisposes to criminal behavior (as data from our clinic suggest), it is also possible that the effect on the rate of criminality of this rise in consumption would swamp the decrease that resulted from decriminalization. We would have just as much crime in aggregate as before, but many more addicts. . . .

Even the legalizers' argument that permitting the purchase and use of drugs as freely as Milton Friedman suggests will necessarily result in less governmental and other official interference in our lives doesn't stand up. To the contrary, if the use of narcotics and stimulants were to become virtually universal, as is by no means impossible, the number of situations in which compulsory checks upon people would have to be carried out, for reasons of public safety, would increase enormously. Pharmacies, banks, schools, hospitals—indeed, all organizations dealing with the public—might feel obliged to check regularly and randomly on the drug consumption of their employees. The general use of such drugs would increase the locus standi of innumerable agencies, public and private, to interfere in our lives; and freedom from interference, far from having increased, would have drastically shrunk.

The present situation is bad, undoubtedly; but few are the situations so bad that they cannot be made worse by a wrong policy decision.

The extreme intellectual elegance of the proposal to legalize the distribution and consumption of drugs, touted as the solution to so many problems at once (AIDS, crime, overcrowding in the prisons, and even the attractiveness of drugs to foolish young people) should give rise to skepticism. Social problems are not usually like that. Analogies with the Prohibition era, often drawn by those who would legalize drugs, are false and inexact: it is one thing to attempt to ban a substance that has been in customary use for centuries by at least nine-tenths of the adult population, and quite another to retain a ban on substances that are still not in customary use, in an attempt to ensure that they never do become customary. Surely we have already slid down enough slippery slopes in the last 30 years without looking for more such slopes to slide down.

# EXPLORING THE ISSUE

## Should "Recreational" Drugs Be Legalized?

### Critical Thinking and Reflection

1. How harmful are illegal drugs? Are they more dangerous than alcohol? Can we distinguish among them, in order to relax and end some prohibitions and retain others? Is greater enforcement possible?
2. Is the history of the prohibition of alcohol relevant in revealing the consequences of prohibition? Are the indicted substances sufficiently different so that comparisons are not useful?
3. In view of crowded prisons, should we consider alternative means of punishment for some categories of drug offenders? Does prohibition inspire its violation?
4. Why shouldn't we have a civil right to do what may be harmful to ourselves?

### Is There Common Ground?

Advocates of legalization mostly believe that it must be accompanied by restraints on drug usage. Just as alcohol is subject to restrictions regarding its manufacturing and sale, and states vary in their requirements regarding the sale of alcohol, so legal drugs may be subject to strict controls. Absolute libertarians will dissent, arguing that there should be no regulation, but a vast majority of Americans would disagree. It would be likely that legalization would involve laws on purity of contents and other requirements that apply to alcohol and other legal drugs.

It is possible that supporters of prohibition may distinguish among the illicit drugs based on present awareness of their different effects. Defenders of drug prohibition might consent to the sale of medical marijuana, due to the claim that its use can reduce the pain of certain diseases. However, the experience in California and elsewhere is that licensing medical marijuana is likely to lead to the easy medical dispensing of medical marijuana to persons who are not legally entitled to it.

### Additional Resources

The *National Review* on February 12, 1996 published an interesting collection of essays in support of drug legalization. William F. Buckley, Jr., the founder and editor of *National Review,* refers to drug prohibition as a "plague." The other essays are by a former political science professor, a big city mayor, a former chief of police, a district judge, a psychiatrist, and a law professor. Together they provide a comprehensive consideration of virtually all of the social, moral, and political issues involved in drug restriction and toleration. James Ostrowski, "Thinking About Drug Legalization," in the *Cato Policy Analysis,* May 25, 1989, concludes that the overall crime rate has increased as a result of prohibition. Other Cato Institute analyses are available on the Internet. Joel Gray, in "The Case for Legalizing All Drugs Is Unanswerable," in *The Observer,* September 11, 2009, goes further in arguing that narcotics profits fuel war and terrorism.

Those who would continue to wage the war on drugs, with more criminal prosecution, and with more success, urge that we retain drug prohibition. Robert Maginnis has sought to refute each of the arguments for legalization in his on-line essay, "Legalization of Drugs: The Myths and the Facts." The Office of National Drug Control Policy, in "2003 National Drug Control Policy," argued that marijuana is a gateway drug (that is, that it leads to the use of more dangerous drugs). The federal Drug Enforcement Agency (DEA) has published online a number of essays arguing that marijuana is a dangerous drug that has a high potential for abuse. The DEA has noted that medical organizations have rejected the use of marijuana as a medicine.

# Internet References . . .

In addition to the Internet sites listed below, type in key words, such as "China military threat," "American world leadership," "torture," or "Middle Eastern profiling" to find other listings.

## U.S. State Department

View this site for understanding into the workings of a major U.S. executive branch department. Links explain exactly what the department does, what services it provides, and what it says about U.S. interests around the world, as well as provide other information.

**www.state.gov**

## Marketplace of Political Ideas/University of Houston Libraries

Here is a valuable collection of links to campaign, conservative/liberal perspectives, and political party sites. There are general political sites, Democratic sites, Republican sites, third-party sites, and much more.

**http://info.lib.uh.edu/politics/markind:htm**

## United States Senate Committee on Foreign Relations

This site is an excellent up-to-date resource for information about the United States' reaction to events regarding foreign policy.

**www.senate.gov/~foreign/**

## Woodrow Wilson School of Public and International Affairs

This center of scholarship in public and international affairs, based at Princeton University, sponsors more than twenty research centers. Among its many links is the Princeton Center for Globalization and Governance, which explores the academic and policy dimensions of globalization and international governance.

**www.wws.princeton.edu/mission/mission.html**

## American Diplomacy

*American Diplomacy* is an online journal of commentary, analysis, and research on U.S. foreign policy and its results around the world.

**www.unc.edu/depts/diplomat/**

## Foreign Affairs

This page of the well-respected foreign policy journal *Foreign Affairs* is a valuable research tool. It allows users to search the journal's archives and provides indexed access to the field's leading publications, documents, online resources, and so on. Link to dozens of other related Web sites from here too.

**www.foreignaffairs.org**

# UNIT 4

# America and the World

*A*t one time the United States could isolate itself from much of the world, and it did. But today's America affects and is affected—for good or ill—by what happens anywhere on the planet. Whether the topic is ecology, finance, war, or terrorism, America is integrally tied to the rest of the world. The United States, then, simply has no choice but to act and react in relation to a constantly shifting series of events; the arguments turn on over whether it acts morally or immorally, wisely or foolishly, what methods are morally justified in protecting the American homeland from attack? Do they include warrantless wiretapping and indefinite detention of suspected terrorists? Does global warming caused by humans threaten the future of the planet, and, if so, what responsibility does the United States have in the international effort to curb it?

- Is Indefinite Detention of Suspected Terrorists Justified?
- Do We Need to Curb Global Warming?
- Is Warrantless Wiretapping Ever Justified to Protect National Security?

# ISSUE 19

## Is Indefinite Detention of Suspected Terrorists Justified?

**YES: Jack Goldsmith**, from "Long-Term Terrorist Detention and a U.S. National Security Court," *Legislating the War on Terror: An Agenda for Reform* (Brookings Institution Press, 2009)

**NO: Sarah H. Cleveland**, from "The Legal, Moral and National Security Consequences of 'Prolonged Detention,'" *Subcommittee on the Constitution of the U.S. Senate Committee on the Judiciary* (June 9, 2009)

### ISSUE SUMMARY

**YES:** Former Department of Justice attorney Jack Goldsmith argues that, in dealing with terrorism, the elective branches have the authority and justification to establish procedures for noncriminal military detention of an extended nature.

**NO:** Department of State counselor Sarah H. Cleveland believes that unlimited detention of suspected terrorists does not contribute to national security, while it undermines the constitutional defense of habeas corpus.

**S**eptember 11, 2001 was the day that changed the United States forever. It was, of course, the tragic day on which four American commercial airplanes carrying passengers were hijacked by nineteen terrorists who crashed two of the planes into the World Trade Center skyscrapers in New York City, a third into the Pentagon in Washington, D.C., and the fourth into an open field in rural Pennsylvania. More than 3,000 people died. Ever since, Americans have been cautioned to be alert to suspicious acts, to state their business on entering major office buildings, to submit to inspection of their luggage and laptop computers, and even to personal searches before boarding planes.

As America turned to confront a danger it had never before encountered, the nation has had to reexamine the balance between liberty and security. Combating terrorist groups involved something other than conventional warfare waged against the uniformed army of a foreign power. In the absence of open aggressive action, it is difficult to identify an enemy that knows no national boundaries, carries no nation's flag, acts secretly and strikes suddenly.

To combat these enemies, Congress authorized President George W. Bush to retaliate. When suspected terrorists were captured, they were questioned in order to learn where and how and against whom the United States and its allies should retaliate. Many suspects were sent to the U.S. base at Guantànamo Bay in Cuba, not within the United States and yet clearly subject to American military rule. The Bush administration concluded that the Geneva Conventions (to which the United States is a signatory), which prescribed humane treatment of prisoners, did not apply to terrorists who were not lawful combatants.

At different times since 9/11, suspected terrorists captured by American military forces and the CIA (Central Intelligence Agency) have been subjected to unusual and sometimes cruel treatment—physical punishment, sleep deprivation, humiliating circumstances, waterboarding (simulated drowning)—in the hope of obtaining valuable information.

Apart from harsh interrogation techniques, the most fundamental challenge to American law came in the denial of habeas corpus, the right of a prisoner to be brought before a judge and to learn the charges on which he is held. The American Constitution states that the right to habeas corpus can be suspended only when the public safety requires it as a result of rebellion or invasion. It has been very rarely suspended.

When the U.S. Supreme Court stated in 2004 (in *Hamdi v. Rumsfeld*) that habeas corpus extends beyond domestic boundaries, Congress sought to enhance presidential power to limit prisoners' rights. Some prisoners were handed over to foreign nations, where there would be no American oversight to curb cruel, inhuman, and degrading treatment. Their confinement rarely resulted in prosecutions and often resulted in indefinite detention. In 2006 (in *Hamdan v. Rumsfeld*), the Supreme Court concluded that the procedures of military commissions violated the Uniform Code and the Geneva Conventions, and that prisoners must be tried under regularly constituted courts-martial.

The difficulty of safeguarding the United States while respecting the rights of accused persons was evident in the initial actions of President Barack Obama, when he inherited his predecessor's policies. Obama proposed several categories of prisoners—those who could be criminally prosecuted, those who should be transferred for prosecution by another country, those who could be settled in other than their native country because of their fear of punishment, and those who would need to be accepted by the United States—leaving those too dangerous to be released, but who cannot be tried. In refusing to release torture allegations by a former Guantànamo Bay prisoner and seeking to prevent disclosure of secret actions, President Obama seemed to concur to some extent with the Bush administration's defense of indefinite detention.

In the following selections, Jack Goldsmith supports indefinite detention because it reflects the need to find new methods of dealing with new dangers the nation has never before experienced. Sarah Cleveland rejects indefinite detention both as an unworkable solution of a difficult issue of national security and unwarranted as a violation of American law.

# YES ⬅

## Long-Term Terrorist Detention and a U.S. National Security Court

The principle that a nation at war has the power to hold members of the enemy's armed forces until the cessation of hostilities is as old as warfare itself and should be uncontroversial. The purpose of military detention, former Justice Sandra Day O'Connor explained in 2004, "is to prevent captured individuals from returning to the field of battle and taking up arms once again." As the Nuremberg Tribunal noted, the capture and detention of enemy soldiers is "neither revenge, nor punishment, but solely protective custody, the only purpose of which is to prevent the prisoners of war from further participation in the war. Military detention of enemy soldiers is the military equivalent of the long-standing practice of noncriminal administrative or preventive detention of dangerous persons such as the mentally ill, those infected with contagious diseases, or sexual predators.

The wisdom of the rule of detention becomes clear as more is learned about what has happened to some of the Guantánamo detainees who have been released. Although reports about the severity of the problem differ, it is clear that a good number of the detainees released on the grounds that they were "nondangerous" have ended up back on the battlefield, shooting at Americans or non-American civilians abroad. One such person, Said Ali al-Shihri, became the deputy leader of al Qaeda's Yemeni branch and is suspected of involvement in the 2008 bombing of the U.S. embassy in Yemen.

Yet if the detention rule is so clear, why is the use of detention so controversial in the war against al Qaeda and its affiliates? One reason is that many observers believe that the nation is not, or cannot be, at war with nonstate actors. That is simply wrong. The United States has fought congressionally authorized wars against nonstate actors such as slave traders and pirates. During the Mexican-American War, the Civil War, and the Spanish-American War, U.S. military forces engaged military opponents who had no formal connection to the state enemy. Presidents also have used force against nonstate actors outside of congressionally authorized conflicts. President McKinley's use of military force to put down the Chinese Boxer Rebellion was directed primarily at nonstate actors. President Wilson sent more than 7,000 U.S. troops into Mexico to pursue Pancho Villa, the leader of a band of rebels opposed to the recognized Mexican government. And President Clinton authorized cruise missile strikes

From *Legislating the War on Terror: An Agenda for Reform* by Benjamin Wittes, ed. (Brookings Institution Press, 2009), pp. 76–80, 93. Copyright © 2009 by Georgetown University Law Center and Brookings Institution Press. Reprinted by permission.

against al Qaeda targets in Sudan and Afghanistan. In all of those instances, presidents, acting in their role as commander-in-chief, exercised full military powers against nonstate actors—sometimes with congressional authorization and sometimes without.

Consistent with those precedents, every branch of the U.S. government today agrees that the nation is in an "armed conflict" (the modern legal term for "war") with al Qaeda, its affiliates, and other Islamist militants in Afghanistan, Iraq, and elsewhere. Former president Bush took that view in September 2001, and President Obama shows no sign of adopting a different stance. Congress embraced the same view in the September 2001 Authorization for Use of Military Force (AUMF) and reaffirmed it in the Military Commissions Act of 2006 (MCA). And the Supreme Court has stated or assumed that the country is at war many times.

Why, then, has there been so much controversy about holding enemy soldiers in Guantánamo? Part of the reason is the suspicion of abuse of prisoners there. But even if there were no such suspicions, the war on terror has three characteristics that, taken together, make a military detention authority problematic:

—First, in most prior wars, it was easy to determine who was a member of the enemy armed forces because those people wore uniforms and usually fought for a nation-state. In this war, the enemy wears no uniforms and blends in with civilians. That unfortunate fact dramatically increases the possibility of erroneous detention.

—Second, this war, unlike any other in U.S. history, seems likely to continue indefinitely; indeed, no one knows what the end of the war will look like. That means, among other things, that mistaken detentions might result in the long-term or even indefinite detention of an innocent person.

—Third, even if mistakes are not made, indefinite detention without charge or trial strikes many as an excessive remedy for "mere" membership in an enemy terrorist organization, especially since a detainee may, after some period, no longer pose a threat to the United States.

These three concerns do nothing to eliminate the need for detention to prevent detainees from returning to the battlefield, but they do challenge the traditional detention paradigm. And while many observers believe that the country can meet that need by giving trials to everyone that it wants to detain and then incarcerating those individuals under a theory of conviction rather than of military detention, I disagree. For many reasons, it is too risky for the U.S. government to deny itself the traditional military detention power altogether and commit itself instead to trying or releasing *every* suspected terrorist.

For one thing, military detention will be necessary in Iraq and Afghanistan for the foreseeable future. For another, the country likely cannot secure convictions of all of the dangerous terrorists at Guantánamo, much less all future dangerous terrorists, who legitimately qualify for noncriminal military detention. The evidentiary and procedural standards of trials, civilian and military alike, are much higher than the analogous standards for detention. With some terrorists too menacing to set free, the standards will prove difficult to satisfy. Key evidence in a given case may come from overseas, and verifying it, understanding its provenance, or establishing its chain of custody in the manner typically required in criminal trials may be difficult. That problem is exacerbated when evidence is gathered on a battlefield or during an armed skirmish, and it only grows larger when the evidence is old and stale. And perhaps most important, the use of such evidence in a criminal process may compromise intelligence sources and methods, requiring the disclosure of the identities of confidential sources or the nature of intelligence-gathering techniques.

Opponents of noncriminal detention observe that despite these considerations, the government has successfully prosecuted some al Qaeda terrorists—in particular, Zacharias Moussaoui and Jose Padilla. That is true, but it does not follow that prosecutions are achievable in every case in which disabling a terrorist suspect is a surpassing government interest. Moreover, the Moussaoui and Padilla prosecutions highlight an underappreciated cost of trials, at least in civilian courts. Those trials were messy affairs that stretched, and some observers believe broke, ordinary U.S. criminal trial conceptions of conspiracy and the rights of the accused, among other things. The Moussaoui trial, for example, watered down the important constitutional right of the defendant to confront witnesses against him in court, and the Padilla trial rested on an unprecedentedly broad conception of conspiracy law. An important cost of trying all cases is that the prosecution will invariably bend the law in ways that are unfavorable to civil liberties and due process, and those changes, in turn, will invariably spill over into nonterrorist prosecutions, thus skewing the larger criminal justice process.

A final problem with using any trial system, civilian or military, as the sole lawful basis for terrorist detention is that the trials can result in short sentences (as the first military commission trial did) or even acquittal of a dangerous terrorist. In criminal trials, defendants often go free because of legal technicalities, government inability to introduce probative evidence, and other factors besides the defendant's innocence. These factors are all exacerbated in terrorist trials by the difficulty of getting information from the place of capture, by restrictions on access to classified information, and by stale or tainted evidence. One way to get around the problem is to assert the authority, as the Bush administration did, to use noncriminal military detention for persons acquitted or given sentences too short to neutralize the danger that they pose. But such authority would undermine the whole purpose of trials and render them a sham. As a result, putting a suspect on trial can make it hard to detain terrorists that the government deems dangerous. For example, the government would have had little trouble defending the indefinite detention of Salim Hamdan, Osama bin Laden's driver, under a military detention rationale. Having put him on trial before a military commission, however, it was stuck with the light sentence that Hamdan has now completed at home in Yemen.

As a result of these problems, insistence on the exclusive use of criminal trials and the elimination of noncriminal detention would significantly raise the chances of releasing dangerous terrorists who would return to kill Americans or others. Since noncriminal military detention is clearly a legally available option—at least if it is expressly authorized by Congress and includes adequate procedural guarantees—that risk should be unacceptable. In past military conflicts, the release of an enemy soldier posed risks. But they were not dramatic risks, for there was only so much damage a lone actor or small group of individuals could do. Today, however, that lone actor can cause far more destruction and mayhem, because technological advances are creating ever-smaller and ever-deadlier weapons. It would be astounding if the pre–9/11 U.S. legal system had struck the balance between security and liberty in a manner that precisely and adequately addressed the modern threats posed by asymmetric warfare. Today the country faces threats from individuals that are of a different magnitude than the threats posed by individuals in the past; government authorities should reflect that change.

Nonetheless, in supplementing its trial system with a detention system, the United States must design the detention system with careful attention to the three problems with detentions identified above: the possibility of detaining an innocent person, the indefinite duration of the war, and the possibility that terrorists will become less dangerous over time. While those problems do not argue for eliminating military detention, they do not argue for simply abiding by the Geneva Conventions either. A dirty little secret is that the United States already provides the Guantánamo detainees with rights that far exceed the requirements of the Geneva Conventions. That said, it does not offer enough process to overcome the anxieties that the three problems generate. The problems with indefinite detention for modern terrorists argue for a more rigorous process and for higher standards than were available for noncriminal military detention in past wars with nation-states. They argue as well for individualizing both the detention assessment and the determination of which detainees are ready for release. They argue, in short, for updating the traditional military detention model to address the novel problems presented by terrorism and to ensure that it is consistent with modern notions of due process . . .

Once one accepts the need for some system of noncriminal military detention, suddenly much less is at stake in the debate over a national security court than the heat generated by that debate would suggest. That is because any system of long-term noncriminal detention of terrorists must and will be supervised by federal judges. At a minimum, federal judges will exercise constitutional habeas corpus jurisdiction over the incarceration of suspected terrorists, thereby having the final legal say over any detention system. In addition, Congress will likely establish statutory federal court review over any detention program that it establishes, as it has already attempted to do once. So one way or another, Article III judges will be in the detention game, helping to regularize, legalize, and legitimize the detention process while reviewing the adequacy of the factual basis for each detention judgment. . . .

Almost five years ago, the 9/11 Commission stated that "Americans should not settle for incremental, ad hoc adjustments to a system designed generations ago for a world that no longer exists." And yet that is precisely what the country has done since the commission published those words. It is time for the president and Congress to work together to address the terrorist detention problem in a comprehensive way. If a detention system becomes part of the solution, as I believe it should, then a national security court will be part of the solution as well. It is far better to have a well-designed national security court—a court designed in a systematic way by political leaders—than to have courts making ad hoc decisions in the rough-and-tumble of high-stakes litigation.

Sarah H. Cleveland

 **NO**

# The Legal, Moral and National Security Consequences of 'Prolonged Detention'

To the world, Guantanamo is not a place. Guantanamo stands for prolonged detention outside accepted standards of the rule of law and fundamental justice. "Closing Guantanamo" therefore requires more than simply closing a particular prison facility. It requires fundamentally redirecting U.S. policy regarding terrorism suspects. If this Administration closes Guantanamo by creating another system of prolonged detention without trial—even a system with substantially more extensive procedural protections—to the world Guantanamo will have been remade in its own image. . . .

The U.S. Supreme Court concluded in *Hamdi v. Rumsfeld* that international law allows states to apprehend enemy troops in a traditional conflict and to hold them until the end of that conflict. The United States urgently needs to adopt procedural protections for such detentions consistent with our Constitution, the law of the territorial state, and international humanitarian and human rights law, through a status of forces agreement with Afghanistan or equivalent regime. But rather than detentions in Afghanistan, it is the claim of a roving power to detain persons seized outside a traditional theater of combat that has brought the United States widespread international condemnation, eroded our moral authority, and inspired new converts to terrorism. . . .

## I. Prolonged Detention Is Unwarranted as a Matter of Law and Policy

Our Constitution does not recognize a roving power to detain dangerous persons as a substitute for criminal trial. "Liberty is the norm" under our legal system, and the protection of personal liberty against arbitrary confinement is one of the hallmarks of our Constitution. The "charge and conviction" paradigm—with its network of constraints on governmental power—is the norm. Predictions of future dangerousness, unlike proof of past criminal acts, are notoriously unreliable. While the government has been recognized as having authority to confine persons without criminal charge in certain historically circumscribed exceptions, such as civil commitment and

From the U.S. Senate, June 9, 2009.

quarantine for public health purposes, these exceptions have been "carefully limited" and "sharply focused." Danger alone has never sufficed; nor has the government's understandable desire to overcome the barriers imposed by the Constitution on prosecution or conviction.

The power to detain enemy belligerents until the end of an armed conflict, long recognized under international humanitarian law, is one such exception. This authority is based on the presumption that the exigencies of armed conflict require a power to detain—because privileged belligerents cannot be criminally prosecuted for waging war; because even where criminal prosecution is available, evidence is difficult to properly preserve and an obligation to prosecute would be disruptive to ongoing military operations, and because from a humanitarian perspective, incapacitating killing enemy soldiers through detention is preferable to killing them.

Such detention, however, traditionally has been constrained by four presumptions: (1) Enemy belligerents are easy to identify, thus limiting the possibility of error. In a traditional international armed conflict, enemy belligerents are generally identifiable through objective indicia: they wear the uniform or insignia of the enemy state; they carry the passport or identification of that state; they are captured while waging war on behalf of the enemy state. (2) The conflict will be limited to a geographically defined space. (3) Detention may last only until the end of the conflict. (4) Detention may only be for the purpose of preventing return to the battlefield. . . .

This authority to detain becomes stretched impossibly, however, when extended to persons seized outside a theater of armed conflict. The risk of error becomes exponentially greater. Persons who are seized outside the area of conflict, while not directly participating in armed conflict, but while in their homes, at work, or on the street, lack any objective indicia of combatency, making the lack of criminal process to determine their culpability all the more problematic. The military imperatives that justify tolerating detention in armed conflict also do not pertain. Outside of the theater of combat the regular criminal justice system is more readily available. Ordinary courts presumably are open and functioning at the locus of the arrest, as well as in the United States. Military exigencies do not complicate the preservation of evidence, and pursuing such a criminal prosecution does not disrupt ongoing military operations.

These considerations are further compounded if the claimed conflict is a "global" conflict against al Qaeda, the Taliban and affiliated groups—participants are much harder to identify, the enemy is not geographically contained, and an "end" to the conflict may not occur in our lifetime. The President recognized in his May 21 speech that "we know this threat will be with us for a long time." Under these circumstances even if non-battlefield detentions could be contemplated under the international law of armed conflict, they likely would be unconstitutional. Falling far outside any traditional exceptions to the charge-and-conviction paradigm, the circumstances of non-battlefield criminal acts simply do not provide a compelling justification for permitting the government to circumvent the traditional constraints of the criminal law.

## II. Comparative Prolonged Detention Is Not Supported by Our Democratic Allies

Prolonged detention of non-battlefield detainees is viewed as illegitimate by the advanced democracies who are our allies and undermines their cooperation with our global counterterrorism efforts. Proponents of a new U.S. system of "preventive detention" often claim that other countries employ similar tactics. But . . . no other European or North American democracy has resorted to long-term detention without charge outside of the deportation context. . . .

Adoption of a prolonged detention regime in the face of rejection of such a system by our European and Canadian allies will undermine their willingness to cooperate with the United States in intelligence sharing and the transfer of terrorism suspects, as well as in the relocation of Guantanamo detainees. European allies participating in the conflict in Afghanistan already transfer persons who are seized directly to Afghan custody, rather than transfer them to the United States. . . .

Most important, there is no evidence that preventive detention works. Comparative studies of terrorism stretching back more than twenty years have concluded that draconian measures—such as prolonged detention without trial—are not proven to reduce violence, and can actually be counterproductive. . . .

Indefinite detention is indeed a hallmark of repressive regimes such as Egypt, Libya, and Syria, which presently hold hundreds of people in prolonged detention, as well as notorious past regimes such as apartheid-era South Africa, which held tens of thousands of government opponents in preventive detention as security threats during the last decades of white rule. The use of prolonged detention also commonly goes hand-in-hand with other forms of human rights abuse such as the use of torture and cruel, inhuman or degrading treatment. . . .

The critical question for our country going forward is whether we will break with these past practices sufficiently to restore our credibility as an international leader in human rights. By contrast, if the United States accepts the premise that we may incarcerate people without trial in order to keep us safe, we would encourage other government's use of prolonged detention in response to security threats, both real and perceived. This could be equally true for a country like Mexico in addressing violent drug-related activities and for Russia in dealing with Chechen rebels. . . .

In sum, should the United States take the unprecedented step of implementing indefinite detention without trial for terrorism suspects, it would have profound consequences for the rule of law globally and for U.S. foreign policy. By acting outside accepted legal standards, we would embolden other nations with far worse human rights records to adopt sweeping regimes for long-term detention. Further erosion of the rule of law in nations such as Egypt and Pakistan could further destabilize these states, with dire consequences for global security. Moreover, taking a position so far out of step with our European and North American allies would undermine our ability to gain their critical cooperation in international counterterrorism efforts.

# III. Closing Guantanamo Does Not Warrant Establishing a New Detention Regime

Guantanamo should never have happened, and the fundamental errors of law and policy that led to its creation are well known: the Administration claimed a sweeping power to detain terrorism suspects from around the globe; detainees were denied relevant protections of the Geneva conventions, including the protection of Common Article III; detainees were denied any legal process to determine the validity of their detention—including habeas corpus and the minimal determination required under Article V of the Third Geneva Convention; detainees were denied the protection of the U.S. Constitution and international human rights law; and torture and cruel, inhuman or degrading treatment were employed to justify detention and to extract information.

Guantanamo has created massive problems not of this Administration's creation. But given the fundamental violations of basic rights that have occurred on Guantanamo, we cannot "close" Guantanamo without making a sharp break with the past and renouncing prolonged detention of the Guantanamo detainees, regardless of any procedural trappings that might now be provided.

So what alternatives are available to us? The path for closing Guantanamo has been well hewn by others. We should criminally prosecute those who have violated our criminal laws. Persons whom we decide not to prosecute but who have violated the laws of other states may be transferred to those countries for trial, with meaningful assurances that due process and international human rights law will be respected. Persons found eligible for release whose home country will not take them or who cannot be returned due to a fear that they will be tortured may be transferred to a third country, if necessary with assurances protecting their security (including monitoring by multiple parties such as U.S. embassy personnel and the International Committee of the Red Cross). If necessary, others may be transferred to third countries with conditions that they will be placed under some form of monitoring, subject always to due process and human rights guarantees. And as controversial as this is for some segments of the American public, some of the detainees will need to be accepted by the U.S. The European Union, for example, has made it clear that U.S. acceptance of some responsibility for the Guantanamo detainees is a condition for its assistance.

We must continue to challenge the premise that there is a fifth category of detainees who are "too dangerous to be released, but who cannot be tried." The proposal for prolonged detention remains a solution in search of a problem. As other witnesses are attesting at this hearing, there is no evidence that our criminal justice system is not up to the task of trying terrorism suspects. . . .

Certainly, the fact that a person was tortured in detention, or that a person was detained on the basis of information extracted by torture, cannot be a proper basis for prolonged detention, given that we have renounced coerced evidence as a basis for prosecution. To conclude that a person who could not be prosecuted as a result of torture could nevertheless be detained indefinitely on that basis would illegitimate U.S. efforts in the struggle to abolish torture and to promote fair trial process around the world.

The fact that a detention may be based on hearsay similarly highlights the unreliability of the basis for detention. Our rules of evidence excluding hearsay, entitling defendants to confront the evidence against them, and requiring proof beyond a reasonable doubt, are designed to ensure accuracy and to prevent people from being incarcerated in error. On the other hand, if the option of long-term detention without trial is available, the temptation will always exist for the government to decide that difficult cases "cannot be tried," and thus to skirt the strictures of the criminal process. But a legal regime that allows a government to guarantee that persons it fears will be incarcerated is not a regime based on the rule of law. . . .

I understand that federal criminal trials of Guantanamo detainees might be fraught for any number of evidentiary reasons, might be embarrassing, might result in acquittals, and might provide the accused with legal and public relations leverage they may not enjoy in a different forum. But many of these inconveniences will arise in any judicial process, including one designed to implement prolonged detention, and most have proven not to be deal breakers in the more than 100 international terrorism cases tried in our federal courts.

Even if a category five person does exist, the overall costs to our national security of establishing a scheme of indefinite detention without trial are greater than any potential benefit, given the departure from historic American legal protections against arbitrary detention, and the fact that such detentions will likely apply to a disproportionately Islamic population and will complicate the ability of allies to cooperate in intelligence sharing and the transfer of terrorism suspects.

Finally, and perhaps most critically, our mistakes of the past must not be allowed to drive mistakes of the future. There are at least three reasons why the problems we confront today on Guantanamo should not be problems going forward:

1. *Torture will not be used.* The President has reaffirmed that the United States renounces torture and cruel treatment. To the extent that criminal prosecutions of the current detainees is complicated by the fact that they were detained based on testimony coerced from themselves or others, this should not be a problem in the future.

2. *Future evidence can be preserved.* The Guantanamo detainees were seized and transferred to Guantanamo with the erroneous expectation that they would never appear before any court, let alone be criminally prosecuted. If terrorism suspects are seized in the future with the expectation that they must be criminally tried, evidence and the chain of custody can be properly preserved.

3. *The criminal law is available.* We now have broader laws criminalizing terrorist activity outside the United States than existed prior to September 11, 2001. Given the breadth, flexibility and extraterritorial reach of our criminal laws in the context of counterterrorism, including our material support and conspiracy laws, it is hard to imagine conduct that could justify administrative detention in accordance with a properly circumscribed interpretation of our Constitution and international humanitarian or human rights law, and yet fall below the threshold for prosecution. If the evidence we have against someone

is insufficient to prosecute under these standards, it is an insufficient basis for detention. . . .

Prolonged detention without trial offends the world's most basic sense of fairness. Our government acquires its legitimacy, and its moral authority as a leader in both counterterrorism efforts and human rights, by acting in accordance with law. President Obama proposes to establish prolonged detention within the rule of law. But skating at the edge of legality was the hallmark of the counterterrorism policies of the past Administration; it should not be the hallmark of this one. For the United States to ratify the principle that our government may hold people indefinitely based on the claim that they cannot be tried but are too dangerous to be released, would be, as Justice Robert Jackson warned in his dissent in *Korematsu,* to leave a loaded weapon lying around ready to be picked up by any future government, at home or around the globe.

# EXPLORING THE ISSUE

## Is Indefinite Detention of Suspected Terrorists Justified?

## Critical Thinking and Reflection

1. In the post-9/11 world, do we need to find a new balance between individual liberties and national security? What are the limits of each?
2. What are we to do with terrorist suspects we cannot try in criminal courts without revealing information harmful to national security or to our agents and informers in the field?
3. In the current atmosphere, what are the advantages of using military tribunals to try high-level terrorist suspects? What considerations would argue against the use of such tribunals?

## Is There Common Ground?

For the time being there seems to be, if not common ground, at least a kind of suspension of hostilities between the two sides of this argument. That is the result of the case of Khalid Sheikh Mohammed (KSM), reportedly the mastermind of the 9/11 attacks. The Bush administration in 2008 began preparing a trial for KSM in a military tribunal at Guantanamo base in Cuba. This set off protests by human-rights groups, and in 2009 the Obama administration's Attorney General, Eric Holder, scrapped the military tribunal and began preparations to try KSM in a Manhattan federal court. This was stiffly resisted by New York-based politicians, including powerful Democrats such as Senator Charles Schumer. Reluctantly, Holder then retreated to the military tribunal option. The complaints from human rights groups have resumed, albeit in very muted fashion, perhaps because, with a presidential election pending, human rights groups are reluctant to criticize a president who has given much verbal support to their positions.

## Additional Resources

Laura K. Donahue, *The Cost of Counterterrorism: Power, Politics, and Liberty* (Cambridge University Press, 2008), suggests that the proliferation of biological and nuclear weapons may lead the United States and Great Britain to enact broadly restrictive measures. Professor Donahue is critical of some restrictions that have already been adopted.

U.S. Circuit Judge Richard Posner is more sympathetic to those restrictions, as he makes clear in the title of his book, *Not a Suicide Pact: The*

*Constitution in a Time of National Emergency* (Oxford University Press, 2006). Posner argues that terrorism is neither war nor crime and requires a recognition of measures that may be at the same time illegal and morally necessary.

A nuanced view of the difficult choices is made by Michael Ignatieff in *The Lesser Evil: Political Ethics in an Age of Terror* (Princeton University Press, 2004). He poses the dilemma that free nations confront: "When democracies fight terrorism, they are defending the proposition that their political life should be free of violence. But defeating terror requires violence. It may also require coercion, deception, secrecy, and violation of rights. How can democracies resort to these means without destroying the values for which they stand?" The USA Patriot Act of 2001 provoked the writing of thoughtful books that raise the very questions of law and security that the United States grapples with today. Among these are Howard Ball, *The USA Patriot Act of 2001: Balancing Civil Liberties and National Security: A Reference Handbook* (ABC-CLIO, 2004) and Amitai Etzioni, *How Patriotic Is the Patriot Act? Freedom versus Security in the Age of Terrorism* (Routledge, 2004).

More recent articles on opposing sides can be found in *Commentary, The New York Review of Books, The National Interest, The American Prospect, The National Review,* and *The Nation.*

344

# ISSUE 20

## Do We Need to Curb Global Warming?

**YES: Gregg Easterbrook**, from "Case Closed: The Debate About Global Warming Is Over," *Issues in Governance Studies* (June 2006)

**NO: Larry Bell**, from *Climate of Corruption: Politics and Power Behind the Global Warming Hoax* (Greenleaf Book Group, 2011)

### ISSUE SUMMARY

**YES:** Editor Gregg Easterbrook argues that global warming, causing deleterious changes in the human condition, is a near certainty for the next few generations.

**NO:** Professor Larry Bell insists that the climate models predicting global warming are speculative at best, and in some cases based upon manipulated data.

**W**hether or not he actually said it, Mark Twain has often been quoted as saying, "Everyone talks about the weather, but no one does anything about it." Today, many scientists and others think that we are doing something about it—something bad. Their contention is that, for roughly the last century, human activities have been generating increasing amounts of carbon dioxide and other "greenhouse gases," that these gases have been heating the planet, that these temperature increases are already having a deleterious effect on human and animal life, and, unless they are checked, may soon produce catastrophic and irreversible consequences for the planet.

The scientists who have reached these alarming conclusions have justified them in many densely argued presentations, papers, and published works. Other scientists, although apparently fewer in number, have dissented from some or all of those conclusions, and they, too, have marshaled the typical array of graphs, charts, and equations that scientists commonly use to illustrate their findings.

What is not in dispute between the two sides is that humans are producing increasing amounts of carbon dioxide from a wide variety of fuels, that the carbon content of the global atmosphere has been slowly increasing since early in the last century (although much of it was produced before

1940, when modern industry really started taking off), that carbon dioxide warms the lower troposphere, and that the globally averaged surface temperature of the Earth is at least 1 degree Fahrenheit warmer than it was about a century ago. What they disagree upon is whether the increase in average temperature is due to the increase in the production of carbon dioxide by humans.

Scientists, of course, disagree about many things, and their debates play a vital role in scientific progress. The natural inclination of nonscientists is to let them fight it out among themselves, in the expectation that the truth will eventually emerge. Why, then, include the topic of global warming in a book of political issues? Isn't that a little presumptuous?

It would be, if the topic concerned only the scientific community. If the argument were about the expansion of the universe or the speed of neutrinos, it would be better for students of politics to stand back and let the scientists sort it out. But the global warming debate is inescapably tied to politics because it involves the future of the human race. If man-made global warming is a fact, within a generation coastal cities like New York could be wiped out, gigantic farming regions could be destroyed by drought, tropical diseases like malaria could migrate north, and hurricanes the size of Katrina could become endemic; the only way to head off these consequences would be for the world's political leaders to take immediate steps to curtail the use of fossil fuels; they must take the lead in moving us toward electric cars, banning coal-fired power plants, and discouraging the burning of oil and its derivatives. But if the global warming alarm is bogus, the future of the planet faces a different but no less serious threat. In headlong pursuit of "green energy," governments would have to force major industries to either shut down or change over to largely untested energy sources like wind and solar. Unemployment, already at crisis levels, would quickly rise, and hard-pressed consumers would pay more for energy. So would nations as a whole in the industrialized world, as they spent hundreds of billions subsidizing developing countries to persuade them to follow the green path. The result could be stagnation in much of the developing world and economic ruin of the industrialized countries.

Either way, the stakes are much too high to leave the debate entirely up to the scientists. Not surprisingly, then, global warming has become a major political issue in domestic and international politics. On the world stage, green politics made its first major appearance in 1997, in Kyoto, Japan, where the heads of state of 191 nations met to negotiate what came to be known as the Kyoto Protocol. Its goal was to reduce worldwide greenhouse gases to 5.2 percent below 1990 levels between 2008 and 2012. To achieve that end, it set specific emission reductions targets for each industrialized nation, but excluded developing countries, even rapidly developing ones like India and China.

President Bill Clinton was one of the main authors of the Kyoto Protocol, but it never got much traction in the United States. Even before it was drafted, the U.S. Senate passed a resolution by 95-0 saying the United States should not sign any carbon-emission cuts that failed to apply to developing countries or that would "result in serious harm to the economy of the United States."

Clinton's successor, George W. Bush, declined even to submit Kyoto to the Senate for ratification.

Despite Congress's bipartisan wariness, Democrats have been more receptive than Republicans to Kyoto's spirit and intent. After the 2008 election of a Democratic president and a large Democratic majority in Congress, the green movement hoped to revive Kyoto by pushing for legislation that Democrats called "cap and trade." (Republicans called it "cap and tax.") This proposed law would set limits ("cap") on the total amount of greenhouse gases that could be emitted nationally. Those companies coming in under the allowable limits because of efficient emission controls could then sell ("trade") their leftover allowances to others lacking such controls.

Despite a 256-175 Democratic majority in the House, cap and trade passed by a slim 219-212 margin in June of 2009. Supporters were disappointed not only by the narrow margin but also by the tardiness of the whole process. The previous December, President Obama attended the United Nations Climate Change Conference in Copenhagen, Denmark, and he had hoped to be able to bring with him a copy of the United State's first cap-and-trade law. Arriving instead empty-handed, he tried to assure the other delegates that the legislation was in the pipeline, but the general mood of the meeting was gloomy; without guaranteed U.S. cooperation, the chances of meaningful international action against global warming were slim at best. The final blow to cap-and-trade came in July 2009, when the bill arrived in the Senate. Majority Leader Harry Reid decided not to bring it to the floor, saying that Republican opposition doomed any chances of passage. But some Democratic Senators, especially from coal-mining states, were also opposed to it.

Whatever the eventual fate of cap-and-trade and other measures aimed at curbing carbon emissions, the larger debate over global warming will continue until one side or the other prevails. That, however, is unlikely to happen soon, for both sides seem equally vigorous and confident in presenting their cases—as we see in the following selections. *New Republic* editor Gregg Easterbrook argues that global warming, causing deleterious changes in the human condition, is a near certainty for the next few generations; architecture professor Larry Bell insists that the climate models predicting global warming are speculative at best, and in some cases based upon manipulated data.

# YES ⬅

Gregg Easterbrook

# Case Closed: The Debate About Global Warming Is Over

. . .

## The Scientific Verdict Is In

When global-warming concerns became widespread, many argued that more scientific research was needed before any policy decisions. This was hardly just the contention of oil-company executives. "There is no evidence yet" of dangerous climate change, the National Academy of Sciences declared in 1991. A 1992 survey of members of the American Geophysical Union and American Meteorological Society, two professional groups of climatologists, found only 17 percent believed there was a sufficient ground to declare an artificial greenhouse effect in progress. In 1993 Thomas Karl, director of the National Climatic Data Center, said there exists "a great range of uncertainty" regarding whether the world is warming. My own contrarian 1995 book about environmental issues, *A Moment on the Earth,* spent 39 pages reviewing the nascent state of climate science and concluded that rising temperatures "might be an omen or might mean nothing." Like others, I called for more research.

That research is now in, and the scientific uncertainty that once justified skepticism has been replaced by near-unanimity among credentialed researchers that an artificially warming world is a real phenomenon posing real danger. The American Geophysical Union and American Meteorological Society, skeptical in 1992, in 2003 both issued statements calling signs of global warming compelling. In 2004 the American Association for the Advancement of Science declared in its technical journal *Science* that there is no longer any "substantive disagreement in the scientific community" that artificial global warming is happening and could become dangerous. In 2005, the National Academy of Sciences joined the science academies of the United Kingdom, Japan, Germany, China and other nations in a joint statement saying, "There is now strong evidence" that Data Center said research now supports "a substantial human impact on global temperature increases." And this month the Climate Change Science Program, the George W. Bush Administration's coordinating agency for global-warming research, declared it had found "clear evidence of human influences on the climate system."

Case closed.

In roughly the last decade, the evidence of artificial global warming has gone from sketchy to overpowering. That does not mean that substantial

From *Issues in Governance Studies,* June 2006. Copyright © 2006 by Brookings Institution Press. Reprinted by permission.

uncertainties don't remain. All researchers agree that knowledge of Earth's climate is rudimentary. (For instance, would a warming world be wetter or drier? Your guess is as good as the next Ph.D. climatologist's.) And considering that the most sophisticated meteorological computer models cannot predict the weather next week, computer predictions of future temperatures are expensive guesswork at best. But incomplete knowledge does not diminish the seriousness of climate change. Some continue to argue, "Because there are significant uncertainties, science cannot issue meaningful warnings about the greenhouse effect." This reasoning is akin to putting a live round in a revolver, spinning the chamber and saying, "Because there are significant uncertainties regarding the location of the bullet, firearms experts cannot issue meaningful warnings about whether to place the gun to your head." Warnings can be imperative even when much remains unknown.

Emissions of artificial greenhouse gases continue to rise at a brisk pace worldwide. Even if reforms are enacted, it seems cast in stone that sometime during the 21st century, atmospheric concentrations of carbon dioxide—the primary greenhouse gas emitted by human activity—will reach double their preindustrial level. This makes a warming world a near certainty for the next few generations.

# Would Artificial Global Warming Be Bad?

Bearing in mind that projections are speculation, the current scientific consensus estimate is that if carbon dioxide in the atmosphere doubles, global temperatures will increase by 4–6 degrees Fahrenheit during this century. Everything from pop-culture presentations of global warming to political and pundit commentary has assumed that such a warming world would be a place of horrors. The big-studio 2004 movie *The Day After Tomorrow* depicted an artificial greenhouse effect wiping out much of Western society in mere days. No effects remotely resembling what happened in *The Day After Tomorrow* have ever been observed in nature, and scientists viewed the movie as little more than two hours of pretentious drivel. While the sort of "instant doomsday" scenarios favored by global warming alarmists cannot be ruled out, they are highly unlikely.

Nor should it be assumed that a warming world would, in itself, be cause for concern. Consensus science shows the world has warmed about 1 degree Fahrenheit during the last century: that warming moderated global energy demand and lengthened growing seasons, both of which are positives. Some researchers think the warming of the 20th century extended the range of equatorial diseases. But even if this was so, the initial phase of artificial global warming appears to have had a net benefit.

Further warming would likely confer some additional benefits. A vast area of the former Soviet Union might open to agricultural production, while large permafrost regions in Russia and Canada might open to petroleum exploration or even residential development. (For the purposes of this briefing, we are contemplating only impacts on human society, skipping whether such possibilities as melting the permafrost may be good or bad in the abstract ecological sense.) Extended global warming might make Antarctica habitable again—before ice ages began, it was lush—thus adding an entire continent to the part of the world useful to people. And global warming might make my hometown of Buffalo, New York, a vacation paradise where Hollywood celebrities compete to snatch up prime lakefront real estate.

But though there could be benefits to a warming world, the bad is likely to outweigh the good. Here are the main dangers:

- **Significant extension of the range of equatorial diseases.** The equator is the world's most disease-prone region. If global temperatures rise by several degrees Fahrenheit, the equatorial disease zone may extend much farther north and south, further afflicting impoverished nations and increasing the odds that air travelers bring equatorial diseases with them to the northern and southern nations that today have low rates of most communicable illnesses.
- **Sea-level rise.** The 2005 statement by the National Academy of Sciences endorsed an estimate that artificial global warming will cause sea levels to rise from 4 to 35 inches in the coming century. The low end of that range would flood parts of Micronesia; the midpoint would inundate much of Bangladesh, and make the survival of New Orleans in any future hurricane problematic; the high end would flood coastal cities worldwide. Coastal cities could be abandoned and new cities built inland, but the cost would be breathtaking—and almost surely exceed the cost of reforms to slow greenhouse emissions in the first place.
- **Melting ice.** Melting glaciers and ice sheets may alter the primary Atlantic Ocean current that warms Europe, causing European Union nations to become significantly colder even as global average temperatures rise. Studies suggest that some Atlantic Ocean currents are already changing.
- **Altering the biology of the sea.** Major shifts of ocean currents have occurred in the past, and in the geologic record, are associated with mass extinctions of marine organisms. This suggests that greenhouse-induced changes in the oceans might harm fish stocks. While it is also possible that greenhouse-induced ocean current changes would be beneficial to fish stocks, the gamble is a major one, as much of the seas are already overfished and much of the developing world relies on fish for dietary protein.
- **Misery in poor nations.** Developing nations might be impacted by global warming much more than wealthy nations. Setting aside Antarctica, the largest chunks of the world's cold land mass are in Alaska, Canada, Greenland and Russia. Extended global warming might make these areas significantly more valuable, while rendering low-latitude poor nations close to uninhabitable. Summer temperatures of 110 degrees Fahrenheit are already common in Pakistan, where most of the population has no access to air conditioning and only sporadic electric power for fans. Imagine the human suffering if 115 degree days became common.

Beyond these concerns is the great danger of artificial global warming—namely, climate change. Global warming and climate change sound like the same thing, but are different. If the world became warmer while climate remained the same, the change would be manageable. In that scenario, the benefits might outweigh the harm. Significant climate change, by contrast, could cause awful problems.

The first danger of climate change involves storms and wind. Tropical storm activity is currently in an up cycle. Whether this is caused by artificial global warming or by natural variability is not known, but the weight of evidence points toward artificial greenhouse gases. Continued global warming may cause more and stronger hurricanes in the Atlantic and typhoons in the Pacific. More frequent or powerful tropical storms might not just wreak havoc with America's Gulf Coast cities; they could bring regular misery to coastal areas of Central America, Indonesia, Malaysia, Bangladesh and other nations. North and south of the tropical-storm band, tornadoes, strong thunderstorms and torrential rains might increase. (There are already indications that rainfall in much of North America is becoming less frequent but more intense.) If jet streams or other major winds increase, air travel and air cargo could be impacted or even become impractical during some parts of the year, and the globalized economy increasingly depends on air travel and air cargo.

The second danger of climate change lies in activating the unknown. We live in an "interglacial," a warm period between ice ages; our interglacial is called the Holocene. Ice-core readings from the interglacial period that preceded ours, called the Eemian, suggest that it was common then for global temperatures to shift from warm to cool and back again, with climate havoc ensuing. Why these shifts occurred is unknown. But during our era, Earth's climate has been magnificently stable—almost strangely so. For roughly the last 8,000 years, coinciding with the advent of the controlled agriculture on which civilization is based, global temperatures, ocean currents, rainfall patterns and the timing of the seasons have varied by only small amounts. Scientists don't know why the climate has been so stable during the last 8,000 years. We do know that stable climate is associated with civilization, while climate change is associated with mass extinctions. We would be fools to tempt that equation.

The third and gravest danger of climate change is disruption of global agriculture. The predicted Malthusian calamities of the postwar era have not occurred. For instance, none of the mass starvations predicted by Paul Ehrlich have happened, though the world population has doubled since Ehrlich said mass famines were just around the corner. The reason Malthusian calamities have not occurred is that global agricultural yields have increased faster than population growth. But the world's agricultural system is perilously poised, barely covering global needs. Suppose climate change shifted precipitation away from the breadbasket regions of the six food-producing continents, sending rain clouds instead to the world's deserts. Over the generations, society will adjust. But years or decades of global food shortages might stand between significant climate shifts and agricultural adjustment. Huge numbers of people might die of malnourishment, while chaos rendered impossible social progress in many developing nations and armies of desperate refugees came to the borders of the wealthy nations.

In 2005, the United Nations Food and Agriculture Organization reported that "chronic hunger is on the decline." Despite rising global population, malnourishment is now believed to be at the lowest level in human history. Because food is in oversupply in the West and malnutrition is declining generally, commentators have begun to take food supply for granted. Climate change that disrupts the agricultural system on which the global economy is based—and almost all successful nations are agricultural nations—could spark a worldwide calamity. Do we really want to stick a bullet into a revolver, spin the chamber and see what happens with global food production?

## Are There Cheap Solutions?

If you think the Kyoto Protocol on greenhouse gas emissions can save the world from artificial global warming, think again. The United States has withdrawn from the Kyoto mechanism—and advocating a reversal of that decision seems a waste of everyone's time, since there is no chance the Senate will ever ratify a treaty that grants the United Nations authority over U.S. domestic policymaking. The United States would ignore any attempt by the United Nations to exercise such authority, of course—but then why bother with an empty treaty? Most nations that have ratified the Kyoto treaty are merrily ignoring it. Canada, for example, frequently hectors the United States about being an environmental offender, yet its greenhouse gas emissions are currently 24 percent above the level mandated by Kyoto—and Ottawa has no meaningful program to change that. Canada's greenhouse gas emissions are also rising faster than greenhouse gas emissions in the United States. Even Japan, which staked much of its international prestige on an agreement signed in its glorious ancient capital city, is turning a blind eye to the treaty's requirements: Japan's emissions of greenhouse gases are 9 percent above the promised level.

At current rates only Russia, Germany and the United Kingdom are close to complying with the Kyoto mandates, and most of the compliance by Russia and Germany is the result of backdated credits for the closing of Warsaw Pact-era power plants and factories that had already been shuttered before the Kyoto agreement was initialed in 1997. Meanwhile, developing nations especially India and China are increasing their greenhouse gas emissions at prodigious rates—so much so that in the short term developing nations will swamp any reductions achieved by the West. Since 1990, India has increased its emissions of greenhouse gases by 70 percent and China by 49 percent, versus an 18 percent increase by the United States. China is on track to pass the United States as the leading emitter of artificial greenhouse gases. If current trends continue, the developing world will emit more greenhouse gases than the West by around 2025. And here's the real kicker: even if all the provisions of the Kyoto Protocol were enforced to perfection, atmospheric concentrations of greenhouse gases in the year 2050 would be only about 1 percent less than without the treaty.

These can sound like reasons to despair about combating artificial global warming, but they are not. Rather, they are reasons to shifts gears from the overly ponderous Kyoto approach to a market-driven, innovation-based approach. The latter approach may not only work much better than Kyoto but be relatively cheap. This is the Big Thought that's missing from the global warming debate: there may be an optimistic path that involves affordable reforms that do not stifle prosperity. Greenhouse gases are an air pollution problem[1] and *all* previous air pollution problems have been addressed much faster than expected, at much lower cost than projected.

True, previous air pollution problems have been national or regional in character; greenhouse gases are a global issue whose resolution must involve all nations. But this does not mean greenhouse gases cannot be overcome using the same tools that have worked against other air pollution problems. In the last 30 years, the United States has substantially reduced air pollution—during the same period the United States population and economy have both boomed. If air pollution can be reduced even as a national economy grows, there is good reason to hope that greenhouse gases can be reduced even as the global economy grows.

Nor do developing nations need an "era of pollution" in order to industrialize. In the 19th century, it was true that air pollution and industrialization were inexorably linked: then, the unregulated smokestack was essential to manufacturing advancement. Today power plants and factories are being built that emit only a fraction of the air pollution of their predecessors—and efficient, low-polluting facilities tend to have the highest rates of return. Already China to a great extent and India to a lesser extent are switching to low-pollution approaches to power production and manufacturing, observing that low-polluting industry not only is good for the environment but for the bottom line. Fifteen years ago, smog was rising at dangerous rates in Mexico City. Mexico adopted anti-pollution technology and now Mexico City smog is in decline, even as the city booms economically and its population grows. Such examples suggest that the air pollution controls that have worked so well in the United States can be expanded to the world. And if the whole world can act against air pollution, maybe the whole world can act against greenhouse gas.

Consider that a little more than three decades ago in the United States rising urban smog from automobiles was widely viewed as an unsolvable problem, just as artificial global warming is widely described as unsolvable today. During the early 1970s, Los Angeles averaged more than 100 Stage One smog alerts annually, while automakers declared that building low-emission cars would raise the price of an automobile by $10,000 or more (in current dollars), if not be technically impossible. In 1970, Congress created an ambitious national smog-reduction goal and gave automakers a strong incentive to comply—devise anti-smog technology if you want to keep selling cars. Engineers turned their attention to the task and in less than a decade a cheap and effective anti-smog device—the catalytic converter—was perfected.

Today, any make or model new car purchased in the United States emits about 1 percent of the amount of smog-forming compounds per mile as a car of 1970, and the cost of the anti-smog technology is less than $100 per vehicle. Air pollution in Los Angeles, as in most other American cities, has declined spectacularly fast, at unexpectedly low cost. Nationally, smog-forming emissions have declined by almost half since 1970, even though Americans now drive their vehicles more than twice as many miles annually. In the last five years combined, Los Angeles has experienced just one Stage One smog alert.

Now consider acid rain, which is caused mainly by the emission of sulfur compounds by coal-fired power plants. In the 1980s, it was said that acid rain would cause a "new silent spring" for the Appalachians, which are downwind from the coal-fired generating stations of the Midwest. Supposedly, by now, the Appalachians would be a dead zone. In 1991, Congress enacted a program that allowed power plants to trade acid-rain emissions permits, without government involvement. The permits annually decline in value, forcing reductions. Any power plant that cut its emissions below a legal maximum could sell its extra credits on the open market. Given a profit incentive, power-plant engineers and managers rapidly found ways to "overcontrol," cutting emissions more than the law required. Since 1990, acid rain emissions have declined by 36 percent, even as the amount of coal burned for power has risen. When the permit-trading program was enacted, reducing acid rain was expected to cost about $2,000 a ton (in current dollars). Instead most permits of the 1990s sold for about $200 a ton, meaning acid rain control cost only about 10 percent as much as predicted. The reason the phrase "acid rain" has largely vanished from American politics is that acid rain is no longer a problem in the United States—and the Appalachian forests are currently in their best health since Europeans first laid eyes on them. Big cuts in acid rain, considered impossible just two decades ago, happened faster and at a much lower price than anyone would have guessed, and without any harm at all to the economy. . . .

What world leaders most urgently need to know today about global warming is not what computer models say the temperature will be, say, in Paraguay in 2063 or any similar conjecture. Rather, they need to know if a program of mandatory greenhouse gas reduction via market-based trading will work without harming the global economy. If the answer is "yes," then an artificial greenhouse effect is not destiny. The only way to find out if the answer is yes is to start greenhouse trading programs that include mandatory reductions.

A significant fraction of corporate America already assumes that mandatory greenhouse reductions are inevitable and is simply waiting for Washington to say a single word: "Go." Leader companies such as DuPont, General Electric, 3M and others have already instituted corporate-wide greenhouse gas reduction programs and are running them without loss of profits—and cutting greenhouse emissions even as their manufacturing output increases.

The Kyoto Protocol might not have been right for the United States, but a mandatory program of greenhouse gas reduction is. For decades, the United States has led the world in technology development, economic vision and pollution control. Right now the catalytic converter and "reformulated" gasoline, anti-smog technology invented here, are beginning to spread broadly throughout developing nations. If America were to impose greenhouse gas reductions on a solely domestic basis—keep the United Nations out of this—it is likely that the United States would soon develop the technology that would light the way for the rest of the world on reducing global warming. The United States was the first country to overcome smog (ahead of the European Union by years), the first to overcome acid rain, and we should be first to overcome global warming. Once we have shown the world that greenhouse gas emissions can be reduced without economic harm, other nations will follow our lead voluntarily. The United States needs to start now with mandatory greenhouse gas reductions not out of guilt or shame, but because it is a fight we can win.

# Note

1. It can be argued that carbon dioxide is not a pollutant because plants, rain and rocks participate in a natural carbon dioxide cycle much greater in scope than artificial emissions of this gas. The point is not merely theoretical: that carbon dioxide is emitted naturally in large quantities probably means carbon dioxide does not fall under the aegis of the Clean Air Act, which regulates only "pollutants." Probably any binding federal program of greenhouse gas reduction will require new legislation from Congress, not merely an interpretation of the Clean Air Act. But for the sake of shorthand, carbon dioxide can be called "air pollution" because artificial greenhouse gases act like pollution, by causing environmental problems.

# Climate of Corruption: Politics and Power Behind the Global Warming Hoax

## . . . The Big Climate Crisis Life

Spaceship Earth reporting . . . all systems functioning . . . thermal controls optimum. Thank you, God.

Larry Bell

Conscientious environmentalism does not require or benefit from subscription to hysterical guilt over man-made climate crisis claims. Perhaps some may argue that unfounded alarmism is justifiable, even necessary, to get our attention to do what we should be doing anyway: for example, conserve energy and not pollute the planet. Hey, who wants to challenge those important purposes?

But what about examining motives? For example, when those who are twanging our guilt strings falsely portray polar bears as endangered climate victims to block drilling in Alaska's Arctic Natural Wildlife Reserve (ANWR), and when alarmists classify $CO_2$ as an endangering pollutant to promote lucrative cap-and-trade legislation and otherwise unwarranted alternative energy subsidies. What if these representations lack any sound scientific basis? Is that okay?

## The Hot Spin Cycle

Cyclical, abrupt, and dramatic global and regional temperature fluctuations have occurred over millions of years, long before humans invented agriculture, industries, automobiles, and carbon-trading schemes. Many natural factors are known to contribute to these changes, although even our most sophisticated climate models have failed to predict the timing, scale (either up or down), impacts, or human influences. While theories abound, there is no consensus, as claimed, that "science is settled" on any of those theories—much less is there consensus about the human influences upon or threat implications of climate change.

Among these hypotheses, man-made global warming caused by burning fossils has been trumpeted as an epic crisis. $CO_2$, a "greenhouse gas," has been identified as a primary culprit and branded as an endangering "pollutant." This, despite the fact that throughout Earth's history the increases in the atmospheric $CO_2$ level have tended to follow, not lead, rising temperatures. It should also be understood that $CO_2$ accounts for only 0.04 of 1 percent of the atmosphere, and about 97 percent of that tiny trace amount comes from naturally occurring sources that humans haven't influenced.

The big lie is that we are living in a known climate change crisis. Climate warming and cooling have occurred throughout the ages. Is the Earth warming right now? Probably not, but what if it is? It might be cooling next year. The models that predict a crisis are speculative at best, and two recent events have cast even more doubt on their accuracy. One relates to undisputable evidence that influential members of the climate science community have cooked the books to advance their theories and marginalize contrary findings. The other problem is evidence provided directly by Mother Nature herself that the global climate appears to have entered a new cooling cycle.

Public exposure of hacked e-mail files retrieved from the Climate Research Unit (CRU) at Britain's University of East Anglia revealed scandalous communications among researchers who have fomented global warming hysteria. Their exchanges confirm long-standing and broadly suspected manipulations of climate data. Included are conspiracies to falsify and withhold information, to suppress contrary findings in scholarly publications, and to exaggerate the existence and threats of man-made global warming. Many of these individuals have had major influence over summary report findings issued by the United Nations' IPCC. This organization has been recognized as the world authority on such matters, and it shares a Nobel Prize with Al Gore for advancing climate change awareness.

Among the more than three thousand purloined CRU documents is an e-mail from its director, Philip Jones, regarding a way to fudge the data to hide evidence of temperature declines: "I've just completed Mike's *Nature* [journal] trick of adding the real temperatures to each series for the past 20 years [i.e., from 1981 onward] and from 1961 for Keith's *to hide the decline* [emphasis mine]." "Mike," in this instance, refers to climatologist Michael Mann, who created the now infamous "hockey stick" chart that has repeatedly appeared in IPCC reports, as well as in Al Gore promotions, to portray accelerated global warming beginning with the Industrial Revolution—hence, caused by humans. The chart has been thoroughly debunked thanks to careful analyses by two Canadian researchers who uncovered a variety of serious problems. Included are calculation errors, data used twice, and a computer program that produced a hockey stick out of whatever data was fed into it.

Some of the e-mails reveal less than full public candor about what scientists don't know about past temperatures. For example, one from Edward Cook, director of tree ring research at the Lamont-Doherty Earth Laboratory, to CRU's deputy director Keith Briffa on September 3, 2003, admitted that little could be deduced regarding past Northern Hemisphere temperatures from the tree ring proxy data Mann used: "We can probably say a fair bit about [less than] 100-year extra-tropical NH temperature variability . . . but honestly know f**k-all [expletive deleted] about what the [more than] 100-year variability was like with any certainty."

Correspondence leaves no doubt that the members of the network were concerned the cooling since 1998 they had observed would be publicly exposed. In an October 26, 2008, note from CRU's Mick Kelly to Jones, he comments, "Yeah, it wasn't so much 1998 and all that I was concerned about, used to dealing with that, but the possibility that we might be going through a longer 10-year period of relatively stable temperatures . . ." He added, "Speculation but if I see this possibility, then others might also. Anyway, I'll maybe cut the last few points off the filtered curve before I give the talk again as that's trending down as a result of the effects and the recent cold-ish years."

Another e-mail to Michael Mann (which James Hansen at NASA was copied on), sent by Kevin Trenberth, head of the Climate Analysis Section of the US National Center for Atmospheric Research, reflected exasperation concerning a lack of global warming evidence: "Well, I have my own article on where the heck is global warming. We are asking here in Boulder where we have broken records the past two days for the coldest days on record. We had four inches of snow." He continued, "The fact is that we can't account for the lack of warming at the moment, and it is a travesty that we can't . . . the data is surely wrong. Our observing system is inadequate."

Trenberth, an advisory IPCC high priest and man-made global warming spokesperson, didn't waste a publicity opportunity to link a devastating 2005 US hurricane season to this cause. After ignoring admonitions from top expert Christopher Landsea that this assumption was not supported by known research, Trenberth proceeded with the unfounded claim that dominated world headlines.

Clearly, members of the CRU e-mail network used their considerable influence to block the publication of research by climate crisis skeptics, thus preventing inclusion of contrary findings in IPCC reports. In one e-mail, Tom Wigley, a senior scientist and Trenberth associate at the National Center for Atmospheric Research, shared his disdain for global warming challengers, common among global warming proponents: "If you think that [Yale professor James] Saiers is in the greenhouse skeptics camp, then, if we can find documentary evidence of this, we could go through official [American Geophysical Union] channels to get him ousted."

Possibly one of the most serious and legally hazardous breaches of professional accountability is seen in an e-mail from Jones to Mann concerning withholding of taxpayer-supported scientific data: "If they ever hear there is a Freedom of Information Act now in the UK, I think I'll delete the file rather than send it to anyone." He then asks Mann to join him in deleting official IPCC-related files: "Can you delete any e-mails you may have had with Keith re: AR4 [the IPCC's Fourth Assessment Report]?" A different e-mail from Jones assures Mann of the way some troublesome contrarian research will be handled: "I can't see either of these papers being in the next IPCC report. Kevin and I will keep them out somehow, even if we have to redefine what the peer-reviewed process is!"

A Jones letter to his colleagues instructed them, "Don't any of you three tell anyone that the UK has a Freedom of Information Act." Still another stated, "We also have a data platform act, which I will hide behind."

The CRU fallout is spreading: It now includes broader allegations by a Russian scientific group that climate-change data obtained from that country has been cherry-picked to overstate a rise in temperatures. Russia accounts for a large portion of the world's landmass, and incorrect data there would affect overall global temperature analyses.

Two things are clear from the CRU emails: (1) Perpetrators of climate science fraud have routinely conspired to exaggerate temperature increases since the Industrial Revolution, and (2) these same perpetrators virtually ignored comparable and even warmer times that preceded this period, as well as prolonged temperature declines since this period, that contradict greenhouse theory and model predictions. Other explanations that conform much more closely to observed fluctuations have been dismissed or aggressively attacked. These practices have produced unsupportable alarmist statements trumpeted in the world press that continue to influence multitrillion-dollar US and international policy decisions—decisions based upon a contrived crisis of hysteria . . . a climate of corruption.

# Chilling News for "Warm-Mongers"

The climate is always changing, in long and short cycles, and mankind has survived and thrived in conditions that have varied greatly from what they are right now.

It is apparent that our planet is once again experiencing a global cooling trend, just as it did quite recently between 1940 and 1975, when warnings of a coming new ice age received front-page coverage in the *New York Times* and other major publications. NASA satellite measurements of the lower atmosphere, where warming greenhouse models predicted effects would be greatest, stopped rising as a decadal trend after 1998 *despite increased levels of $CO_2$*. Measurements recorded by four major temperature-tracking outlets showed that world temperatures plummeted by more than 1 degree Fahrenheit (1°F) during 2007. This cooling approached the total of all the warming that had occurred over that past 100 years. In other words, temperatures worldwide and collectively never rose more than 1°F in a century. 2008 was significantly colder than 2007 had been. Although models predicted that the year 2008 would be one of the warmest on record, it actually ranked fourteenth coldest since satellite records commenced in 1979, and the coldest since 2000.

If ordinary citizens don't receive or heed scientific reports, many may legitimately question global warming assertions from direct experience. Take the year 2007, for example. North America had the most snow it's recorded in the past 50 years. A Boston storm in December dumped 10 inches of snow, more than the city typically receives in that entire month, and Madison, Wisconsin, had the highest seasonal snowfall since record keeping began. Record cold temperatures were recorded in Minnesota, Texas, Florida, and Mexico.

Those trends continued into the following 2 years. During October 2008, Oregon temperatures mid-month dipped to record lows, and Boise, Idaho, received its earliest-ever recorded snowfall. December 2008 witnessed 3.6 inches of snow in the Las Vegas Valley, the most to have fallen at that time of year since 1938, when record keeping began. Houston witnessed its earliest-ever recorded snowfall on December 4, 2009.

A blizzard on February 20, 2010, broke a Washington, DC, 110-year-old annual snowfall record of 55 inches as well as seasonal records in Baltimore and Philadelphia. Then, on February 26 and 27, another storm that pummeled New York City for 2 days broke a monthly snowfall record (37 inches) in Central Park that had stood for 114 years; the previous record for February was 28 inches in 1934, and the largest for any month was 30.5 inches in March 1896.

Most people's perceptions about warming and cooling trends depend on where they happen to reside and the time range they have experienced for reference. During July 2010, those throughout New England witnessed temperatures among the ten warmest recorded during that month in about a century, while temperatures in southeastern US states registered below normal. Simultaneously, Los Angeles broke a coldest July day record set in 1926, Australia since 1966, and the southern cone of South America saw the coldest July in half a century. Freezing temperatures in eastern Bolivia (normally above 68°F) killed millions of fish in three major rivers, characterized there as an environmental catastrophe.

Going back to 2007, Baghdad saw its first snowfall ever recorded, and China experienced its coldest winter in 100 years. Record cold temperatures were also recorded in Argentina, Chile, and yes, even Greenland. The end of 2007 set a record for the largest Southern Hemisphere sea ice expanse since satellite altimeter monitoring began in 1979, it was about 1 million square kilometers more than the previous 28-year average. In 2008, Durban, South

Africa, had its coldest September night in history, and parts of that country experienced an unusual late-winter snow. A month earlier, New Zealand officials at Mount Ruapehu reported the largest snow accumulation ever.

According to records collected by NASA, the National Oceanographic and Atmospheric Administration (NOAA), and the Hadley Centre for Climate Change, 2008 was cooler than 2007, making it the coldest year thus far of the 21st century. And this has occurred while atmospheric $CO_2$ levels have continued to rise.

This picture is far different from much of the information presented in the media. As a case in point, a 2008 Associated Press report claimed that the 10 warmest days recorded have occurred since the time of President Bill Clinton's second inaugural in January 1997. The report quoted James Hansen, who heads NASA's Godard Institute for Space Studies (GISS); Hansen is a principal adviser to Al Gore and has been a primary source of much global warming alarmism. NASA later issued corrections. In reality, the warmest recorded days—in descending order-occurred in 1934, 1998, 1921, 2006, 1931, 1934, 1953, 1990, 1938, and 1939. As Jay Lehr, a senior fellow and science director at the Heartland Institute, stated on CNN's *Lou Dobbs Tonight* program in December 2008, "If we go back in really recorded human history, in the 13th century we were probably 7 degrees Fahrenheit warmer than we are now."

Bear in mind that monthly, annual, decadal and much longer temperature fluctuations are fundamental aspects of Earth's dynamic climate history. Also remember that incredibly complex and interactive mechanisms and effects of those changes are geographically distributed in ways that confound global generalization. Most recently, NOAA's National Climatic Data Center reported that March, April, May and June of 2010 set records for the warmest year worldwide since record-keeping began in 1880. However, June was actually cooler than average across Scandinavia, southeastern China, and the northwestern US according to the same report.

NOAA ground stations reported the June average to be 1.22°F higher than normal, while NASA satellite data showed the average to be only 0.79°F above a 20-year average. This made June 2010 the second warmest in the short 32-year satellite temperature record, and the first six months of 2010 were also the second warmest. So what can we really deduce from all of this to predict a trend? Not much of anything, and certainly nothing to be alarmed about.

# Climate, Carbon, and Conspirators

So, who stands to gain from climate science corruption? There are many culprits, and they are becoming ever more powerful. Principal among these are certain agenda-driven federal government regulatory agencies, alternative energy and environmental lobbies, and yes, the UN and other organizations that seek global resource and wealth redistribution. Many of these organs of misinformation are joined at a common colon.

The IPCC has long served as the authoritative source of alarmist climate change predictions cited in media and activist warm-mongering campaigns. A richly funded example is Al Gore's Alliance for Climate Protection

(ACP), which has routinely enlisted celebrities in advertising for united action against a "climate crisis." In reality, the IPCC only conducts literature reviews, although many of the publications it selectively cites are produced by the same influential people that author its reports. Moreover, illuminating CRU e-mails revealed that a small group within that organization actively worked to prevent research findings that contradicted their biases from being published in leading journals, hence blocking dissenting views from being reviewed and cited in IPCC reports.

Global warming doom-speakers and promoters of fossil energy alternatives are united behind carbon-capping politics. Climate change alarm drives the development and marketing of technologies that are otherwise uncompetitive without major government support. Unwarranted climate fear, combined with legitimate public concern about fossil-fuel depletion and dependence upon foreign oil, is promoted to justify to taxpayers and consumers the use of more costly energy options. Media campaigns portray images of dying polar bears as fossil fuel-generated carbon casualties to support arguments against drilling in ANWR and, by association, other national oil and natural gas reserves. Fossil-fuel prices rise higher, assisted by massive $CO_2$ sequestration costs and de facto cap-and-trade taxes, so consumers pay more, making alternatives seem all the more attractive.

Does it seem remarkable that the US Environmental Protection Agency (EPA) applied a global warming argument to declare that $CO_2$, the natural molecule essential for all plant life, is a "pollutant"? Might that possibly have to do with a larger agenda supported by the EPA and other organizations, such as wind and solar power lobbies and prospective carbon brokers, to limit fossil fuel use by requiring costly carbon sequestration, in turn making alternatives more price competitive, justifying subsidies, and supporting cap-and-trade schemes? But of course, those purposes wouldn't fall within EPA responsibilities, would they? And they wouldn't make any sense at all if man-made carbon emissions didn't pose a dire climate threat.

Yet consider the implications of the suppressed EPA "Internal Study on Climate" report that was kept under wraps, its author silenced, due to pressure to support the agency's agenda to regulate $CO_2$. Alan Carlin, a senior research analyst at the EPA's National Center for Environmental Economics (NCEE), had stated in that report that after examining numerous global warming studies, his research showed the available observable data to invalidate the hypothesis that humans cause dangerous global warming. He concluded, "Given the downward trend in temperatures since 1998 (which some think will continue until at least 2030), there is no particular reason to rush into decisions based upon a scientific hypothesis that does not appear to explain most of the available data."

After serving with the EPA for 38 years, Alan Carlin was taken off climate-related work and was forbidden from speaking to anyone outside the organization on endangerment issues such as those in his then-suppressed report. A then-proposed "endangerment finding" under the Clean Air Act would enable the EPA to establish limits on $CO_2$ and other GHG concentrations as threats to public health, directly supporting cap-and-trade carbon regulations. That finding is now in force.

Bowing to pressure from global warming alarmists, the US Department of the Interior (DOI) placed polar bears on its Endangered Species Act list in 2008. Reported threats of massive melting in their habitats prompted this action. While the act's purview doesn't extend to actually regulating GHGs, there is little doubt that the classification establishes the species as poster cubs for the man-made global warming movement. It also supports environmentalist opposition to oil and gas drilling in ANWR.

But are polar bear populations really declining, as tragically depicted in Al Gore's film, *An Inconvenient Truth?* Apparently not, according to Mitchell Taylor, manager of Wildlife Research for the Government of the Canadian Territory of Nunavut, which monitors these conditions: "Of the thirteen populations of polar bears in Canada, eleven are stable or increasing in number. They are not going extinct [nor do they] even appear to be affected at present . . . [It is] silly to present the demise of polar bears based on media-assisted hysteria."

Cap-and-trade legislation, a major priority of President Barack Obama's administration, has no defensible purpose without a supporting global warming rationale. It also makes no sense from an economic standpoint. It will place onerous cost burdens upon energy consumers, continue to drive businesses overseas, and offer no real climate or environmental benefits whatsoever. Such legislation will multiply the price of electricity by dramatically increasing coal plant construction and operating costs for $CO_2$ sequestration. While intended to make such "renewables" as wind and solar more attractive, even this legislation won't make them competitive without large tax-supported subsidies. A new stock exchange would then be created that treats ("bad") carbon as a valuable ("good") commodity, providing billions of profits for operators.

Al Gore, now a very wealthy "green energy" proponent, strongly lobbies for carbon-emission trading through a London-based hedge fund called Generation Investment. He cofounded the company with David Blood, former head of investment management at Goldman Sachs, which in turn is a large shareholder in the Chicago Climate Exchange, a "voluntary pilot agency" established in 2003 to advance trading in US carbon emissions. Both organizations are working hard to persuade governments to block new power plants that use fossils. Gore exuberantly told members at a March 2007 Joint House Hearing of the Energy and Science Committee: "As soon as carbon has a price, you're going to see a wave [of investment] in it. . . . There will be unchained investment."

Perhaps the most serious public deception perpetrated by this "war against climate change" (e.g., the carbon enemy) is the notion that cleaner, sustainable options are *available* in sufficient abundance to replace dependence upon fossil resources that currently provide about 85 percent of all US energy. Regrettably, this is broadly recognized not to be the case at all. Ironically, many of the same groups that champion environmental and human causes are inhibiting progress toward vital solutions.

Extravagantly funded media campaigns continue to advertise a "climate change crisis," despite obvious evidence that the Earth began cooling once more at least a decade ago. Meanwhile, America's energy and industrial progress is being held hostage by political and legal pressures applied by groups that no one elected to represent us, and industries and other businesses that provide jobs and revenues are being driven overseas. And, as artificially manipulated energy costs continue to add unsustainable burdens to already out-of-control government borrowing and spending deficits, those impacts will fall hardest upon people who can least afford them.

# . . . Setting the Records Straight

## The Science Unanimity Myth

Widely circulated statements that scientists unanimously agree about global warming and human contributions to it or the importance and consequences of it are patently false. The apparent purpose of such claims is to discredit those with opposing viewpoints, deriding them with contempt previously reserved for those who deny the Holocaust, the dangers of tobacco, and the achievements of NASA's Apollo program. Al Gore has little tolerance for unbelievers, as evidenced in this statement: "Fifteen percent of the population believes the Moon landing was staged in a movie lot in America, and somewhat fewer believe the Earth is flat. I think they should all get together with the global warming deniers on a Saturday night and party."

"Scientific consensus" representations attached to scary climate projections have played well to legitimize highly speculative research conclusions useful to justify additional funding, sell newspapers, and enhance television audience ratings. But several petitions and surveys involving science communities present a far from unified picture.

- In 1992, a "Statement of Atmospheric Scientists on Greenhouse Warming" that opposed global controls on GHG emissions drew about 100 signatures, mostly from American Meteorological Society technical committee members.
- In 1992, a "Heidelberg Appeal," which also expressed skepticism on the urgency of restraining GHG emissions, drew more than 4,000 signatures from scientists worldwide.
- In 1996, a "Leipzig Declaration on Climate Change" that emerged from an international conference addressing the GHG controversy, was signed by more than 100 scientists in climatology and related fields.
- In 1997, a survey of American state climatologists (the official climate monitors in each of the fifty states) found 90 percent agreed that "scientific evidence indicates variations in global temperatures are likely to be naturally occurring and cyclical over very long periods of time."
- In 2001, the American Association of State Climatologists concluded that "climate prediction is complex, with many uncertainties; the AASC recognizes climate prediction is an extremely difficult undertaking. For time scales of a decade or more, understanding the empirical accuracy of such prediction—called verification—is simply impossible, since we have to wait a decade or more to assess the accuracy of the forecasts."

- In May 2007, a survey of 530 climate scientists by the Heartland Institute revealed that only about one-half agreed that "climate change is mostly the result of anthropogenic causes," and only one-third of those agreed that "climate models can accurately predict conditions in the future."
- In April 2008, the results of a survey of 489 scientists, conducted by the Statistical Assessment Service (STATS), indicated that most (74 percent) believed that some human-induced greenhouse warming has occurred, up from 41 percent reported in the 1991 Gallup survey. Only 41 percent of those polled, however, said they were directly involved in any aspect of global climate science.
- In 2008, a US Senate minority report issued by Senator James Inhofe (R-OK) presents the testimony of 650 climate-related scientists from around the world who strongly challenge global warming crisis claims. They include a Nobel laureate and former IPCC study participants.
- In March 2009, more than 600 skeptical people attended a conference organized by the Heartland Institute in New York City to protest cap-and-trade regulations favored by President Obama that would roll GHG emissions back to 1990s levels. President Vaclav Klaus of Czech Republic delivered the keynote speech. Speaking again the next day to Columbia University faculty and students, he reaffirmed his strong opposition to a concept that global warming is man-made. "The problem is not global warming . . . by the ideology which uses or misuses it—it has gradually turned the most efficient vehicle for advocating extensive government intervention into all fields of life and for suppressing human freedom and economic prosperity."

Scientific questions and disputes will never be resolved by opinion poll tabulations. If that were the case we might now be fleeing in seal-oil fueled snowmobiles the ravages of the miles-thick glaciers predicted a few decades ago. Yet it is disingenuous to suggest that the debate is over. Or if it is, that will come as a big disappointment to those with a few remaining contrary opinions that they may be required to abandon by majority vote. In fact, some man-made warming proponents are attempting to discredit skeptical scientific opinions out of existence altogether.

For instance, in a December 2004 article titled "Beyond the Ivory Tower: The Scientific Consensus on Climate Change," published in the journal *Science*, Naomi Oreskes, a University of California–San Diego history professor, reported that her search of the Internet under the term "climate change" turned up 928 studies, based on which she cheerfully concluded that there was complete scientific agreement.

Few, if any, scientific papers claim to "refute" the theory of human-induced warming, and a search under the term "climate cycles" rather than "climate change" would have produced a different result. Hundreds of studies have been published that discuss potentially important and dominant natural forces that influence global warming and cooling over both short and very long periods, including solar climate-forcing factors (hereafter referred to at times simply as climate forcings).

Issues of debate cannot be resolved by claims that a consensus among authorities has settled the matters so long as a minority, even a small one, believes otherwise. Objective science and progress have always been advanced by those who have proven that simple lesson.

If global warming crisis skeptics and deniers are heretics, they may perhaps take some comfort in the fact that their numbers are rapidly growing. This is particularly true in the US. A 2010 Gallup poll indicates that the percentage of respondents who said they worry "a great deal" about global warming was only 28 percent, down from 33 percent in 2009 and 41 percent in 2007, when worry peaked. Global warming ranked last of eight environmental issues listed in the survey.

Gallup also conducted a 2010 poll that asked the question "Thinking about what is said in the news, in your view is the seriousness of global warming generally exaggerated, generally correct, or generally underestimated?" In just 4 years the percentage of Americans who believe global warming has been exaggerated has grown by 60 percent, constituting 48 percent of the respondents.

## Embracing Changes and Challenges

Two realities are quite clear: (1) that the short era of inexpensive energy resources is nearing an end; and (2) that there are no single or simple solutions. No known technology advancement or combination of advancements will satisfy the needs of uncontrolled consumption. The future we experience and introduce to those who follow will depend instead upon our human resources of vision, intellect, creativity, and discipline. We must apply all available means to expand the development and use of renewable as well as other resources, yet recognize their realistic limitations. We must strive to implement efficient processes and systems that minimize, recycle, and reuse wastes. We must apply personal and corporate lifestyles that do more with less, recognizing that this makes good economic and moral sense.

Our human ability to gain knowledge about changes we are imposing upon our planet provides opportunities to adapt our living habits, industries, and technologies to prevent avoidable surprises that lead to unfortunate events. Earth-sensing satellite observations and advancements in information technology are yielding a better understanding of nature's complexities and intricacies. This better understanding provides us with lessons we can apply to be more positive contributors. Humans are also blessed with gifts of curiosity, intelligence, and compassion, all of which enable us to recognize our responsibilities and interdependencies within a larger world community.

There is inescapable evidence that human activities are impacting Earth's environment and ecosystems, often not for the better. Air, water, and land pollution are an expanding global reality. Scientists who study these matters do us great service in pointing such things out and helping us to do better. We are not beneficially served, however, by exaggerated statements—purporting to be based upon science—that are calibrated to get maximum public attention. Alarmism, however well intentioned, is not conducive to sound judgment and reasoned responses.

Failure to rapidly develop essential energy capacities will have widespread, destructive social and economic consequences that will be particularly burdensome upon the poorest among us. A 3-decade-long blockage of US nuclear power development has already caused depletion of natural gas that could have been conserved or applied for other, more appropriate fuel and feedstock purposes. This has contributed to high natural gas prices that have forced many US energy- and chemical-intensive industries overseas, along with the jobs and tax revenues they might have otherwise provided.

Expansion of existing energy production capacity infrastructures, and creation of new ones, requires lots of time and investment in a friendly legislative environment. This applies to nuclear plant licensing; fossil drilling; refinery construction; clean coal and coal shale development; organic and fossil synthetic liquid fuels; and yes, wind farms. While coal is our most abundant long-term fossil source, onerous and unwarranted $CO_2$ sequestration mandates, in combination with prospective carbon caps, will continue to kill incentives to build new coal-fired plants. US coal use decreased in relation to oil and gas over a 50-year [sic] period between about 1910 and 1940, and transitioning back to cleaner and liquid derivative technologies may require decades under the best circumstances. Time is very much of the essence.

Some groups and individuals advertised as "environmentalists" seem to want society to return to what they regard as the simpler, ecologically superior lifestyle of the past. This is neither possible nor desirable. Looking back, earlier tribes may have had lighter ecological footprints only because there weren't nearly as many feet then. Their lives were much harder and shorter than ours, and they used substantially more land per capita to survive and raise larger families.

We can, however, learn much from the past. From a truly "big picture" time perspective, we can readily observe that Earth's climate has changed often and dramatically over long, short, and irregular cycles, with no influence from our ancestors. From a human perspective, we can take heart that our species has adapted to rapid and severe climate shifts on numerous occasions, and the worst by far were periods of cold. We can relearn ways that indigenous peoples in all climate zones have applied logical conservation principles in dwelling construction that make resourceful use of sunlight and natural ventilation.

There should be no doubt that we humans are highly resilient creatures with remarkable abilities to survive in difficult times. In 2002, a report issued jointly by the Ocean Studies Board, the Polar Research Board, and the Board on Atmospheric Sciences and Climate of the National Research Council—titled 'Abrupt Climate Change: Inevitable Surprises"—advocated preparation without panic: "The climate record for the past 100,000 years clearly indicates that the climate system has undergone periodic and extreme shifts, sometimes in as little as a decade or less . . . Societies have faced both gradual and abrupt changes for millennia and have learned to adapt."

The report went on to advise: "It is important not to be fatalistic about the threats of abrupt climate change . . . Nevertheless, because climate change will likely continue in the coming decades, denying the likelihood or down-playing the relevance of abrupt changes could be costly."

How do we prepare for rapid climate change? Consider that the most important impact, whether average temperatures rise or drop, will be upon energy demands. A warmer climate will increase crop yields, just as it always has, along with power consumption for air-conditioning. A cooler climate may further accelerate population shifts from US northern states to the Sun Belt, also increasing air-conditioning demands but increasing fuel consumption for winter heating in much of the country as well. Those who pay attention will have noticed that US temperatures, which had warmed until the mid-1940s, then cooled through the late 1970s, warmed until the late 1990s, and now seem to be cooling again, potentially for decades to come. All this is despite steady and "alarming" increases in human $CO_2$ releases and other activities.

Apart from climate, each of us affects the course of human events, adaptation, and technological, social, and economic progress through our choices and actions. Individually and collectively, we change the world for better or worse in a variety of important ways. We determine which businesses and products will be successful in the marketplace through our purchasing power. We decide how many resources we will consume, how much waste will be created, and whether waste will be recycled, based upon priorities that guide how we live. We influence our children and others around us through our conservation outlooks and the examples we put into practice. And we determine whom we trust to lead us and implement policies we believe in through active participation and informed votes in local, state, and national electoral processes that affect the political climate. That's the climate crisis that we urgently need to address.

# EXPLORING THE ISSUE

## Do We Need to Curb Global Warming?

## Critical Thinking and Reflection

A thought experiment: suppose global warming is indeed taking place. Is that necessarily a bad thing? During the so-called medieval warming period, from A.D. 1000 to 1300, when northern Europe warmed appreciably, England is said to have established wineries and Greenland was actually green. If global warming were to occur again, much of Siberia and northern Canada might be able to support crop cultivation, increasing the world's food supply. The point is, wouldn't there be desirable as well as undesirable effects resulting from global warming? But would we want to risk such a tradeoff if we knew that the same increased warming would probably make some already hot regions uninhabitable?

## Is There Common Ground?

There should be. No one on either side of the debate over global warming should be complacent about smoke-belching factories and generating plants. Since 1970, the United States has made significant progress toward getting rid of them. President Nixon signed the Clean Air Act that year, and since then the emission of six major pollutants, including carbon monoxide, ozone, and lead, has been cut in half. Remarkably, these reductions came during a period of rapid economic growth, when the U.S. economy grew by more than 187 percent and U.S. energy consumption by 47 percent. This is not to suggest that America can sit back on its laurels while congratulating itself. On the contrary, it should stir us to greater efforts, for it shows that a nation can clean up its act without destroying its economy.

## Additional Resources

Al Gore's *An Inconvenient Truth* (Rodale Books, 2006) and Gore's Oscar-winning film based on it caused a sensation in the United States, the United Kingdom, and other countries. The film is still often used in high school and college classrooms, although a High Court judge in the United Kingdom has ruled that the film can be shown only in secondary schools after students have been warned that it contains nine major errors, including Gore's assertion that global warming will cause a sea-level rise of up to 20 feet in some areas and that polar bears are drowning because of melting ice. More recently, Gore defended his work in a *Rolling Stone* article ("Climate of Denial," June 22, 2011) calling his critics "Polluters and Ideologues" and accusing them of "slanderous insults." Walter Russell Mead replied in a three-part blog "The Failure of Al Gore" in www.the-american-interest.com (June 24 and 27, July 1, 2011). In *Changing Planet, Changing Health* (University of California Press, 2011), Paul Epstein and Dan Ferber make the case that global warming threatens the health of people throughout the world; they also suggest means of countering it. Roy W. Spencer's *Climate Confusion* (Encounter Books, 2010) dismisses such concerns as "hysteria," more myth than science. Point-by-point rebuttals of the major claims of the global-warming warners are given by Iain Murray in "Gorey Truths," *National Review Online* (www.nationalreview.com), June 22, 2008. A more even-handed review of the pros and cons of global warming (although it gives the warming side the last word) is presented by Michael Totty in "What Global Warming?" *Wall Street Journal* (December 6, 2009).

# ISSUE 21

## Is Warrantless Wiretapping Ever Justified to Protect National Security?

**YES: Andrew C. McCarthy,** from "How to 'Connect the Dots'," *National Review* (January 30, 2006)

**NO: Al Gore,** from "Restoring the Rule of Law," from a Speech Presented to The American Constitution Society for Law and Policy and The Liberty Coalition (January 15, 2006)

### ISSUE SUMMARY

**YES:** Former federal prosecutor Andrew C. McCarthy supports the National Security Agency program of surveillance without a warrant as an effective means of protecting national security that employs the inherent power of the president to protect the country against subversion.

**NO:** Former vice president Al Gore views the warrantless wiretapping of American citizens as a brazen violation of the Constitution and of specific acts of Congress that have spelled out the circumstances under which a president may receive judicial permission to wiretap or otherwise invade the privacy of citizens.

$A$mericans overwhelmingly believe in the right to privacy. They subscribe to the old adage that a man's home is his castle (adding that a woman's home is hers). Yet the Constitution makes no explicit mention of a right to privacy. Controversy revolves not around the right to privacy but under what circumstances there are conflicting societal interests that would curtail it.

As it has on earlier occasions, privacy rights became a political issue when, shortly after the terrorist attack on September 11, 2001, on the World Trade Center in New York and the Pentagon in Washington, D.C., President Bush issued a secret executive order authorizing the National Security Agency to conduct warrantless electronic surveillance of telecommunications into and out of the United States of persons who might be linked to al Qaeda or other terrorist organizations. Some NSA surveillance involved persons in the United States.

The classified presidential authorization was made known to select members of the congressional leadership and intelligence committees, but was concealed from public knowledge until *The New York Times* reported it in December 2005, more than a year after it acquired information regarding it. (President Bush's administration had sought to have the newspaper not publish the article.)

The 1978 Foreign Intelligence Surveillance Act (FISA) had barred electronic surveillance of persons within the United States without the approval of a newly established Foreign Intelligence Surveillance Court. Before the public revelation of warrantless wiretapping, President Bush stated, with regard to domestic surveillance, "Constitutional guarantees are in place when it comes to doing what is necessary to protect our homeland, because we value the Constitution." He later maintained that warrantless surveillance was justified in dealing with international communications that threaten nation security, and that such surveillance was implicitly authorized by the 2001 congressional Authorization for Use of Military Force adopted days after 9/11. Supporting the president, some legal authorities argued that Congress cannot interfere with the means and methods the president uses to engage an enemy.

Critics of warrantless wiretapping hold that FISA established a clear and exclusive procedure for authorizing emergency wiretaps. They charge that such wiretaps by the president, when based upon the claim of "inherent authority," risk unauthorized government recording of the communications of a wholly domestic character.

Publication by the *Times* precipitated widespread public debate regarding the right to privacy and the legality of warrantless electronic surveillance of American citizens. Despite later revelations by the *Times* and the *Washington Post*, details of the extent of wiretapping or other secret interception of messages have not been revealed. Defending this silence, White House Press Secretary Scott McClellan said, "There's a reason we don't get into discussing ongoing intelligence activities, because it could compromise our efforts to prevent attacks from happening."

As for the success of warrantless wiretapping, General Michael Hayden, Principal Deputy Director for National Intelligence, stated, "The program has been successful in detecting and preventing attacks inside the United States." Along with administration officials, General Hayden has asserted, "Had this program been in effect prior to 9/11, it is my professional judgment that we would have detected some of the 9/11 Al Qaeda operatives in the United States, and we would have identified them as such."

Many members of both parties disagreed with the president's secret executive action. It is unlikely that all the facts regarding the extent of the program or what it achieved will be known for years, but the constitutional questions require answers.

Former federal prosecutor Andrew McCarthy defends secret surveillance as having been widely used (although sometimes abused) and wholly within the president's power. Former presidential candidate Al Gore believes that this activity is dangerous, unnecessary, and violates the rule of law.

# YES ⤶     Andrew C. McCarthy

# How to 'Connect the Dots'

**W**ashington's scandal *du jour* involves a wartime surveillance program President Bush directed the National Security Agency to carry out after al-Qaeda killed nearly 3,000 Americans on September 11, 2001. The idea that there is anything truly scandalous about this program is absurd. But the outcry against it is valuable, highlighting as it does the mistaken assumption that criminal-justice solutions are applicable to national-security challenges.

The intelligence community has identified thousands of al-Qaeda operatives and sympathizers throughout the world. After Congress overwhelmingly authorized the use of military force immediately following the 9/11 attacks, the president, as part of the war effort, ordered the NSA to intercept the enemy's international communications, even if those communications went into and out of the United States and thus potentially involved American citizens. According to reports from the *New York Times*, which shamefully publicized leaks of the program's existence in mid-December 2005, as many as 7,000 suspected terrorists overseas are monitored at any one time, as are up to 500 suspects inside the U.S.

As is typical of such wartime operations, the NSA program was classified at the highest level of secret information. It was, nevertheless, completely different from the kind of rogue intelligence operations of which the Nixon era is emblematic (though by no means the only case). The Bush administration internally vetted the program, including at the Justice Department, to confirm its legal footing. It reviewed (and continues to review) the program every 45 days. It briefed the bipartisan leadership of Congress (including the intelligence committees) at least a dozen times. It informed the chief judge of the federal Foreign Intelligence Surveillance Court (FISC), the tribunal that oversees domestic national-security wiretapping. And it modified the program in mid-2004 in reaction to concerns raised by the chief judge, national-security officials, and government lawyers.

Far from being a pretextual use of war powers to spy on political opponents and policy dissenters, the NSA program has been dedicated to national security. More to the point, it has saved lives, helping break up at least one al-Qaeda conspiracy to attack New York City and Washington, D.C., in connection with which a plotter named Lyman Faris was sentenced to 20 years' imprisonment.

From *The National Review,* January 30, 2006. Copyright © 2006 by National Review, Inc, 215 Lexington Avenue, New York, NY 10016. Reprinted by permission.

As potential scandal fodder, so unremarkable did the NSA program seem that the *Times* sat on the story for a year—and a year, it is worth noting, during which it transparently and assiduously sought to exploit any opportunity to discredit the administration and cast it as a mortal threat to civil liberties. The leak was not sprung until the eleventh hour of congressional negotiations over renewal of the Patriot Act—at which point it provided ammunition to those who would gut Patriot's crucial post-9/11 domestic surveillance powers and simultaneously served as a marketing campaign for *Times* reporter James Risen, who just happened to be on the eve of publishing a book about, among other things, Bush's domestic "spying."

In fact, so obviously appropriate was wartime surveillance of the enemy that Rep. Jane Harman, the ranking Democrat on the House Intelligence Committee, issued a statement right after the *Times* exposed the program, saying: "I have been briefed since 2003 on a highly classified NSA foreign collection program that targeted Al-Qaeda. I believe the program is essential to US national security and that its disclosure has damaged critical intelligence capabilities." (With partisan "scandal" blowing in the wind, Harman changed her tune two weeks later, suddenly deciding that the "essential" program was probably illegal after all.)

⋅◦❀◦⋅

If President Bush's reelection is any indication, what most Americans will care about is that we are monitoring the enemy. Chances are they won't be overly interested in knowing whether that monitoring is done on the president's own constitutional authority or in accordance with a statutory scheme calling for judicial imprimatur. Nevertheless, the Left is already indulging in loose talk about impeachment. Even some Republican "moderates," such as Arlen Specter, say the domestic-spying allegations are troubling enough that hearings are warranted. So it's worth asking: What is all the fuss about?

At bottom, it is about a power grab that began nearly three decades ago. Ever since it became technologically possible to intercept wire communications, presidents have done so. All of them, going back to FDR, claimed that the powers granted to the chief executive under Article II of the Constitution allowed them to conduct such wiretapping for national-security purposes. Particularly in wartime, this power might be thought indisputable. The president is the commander in chief of the armed forces, and penetrating enemy communications is as much an incident of war-fighting as bombing enemy targets is.

But surveillance power has been abused—and notoriously by President Nixon, whose eavesdropping on political opponents was the basis of a draft article of impeachment. Watergate-era domestic-spying controversies dovetailed with important developments in the law of electronic surveillance. In 1967, the Supreme Court, in *Katz* v. *United States*, held that Fourth Amendment protection against unreasonable searches extended to electronic surveillance—meaning that eavesdropping without a judicial warrant was now presumptively unconstitutional. Congress followed by enacting a comprehensive scheme, known as "Title III," that required law-enforcement agents to obtain a court warrant for probable cause of a crime before conducting electronic surveillance. Yet both *Katz* and Title III recognized inherent presidential authority to conduct *national-security* monitoring without being bound by the new warrant requirement.

The Supreme Court undertook to circumscribe this inherent authority in its 1972 *Keith* decision. It held that a judicial warrant was required for national-security surveillance if the target was a purely *domestic* threat—the Vietnam-era Court giving higher priority to the free-speech interests of "those suspected of unorthodoxy in their political beliefs" than to the safety of those who might be endangered by domestic terrorists. Still, the Court took pains to exempt from its ruling the "activities of *foreign* powers or their agents" (emphasis added).

The true power grab occurred in 1978, when Congress enacted the Foreign Intelligence Surveillance Act. FISA attempted to do in the national-security realm what Title III had done in law enforcement: erect a thoroughgoing legal regime for domestic eavesdropping. And therein lies the heart of the current dispute. If the president has inherent authority to conduct national-security wiretapping, it is a function of his constitutional warrant. It is not a function of Congress's having failed until 1978 to flex its own muscles. A constitutional power cannot be altered or limited by statute. Period.

But limiting presidential authority is precisely what FISA purports to do. It ostensibly prohibits national-security eavesdropping (and, since 1994, physical searches) unless the executive branch can satisfy a federal judge—one of eleven who sit on a specially created Foreign Intelligence Surveillance Court—that there is probable cause that the subject it seeks to monitor is an "agent of a foreign power" (generally either a spy or a member of a foreign terrorist organization).

FISA does not aim to restrict the power to eavesdrop on *all* conversations. Communications that are entirely foreign—in that they involve aliens communicating overseas, for example—are exempted, as are conversations that *unintentionally* capture "U.S. persons" (generally, American citizens and permanent resident aliens), as long as these communications are intercepted outside the U.S. But where it does apply, FISA holds that the president—the constitutional officer charged with the nation's security—is powerless to eavesdrop on an operative posing a threat to the United States unless a judge—who need not possess any national-security expertise—is persuaded that the operative is a genuine threat. One suspects that such a system would astonish the Founders.

⁓⊙⁓

Does the NSA program violate FISA? That question is difficult to answer with certainty. The program remains highly classified, and many of its details are not publicly known, nor should they be. Much has been made of the fact that FISA approval is required to intercept calls into or out of the United States if an American is intentionally being targeted. But scant attention has been given to FISA's caveat that such conversations are protected only if their participants have a *reasonable expectation of privacy*. It is difficult to imagine that Americans who make or receive calls to war zones in, say, Afghanistan or Iraq, or to al-Qaeda operatives anywhere, can reasonably expect that no one is listening in.

Nevertheless, it would not be surprising to learn that at least some of the NSA monitoring transgresses the bounds of FISA. For example, the statute mandates—without qualification about the reasonable expectation of privacy—that the government seek a judicial warrant before eavesdropping on any international call to or from the U.S., if that call is intercepted *inside* our borders. A distinction based on where a call is intercepted made sense in 1978. Back then, if a conversation was intercepted inside our borders, its participants were almost certain to include at least one U.S. person. But modern technology has since blurred the distinction between foreign and domestic telephony. Packets of digital information are now routed through switches inside countries (including, predominately, the U.S.) where neither the sender nor the recipient of the call is located. The NSA has capitalized on this evolution, and is now able, from within the U.S., to seize calls between Tikrit and Kabul, or between Peshawar and Hamburg. If done without a warrant, those intercepts present no FISA problem, because all the speakers are overseas. But it's hard to believe that the NSA is using this technology *only* to acquire all-foreign calls, while intercepting calls between, say, New York and Hamburg only from locations *outside* the U.S.

Perhaps that is why the Bush administration's defense has been light on the abstruse details of FISA and heavy on the president's inherent Article II power—although carefully couched to avoid offending Congress and the FISC with suggestions that FISA is at least partly unconstitutional. Essentially, the administration argues that FISA is beneficial in ordinary times and for long-term investigations, but that it did not and cannot repeal the president's independent constitutional obligation to protect the country: an obligation that was explicitly reserved even by President Carter, who signed FISA; that has been claimed by every president since; and that is uniquely vital in a war against thousands of stateless, stealthy terrorists, in which both a "probable cause" requirement and a sclerotic bureaucracy for processing warrant applications would be dangerously impractical.

In advancing this argument, the administration finds much support in the one and only decision ever rendered by the Foreign Intelligence Court of Review—the appellate court created by FISA to review FISC decisions. That decision came in 2002, after a quarter-century of FISA experience. Tellingly, its context was a brazen effort by the FISC to reject the Patriot Act's dismantling of the "wall" that prevented intelligence agents and criminal investigators from pooling information. In overruling the FISC, the Court of Review observed that "all the other courts to have decided the issue [have] held that the President did have inherent authority to conduct warrantless searches to obtain foreign intelligence information." Notwithstanding FISA, the Court thus pronounced: "We take for granted that the President does have that authority."

The administration has also placed great stock in Congress's post-9/11 authorization of "all necessary and appropriate force" against those behind the terrorist attacks. While this resolution did not expressly mention penetrating enemy communications, neither did it explicitly include the detention of enemy combatants, which the Supreme Court, in its 2004 *Hamdi* decision, found implicit in the use-of-force authorization because it is a "fundamental incident of waging war." Capturing intelligence, of course, is as much a component of waging war as capturing operatives. Any other conclusion would lead to the absurdity of the president's having full discretion to kill terrorists but needing a judge's permission merely to eavesdrop on them.

FISA aside, the administration stresses that the NSA program fits comfortably within the Fourth Amendment. That Amendment proscribes *unreasonable* searches, not warrantless ones—and it is thus unsurprising that the Supreme Court has recognized numerous exceptions to the warrant requirement that are of far less moment than the imperative to protect the country from attack. Plainly, there is nothing unreasonable about intercepting potential enemy communications in wartime. Moreover, the courts have long held that searches conducted at the border are part of the sovereign right of self-protection, and thus require neither probable cause nor a warrant. Cross-border communications, which might well be triggers of terror plots, are no more deserving of constitutional protection.

⋅⟨◉⟩⋅

Critics have made much of a lengthy analysis published on January 6, 2006, by the Congressional Research Service that casts doubt on the administration's core contentions. Media have treated the report as bearing special weight because the CRS is a nonpartisan entity. But that does not mean the CRS is *objective.* "The sole mission of CRS," it explains on its website, "is to serve the United States Congress." Yet the issue at stake is precisely a separation-of-powers dispute.

While the CRS study is an impressive compilation of the relevant law, it resorts to a fairly standard tactic for marginalizing executive power: reliance on the concurring opinion by Supreme Court Justice Robert Jackson in a 1952 case involving President Truman's failed effort to seize steel mills—a move Truman justified by referring to the exigencies of the Korean War. Jackson saw executive power as waxing or waning along a three-stage scale, depending on whether a president acted with the support, the indifference, or the opposition of Congress. On this theory, a statute like FISA could curb a president's inherent constitutional authority. The fatal problem with the Jackson construct, however, has always been that it makes Congress, not the Constitution, the master of presidential authority. It disregards the reality that the executive is a coequal branch whose powers exist whether Congress acts or not. But the CRS prefers Jackson's conveniently airy formula, which failed to command a Court majority, to relevant opinions that don't go Congress's way, such as that of the Foreign Intelligence Court of Review—which, unlike the Supreme Court, was actually considering FISA.

Frustrated by its inability to move public opinion, the Left is now emphasizing the large "volume of information harvested from telecommunication data and voice networks," as the *Times* breathlessly put it, "without court-approved warrants." But this is pure legerdemain. When we refer to "information" from "telecommunication data," we are talking about something that, legally, is worlds apart from the content of telephone calls or e-mail messages.

These data do not include the substance of what people privately say to one another in conversations, but rather comprise statistical facts about the use of telecommunications services (for example, what phone number called another number, the date and time of the call, how long it lasted, etc.). Court warrants have never been required for the acquisition of such information because, as the Supreme Court explained over a quarter-century ago in *Smith* v. *Maryland*, telecommunications data do not implicate the Fourth Amendment. All phone and e-mail users know this information is conveyed to and maintained by service providers, and no one expects it to be private.

Analyzing such data is clearly different from monitoring the calls and e-mails themselves. For our own protection, we should want the government to collect as many of these data as possible (since doing so affects no one's legitimate privacy interests) in order to develop investigative leads. That's how a country manages to go four years without a domestic terror attack.

Yet the Left's rage continues, despite the public's evident disinterest in the mind-numbingly technical nature of the dispute, and despite the obvious truth that the NSA program was a bona fide effort to protect the nation from harm, not to snoop on Americans—only a tiny fraction of whom were affected, and those with apparent good reason. The controversy is a disquieting barometer of elite commitment to the War on Terror. As recently as two years ago, when "connecting the dots" was all the rage, liberals ignored eight years of Clintonian nonfeasance and portrayed the Bush administration as asleep at the switch while terrorists ran amok. Now they ignore President Clinton's insistence on the very same executive surveillance power that the current administration claims and caricature Bush as the imperial president, shredding core protections of civil liberties by exaggerating the terror threat. Either way you slice it, national security becomes a game in which necessary decisions by responsible adults become political grist, and, if they get enough traction, phony scandals. What remains real, though, is the danger to Americans implicit in any system that can't tell a war from a crime.

**Al Gore**                                          ➔ **NO**

# Restoring the Rule of Law

The Executive Branch of the government has been caught eavesdropping on huge numbers of American citizens and has brazenly declared that it has the unilateral right to continue without regard to the established law enacted by Congress to prevent such abuses.

It is imperative that respect for the rule of law be restored.

So, many of us have come here to Constitution Hall to sound an alarm and call upon our fellow citizens to put aside partisan differences and join with us in demanding that our Constitution be defended and preserved.

It is appropriate that we make this appeal on the day our nation has set aside to honor the life and legacy of Dr. Martin Luther King, Jr., who challenged America to breathe new life into our oldest values by extending its promise to all our people.

On this particular Martin Luther King Day, it is especially important to recall that for the last several years of his life. Dr. King was illegally wiretapped—one of hundreds of thousands of Americans whose private communications were intercepted by the U.S. government during this period.

The FBI privately called King the "most dangerous and effective negro leader in the country" and vowed to "take him off his pedestal." The government even attempted to destroy his marriage and blackmail him into committing suicide.

This campaign continued until Dr. King's murder. The discovery that the FBI conducted a long-running and extensive campaign of secret electronic surveillance designed to infiltrate the inner workings of the Southern Christian Leadership Conference, and to learn the most intimate details of Dr. King's life, helped to convince Congress to enact restrictions on wiretapping.

The result was the Foreign Intelligence and Surveillance Act (FISA), which was enacted expressly to ensure that foreign intelligence surveillance would be presented to an impartial judge to verify that there is a sufficient cause for the surveillance. I voted for that law during my first term in Congress and for almost thirty years the system has proven a workable and valued means of according a level of protection for private citizens, while permitting foreign surveillance to continue.

Yet, just one month ago, Americans awoke to the shocking news that in spite of this long settled law, the Executive Branch has been secretly spying on large numbers of Americans for the last four years and eavesdropping on "large

From a speech by former Vice President Al Gore, January 16, 2006. The event was co-sponsored by The American Constitution Society for Law and Policy and The Liberty Coalition. Reprinted by permission.

volumes of telephone calls, e-mail messages, and other Internet traffic inside the United States." The New York Times reported that the President decided to launch this massive eavesdropping program "without search warrants or any new laws that would permit such domestic intelligence collection."

During the period when this eavesdropping was still secret, the President went out of his way to reassure the American people on more than one occasion that, of course, judicial permission is required for any government spying on American citizens and that, of course, these constitutional safeguards were still in place.

But surprisingly, the President's soothing statements turned out to be false. Moreover, as soon as this massive domestic spying program was uncovered by the press, the President not only confirmed that the story was true, but also declared that he has no intention of bringing these wholesale invasions of privacy to an end.

At present, we still have much to learn about the NSA's domestic surveillance. What we do know about this pervasive wiretapping virtually compels the conclusion that the President of the United States has been breaking the law repeatedly and persistently.

A president who breaks the law is a threat to the very structure of our government. Our Founding Fathers were adamant that they had established a government of laws and not men. Indeed, they recognized that the structure of government they had enshrined in our Constitution—our system of checks and balances—was designed with a central purpose of ensuring that it would govern through the rule of law. As John Adams said: "The executive shall never exercise the legislative and judicial powers, or either of them, to the end that it may be a government of laws and not of men."

An executive who arrogates to himself the power to ignore the legitimate legislative directives of the Congress or to act free of the check of the judiciary becomes the central threat that the Founders sought to nullify in the Constitution—an all-powerful executive too reminiscent of the King from whom they had broken free. In the words of James Madison, "the accumulation of all powers, legislative, executive, and judiciary, in the same hands, whether of one, a few, or many, and whether hereditary, self-appointed, or elective, may justly be pronounced the very definition of tyranny."

Thomas Paine, whose pamphlet, "On Common Sense" ignited the American Revolution, succinctly described America's alternative. Here, he said, we intended to make certain that "the law is king."

Vigilant adherence to the rule of law strengthens our democracy and strengthens America. It ensures that those who govern us operate within our constitutional structure, which means that our democratic institutions play their indispensable role in shaping policy and determining the direction of our nation. It means that the people of this nation ultimately determine its course and not executive officials operating in secret without constraint.

The rule of law makes us stronger by ensuring that decisions will be tested, studied, reviewed and examined through the processes of government that are designed to improve policy. And the knowledge that they will be reviewed prevents over-reaching and checks the accretion of power.

A commitment to openness, truthfulness and accountability also helps our country avoid many serious mistakes. Recently, for example, we learned from recently classified declassified documents that the Gulf of Tonkin Resolution, which authorized the tragic Vietnam War, was actually based on false information. We now know that the decision by Congress to authorize the Iraq War, 38 years later, was also based on false information. America would have been better off knowing the truth and avoiding both of these colossal mistakes in our history. Following the rule of law makes us safer, not more vulnerable.

The President and I agree on one thing. The threat from terrorism is all too real. There is simply no question that we continue to face new challenges in the wake of the attack on September 11th and that we must be ever-vigilant in protecting our citizens from harm.

Where we disagree is that we have to break the law or sacrifice our system of government to protect Americans from terrorism. In fact, doing so makes us weaker and more vulnerable.

Once violated, the rule of law is in danger. Unless stopped, lawlessness grows. The greater the power of the executive grows, the more difficult it becomes for the other branches to perform their constitutional roles. As the executive acts outside its constitutionally prescribed role and is able to control access to information that would expose its actions, it becomes increasingly difficult for the other branches to police it. Once that ability is lost, democracy itself is threatened and we become a government of men and not laws.

The President's men have minced words about America's laws. The Attorney General openly conceded that the "kind of surveillance" we now know they have been conducting requires a court order unless authorized by statute. The Foreign Intelligence Surveillance Act self-evidently does not authorize what the NSA has been doing, and no one inside or outside the Administration claims that it does. Incredibly, the Administration claims instead that the surveillance was implicitly authorized when Congress voted to use force against those who attacked us on September 11th.

This argument just does not hold any water. Without getting into the legal intricacies, it faces a number of embarrassing facts. First, another admission by the Attorney General: he concedes that the Administration knew that the NSA project was prohibited by existing law and that they consulted with some members of Congress about changing the statute. Gonzalez says that they were told this probably would not be possible. So how can they now argue that the Authorization for the Use of Military Force somehow implicitly authorized it all along? Second, when the Authorization was being debated, the Administration did in fact seek to have language inserted in it that would have authorized them to use military force domestically—and the Congress did not agree. Senator Ted Stevens and Representative Jim McGovern, among others, made statements during the Authorization debate clearly restating that that Authorization did not operate domestically.

When President Bush failed to convince Congress to give him all the power he wanted when they passed the AUMF, he secretly assumed that power anyway, as if congressional authorization was a useless bother. But as Justice

Frankfurter once wrote: "To find authority so explicitly withheld is not merely to disregard in a particular instance the clear will of Congress. It is to disrespect the whole legislative process and the constitutional division of authority between President and Congress."

This is precisely the "disrespect" for the law that the Supreme Court struck down in the steel seizure case.

It is this same disrespect for America's Constitution which has now brought our republic to the brink of a dangerous breach in the fabric of the Constitution. And the disrespect embodied in these apparent mass violations of the law is part of a larger pattern of seeming indifference to the Constitution that is deeply troubling to millions of Americans in both political parties. . . .

Whenever power is unchecked and unaccountable it almost inevitably leads to mistakes and abuses. In the absence of rigorous accountability, incompetence flourishes. Dishonesty is encouraged and rewarded.

Last week, for example, Vice President Cheney attempted to defend the Administration's eavesdropping on American citizens by saying that if it had conducted this program prior to 9/11, they would have found out the names of some of the hijackers.

Tragically, he apparently still doesn't know that the Administration did in fact have the names of at least 2 of the hijackers well before 9/11 and had available to them information that could have easily led to the identification of most of the other hijackers. And yet, because of incompetence in the handling of this information, it was never used to protect the American people.

It is often the case that an Executive Branch beguiled by the pursuit of unchecked power responds to its own mistakes by reflexively proposing that it be given still more power. Often, the request itself it used to mask accountability for mistakes in the use of power it already has.

Moreover, if the pattern of practice begun by this Administration is not challenged, it may well become a permanent part of the American system. Many conservatives have pointed out that granting unchecked power to this President means that the next President will have unchecked power as well. And the next President may be someone whose values and belief you do not trust. And this is why Republicans as well as Democrats should be concerned with what this President has done. If this President's attempt to dramatically expand executive power goes unquestioned, our Constitutional design of checks and balances will be lost. And the next President or some future President will be able, in the name of national security, to restrict our liberties in a way the framers never would have thought possible.

The same instinct to expand its power and to establish dominance characterizes the relationship between this Administration and the courts and the Congress.

In a properly functioning system, the Judicial Branch would serve as the constitutional umpire to ensure that the branches of government observed their proper spheres of authority, observed civil liberties and adhered to the rule of law. Unfortunately, the unilateral executive has tried hard to thwart the ability of the judiciary to call balls and strikes by keeping controversies out of its hands—notably those challenging its ability to detain individuals without legal process—by appointing judges who will be deferential to its exercise of power and by its support of assaults on the independence of the third branch.

The President's decision to ignore FISA was a direct assault on the power of the judges who sit on that court. Congress established the FISA court precisely to be a check on executive power to wiretap. Yet, to ensure that the court could not function as a check on executive power, the President simply did not take matters to it and did not let the court know that it was being bypassed. . . .

The Executive Branch, time and again, has co-opted Congress' role, and often Congress has been a willing accomplice in the surrender of its own power.

Look for example at the Congressional role in "overseeing" this massive four year eavesdropping campaign that on its face seemed so clearly to violate the Bill of Rights. The President says he informed Congress, but what he really means is that he talked with the chairman and ranking member of the House and Senate intelligence committees and the top leaders of the House and Senate. This small group, in turn, claimed that they were not given the full facts, though at least one of the intelligence committee leaders handwrote a letter of concern to VP Cheney and placed a copy in his own safe.

Though I sympathize with the awkward position in which these men and women were placed, I cannot disagree with the Liberty Coalition when it says that Democrats as well as Republicans in the Congress must share the blame for not taking action to protest and seek to prevent what they consider a grossly unconstitutional program. . . .

Fear drives out reason. Fear suppresses the politics of discourse and opens the door to the politics of destruction. Justice Brandeis once wrote: "Men feared witches and burnt women."

The founders of our country faced dire threats. If they failed in their endeavors, they would have been hung as traitors. The very existence of our country was at risk.

Yet, in the teeth of those dangers, they insisted on establishing the Bill of Rights.

Is our Congress today in more danger than were their predecessors when the British army was marching on the Capitol? Is the world more dangerous than when we faced an ideological enemy with tens of thousands of missiles poised to be launched against us and annihilate our country at a moment's notice? Is America in more danger now than when we faced worldwide fascism on the march—when our fathers fought and won two World Wars simultaneously?

It is simply an insult to those who came before us and sacrificed so much on our behalf to imply that we have more to be fearful of than they. Yet they faithfully protected our freedoms and now it is up to us to do the same. . . .

A special counsel should immediately be appointed by the Attorney General to remedy the obvious conflict of interest that prevents him from investigating what many believe are serious violations of law by the President. We have had a fresh demonstration of how an independent investigation by a special counsel with integrity can rebuild confidence in our system of justice. Patrick Fitzgerald has, by all accounts, shown neither fear nor favor in pursuing allegations that the Executive Branch has violated other laws.

Republican as well as Democratic members of Congress should support the bipartisan call of the Liberty Coalition for the appointment of a special counsel to pursue the criminal issues raised by warrantless wiretapping of Americans by the President.

Second, new whistleblower protections should immediately be established for members of the Executive Branch who report evidence of wrongdoing—especially where it involves the abuse of Executive Branch authority in the sensitive areas of national security.

Third, both Houses of Congress should hold comprehensive—and not just superficial—hearings into these serious allegations of criminal behavior on the part of the President. And, they should follow the evidence wherever it leads.

Fourth, the extensive new powers requested by the Executive Branch in its proposal to extend and enlarge the Patriot Act should, under no circumstances be granted, unless and until there are adequate and enforceable safeguards to protect the Constitution and the rights of the American people against the kinds of abuses that have so recently been revealed.

Fifth, any telecommunications company that has provided the government with access to private information concerning the communications of Americans without a proper warrant should immediately cease and desist their complicity in this apparently illegal invasion of the privacy of American citizens.

Freedom of communication is an essential prerequisite for the restoration of the health of our democracy.

It is particularly important that the freedom of the Internet be protected against either the encroachment of government or the efforts at control by large media conglomerates. The future of our democracy depends on it.

I mentioned that along with cause for concern, there is reason for hope. As I stand here today, I am filled with optimism that America is on the eve of a golden age in which the vitality of our democracy will be re-established and will flourish more vibrantly than ever. Indeed I can feel it in this hall.

As Dr. King once said, "Perhaps a new spirit is rising among us. If it is, let us trace its movements and pray that our own inner being may be sensitive to its guidance, for we are deeply in need of a new way beyond the darkness that seems so close around us."

# EXPLORING THE ISSUE

## Is Warrantless Wiretapping Ever Justified to Protect National Security?

## Critical Thinking and Reflection

1. Does the president have the authority to engage in secret surveillance?
2. Is there a constitutional conflict between constitutional liberties and national security?
3. Can Congress deny the power to wiretap or otherwise invade private behavior?
4. Is the president subject to fewer restrictions in intercepting communications by or with foreigners?
5. Where should we draw a line between civil rights and national security?
6. To what extent should the government be permitted to examine private medical and other personal records?
7. Under what circumstances may the president suspend the writ of habeas corpus?
8. How does the Foreign Intelligence Surveillance Act change government policy?
9. Should the president be exempt from lawsuits when dealing with national security?
10. Should the constitution be amended in order to give greater latitude to presidential security measures?

## Is There Common Ground?

Although advocates of warrantless wiretapping have urged that it be made permanent, administration officials in the last years of President George W. Bush and the early years of President Barack Obama have maintained that there have been no instances of electronic surveillance without court-approved warrants. Similarly, there have been very few charges of excessive use of other security measures under the revised Patriot Act. Although disagreement persists as to how much valuable information for national security can be obtained by actions that may violate individual liberty, a sense of greater national security may permit a reassessment of the extent to which individual rights need to be curtailed in order to ensure the nation's safety. Negative public reaction to the very minor invasion of privacy affected by airline searches of passengers has been met by government efforts to deal more efficiently and less intrusively with the potential threat.

# Additional Resources

Jonathan White has written extensively on national security, and his *Terrorism and Homeland Security, Fifth Edition* (Wadsworth, 2005) has long been considered a leading work in the field. Ellen Frankel Paul, Fred D. Miller, Jr., and Jeffrey Paul have edited *The Right to Privacy* (Cambridge University Press, 2000), a series of wide-ranging essays by philosophers and academic lawyers, examining various aspects of privacy, including its role in American constitutional laws and the ways it influences public policy.

The difficulty that the government has in striking an appropriate balance between individual freedom and national security is mirrored in the close division in public sentiment. CNN/USA Today/Gallup Polls 5 months apart in 2006 showed a shift of public support for warrantless wiretapping from a slim majority in favor to a similarly slim majority opposing. Such shifts have taken place since, suggesting that the relationship and possible conflict between personal liberty and national security will not be resolved in a dangerous world.

# Contributors to This Volume

## EDITORS

**GEORGE McKENNA** is professor emeritus and former chair of the Department of Political Science, City College of New York. He has written or edited eight books on politics and society, including his latest, *The Puritan Origins of American Patriotism* (Yale, 2007). He is currently working on a biography of Booker T. Washington.

**STANLEY FEINGOLD,** recently retired, held the Carl and Lily Pforzheimer Foundation Distinguished Chair for Business and Public Policy at Westchester Community College of the State University of New York. He received his bachelor's degree from the City College of New York, where he taught courses in American politics and political theory for 30 years, after completing his graduate education at Columbia University. He spent four years as visiting professor of politics at the University of Leeds in Great Britain, and he has also taught American politics at Columbia University in New York and the University of California, Los Angeles. He is a frequent contributor to the *National Law Journal* and *Congress Monthly,* among other publications.

# AUTHORS

**DICK ARMEY** served for 18 years as a Republican member of the House of Representatives from Texas before he became the leader of FreedomWorks, one of the earliest groups in the Tea Party movement.

**LARRY BELL** is professor of architecture at the University of Houston, is the founder and director of the Sasakawa International Center for Space Architecture (SICSA).

**STEPHEN BREYER** is associate justice of the United States Supreme Court.

**STEVE BROUWER** is the author, among other books, of *Robbing Us Blind: The Return of the Bush Gang and the Mugging of America* (2004) and *Conquest and Capitalism: 1492–1992* (1998).

**MICHAEL CAIRO** has written on foreign policy formation, human rights, and national security. He has taught at Virginia Commonwealth University, Southern Illinois University at Carbondale, the University of Wisconsin at Stevens Point, and Georgetown College.

**SARAH H. CLEVELAND,** professor of human and constitutional rights, Columbia Law School, is an attorney and former Rhodes Scholar. She was recently named counselor to the U.S. State Department on foreign relations issues, including human rights cases.

**THEODORE DALRYMPLE** is fellow at the Manhattan Institute and contributing editor of *City Journal*. He is a retired physician who practiced in a British inner-city prison and hospital.

**JIM DEMINT,** United States senator from South Carolina since 2005, serves on four different senatorial committees, including the Joint Economic Committee and the Committee on Banking, Housing, and Urban Affairs.

**CHRISTOPHER C. DeMUTH** is president of the American Enterprise Institute for Public Policy Research. He has served in several administrative capacities in the executive branch of the federal government and on the faculty of the Kennedy School of Government at Harvard University.

**CURTIS S. DUBAY** is a senior analyst of tax policy at The Heritage Foundation. He previously served as senior economist at the Tax Foundation.

**GREGG EASTERBROOK** is a writer, lecturer, and a senior editor of *The New Republic*. He was a fellow at the Brookings Institution and is the author of *The Progress Paradox* and the forthcoming *Sonic Boom*.

**IRWIN GARFINKEL** is professor in the School of Social Work at Columbia University in New York. He is the author of numerous books and articles on social policy.

**ROBERT P. GEORGE** is the McCormick Professor of Jurisprudence and director of the James Madison Program in American Ideals and Institutions at Princeton University. Recently, he was appointed by President George W. Bush to the President's Council on Bioethics. He previously served on the U.S.

Commission on Civil Rights and as a judicial fellow at the Supreme Court of the United States.

**JACK GOLDSMITH,** Professor at Harvard Law School and author of *The Terror Presidency: Law and Judgment Inside the Bush Administration* (2007), served under President George W. Bush as United States Assistant Attorney General for the Office of Legal Counsel.

**MARY GORDON** is a novelist and short-story writer. She is the author of *Penal Discipline: Female Prisoners* (Gordon Press, 1992), *The Rest of Life: Three Novellas* (Viking Penguin, 1993), and *The Other Side* (Wheeler, 1994).

**AL GORE** was the vice president of the United States, 1993–2001, and the Democratic candidate for president in 2000. He is the author of two books on environmental issues: *Earth in the Balance: Ecology and the Human Spirit* (Plume Books, 1992) and *An Inconvenient Truth* (Rodale Books, 2006), and the narrator of a documentary film based on the latter book.

**DAVID GRAY ADLER** is a professor at Idaho State University and the author of books and articles on foreign policy and presidential war powers.

**MARK GREEN** is a political activist and frequent candidate who worked and wrote with consumer advocate Ralph Nader. He is coeditor, with Eric Alterman, of *The Book on Bush: How George W. (Mis)leads America* (Viking, 2004).

**ROBERT GREENSTEIN** is the founder and executive director of the Center on Budget and Policy Priorities. Among other federal positions he holds is his membership on the Bipartisan Commission on Entitlement and Tax Reform.

**LEE H. HAMILTON,** who served in the U.S. House of Representatives for 34 years, was vice chairman of the 9/11 Commission and currently serves on the President's Homeland Security Advisory Council.

**HENRY HUDSON** is U.S. federal judge in the U.S. District Court for the Eastern District of Virginia. He was appointed by President George W. Bush in 2002.

**ANTHONY KENNEDY** is an associate justice of the United States Supreme Court. He was appointed in 1988 by President Ronald Reagan.

**MATT KIBBE** is president and CEO of FreedomWorks. He has been with the organization (previously known as Citizens for a Sound Economy) for over 12 years. An economist by training, Matt Kibbe is a well-respected national public policy expert, bestselling author and political commentator. Newsweek has called Kibbe "one of the masterminds" of Tea Party politics, expertise which has led to frequent appearances on national news shows including FOX News, NBC, ABC News, CNN, MSNBC, FOX Business, PBS, and CSPAN.

**EZRA KLEIN** is a blogger and columnist for *The Washington Post, Bloomberg, Newsweek,* and a contributor to MSNBC.

**JILL LEPORE** is a professor of American history at Harvard University; a regular contributor to *The New Yorker;* and the author of *A Is for American,* a study of language and politics in America's first century.

**YUVAL LEVIN** is fellow at the Ethics and Public Policy Center in Washington, DC. He is also senior editor of *The New Atlantis* and a contributing editor to *National Review.*

**GLENN C. LOURY** is university professor, professor of economics, and director of the Institute on Race and Social Division at Boston University.

**JEFF MADRICK** is the editor of *Challenge* magazine, the author of *The End of Affluence* (1995) and other books, a frequent contributor to *The New York Review of Books*, and a visiting professor of humanities at The Cooper Union in New York.

**ANDREW C. McCARTHY** was the U.S. attorney who led the 1995 terrorism prosecution that resulted in the conviction of Islamic militants for conducting urban terrorism, including the 1993 World Trade Center bombing. His essays have been published in *The Weekly Standard, Commentary, Middle East Quarterly*, and other publications.

**WILFRED M. McCLAY** holds the SunTrust Chair of Humanities at the University of Tennessee at Chattanooga.

**THEODORE B. OLSON** served as an assistant attorney general in the Reagan administration (1981–1984). In private legal practice, Olson later successfully represented presidential candidate George W. Bush in the Supreme Court case *Bush v. Gore* (2000).

**LEE RAINWATER** is professor of sociology emeritus and research director of the Luxembourg Income Study. His books include Poor Kids in a Rich Country: America's Children in Comparative Perspective, with Timothy M. Smeeding, Russell Sage Foundation, 2003; Income Distribution in OECD Countries, with Anthony B. Atkinson and Timothy M. Smeeding, OECD, 1995; Public/Private Interplay in Social Protection with Martin Rein, (eds.), M.E. Sharpe and Co., 1986; What Money Buys: Inequality and the Social Meaning of Income, New York: Basic Books, 1974; Behind Ghetto Walls: Black Families in a Federal Slum, Chicago: Aldine Publishing Company, 1970; and And the Poor Get Children: Sex, Contraception and Family Planning in the Working Class, Chicago: Quadrangle Books, Inc., 1960.

**MARK J. ROZELL** is a professor at George Mason University and the author and editor of books and articles on religion and politics, executive privilege, and southern and state politics.

**JOHN SAMPLES** is the director of the Cato Institute Center for Representative Government. He is a frequent contributor to *The American Spectator* and other publications.

**ANTONIN SCALIA** is an associate justice of the United States Supreme Court. He was appointed in 1986 by President Ronald Reagan.

**SAM SHULMAN** is a New York writer whose work appears in *New York Press,* the *Spectator* (London), and JewishWorldReview.com.

**TIMOTHY SMEEDING** is a professor of economics and public affairs at the University of Wisconsin-Madison, and the author and editor of books on poverty and wealth in the United States.

**GEORGE CARAM STEEH** was appointed United States District Judge in 1998 by President Clinton. He previously served as a Macomb County Circuit Court Judge from 1990 until 1998, after serving for two years as a District Court Judge in Mt. Clemens. Judge Steeh received a BA from the University of Michigan in 1969, and his JD from the University of Michigan Law School in 1973.

**JOHN PAUL STEVENS** was an associate justice of the United States Supreme Court. He was appointed in 1975 by President Gerald Ford and served until his retirement in 2010.

**BRYAN STEVENSON** is a faculty member of the New York University School of Law and Executive Director of the Equal Justice Initiative, an organization that focuses on criminal justice reform.

**WALTER E. WILLIAMS** is the John M. Olin Distinguished Professor of Economics at George Mason University.

**JOHN C. YOO,** a professor of law at Boalt Hall, University of California, Berkeley, served as deputy assistant attorney general in the Office of Legal Counsel in the U.S. Department of Justice from 2001 to 2003. He is the author of *The Powers of War and Peace* (University of Chicago, 2005) and *War by Other Means: An Insider's Account of the War on Terrorism* (Grove/Atantic, 2006).

**HOWARD ZINN**, historian, playwright, and social activist, is best known for his book, *A People's History of the United States*. He has taught at Spelman College and Boston University, and has been a visiting professor at the University of Paris and the University of Bologna.